Light, air & openness

Paul Overy

Light, air & openness

Modern architecture between the wars

with 66 illustrations

Thames & Hudson

For Tag

Half-title Queen Alexandra Sanatorium,
Davos, Switzerland, 1907
Otto Pfleghard and **Max Haefeli**

Frontispiece Radun Sanatorium Boarding House,
Luhačovice, Czechoslovakia (now Czech Republic), 1927
Bohuslav Fuchs

First published in the United Kingdom in 2007 by
Thames & Hudson Ltd, 181A High Holborn,
London WC1V 7QX

www.thamesandhudson.com

British Library Cataloguing-in-Publication Data
A catalogue record for this book is available from the
British Library

ISBN 978-0-500-34242-8

Printed and bound in Slovenia by MKT Print d.d.

Contents

Introduction

The Zonnestraal Sanatorium near Hilversum (1925–31) is one of the most spectacular of early 20th-century modernist buildings. Designed for the Dutch Diamond Workers' Union (ANDB) by Jan Duiker and Bernard Bijvoet, in collaboration with the structural engineer Jan Gerko Wiebenga, the sanatorium is well known from reproduction in histories of 20th-century architecture – although relatively few people have seen it. Surrounded by the birch and pine woods of the Loosdrechtse Bos, the low white concrete-and-glass pavilions are not easy to find. My own first visit to Zonnestraal was on a bitterly cold, icily clear late November afternoon in the early 1990s. I was driven there by a Dutch friend, Frank den Oudsten, who had photographed and filmed the Zonnestraal complex some ten years earlier. He had not been back since and we had some difficulty in locating it, taking several wrong turnings and having to ask directions a number of times. When we finally found the buildings it was almost dark, except for the cold sharp light of the already sunken sun reflected in the wintery late-afternoon sky.

Framed by the dark outlines of pine trees and eerily illuminated, the central-services building of the sanatorium complex was still in operation – although much changed from its original almost ethereal appearance. Splaying out into the woods behind it, the wings of the disused Dresselhuys pavilion appeared pale and unearthly in the last reflected light of the cold November sky and the pale wintery light of the rising moon. This had once housed the individual patients' rooms – with long balconies for outdoor bedrest, so that they could regain their strength while lying in the sunshine and fresh air. But as we approached closer it was clear that the pavilion was now in a desperate state of ruin. Its concrete walls were grotesquely cracked and stained. Shattered windows hung open from rusted and twisted hinges, steel reinforcing rods protruded where the concrete had fallen away from the floors, ceilings and walls, steps were broken and cracked, drifted with dead leaves and twigs. Glass from the shattered metal-framed windows and doors crackled like ice under foot. The small cell-like rooms with their wide airy windows which had opened directly onto the fresh resin-scented woods were now overrun by intruding branches and brambles that grew up to, into, and sometimes through them. The relationship of the sanatorium buildings to the surrounding woods must always have appeared strangely symbiotic, even when they were pristine and first in use. Increasingly, the woods had encroached over the years. By the 1990s, the trees and undergrowth had penetrated into the deserted pavilion – as if mocking the modernist practice of positioning 'real' plants against austere geometric surfaces in place of the 'representational ornament' of an earlier era.

Zonnestraal means sunbeam or sunray in Dutch: a symbol of the belief in the healing power of the sun for the treatment of tuberculosis and related lung diseases during the early decades of the 20th century. But my first sight of this iconic building was by the light of the rising moon. (The visionary writer Paul Scheerbart foresaw in

Zonnestraal Sanatorium, central-services building,
Hilversum, The Netherlands, 1925–31
Jan Duiker and **Bernard Bijvoet**

1914 a modern glass architecture that would let in 'the light of the sun, the moon and the stars'.)[1] The eerie and unearthly light seemed appropriate to the sanatorium's condition – no longer pristine and perfect as in the reproduced black-and-white photographs that made it internationally famous, but a crumbling and decaying ruin. The uncanniness of its situation, the sense of neglect, of a superseded and almost forgotten past overlaid an awareness of the idealistic hope and optimism that had inspired the Zonnestraal's commissioning and design. Yet despite its neglect and ruin, the entire utopian dream of early 20th-century modernist architecture and design seemed to be concentrated in these buildings. The refined precision of their elementary geometry and purity of line was still discernible, even emphasized by ruin and the rampant vitality of invasive vegetation – but in ways that now seemed poignant, part of an already distant and seemingly irrecoverable past.

When Zonnestraal was fully operational as a sanatorium its elegant white-painted concrete walls and shimmering sheets of rolled glass must have spectacularly embodied the modernist belief in sunlight, fresh air and openness, hygiene and health. The surrounding pine woods scenting the fresh air that flowed into the patients rooms through the huge windows, the enormous swathes of glass creating an almost unbelievable intensity of light which would have given patients and staff a sense of continual emotional and spiritual uplift – even on grey or dull days. Despite the ruinous state into which the sanatorium had sunk by the end of the 20th century, it was possible to imagine it in its heyday: the convalescent patients propped up in their beds on the long balconies, quietly resting in front of the wide windows of their rooms that looked out into the woods – or working in the occupational-therapy pavilions designed in a more vernacular style, set separately among the trees.

The sanatorium was designed for patients who had already undergone some treatment for tuberculosis to rest and recover their strength. Its aim was to mediate 'the relationship between being ill and being healed', to help patients gradually resume their place in 'the multiplicity of social life'.[2] Occupational therapy enabled them to bridge the gap between illness that demanded complete rest, and their final return to work.[3] Once they had recovered sufficiently, the patients moved from the sanatorium itself to individual small cabins in the woods – where they would continue to build their strength prior to their return to the outside world – and later on to after-care accommodation 'where they could live, reunited with their families, until they were deemed fit enough to return to life outside the sanatorium'.[4] These facilities were designed to provide a progression from bedrest and constant medical attention, through a regime that combined regular exercise and frequent rest, to therapeutic work, partial independence and (eventually) complete rehabilitation – all in surroundings that offered the maximum of open space, fresh air and sunlight.

Light, air & openness

A preoccupation with cleanliness, health, hygiene, sunlight, fresh air and openness characterized modern architecture of the years between the two world wars. Representations of the need for 'light, air and openness' and a particular concern with health and hygiene feature prominently in the written texts, photographs and films employed to promote the modern movement during the late 1920s and early 1930s. Light, air, sunshine and spatial openness are skilfully evoked in the opening sequences of *Die neue Wohnung* (The New Dwelling), a documentary promoting modernist housing and domestic design commissioned by the Swiss Werkbund from the German artist and film-maker Hans Richter to accompany a model-housing exhibition in Basel in the summer of 1930.[5] The film begins with a time-lapse sequence of a sunflower raising its head to the sun in response to the light, followed by a series of intertitles:

Light
Air
Sun
Make life possible

(Light of course also makes possible the technology of photography and film.) Shots of newborn chicks and a child sitting in a sunny meadow are intercut with those of a small girl playing in a shadowy interior courtyard, followed by the intertitle 'Walls constrict'. This introduces a sequence showing the dark heavy walls of traditional masonry buildings intercut with shots of plants drooping in sunless courtyards.[6]

In contrast to these Richter shows a series of light and airy modern dwellings with large windows, terraces and balconies, and sliding or folding partitions that enable rooms to be opened out and combined when required. This is strikingly illustrated by a sequence of couples dancing in the open-plan living room of an apartment where the lightweight furniture has easily and conveniently been moved out of the way. When Richter re-edited the film for German audiences he took out the didactic opening montage, and instead emphasized the health-giving and life-enhancing qualities of sunlight, fresh air and openness through a sequence of images of open-air terraces, balconies, patios and sun roofs with people – and particularly children – enjoying the interpenetration of indoor and outdoor space. Similar (and sometimes identical) images evoking openness, sunlight, fresh air and mobility appear in Sigfried Giedion's short polemical text promoting modernist housing, *Befreites Wohnen* (Liberated Living), published a year earlier in 1929. Giedion designed the front cover himself, employing the modernist typographical device of 'typophoto' to reiterate the words '*Licht, Luft und Oeffnung*' (Light, Air and Openness) overlaid repeatedly across a carefully posed photograph of a young couple relaxing in a modern living room, which opens out onto a wide airy terrace overlooking the river Limmat in Zurich.[7] ('*Oeffnung*' means literally 'opening' in German, but in this context 'openness' is a better translation.)

Hospitals and sanatoriums feature prominently in both film and text, and the faith in the curative powers of sunlight and fresh air are evoked by shots of both domestic and sanatorium terraces and balconies. Giedion reproduces three photographs and a plan of Zonnestraal while Richter included sequences shot in a modernist Swiss Alpine sanatorium, showing its glass-enclosed solarium and open sun terraces intercut with shots of children playing on domestic terraces and adults relaxing.[8] These are supplemented by images of fit adults and healthy children enjoying the sunshine and open air in sports, play and leisure activities out of doors – or in the privileged liminal spaces of modernism: balconies, terraces, gardens, roof gardens, and the sheltered areas under buildings raised up on pilotis or concrete columns.[9]

Similar images appeared in *Terrassentyp* by the German architect Richard Döcker, published like Giedion's *Befreites Wohnen* in 1929. Here Döcker promoted the terraced building open to sunlight and fresh air as a new type for public and institutional buildings, offices, hotels, houses and apartments – based on the model of the sanatorium and the hospital, and using his own celebrated sanatorium-like Waiblingen District Hospital (1926–28) near Stuttgart as a detailed case study.[10] Giedion illustrated the clean hygienic white interior of one of the rooms in Döcker's hospital in *Befreites Wohnen*, with its full-width sliding window opening onto a wide terraced balcony looking over the town and the surrounding countryside. With this he contrasted a photograph of a

Children playing on the terrace of Max Ernst Haefeli's Lüscher House, Zurich, 1928–29.
Still from Hans Richter's film *Die neue Wohnung* (The New Dwelling), 1930

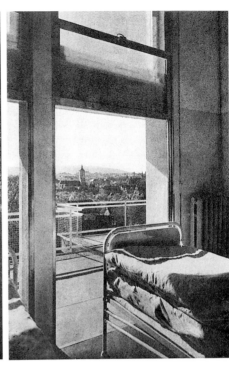

prisoner standing in a narrow, bare, brick-built prison cell, illuminated only by a small barred window – his outstretched arms almost touching the walls on either side.[11]

In such texts the term 'openness' was usually employed rather than 'space', because it more specifically evoked the outdoors and the open air, and (especially) the interconnection and interpenetration of inside and outside: one of the major ideological articles of faith of modernist architecture and design of the 1920s and 1930s. It also suggested a new openness of human relationships, less constricting and binding than previously. Although this did not necessarily imply an identification with the 'open relationship' or the 'open marriage', many made the connection at the time or have done so subsequently. Where the word space (*Raum* in German) was employed it was used to mean sufficient room for people to live and work comfortably together and individually – rather than in the more abstract sense found in later accounts of modernist architecture, such as Giedion's own exhaustive (although in many ways partial and exclusive) *Space, Time and Architecture*, first published in 1941.[12] In the late 1920s, the term *Existenzminimum* achieved wide currency in modernist texts, and Giedion employs it extensively in *Befreites Wohnen*. This is sometimes misunderstood to mean subsistence or substandard housing accommodation. But the aim of 'existence-minimum' housing – particularly as advocated by the innovative municipal-housing department of Frankfurt am Main under its influential and powerful director Ernst May – was to provide the best possible quality of life for tenants within a minimum and

Left Sigfried Giedion, *Befreites Wohnen* (Liberated Living), cover 1929
Centre and right Photographs from *Befreites Wohnen* of a prisoner in his cell, 1928, and a room in Waiblingen District Hospital, architect Richard Döcker, 1926–28 (pls 4 & 5)

affordable space.[13] May and his Frankfurt colleagues tried to incorporate the maximum of light, air and openness within this basic provision.[14] By using modern windows wider than they were tall, lower ceilings, and walls painted in pale colours, rooms could be made lighter and brighter, and easier to heat and keep clean – but also smaller, so that social housing was cheaper to build and less expensive to rent. Giedion's pamphlet appeared shortly before May's department hosted the second congress of the international modernist pressure group CIAM (the Congrès Internationaux d'Architecture Moderne) at Frankfurt in the autumn of 1929, which was devoted to the subject of the existence-minimum dwelling. It was almost certainly intended as a direct contribution to the heated debates and polemics that were to take place there.[15]

Ideas about hygiene and health, light, air, and openness – invoked as the aims of the new architecture in campaigning modernist texts and films such as *Die neue Wohnung, Befreites Wohnen* and *Terrassentyp* – also operated as metaphors that could be applied to the processes of perception and communication. In 1925, the Hungarian artist and designer László Moholy-Nagy claimed that 'The hygiene of the optical, the health of the visible is slowly filtering through'. Moholy was referring to the new means of visual communication of the 20th century such as photographically illustrated newspapers, book and magazines, cinema newsreels, and television, which was already at the experimental stage in the mid-1920s – known as *Fernsehen* ('Far Seeing') in German.[16] Both Giedion and Richter employed 'optical hygiene' to create visual impact in their promotional polemics. Richter used film-editing techniques derived from the Soviet silent cinema and the western European experimental film movement of which he was one of the leading protagonists and practiners, whereas Giedion employed modernist typographical techniques in the design of the cover and layout of *Befreites Wohnen*. These are openly partisan and committed accounts. There is much less emphasis on new aesthetic forms and the impact of new materials and structural innovations than in those texts that were to become the canonical histories of modernist architecture and design.[17] They are direct, succinct and committed representations of modernism and its ideals, produced from within the movement itself. The preoccupations they voice – the importance of health and hygiene, sunlight, fresh air, openness and mobility for a new social architecture – were regarded as crucial issues in modernist circles in Europe and North America in the 1920s and 1930s.

In 1932, the Dutch architect and furniture designer Gerrit Rietveld claimed that Giedion's ideal of '*befreites Wohnen*' (liberated living) was the true goal of modernist architecture, which was often mistakenly perceived as 'a kind of impoverishment or austerity, the omission of everything that is thought to be attractive and pleasing'. Liberated living should rather be seen 'in a social sense' as 'a kind of spatial hygiene' which eliminated everything that was superfluous.[18] Rietveld – whose own work was closely based on the ideals of 'light, air and openness' – believed that the idea of 'liberated living' implied both spatial and intellectual openness.[19] Richard Döcker claimed in *Terrassentyp* that: 'The old traditional form of the closed and finished building block has been exploded, the world enclosed inside the house bursts out and forces its way toward light and sun, seeking to merge with nature and the landscape.'[20] In 1927, he had acted as the supervising site architect for the Weissenhofsiedlung model-housing exhibition in Stuttgart, of which Mies van der Rohe was the artistic director. Here the principles of spatial hygiene, light, air and openness were demonstrated on a spectacular suburban hillside site in a series of apartment buildings and houses designed by fifteen modernist architects from France, Germany, Austria, The Netherlands, Belgium and Switzerland.

This book examines modern architecture between the world wars in terms of the preoccupations with light, air and openness described above. Rather than emphasizing formal and structural innovation, it investigates in greater detail the preoccupations of the period with fresh air, sunlight, health and hygiene, water, cleanliness and whiteness. These issues are considered in the context of class and social control, colonialism and race, and the recurring utopian metaphors of 'the clean machine' and the model factory.[21] Changes that have taken place over time in the physical condition and functional circumstances of modernist buildings emphasize the importance of adopting an archaeological approach to the ideologies that inspired them. The recent restoration and reconstruction of buildings originally intended to have only a short lifespan (and for which modernity and newness were of the essence) can be seen to expose many of the contradictions within modernism itself. The 'reconstructive surgery' applied today to diseased, decaying and obsolete modernist buildings recalls the medical paradigms that inspired such an architecture – exposing the pathos and paradoxes of the original enterprise.

This is not intended to be a comprehensive account of modern architecture between the world wars. Rather it is an examination of aspects of its development which can enrich and enhance our understanding of that architecture's aims and aspirations, as well as its forms. Certain buildings and projects are analysed in detail while others – including some often regarded as seminal or iconic – are discussed relatively briefly, or referred to only in passing. As this account is not solely concerned with formal, aesthetic or structural issues, I have avoided making rigid and inflexible distinctions between modernist architecture and design and what is sometimes termed 'modernistic', *moderne*, or (more recently) 'art deco'. Modernism as a term is deliberately not defined. I hope that its meaning in this particular context will be enriched through the arguments of the following chapters.

1 The city in the country

The commissioning of the Zonnestraal Sanatorium is a remarkable story of the struggle to ameliorate labour conditions in the first decades of the 20th century. At this time over 10,000 people were employed in the diamond-polishing industry in Amsterdam. The fine dust produced while polishing the stones was highly abrasive to human tissue if inhaled. As a result many diamond workers suffered from tuberculosis and other occupationally induced respiratory diseases, often aggravated by the squalid and unhygienic living conditions in which they lived. In the early 1900s, Henri Polak and Jan van Zutphen, the leading figures in the ANDB (Dutch Diamond Workers' Union) – the richest and most powerful union in The Netherlands – had sought ways to help members who suffered from these ailments.[1] Initially, funds came through selling waste copper from the rods used to hold the stones in place while they were being polished with mechanical wheels. The Koperen Stelenfonds (Copper Rod Fund) was set up in 1905 to collect the proceeds of salvaging the broken copper shafts. Previously, this had been sold and the proceeds used as a 'drinking fund' for the diamond workers. To provide further funds Professor Henri ter Meulen of Delft Technical University – after whom one of the two Zonnestraal residential pavilions was named – devised a method of separating the diamond dust from other waste. The insides of the polishing pans were coated with grease to catch the loose dust, which was then reclaimed and resold. Additional dust was salvaged by laundering the overalls worn by the workers, and a laundry was specially built for this purpose. With the money raised through selling the recovered copper waste and diamond dust the Zonnestraal Fund was set up in 1925 to build a new sanatorium in the countryside near Hilversum.

The commission to design the Zonnestraal complex came to Jan Duiker and Bernard Bijvoet through Hendrik Petrus Berlage, the great Dutch architect, theorist, urban planner and socialist. Berlage is best known for the Beurs (or Stock Exchange) in Amsterdam, but he was also the architect of the Amsterdam headquarters of the ANDB.[2] On his recommendation, the union commissioned the two young and unknown architects in 1924 to design the laundry to recover the diamond dust from the workers' overalls. The sparkling appearance of this white-painted glass and reinforced-concrete building signalled the hygienic nature of the cleansing operations that took place inside, and the healing campaign the recovery of the diamond dust would help to sponsor.[3] Shortly after designing the laundry, Duiker and Bijvoet were appointed architects of the Zonnestraal Sanatorium complex at Hilversum. In 1925, Bijvoet moved to Paris, where he worked with the furniture designer Pierre Chareau on the Maison de Verre. He remained in close touch with Duiker and after his death in 1935 completed Duiker's last building, the Gooiland Hotel in the centre of Hilversum.[4] There is a close connection both conceptually and symbolically between the earlier laundry and the sanatorium. A dash of blue added to the original white paint made the sanatorium look even whiter – like the 'blue' that was traditionally added to washing at the time. Part of the central-services building at Zonnestraal contained a laundry. The regular washing of soiled sheets and other linen at high temperatures is one of the most important facilities of a sanatorium or hospital, ensuring cleanliness and hygiene and the destruction of harmful bacteria. The steam laundry was one of the key elements in the industrialization of hygiene in the late 19th and early 20th centuries. The design of the Zonnestraal central-services building with its boilers, laundry, steam and water pipes, and prominent elegant metal chimney – its base encircled by the concrete drum of the main water tank – made explicit those qualities of hygiene and cleanliness that the sanatorium complex as a whole was to embody and represent. It was a powerful image of the 'clean machine', like the boiler rooms and powerhouses of early modernist factories such as the Fagus-Werk in Alfeld an der Leine near Hanover, or the Van Nelle factory in Rotterdam (see chapters 11 and 12).

The new sanatorium was constructed in the grounds of De Pampahoeve, a villa purchased through the Zonnestraal fund as a small interim sanatorium for nineteen patients.[5] A long, low complex based on the layout of early British tuberculosis sanatoriums – although startlingly different in appearance – the Zonnestraal consisted of a central-services building flanked by two residential wings that could accommodate a hundred patients, all of whom were initially male.[6] Further wings were envisaged but never built. Besides the laundry and boilerhouse the central-services building contained a small six-bed intensive-care unit, a medical department and dispensary, baths, showers and a kitchen, with a separate kosher food-preparation area (most workers in the Amsterdam diamond industry were Jewish).[7] An enormous dining and recreation room occupied the whole of the upper floor, which was also used for social activities, theatrical performances and film shows, and special events such as parties for patients' birthdays – or to celebrate their return to the outside world. (Most patients stayed for at least a year, often for eighteen months.) Glazed on all sides from floor to ceiling with a clerestory admitting yet more light, on a sunny day the illumination was almost supernaturally bright. Glass doors led out onto an extensive south-facing terrace, protected by glazed windscreens and the reinforced-concrete roof. Light, air and openness could not have been more generously, or more spectacularly provided.

Each of the residential wings consisted of a pair of two-storey pavilions set at a 45-degree angle to one other, so that every room had an uninterrupted view and received the maximum amount of sunlight. These were linked by corridors to a single-storey lounge between the two wings. Workshops for occupational therapy and accommodation for eighteen young women health-care assistants were provided in separate smaller buildings some distance from the main complex. Two further wings to the south were planned but never built. The central-services building and the first wing of patients' accommodation (the Ter Meulen pavilion) were completed in 1928, together with the reinforced-concrete frame for a second wing, the Dresselhuys pavilion. For financial reasons this was only completed in 1931. During the first three years the sanatorium was in use this spare and elegant (but unclad) concrete skeleton signalled the sanatorium's incompleteness, eerily anticipating its own later dereliction and ruin.

The name Zonnestraal (sunbeam) appropriately characterized the spectacular crystalline construction of wafer-thin concrete and sparkling sheets of glass.[8] The sunbeam (or sunset, or sunrise) was a ubiquitous and popular motif during the period between the wars, frequently found in art-deco ornamentation – and especially in stained-glass windows in lower middle-class speculative housing in western Europe and North America. Such imagery is less often associated with 'international modernist' buildings like Zonnestraal. Here there was no direct attempt to represent the image of the sunbeam, except perhaps through the extraordinary brilliance, whiteness, reflectance and transparency of the concrete-and-glass 'skin' or 'envelope' of the build-ing itself. The original drawn glass was colourless, unlike modern float glass which has

Zonnestraal Sanatorium, Hilversum, The Netherlands, 1925–31, (above) accommodation for health-care assistants, photographed in the 1950s, (right) aerial view, c. 1928

Jan Duiker and Bernard Bijvoet

a greenish tinge. It was not entirely flat, but had a slight ripple (from passing over the manufacturing rollers) which caught and reflected the sunlight.[9] Like the sunbeam, the image of the diamond was a powerful and pervasive visual motif frequently found in decorative architectural features during the early years of the 20th century, and in the art-deco buildings and artifacts of the inter-war years.[10] Berlage's turn-of-the-century diamond workers' union headquarters in Amsterdam incorporated symbolic forms based on diamonds and the processes of cutting and setting the stones.[11] Bruno Taut had glazed his Glass Pavilion for the 1914 Werkbund Exhibition in Cologne with glass lenses, which gave the structure the appearance of an enormous diamond – although actually based on the related forms of crystal. Between the wars the diamond form was seen as subversive or decorative by many of the more purist of modernists. Yet abstracted diamond imagery features frequently in early 20th-century Dutch modernism. Both Piet Mondrian and Theo van Doesburg employed diamond formats for a number of key abstract paintings in the 1920s.[12] As a young man Gerrit Rietveld had worked as a designer for a jewelry firm in Utrecht, and later designed a shop in Amsterdam for the Gold- and Silversmith's Company which featured a large illuminated three-dimensional symbolic form in the shape of a diamond.[13]

The stylized and abstracted diamond imagery of the Zonnestraal is obviously related to its history and function. The buildings were exceptionally pure and austere: their forms as crystalline and clear as the gemstones with which the patients had spent their lives working. While there is no traditional decoration or ornamentation as such, Duiker and Bijvoet introduced elements of diamond imagery and symbolism into the overall design. Seen in plan or from the air, the pattern of the pavilions splayed out around the central-services block appears to be based on the molecular structure of a

diamond.[14] Similar abstracted forms can be deciphered in some of the details of the main sanatorium complex, and in the smaller vernacular-style workshop buildings in the woods designed by Duiker in close collaboration with Bijvoet. This imagery reinforced the association with diamonds – the dust from the polishing of which caused (or aggravated) the diseases the sanatorium was designed to treat, and also helped to finance it. The association emphasizes the paradox of decay in this purest of modernist buildings. For the image of the diamond signifies a crystalline purity that will not wear or weather. Yet far from remaining immaculate and pure as in the photographs taken shortly after its completion, the white surfaces of the Zonnestraal sullied, peeled and cracked far quicker than earlier, more traditionally constructed buildings.[15] It is as if the sanatorium buildings were intended (as was in fact the case) to be temporary structures like exhibition pavilions: to serve their purpose – both functional and symbolic – and then be dismantled and destroyed. It is as if they were not designed to last or resist the effects of the elements, or weather sympathetically as buildings have been designed to do in the past – but to sparkle for a brief utopian moment, and after that moment had passed decay and crumble away.[16]

The diamond has traditionally been a symbol of permanence, indestructibility and eternity, and more recently of modernity. 'A diamond is for ever', was the slogan of an advertising campaign after the Second World War aimed at selling inexpensive engagement rings to couples who had never before possessed such purchasing power.[17] A diamond had been the trademark of the electrical company AEG (Allgemeine Elektrizitäts-Gesellschaft), one of the most powerful and successful capitalist industrial enterprises in the world, with international links and subsidiaries throughout Europe.[18] In *Imperialism, the Highest Stage of Capitalism* Lenin describes how, by means of international trusts and cartels, the manufacturing and distributive concerns of the major imperialist nations ensured themselves an international and virtually worldwide domination in the first decade of the 20th century. Lenin cited as examples of this the German AEG and American GEC electrical companies, which had concluded an agreement in 1907 to cease competitive practices and 'divide the world between themselves'. GEC held the monopoly for the United States and Canada, while AEG controlled the market in Germany, Austria, Russia, The Netherlands, Denmark, Switzerland, Turkey and the Balkans.[19] The diamond was an apt symbol of the power and longevity of AEG as a multinational combine – and indeed of the staying power of capitalism itself.

The ultimate luxury artefact, diamonds were cut and polished by craftsmen who were exploited for their labour and whose work severely damaged their health. But the black workers who mined the raw uncut diamonds in South Africa worked in far worse conditions. Their exploitation was one of the most extreme examples of colonial abuse. Often masked by other ideological issues, colonialism remains one of the hidden agendas of international modernist architecture between the wars: the 'heart of darkness' beneath the pristine white 'skin' of modernist buildings.[20] There is a further paradox. Diamonds are considered the ultimate 'useless' luxury. (Georges Bataille claimed jewels were 'brilliant waste'.) But for the former aristocrats and wealthy bourgeoisie fleeing the Russian Revolution, and for Jews escaping 19th-century pogroms and 20th-century Nazi persecution, jewelry (and diamonds in particular) were a lifeline to survival – 'liquid capital' in a highly portable and easily exchangeable form. Jews formed the majority of diamond workers in the workshop industries of Amsterdam, Antwerp and London, and of the members of the ANDB.[21] They were also often the patrons and commissioners (and sometimes the designers) of modernist buildings, and anti-Semitic denunciations of modern architecture were common between the wars.

Spiritual economy

Perhaps because of its fragility the Zonnestraal has always been regarded as rather special and unique, even among the many extraordinary works of modernist architecture created during the 1920s and 1930s. For the English architect Peter Smithson, writing in the early 1960s, Jan Duiker's works were the 'religious buildings of a faith that died in the thirties' – possessed of a 'slightly mad but quite real poetry' which gave them 'a purity and a faith that we find almost too hard to bear': 'No conventional aids were used in designing them, no history propped them up. What invention and courage this must have demanded!'[22] Smithson argued that Duiker's architecture dealt with problems that were essentially 20th century, 'central to a new sort of society': the sanatorium, the (news) cinema and the middle-class hotel. Forty years later, it is apparent that Duiker was more especially concerned with problems that were specific to the 1920s and 1930s. (His Cineac cinema in central Amsterdam was specifically designed to show newsreels – a medium that is now obsolete, superseded by television.) And it is the quickly changing and short-lived nature of such institutions and the society that produced them that gives these early modernist buildings their particular ephemerality, poignancy and pathos.

Wessel de Jonge, who was responsible with Hubert-Jan Henket for the restoration of the Zonnestraal in the early 2000s, has argued that 'the transitoriness of modern movement architecture can in some cases be understood as part of a design intention'.[23] The sanatorium was designed to be as light as possible using minimum amounts of material. As with many modern-movement buildings of the period, the specifications do not meet present-day construction standards. The thinness of the concrete slabs means 'that there can hardly be any concrete covering the reinforcement', allowing no latitude for slight errors that occurred during the construction process.[24] De Jonge argues that far from being the result of professional ignorance or incompetence, research suggests that Duiker and other like-minded modernists were 'well aware of what they were doing', regarding such 'economy of means' as a 'spiritual economy' that aspired to 'the immaterial'.[25] This belief was shared by the third collaborator on the original project,

Jan Gerko Wiebenga, an innovative structural engineer with experience of working in reinforced concrete since before the First World War, who had recently returned from three years in the United States where he had become familiar with the most up-to-date reinforced-concrete construction techniques.[26] While such spiritual and immaterial aspirations may well have been part of the designers' original intentions, this has had dire consequences for the survival of the buildings.

The specification for the sanatorium was cut to the bone to produce a lean and almost insubstantial appearance in line with Duiker and Wiebenga's ideas about 'material and spiritual economy', and also to economize on materials, building time and costs. The money available from the Zonnestraal Fund was extremely limited and this made an inexpensive method of building essential. The sanatorium was constructed using lightweight reinforced-concrete frames and floors, large areas of single-thickness metal-framed glass, and plaster-and-mesh walls attached to the supporting I-section beams with clamps. That these construction methods would limit the life of the building was probably thought not to be a disadvantage. Duiker seems to have conceived his buildings as temporary replaceable structures. Consequently, Zonnestraal was designed in 'the acceptance of a limited technical lifespan, in line with the functional lifespan of the sanatorium'.[27] (Duiker's own lifespan was also rather short; he died from cancer in his mid-forties in 1935, having produced a small number of technically flawed but justly celebrated and seminal modernist buildings.) In the preparatory meetings for the planning of the sanatorium, the Zonnestraal Board suggested a life expectancy for the buildings of thirty years, in the belief that tuberculosis and related lung diseases to which diamond workers were prone would be eliminated within this period.[28] The forecast was extraordinarily accurate. Used as a military hospital by the occupying Nazi forces during the Second World War, Zonnestraal was returned to its original function after the war. But by the late 1950s the decline of the Amsterdam diamond industry – and the virtual (although it now appears, temporary) elimination of tuberculosis in Europe as the result of immunization and the recently perfected triple-drug therapy – meant the sanatorium was no longer needed for its original purposes.[29] In 1957, it was clumsily altered and extended and converted into a general hospital – almost exactly thirty years after it opened as a sanatorium.

That new buildings would be designed for a short lifespan, to last about thirty years (or a single human generation) was a common idea among modernist architects, designers and theorists in the 1920s. Already in 1914, the Futurists had argued in the Manifesto of Futurist Architecture that: 'Houses will last less long than we. Each generation will have to build its own city.'[30] In an article published in 1925 in a Dutch construction magazine, Theo van Doesburg argued 'we are not building for eternity any more': '*Light, open, clear* and, above all, *temporary* – those are the tasks for the new architecture. Temporary but not superficial; open and clear but not empty and hollow; light but not flimsy.'[31] In *Befreites Wohnen* Giedion emphasized the limited lifespan of the modern house designed on the principles of 'light, air and openness' to a much greater extent than in any other of his writings, and included a passage from an interview with Henry Ford as an epigraph at the beginning of his short book:

> The form of the house will be transformed with the same speed as changes take place in clothes' styles, and even household management will undergo a revolution. In the past this took a long time, but from now on progress will be very swift. An evolution in housing was not possible until the present because the dwelling was so massively built that no one knew how to recast it in another form.[32]

Referring explicitly to the Futurists' manifesto, Giedion maintained that the life of a house was determined by its usefulness and that it should be replaced after a limited time, like the mass-produced motorcar.[33] By the beginning of the 21st century, the ephemeral nature and short lifespan of most modern commercial buildings is universally recognized, although certain institutional and most residential buildings are still expected to last indefinitely. Pointing out that today 'offices have a useful life of approximately ten years, factories eight years and shops only five years', Hubert-Jan Henket has argued that as a consequence the 'emotional appreciation' of a 20th-century building 'is often longer-lasting than its functional viability'.[34]

Zonnestraal continued in use as a general hospital for some years, and later became a geriatric unit – the building decaying like its inmates. The south wing of the 1931 Dresselhuys pavilion was abandoned in 1973 and the remaining wings served administrative functions until the early 1980s, after which the pavilion was left to decompose and be vandalized. Eventually, the whole complex became redundant, and despite attempts to raise money for its restoration large parts of it gradually deteriorated into a ruinous state during the 1980s. That these buildings had been a sanatorium and hospital made their ruin seem all the more poignant and disturbing, as if they themselves had succumbed to sickness and bodily deterioration. This was even more painful because it was allowed to happen in The Netherlands, a country more sensitive than most to its early 20th-century modernist heritage, where many of what the Dutch call 'young monuments' have been restored over the last two decades – usually long before they had fallen into the shocking state of ruin and dereliction of Zonnestraal during the 1980s and 1990s. Finally, after discussions and debates that lasted over two decades, the sanatorium began to be restored in the early years of the 21st century.

The sanatorium movement

At the turn of the 19th and 20th centuries, tuberculosis was the single greatest killer of adults in Europe and the United States. It particularly attacked younger men and women and its effect on the work force of the western world approached catastrophic proportions – comparable with AIDS in Africa at the beginning of the 21st century.[35]

Many European countries and the United States instituted national campaigns in an attempt to eradicate the disease. (The National Association for the Prevention of Consumption and Other Forms of Tuberculosis was founded in Britain in 1899.) In 1902, the International Central Bureau for the Campaign against Tuberculosis was established. During the first decades of the 20th century, the 'war on disease' – like war itself – was pursued on an international scale. Associated with dirt, lack of sunlight and fresh air, and poor living and working conditions, the number of sufferers had greatly increased during the First World War. In Germany, the number of cases doubled in the last two years of the war when no soap was available. After the war, the campaign to combat the disease was waged with renewed vigour. Tuberculosis attacked the young and fit in a manner that was directly equated with the way in which they had been the victims of technological warfare. The disease became a powerful metaphor of the failings of the human body.[36] Great emphasis was put on fresh air, 'through draughts', or 'cross ventilation' in the prevention of tuberculosis. At the end of the 19th century, it was reported to the Sanitary Institute of Great Britain that the incidence of the disease was some 50 per cent higher in back-to-back housing than in housing with cross or through ventilation. Cleanliness, hygiene, sunshine and fresh air were regarded as equally essential in the treatment or prevention of many other ailments – particularly the infectious diseases of childhood and the two other great 'scourges' of late 19th-century and early 20th-century urban life: cholera and typhoid.

The aim of the sanatorium movement was to demonstrate that the human body could be rested, relaxed and returned to health and potency through a period of separation from the unhygienic living conditions of much urban (and rural) life and exposure to fresh air and sunlight. The campaign to defeat tuberculosis continued to depend on sanatoriums with treatments centred on bedrest, fresh-air-and-sunlight regimes and controlled diet throughout the first part of the 20th century, until the successful introduction of triple-drug chemotherapy and inoculation in the mid-1950s.[37] Combined with improved living standards and the pasteurization of milk this served virtually to eliminate the disease in western Europe and North America at the time. During the late 20th and early 21st centuries there has been a resurgence of tuberculosis cases throughout the world. Britain has the highest incidence of tuberculosis in the major western European countries, and worldwide the disease is the major killer of young women today. The efficacy of fresh air and sunlight as a treatment for tuberculosis has been questioned in retrospect.[38] But many medical specialists today still believe that exposure to sunlight has an important effect on the prevention of tuberculosis and indeed other diseases such as cancer.[39]

From the second half of the 19th century, sanatoriums located in mountain or woodland areas provided treatment for tuberculosis through bedrest and exposure to fresh air and sunlight. The *Luft und Liegekur* – a combination of the *Luftkur* (based on fresh air) and the *Liegekur* (based on lying down and complete rest) – was widely prescribed in Europe and the United States, even before the discovery of the bacillic origins of the disease in the early 1880s. For most of the 19th century tuberculosis had been considered a hereditary disease, but in 1882 while working at the Imperial Health Office in Berlin the physician and microbiologist Robert Koch identified the bacillus *Mycobacterium tuberculosis* as its cause. Koch's discovery was taken as proof the disease was contagious, and resistance to it weakened by bad housing, overwork, malnutrition, overcrowding and alcoholism: confirming that a cure demanded isolation and treatment in specially designed and equipped sanatoriums. This became generally accepted during the late 1880s and 1890s, and by the early 20th century a demand had been created for new building types and new kinds of medical equipment and furniture.[40]

The German physician Hermann Brehmer had founded the first sanatorium for the treatment of pulmonary tuberculosis in 1854 in the mountain village of Görbersdorf in Silesia (now Sokołowsko, Poland). Brehmer mistakenly believed the reduced atmospheric pressure at relatively high altitudes would enable the heart to pump more efficiently, and that this would improve the general metabolism of the body and increase its capacity to overcome disease.[41] He was encouraged in his belief by the explorer Alexander von Humboldt who (also erroneously) assured him that tuberculosis did not exist in mountainous countries. Although their belief was mistaken, sanatoriums continued to be opened in mountainous areas well into the 20th century. The almost mystical association of mountains with physical and spiritual renewal – one of the enduring myths of Romanticism, particularly in German-speaking Alpine countries – was a major factor in the success of the sanatorium movement. As Thomas Dormandy has argued in his cultural history of the disease, the extraordinary dominance of ideas 'entirely devoid of experimental basis or empirical proof' probably owed 'more to the lyric poetry of Goethe, the songs of Schubert, and the vision of moonlit forests and snow-capped mountain peaks by Caspar David Friedrich, than to scientific mumbo-jumbo about metabolic purification'.[42] The legacy of Brehmer's belief continues today, as does that of another of his innovations: the placing of wooden seats at regular intervals along the forest paths near Görbersdorf to help patients complete their prescribed walks, from which derives the worldwide tradition of siting benches in parks and on woodland paths.

From 1876, Brehmer's former patient and student Peter Dettweiler developed Brehmer's ideas at a sanatorium in Falkenstein, situated in the Taunus Mountains near Frankfurt. As well as carefully graduated open-air walks and other forms of exercise, Dettweiler's regime included measured periods of rest in sheltered *Liegehallen* (covered balconies) or open terraces that were to become the characteristic design features of tuberculosis sanatoriums. Here patients could rest for long periods in reclining chairs in the fresh air and receive heliotherapy (sun therapy) while inhaling the scent of the pine woods – an early form of aromatherapy.[43] An open-air regime consisting of long periods of complete rest and immobility (combined with a large intake of protein and carbohydrates and graduated walks) was introduced in 1888 by Otto Walther at his Nordrach-in-Baden sanatorium, a former glass factory 450 metres above sea level in the Black Forest. Walther's ideas were widely adopted outside Germany – especially in Britain from where many of his patients came, and where sanatoriums were founded with names such as Nordrach in Wales, Nordrach on Dee, and Nordrach on Mendip.

One of the most successful of all sanatorium locations was Davos: a Swiss mountain resort that became known as 'the tuberculosis capital of Europe'. A local practitioner, Dr Walter Spengler, opened the first sanatorium in Davos in 1862, and he was soon followed by other doctors who opened their own establishments. The village, in an isolated valley, was transformed into a prosperous and extremely fashionable small town whose main industry was the treatment of tuberculosis and other respiratory ailments, attracting patients from Britain, Germany, The Netherlands, Russia and the United States.[44] By 1887, the original population of about one hundred had swollen to 3,000. The writers Robert Louis Stevenson and John Addington Symonds, and the photographer Bill Brandt were among those who stayed there as patients. Davos was also a centre for the treatment of other lung diseases – not always successfully. Theo van Doesburg (who suffered from acute asthma) died suddenly from a heart attack while receiving treatment there in 1931. Thomas Mann set his sanatorium novel *The Magic Mountain* (1924) in Davos, where his wife was treated for six months before the First World War. In Mann's novel, visitors are referred to as 'from the flatland'.[45] However, not all sanatoriums were in mountainous regions and in the early 20th century many were built on the edge of lakes, or in pinewoods such as Alvar Aalto's sanatorium at Paimio in south-west Finland, or the Zonnestraal – located in what was literally the flatland: the low heaths and pine woods of the central Netherlands around Hilversum. Despite this the sanatorium movement continued to be associated with the Romantic mystique of mountains and alpinism, particularly in the German-speaking countries of Europe. This mystique persisted through the 1920s and 1930s with a series of mountain films (*Bergfilme*) made in Germany, but popular throughout Europe.[46]

In 1902, Dr Karl Turban and the architect Jacques Gros designed an 'ideal sanatorium' in Davos where the south-facing wall of each patient's room was constructed entirely of movable panes of glass divided by thin metal frames, very similar to the types of window adopted in modernist buildings during the years between the wars.[47] Fresh air and sunlight treatment were also taken in the often spacious gardens and grounds of sanatoriums, or in the surrounding woods and forests – sometimes in revolving kiosks (known as 'sunboxes') which could be moved to follow the sun, first used by Turban in his Davos sanatorium.[48] This may have influenced the Italian engineer Angelo Invernizzi, the designer of the Casa Girasole (Sunflower House) near Verona – a modernist villa with a dramatic rooftop garden that revolved on its axis to follow the sun, like a sunflower. Among the most spectacular of early 20th-century sanatoriums was Otto Pfleghard and Max Haefeli's Queen Alexandra Sanatorium (1907) at Davos, prominently illustrated in Giedion's *Befreites Wohnen* and

Döcker's *Terrassentyp*, for which the great Swiss constructional engineer Robert Maillart was engineer in charge and Hennebique, the French specialists in reinforced-concrete construction, the contractors.[49] The sanatorium was one of the earliest large-scale reinforced-concrete buildings in Europe, designed in a stripped minimal 'proto-modernist' style with very little decoration, and featured generous terrace-like balconies where patients could receive fresh-air and sunlight treatment lying on beds or recliners (see half-title page).[50] Surrounded by pine trees and situated at a high altitude on a 'ledge' half way up a mountain, it was carefully oriented as a light trap to catch 'all the available sunlight'. Built for English 'consumptive patients of small means', the Queen Alexandra Sanatorium probably inspired Mann's description of the sanatorium in *The Magic Mountain* as it first appeared to the protagonist Hans Castorp on his arrival from Hamburg – when he glimpses 'a long building' with so many balconies that from a distance 'it looked porous, like a sponge'.[51]

Queen Alexandra Sanatorium,
Davos, Switzerland, 1907
Otto Pfleghard and Max Haefeli

25

Rudolf Steiger and Flora Steiger-Crawford's Bella Lui Sanatorium (1928–30) in Montana, which features in Richter's *Die neue Wohnung*, was a later example of the terraced Davos-type sanatorium in Switzerland that also took dramatic advantage of the sloping mountain site. The treatment rooms, kitchen and dining hall (glazed on three sides, with spectacular views) were located on the floor below the entrance level where the music room, offices and living quarters for the senior staff were situated. Above rose several terraced floors of patients' rooms, each of which had an individual balcony facing the sun.[52] In Richter's film, huge metal windows slide back – apparently with no help from human hand (like the camera lens itself) – to reveal panoramic views across the Alpine landscape from the solarium equipped with furniture by Max Ernst Haefeli, whose father had designed the Queen Alexandra Sanatorium with Pfleghard twenty years earlier. Another sequence shows the fourth-floor terrace with a row of elegant metal recliners designed by Haefeli and later marketed for domestic use.[53]

Although its generous sun terraces and enormous glass windows seemed to derive from the Davos-type sanatorium designed for sloping mountain sites, many of the features of the Zonnestraal were drawn from the pavilion plan employed in British sanatoriums, which were often located on the outskirts of towns or cities rather than in the mountains. The layout of 19th- and early 20th-century hospitals and sanatoriums was largely derived from the buildings of religious foundations, with long corridor wards where serried rows of beds could be partitioned off by curtains to form individual (if not very private) cubicles. In place of these, early 20th-century British sanatoriums were designed with separate pavilions providing individual rooms for patients, an access corridor running down one side, and a long terrace with individual balconies for each room on the other.

Before beginning work on Zonnestraal, Duiker visited a number of sanatoriums in Britain with Ben Sajet, a left-wing doctor associated with the Dutch Diamond Workers' Union. The sanatoriums they visited included the Papworth After-Care Colony and Village Settlement near Cambridge, founded by Pendrill Varrier-Jones in 1917, based on Ebenezer Howard's Garden City ideas and wholistic theories of medicine.[54] At Papworth, the central medical and sanatorium buildings – which Varrier-Jones preferred to call a 'convalescent section' – were surrounded by individual wooden chalets for patients (and sometimes their families), and a village settlement with workshops intended to provide a self-contained and self-financing community with work paid at trade-union rates.[55] Zonnestraal drew many of its characteristic elements from such British models, with its central-services building and patients' pavilions overlooking heathland and pine woods, and its small vocational workshop buildings located in the woods. But the long rows of terrace-like balconies opening off each patient's room in the residential pavilions derived more from Swiss mountain sanatoriums, and the brilliance and whiteness of the buildings suggested their snowy settings in the midst of the pine forests and heaths of 'the flatland'. The dazzling white walls, huge shimmering sheets of glass, and daringly thin reinforced-concrete frame devised by Duiker and Wiebenga evoked the construction of modern factories, ships and aeroplanes – those paradigms of the 'clean machine' so often invoked in modernist promotional texts. (The sanatorium was known locally as 'the ship on the heath'.)[56]

Alvar Aalto's Paimio sanatorium, set in dense forest twenty miles east of Turku in Finland on a relatively flat site, had a layout partly based on that of Zonnestraal, which Aalto visited in the summer of 1928 shortly before receiving the commission. Instead of individual balconies leading directly off patients' rooms like Zonnestraal and most of the Davos-type mountain sanatoriums, long terraces were positioned in a subsidiary block – accessible from the corridors on each floor – angled to catch the morning and afternoon sun. Unlike the low-lying two-storey Zonnestraal complex, Paimio was a cliff-like structure on seven floors, even more closely resembling the terraced Davos type. This was because of the need to rise above the dense forest that surrounded the buildings so as to provide adequate sunlight for the patients.[57] The dizzying height of the terraces led some of the more desperate inmates to throw themselves over the parapets, and the topmost seventh-floor terrace was consequently closed.[58]

With their wealthy international clientele many sanatoriums (particularly those in the Alps) resembled grand hotels, which some of the earliest had originally been.[59] In a Futurist manifesto of 1913, F. T. Marinetti had celebrated the grand hotel as an 'annual synthesis of different races'.[60] The international sanatorium of the early decades of the 20th century was even more a 'synthesis of different races' where the guests stayed longer, and sometimes indefinitely. While in Switzerland in the mid-1920s to receive treatment for tuberculosis, the Russian artist and designer El Lissitzky wrote to his future wife Sophie Küppers of a sanatorium he visited that resembled 'an international hotel, full of people'. (No beds were available and Lissitzky had to be treated elsewhere as an outpatient.)[61] Even at the height of the sanatorium movement shortly before and shortly after the First World War, the popularity of spas such as Davos was as much the result of fashion as of the success rate of cures. While cheaper chalet-type sanatoriums served less wealthy middle-class patients, the luxury establishments provided similar facilities to the most exclusive hotels. Brochures and advertisements publicized the quality and abundance of the cuisine and the additional comforts provided.[62] Sanatoriums also evoked the great transatlantic liners of the period, on the decks and terraces of which the voyager could take the air, lie in the sun, bathe in the deck-top swimming pool, or enjoy the healthy salt spray of the sea. A patient in *The Magic Mountain* compares the sanatorium to an ocean liner with its passengers from all over the world.[63] Mann's protagonist Hans Castorp is a young marine engineer who reads *Ocean Steamships* while resting in the recliner on his balcony. The modern sanatorium was a pristine white 'clean machine', a cruise ship that took the patients on a magical voyage lasting many months (or even years) from the old unhygienic and unhealthy world of the past to a new life of physical and mental health, fresh air, sunlight, hygiene and cleanliness. Like liners, sanatoriums were a city without the city.

Arriving at the sanatorium for the first time late in the evening after a long train journey from Hamburg, Castorp is escorted 'noiselessly along the coco matting of the narrow corridor' lit 'by electric lights in white glass shades set in the ceiling', the walls gleaming 'with hard white enamel paint'. He is shown to the room where an American woman has died two days before, but which has been thoroughly fumigated with formalin – 'the proper thing to use in such cases'. In the 'vibrating brilliance' of the ceiling light the room looked 'restful and cheery, with practical white furniture, white washable walls, clean linoleum, and white linen curtains gaily embroidered in modern taste'. There is a white-painted metal bed and a large washbasin where the chromed taps gleam in the electric light. Patients are required to lie out on their balconies not only during the day but also in the evening after dinner from eight to ten (moonbathing rather than sunbathing?). Castorp finds the door to the balcony open, through which the lights of the valley below are visible and the sound of distant dance music from the village can be heard.[64] Oskar Kokoschka recalled that the young English dancer Bessie Bruce (the long-term companion of the architect and designer Adolf Loos), who was being treated for tuberculosis in a sanatorium at Leysin in Switzerland just before the First World War, 'used to climb out of the window and go off dancing with the other patients – those anyway who still had enough life left in them', after the staff had gone to bed.[65] With its cosmopolitan clientele, Mann's International Sanatorium Berghof is largely based on the Davos sanatorium where his wife was a patient in 1912.[66] First conceived shortly after he visited her there, *The Magic Mountain* was intended to be a long short story like *Death in Venice*, which he had been on the verge of completing when he went to Davos.[67] Mann returned to the project only after the First World War, by which time it had taken the form of a very long novel. Although set before the war it is often seen as more an evocation of the immediately post-First World War period and the inter-war modernist sanatorium.

Whether located in mountainous regions or low-lying pine forests, tuberculosis sanatoriums and the destinations commonly recommended to those who suffered from the disease shared the common factor of not being in cities.[68] They constituted the 'other' of the urban, and yet were sites of sociality and relative sophistication: institutions that were cities apart from cities, like monasteries and convents, or ocean liners. Sanatoriums were anti-urban (or at least suburban) models for modernist architecture – so often associated with the urban, or with urbanism. The modernist building opened itself to light, air and openness (elements thought to be typical of the country) while remaining essentially an urban concept. It brought the country into the city, but studiously avoided the picturesque by evoking the model of the institution.

2 The house of health

Sanatoriums exerted a powerful hold on the imaginations of modernist architects and designers as building types and institutional models.[1] Among the first to be designed in a 'modern' or 'modernist' style, purpose-built sanatoriums for tuberculosis and other chronic diseases were some of the most technologically advanced buildings of the first decades of the 20th century. Combining associations of health, hygiene, cleanliness (and easy-to-cleanness), modernity and machine-like precision of operation, they were to have a major influence on modernist architecture and furniture design between the wars. Many of the materials and much of the furniture employed in modernist buildings were developed either for sanatoriums and hospitals, or for the 'model' factories that resembled them in their cleanliness and openness to light and sunshine.[2] Only later were these introduced into domestic designs – and then initially mainly for the wealthy, or those with a professional interest such as doctors, dentists, health and housing officials, and 'philanthropic' industrialists. The hygienic appearance of such designs was seen as a positive factor in the promotion of the modernist lifestyle – although this was often subjected to ridicule by opponents as 'surgical', 'clinical' or 'hospital-like'.

State-of-the-art heating, ventilating and cleaning systems were developed to control the internal environment of sanatorium and hospital buildings – while modern electric-lighting fixtures provided the closest possible equivalent of 'natural' daylight. Such features operated as much at a symbolic as a functional level. The white-painted concrete or white-tiled walls, the easily cleaned white furniture in the patients' rooms, and the 'functional' bent-wood or tubular-steel reclining chairs for resting and relaxing in the open air on balconies or terraces became potent symbols of cleanliness, light, fresh air and openness. Signifying healthiness and freedom from infection according to the socio-medical ideology of the time, they seemed to refuse any possibility of the presence of dirt or germs. The austere white rooms for the patients of sanatoriums were designed not only to be easy to clean but also *to appear to be spotlessly clean* – potent visual symbols of hygiene and health. At the symbolic level, sanatoriums could be regarded as representing 'a kind of exorcism', producing an 'illusion of health' that contrasted with 'the sickness of those they accommodated'.[3] Intended to have a similar reassuring effect on patients as the white coats worn by the medical and clinical staff, the walls and furniture of sanatoriums signified a literal cleanliness, freshness and hygiene,[4] but also evoked purity and spotlessness as abstract ideals.

Combining qualities of light, air and openness with a scrupulous attention to hygiene and cleanliness, sanatoriums became the models for housing, schools and other educational buildings. Simple undecorated forms, smooth washable surfaces and white-painted or light-coloured interior (and often exterior) walls were adopted for domestic and other non-medical buildings, which were frequently equipped with furniture originally designed for sanatoriums made from durable, germ-resistant and easily cleaned materials. Reclining chairs similar or sometimes identical to those used by patients were to become as important an element of the modernist interior as the white (or light) painted walls that evoked the hygienic white-painted rooms and corridors of sanatorium buildings. Not only was the design of much modernist architecture directly or indirectly derived from that of sanatoriums, its promoters also adopted the language of the hygienicist and health-reform movements of the period.[5] Closely linked not only to social and economic reform but also to health and dress reform, modernist architecture and design were energetically and evangelically promoted in terms of hygiene, health, physical fitness and (sometimes) eugenics.[6] Allying themselves with social reformers and healthcare professionals, modernist designers and architects persuaded themselves and their clients that such hygienic and athletic reorganizations of the modern domestic interior would 'ensure a morally and physically healthy society'.[7] In early modernist documents such as Giedion's *Befreites Wohnen*, Richter's *Die neue Wohnung* and Döcker's *Terrassentyp*, images of sanatoriums and clinics were used to promote the idea of the home as a kind of domestic hospital. An illustration in *Befreites Wohnen* depicts a man and a woman relaxing in the shaded undercroft of the younger Haefeli's Rotachhäuser (a 1928 row of modernist model housing in Zurich), which provided the inhabitants with a sheltered space directly open to the air and the garden, while shaded from the sun and protected from rain.[8] The man lies on an early version of Haefeli's sanatorium recliner in a state of total relaxation, while the woman sits reading – like patients in a 'domestic sanatorium', as Beatriz Colomina has observed.[9]

Hygiene, cleanliness and the provision of open-air balconies and terraces for exposure to fresh air and sunlight determined the stylistic features of the many modernist sanatoriums built in the 1920s and 1930s throughout Europe and North America. These ranged from the well-known and well-documented Zonnestraal and Paimio sanatoriums to little-known examples in Czechoslovakia and other parts of central Europe (see frontispiece). In southern climates the type was adapted to the very hot summers: balconies and terraces were angled and recessed to give shade in the middle of the day – as in the Bucegi Sanatorium at Predeal in Romania, designed by the former Dadaist Marcel Janco (Iancu) and his brother Juliu Iancu in 1936.[10] Sanatoriums were also designed for the treatment of conditions other than tuberculosis. In particular, special sanatoriums were constructed on the model of tuberculosis sanatoriums for the mentally ill and those suffering from 'nervous diseases'.[11] Like tuberculosis sanatoriums, these were generally located in peaceful rural or leafy suburban surroundings, as fresh air and sunlight were thought to be equally important for treating nervous disorders by removing the patient from the alienating shocks and *anomie* of the modern metropolis. Among the most celebrated of these was the Purkersdorf Sanatorium near Vienna, founded around 1890 to provide treatment for nervous complaints by Anton Löw and the well-known psychiatrist Richard von Krafft-Ebing.[12] The Secessionist architect and designer Josef Hoffmann was commissioned to design a new building for the sanatorium in 1903–4 with discreetly luxurious accommodation, spa baths, and extensive facilities for electrotherapy and physiotherapy. Set in a large park a few miles outside the city in the valley of the river Wien, the Westend Spa Sanatorium at Purkersdorf attracted a fashionable and well-heeled Viennese clientele who included musicians and writers such as Gustav Mahler, Arnold Schoenberg, Hugo von Hofmannsthal and Arthur Schnitzler. The patients continued to be treated according to Krafft-Ebing's methods – regarded in Austria at the time as a 'rational' and pragmatic alternative to the psychoanalytical 'talking cure' of Freud – one of the main principles of which was the importance of fresh air and good ventilation for the health of the nervous system.[13]

Hoffmann described his Purkersdorf building as having been developed out of 'necessity, need and the importance of hygiene'.[14] In the institution's annual yearbook of 1911 the chief physician Ludwig Stein praised its 'incomparably beautiful and hygienic facility', the 'hygienic and comfortable accommodation of patients', and the 'generous provision of light and air'.[15] Although the sanatorium was constructed with white-painted load-bearing brick walls supporting reinforced-concrete beam-and-slab ceilings (rather than a reinforced-concrete frame), the sheer amount of glass to wall was nonetheless impressive.[16] Hoffmann paid particular attention to providing ingenious opening mechanisms for the windows, allowing the amount of air in each room to be carefully regulated. The architectural critic Joseph August Lux praised the sanatorium as 'a house of health' where the 'lost' were 'recovered', with its 'wide and commodious' windows which admitted 'as much light and air and sun into the building as possible'. According to Lux, it was 'not only the bath facilities and ingenious muscle-strengthening machines' that played such an important role in this, but also the 'light, air, and sun and the beautiful green forest landscape' which streamed through the windows into the buildings and 'into the patient's souls'.[17] With a wide, flat, overhanging roof and sun terraces that opened off the patients' rooms on the upper floor, the white-painted sanatorium shone brilliantly in its leafy pastoral setting. White also predominated inside, intensifying the daylight that poured through the windows and heightening the 'impression of hygienic cleanliness'.[18] The building was equipped with simple electric-light fittings with glass shades, which were considered cleaner and more hygienic than

gas lighting. Electricity was widely used throughout the sanatorium and was probably seen as a metaphor for the well-regulated nervous energy of the healthy individual.

In its pristine simplicity and austere geometric rigour, the Purkersdorf Sanatorium was unlike most other buildings of its time, combining some of the qualities of a luxurious home, a modern hospital and a 'reform' factory. The imagery of the 'clean machine' that would have powerfully impressed a patient or visitor as they approached the new gleaming white building was reinforced as they drew up at the main entrance, over which a metal-and-glass canopy was suspended from two small steel lattice girders.[19] Set among the green fields and woods in its sparkling whiteness, the sanatorium seemed to represent the utmost modernity. As the critic Ludwig Hevesi wrote in 1905, 'everything is new, newer, newest'.[20] With its ranks of electrically powered massage and exercise machines, the 'mechanotherapy' room on the ground floor resembled the carefully ordered control room of a modern factory (see chapters 11 and 12).

Purkersdorf Sanatorium, rear façade, Vienna, 1903–4,
photographed in 2002 while under restoration
Josef Hoffmann

The deliberately repetitive geometrical motifs throughout the main public rooms of the sanatorium and in the patients' own bedrooms were intended to have a calming and beneficial effect. Hoffmann used his own specially designed geometric fabrics, to which he gave the names *Sehnsucht* (Yearning) and *Notschrei* (Cry for Help).[21] Like many of his generation of Viennese middle-class professionals, he had himself undergone treatment for nervous conditions, and was later to spend an extended period in an Alpine sanatorium at Semmering near Vienna in 1919.[22] With its sensitive and rational functionalism, 'the restfulness of rectilinearity', Hoffmann's Purkersdorf Sanatorium was designed to soothe the nerves of its wealthy patients, damaged according to Krafft-Ebing's theories by the speed and cacophony of 'modern life'.[23] Yet at the same time Hoffmann's design allowed the medical staff discreetly to surveil their charges through its clear and rational layout of long straight corridors and partially glazed doors.[24]

About the same time as Hoffmann's Purkersdorf extension was built, Otto Wagner laid out the ground plans of the Am Steinhof psychiatric hospital on the outskirts of Vienna as a series of pavilions 'presented as a sanatorium rather than an asylum'.[25] Wagner himself was responsible for the detailed design of the hospital church, which was richly decorated with gilt-and-marble Secessionist ornament and stained glass by Koloman Moser. Here Wagner incorporated the latest ideas about hygiene: with holy-water fountains like soap dispensers to prevent cross infection, and a floor sloped towards the altar to facilitate cleaning, as many of the patients were incontinent. The poet and feuilletonist (and close friend of Adolf Loos and Karl Kraus) Peter Altenberg – who published a whole book of poems on the subject of health, hygiene and dietetics – spent some time as a patient at Am Steinhof.[26] In 1915, Altenberg published the poem 'Werdet einfach!' (Be Simple!), which begins:

> Be simple!
> Make health, cleanliness of the body and the soul your only luxury!
> Let hygiene and dietetics, those economisers and augmenters of the Life-force be your luxury!
> Even with a tin basin, a sponge and the cheapest good-quality soap one can be clean!
> Let your walls be white-washed, your windows open day and night, your bed healthily hard, a kind of ideal camp bed; the best-quality loden and the best-quality flannel replace your criminal furs!
> Be simple!
> There is a pleasure in simplicity! [...][27]

Lodging mainly in relatively inexpensive hotel rooms for the last decade or so of his life – with few luxuries and even fewer possessions – Altenberg put his ideas of simplicity into practice, living like a patient in a sanatorium until his death from a neglected chill in 1919 at the age of fifty-nine.

Following the stock-market crash of 1929, patients who had stayed for years on end in sanatoriums could no longer afford to do so. In a commentary to *The Magic Mountain* written in 1953, almost thirty years after the novel's first publication, Mann pointed out that institutions like his International Sanatorium Berghof had only been possible 'in a capitalistic economy that was still functioning well and normally':

> Only under such a system was it possible for patients to remain there year after year at the family's expense. *The Magic Mountain* became the swan song of that form of existence. Perhaps it is a general rule that epics descriptive of some particular phase of life tend to appear as it nears its end.[28]

Fashionable sanatorium towns such as Davos increasingly turned to sports tourism. (In recent years it has become the meeting place for the global elite of statesman, politicians and administrators at the World Economic Forum.) More specialized sanatoriums such as Zonnestraal survived the economic slump, although its building programme was delayed and cut. The economies made in construction were to have a dire effect on its condition in later years. After the Second World War, when the regime of isolation, sun and fresh air was superseded by the introduction of effective chemotherapy and inoculation against the disease, many sanatoriums on mountain sites reverted back to (or were converted to) grand hotels with facilities for winter sports.[29] Those on lowland sites or situated on the outskirts of cities were usually turned into general hospitals, like the Zonnestraal.

An openness to fresh air and sunlight, immaculate hygiene and cleanliness, white walls, white-painted (or chromed-metal) furniture and a liberal provision of sun terraces also marked the design of general hospitals and clinics of the inter-war period. Richard Döcker's Waiblingen District Hospital (1926–28) near Stuttgart – ranked by the architectural historians Richard Pommer and Otto Christian with the Zonnestraal and Paimio sanatoriums as 'among the paradigmatic monuments of the neues Bauen'[30] – was planned like a sanatorium with wide, stepped terraces onto which the patients' beds could be wheeled. An angled concrete canopy above the terraces shaded the upper parts of the patient's body when the sun was at its hottest in the middle of the day in summer, while enormous sliding windows ensured that the maximum fresh air and light entered the small six- or eight-bed wards.

In *Terrassentyp*, Döcker advocated the stepped-terrace type as a model not only for hospitals and other institutional or public buildings, but also for hotels, offices, private houses and social housing.[31] He designed two terraced houses for the 1927 Weissenhof-siedlung housing exhibition, which displayed a wide variety of modernist housing types with terraces. Sensitively exploiting the steeply falling terrain, Döcker's long, low, open dwellings appear rooted in the hillside – with long windows and extensive terraces to maximize the effects of sunlight and fresh air on the south-east facing site.[32] Döcker saw the terrace type as unlocking the traditional closed structure of the house, opening the interior to sunshine and fresh air, and merging it organically into the garden and surrounding landscape, 'in contrast to the old idea of shutting out the outside world, which renders a house inappropriate for modern concepts of habitation'.[33]

Many features of the sanatorium also appear in other types of institutional buildings of the period, such as Adolf Schneck's Haus auf der Albe (1930), a holiday retreat for workers in wooded countryside south of Stuttgart which had austere cell-like rooms equipped with balconies and wide windows, and Hannes Meyer's sober ADGB residential trade-union college (1927–30) set in pine forests by a lake at Bernau north of Berlin. Döcker suggested parallels between sanatoriums and hotels in *Terrassentyp*.[34] If sanatoriums sometimes resembled grand hotels, hotels also often resembled sanatoriums. The Isla 'mountain hotel' designed by J. Licht in the late 1920s for a spectacular Alpine site in Arosa had large balconies and verandas off the guest rooms designed in similar fashion to the lying-out balconies of mountain sanatoriums, as also did Lois Welzenbacher's Pension Turm – a tall tower-like hotel building in Hall in the Austrian Tyrol, which featured dramatic cantilevered balconies and a rooftop terrace.[35] Not surprisingly, the Gooiland Hotel (1934–36) in Hilversum, designed by Jan Duiker at the end of his life when he was dying from cancer, also bears a close resemblance to modernist sanatorium or hospital buildings – not least the nearby Zonnestraal.

Shortly before the First World War, Otto Wagner had produced designs for hotels on prominent inner-city sites in Vienna with interior layouts similar to those of hospitals and sanatoriums: the Hotel Wien on the Ringstrasse (1910) and the Hotel on the Karlsplatz (1910–11), although neither was built. In their monograph on Wagner, Heinz Geretsegger and Max Peintner group these together with designs for sanatoriums in a section entitled 'Sanatoria and Hotels'.[36] Wagner's hotel designs were made while he was

Hotel Wien,
Vienna, 1910
Otto Wagner

working on the Stiftung Heilstatte für Lupuskranke, a flat-roofed reinforced-concrete sanatorium for lupus in Vienna built between 1910 and 1913. Shortly after this, in 1914, he made unrealized designs for a heliotherapeutic mountain sanatorium, Palmschloss near Brixen, with long south-facing wards and sun terraces onto which patients beds could be wheeled.[37] During the First World War, Wagner produced a design for a 'bungalow installation for convalescent soldiers which could later be used as a tuberculosis sanatorium', and advocated that after the war tuberculosis sanatoriums should be built near the major cities which could subsequently be adapted as other types of hospital.[38] Wagner clearly thought of the design of hotels and sanatoriums as closely linked. 'What is required of hotel accommodation in nearly all cases,' he wrote, 'is a quiet, clean, hygienic room, where the guest is able to sleep undisturbed and attend to his physical needs.' In place of the 'princely apartments' generally demanded, he proposed austerely fitted rooms of minimum size furnished with 'genuine objects' rather than 'the frippery in current use'.[39] A drawing for the Hotel Wien shows a sanatorium-like interior with a uniformed chambermaid dressed like a nurse cleaning the floor with a vacuum cleaner (the clean machine). Wagner believed that the ideal hotel should have between 400 and 800 beds, which would have produced very large institution-like structures.

Many of the superblocks built by the Vienna municipal-housing department in the 1920s and early 1930s, such as the Karl-Marx-Hof, resembled both grand hotels and sanatoriums from the outside. Although the accommodation was often cramped and basic, the largest of these offered a wide range of communal hygienic and social facilities such as baths, kindergartens, laundries, public libraries, post offices, shops, meeting halls, advice centres – and sometimes also tuberculosis clinics and other general and specialized medical services.[40] The combating of tuberculosis and similar debilitating diseases was one of the direct aims of social housing between the wars. In the conviction that 'only by providing people with a place to sit out in the sun whenever possible was a long term remedy for tuberculosis attainable', Bruno Taut designed each apartment with a balcony facing south or west in the Wohnstadt Carl Legien in Berlin (1928–30).[41] Probably the most extreme example of such beliefs was Peter Behrens's apartment block for the Weissenhofsiedlung in 1927, which was directly inspired by the model of the sanatorium and provided every tenant with an open-air south-facing terrace. Before the First World War, when Walter Gropius, Mies van der Rohe and Le Corbusier were all working as assistants in his Berlin office, Behrens had designed a series of roof terraces on the top of the AEG factory and administrative buildings as part of the series of major design projects undertaken for the German electrical combine. Although they evoked ideas of the 'machine in the garden' or the 'clean machine' promoted by industrial reformers in the early 20th century, these terraces were not designed to benefit the workers but for the use of the AEG executives and as a venue for company functions.[42] After the First World War, however, Behrens had become convinced of the health-promoting qualities of the open-air domestic terrace in the fight against tuberculosis. Since 1922, he had

Karl-Marx-Hof,
Vienna, 1926–30
Karl Ehn

been professor and director of the Meisterschule für Architektur at the Akademie in Vienna, where he had designed a number of apartment blocks for the Social Democrat city council's social-housing programme. Although several of these were realized, his plans for a terraced block of apartments were rejected by the city council as too expensive – as were similar terraced blocks by Adolf Loos and Oskar Strnad.[43] The advantage of a terraced design was that it provided each apartment with the access to sunlight and fresh air he believed to be the key to a healthy hygienic and disease-free environment. By giving each apartment its own terrace or large balcony providing direct access to the open air, Behrens aimed to prevent tuberculosis and other infectious diseases. It was also his intention to assist the treatment of those who suffered from such ailments by making the terraces or balconies large enough to move sickbeds or recliners out onto them on sunny days – as in a sanatorium.[44] He described his ideas in 1926 in the journal of the German Red Cross and shortly afterwards wrote to his former pupil Mies van der Rohe about realizing a terraced block at the Weissenhofsiedlung, of which Mies was artistic director.[45] Behrens sent Mies a copy of his article and a large charcoal sketch to give a clearer idea of his proposals, declaring that: 'If ever this type of terraced block is translated into reality, I believe that it can do a great deal for the health of the people.'[46]

Behrens was one of the few Weissenhof architects to mention hygiene in the published description of his building.[47] Cited as one of the main criteria for the exhibition in the first policy document issued by the organizers in June 1925, this had disappeared from the definitive document of December 1926, perhaps because by this date hygiene seems to have been taken for granted 'as a presumed standard'.[48] While most of the architects who designed individual single-family houses at Weissenhof made some attempt to provide the inhabitants with outside space and fresh air, Behrens's block was intended as a didactic demonstration that this could be achieved in a design for an apartment building which could serve as a model for social housing.[49] As with all the housing at Weissenhof, Behrens's apartments were occupied by middle-class tenants after the exhibition closed. Nevertheless, his intention had been to build a block of model apartments that would serve as a prototype: demonstrating the possibilities of healthy and hygienic social housing for the lower-income families who were most at risk from tuberculosis and other environmentally related diseases by providing outdoor space and fresh air for those who could never afford to live in a separate house with a garden: 'In order to make some impact on tuberculosis, it is apparent that every dwelling, even in a multi-storey building, needs to have a sizable space open to the sky. It is no less necessary to ensure that all dwellings have thorough ventilation.'[50] In his Weissenhof apartment building Behrens used the flat roofs of the lower floors to provide terraces for the upper apartments, while terraces at ground level served the lower apartments. Loos had incorporated a series of stepped terraces in a villa designed in 1912 for the Social Democrat lawyer and reformer Gustav Scheu – who as a municipal councillor and adviser on housing in Vienna after the First World War was largely responsible for persuading Loos to work on social housing in the city. He elaborated this idea in plans for stepped-terrace apartments that were part of the same social housing project for which Behrens produced his terraced designs in 1924.[51] In an unrealized design for a group of middle-class villas on the Côte d'Azur, Loos stepped the terraces and roof gardens asymmetrically – a system that Behrens adopted for his Weissenhof block.[52]

As Karin Kirsch has pointed out, given the preoccupations with health and hygiene at this time it is curious that very few critics seem to have commented on Behrens's concern with attacking the social evil of tuberculosis directly through building reform.[53] This may be because in his desire to provide open-air spaces for every tenant, he appears paradoxically to have produced apartments that were poky and badly lit inside – compromising the provision of healthy and hygienic accommodation that was his major objective. The ingenious if over-complicated designs necessitated certain concessions in the living space to achieve 'the central principle of a hygienic, modern apartment house': a spacious terrace or balcony for each of the eleven apartments.[54] By comparison with the individual Weissenhof houses designed by younger architects, many of which provided generous sun terraces and balconies – or roof gardens in the case of Le Corbusier's houses – Behrens's apartment building appeared clumsy and awkward. Where most of the Weissenhof houses emphasized the interpenetration of inside and outside spaces celebrated by Sigfried Giedion in *Befreites Wohnen* and Hans Richter in *Die neue Wohnung*, in his apartment block Behrens kept the inside and outside separate. And in providing each tenant with a terrace he was unable to aspire to the minimalist elegance of Mies van der Rohe's apartment building with its long unbroken strips of windows and token balconies.

Theo van Doesburg contrasted the 'dim rooms and caverns' of Behrens's building – where 'the small openings for the windows' were 'totally out of proportion with the façades' – with the 'lavish use of glass' in Mies van der Rohe's apartment block, which made the 'rooms, corridors and service quarters' appear 'large and light'.[55] Rather than providing outdoor terraces or roof gardens, Mies's block was designed to give all rooms in the apartments maximum light and fresh air by means of wide windows and cross ventilation. Nevertheless, the housing expert Marie-Elisabeth Lüders criticized this in *Die Form* as creating 'a constant draught over the floor, a cause for no little concern when small children are present'.[56] Lüders also criticized the inward-opening windows on the stair landings, complaining that these created 'an unheard-of danger to children in the house', and that the bars of the balconies were 'set so far apart that children six years old and older can very easily climb through them'.[57] The top storey provided drying space for washing, rather than a roof garden, as was customary in three- or four-storey blocks of social housing in Germany at the time. The individual apartments did not have terraces, but token metal balconies on which little more than a flower-pot or two could be placed, a feature typical of much German modernist social housing of the late 1920s.[58] The purpose of these was representational rather than functional. During the Second World War this 'simple slab dedicated to hygiene' was used as an isolation hospital for children with scarlet fever and diphtheria.[59]

Although clearly obsessed by the fight against tuberculosis, Behrens believed the terraces in his Weissenhof block also served to provide essential space for the tenants to enjoy nature and cultivate plants, arguing that 'it is surely well enough known how deeply the inhabitants of great cities long for open-air activities and closeness to nature, as the profusion of flowers on their tiny balconies often so touchingly shows'.[60] Here he was probably influenced by his contact with Loos and other architects such as Margarete Schütte-Lihotzky who had worked with the Austrian settlers' movement immediately after the First World War and who championed the provision of 'productive' gardens and allotments, following the ideas of the German garden-design specialist Leberecht Migge. In the mid-1920s, Migge was employed to landscape the first suburban estates built for the neue Frankfurt, such as Römerstadt and Praunheim. Individual houses and apartments were generously provided with gardens and allotments, roof gardens and terraces.[61] In Praunheim, the gardens of single-family terrace houses were divided into areas or 'rooms' – one for sitting and relaxing, another for growing vegetables – separated from the neighbouring gardens by wood-and-metal pergolas over which creeping plants could be grown. May commissioned Schütte-Lihotzky to design allotment and garden huts for the Frankfurt estates based on those she had designed for the settlers' movement in Vienna in the early 1920s. The original Austrian versions had been extendable, so as to create permanent living accommodation for their owners, and had formed a model for the design of existence-minimum housing.[62]

Migge also collaborated with Martin Wagner and Bruno Taut on the landscaping and design of many of the neue Berlin estates, including the enormous Hufeisensiedlung (Horse-Shoe Estate) and the quaintly named Onkel Toms Hütte Siedlung (Uncle Tom's Cabin Estate). The Hufeisensiedlung (1925–27) was a spectacular four-storey apartment block designed by Taut and Wagner and landscaped by Migge, providing 1027 apartments in the working-class district of Berlin-Britz. It was built in a horseshoe shape round an extensive and carefully planted communal garden, while balconies and winter gardens were provided for individual apartments. The more suburban Onkel Tom Hütte (1926–31) consisted of 1105 low-rise apartments and 895 single-family houses designed by Taut, Otto Rudolf Salvisberg and Hugo Häring to estate plans laid out by Wagner – set in the densely wooded suburb of Berlin-Zehlendorf, with Migge and Martha Willings-Göhre as landscape architects. Each single-family house was provided with a 200-square-metre garden, and many of the existing forest trees were incorporated into the planting to form a 'Waldsiedlung' (forest Siedlung). Today – like the housing they surround – the green spaces Migge and Willings-Göhre designed are protected by German law as historic monuments.

With its communal provision for individual needs the modern sanatorium was one of the main models for dom kommuny, the apartment blocks with collective eating and social facilities built in the Soviet Union during the late 1920s. The best known of these was Moisei Ginzburg and Ignati Milinis's Narkomfin building in Moscow (1928–30), designed to house fifty employees of the ministry of finance and their families in a six-storey block raised on pilotis. Communal facilities were provided in a smaller building linked to the apartment block by a pedestrian bridge. Its two double-height storeys contained a gymnasium or sports hall on the ground floor, a communal kitchen, dining room, reading room and other recreational rooms on the upper floor, and a summer dining terrace. The communal building was fully glazed on its north façade, directly facing the large communal garden which occupied the park-like grounds of two early 19th-century aristocratic mansions.[63] These buildings were much admired by many western European architects, and by left-wing critics such as the Czech writer and theorist of modernism Karel Teige. As a militant advocate of housing with communal facilities, Teige argued that the feasibility of the collective apartment block could be tested through institutional buildings such as Jaromír Krejcar's Machnáč spa and sanatorium at Trenčianske Teplice in Slovakia.[64] Built between 1930 and 1932 for the Czechoslovakian Association of Private Clerical Workers, with its generous sun terraces, roof gardens and individual balconies, the sanatorium was described by the

Czech architect Ladislav Žák as a 'proto-image of socialist living'.[65] While Teige declared:

> Well, transform this convalescent sanatorium into workers' housing; make the
> rooms apartments for single people, that is, a dwelling without a household or
> household economy, a dwelling without a kitchen; turn the wing with a restau-
> rant and conference rooms into a tenants' club with a cafeteria, a dining room
> and a crèche, and you have a quite precise image of the collective dwelling, with
> a centralized economy, cultural and social institutions [...]. [66]

More than any other protagonist of modernism, Teige promoted the sanatorium as
the model building type, arguing that only social health-care buildings, hospitals and

Narkomfin building,
Moscow, 1928–30
Moisei Ginzburg and **Ignati Milinis**

open-air schools managed to escape 'bourgeois ideology'. As examples he cited the Zonnestraal Sanatorium and Duiker's Open-Air School in Amsterdam (see Chapter 7) along with Hannes Meyer's ADGB Bundesschule (trade-union college) at Bernau, Mart Stam and Werner Moser's Budge Home for the Aged in Frankfurt, and three examples from Czechoslovakia: Bohuslav Fuchs municipal swimming pool and spa in Brno-Zábrdovice, the Vesna Schools for Women's Professions by Fuchs and Josef Polášek, and Krejcar's Trenčianske Teplice sanatorium. These represented for him an antithesis to 'the holy cow of bourgeois ideology and morality: the family and its household', which he believed forced architecture to conform 'to outdated forms of dwelling culture'.[67]

While many were luxuriously appointed, some of the custom-built service apartments popular among the better-off middle classes in western Europe during the 1930s simulated a spartan and hygienic severity that evoked both the *dom kommuny* and the modern sanatorium. With its long, white, concrete access balconies and sculptural zigzagging external staircase, the most strikingly austere in appearance of these was the Isokon apartment building in north-west London by the Canadian architect Wells Coates – which bore a resemblance both to Aalto's cliff-like sanatorium at Paimio and Ginzburg and Milinis's Narkomfin communal apartment building in Moscow.[68] Intended to provide existence-minimum 'pieds-à-terre' for well-heeled middle-class professionals, the Isokon building housed a number of modernist émigrés, such as Walter Gropius, Marcel Breuer and László Moholy-Nagy, who lived there briefly while working in London after leaving Nazi Germany in the mid-1930s.

Set in a north German landscape of pine forests and lakes to the north of Berlin, the ADGB (Allgemeine Deutsche Gewerkschaftsbund) trade-union college took many of its features from the modern sanatorium and the hospital. Designed by Hannes Meyer and Hans Wittwer with students from the Bauhaus, this residential educational complex was planned as a series of separate but connected elements roughly in the form of a Z, staggered to follow the natural contours of the site and to maximize exposure to sunshine and protection from the wind. Financed by a contribution of 50 pfennig from each of the four-and-a-half million union members throughout Germany, the school was designed as an institution for union officials to take short courses in subjects such as trade-union studies, economics, management, industrial hygiene, insurance and labour law.[69] During his stay at Bernau, 'the student would also receive excellent food' and 'physical training to improve his general condition'. Meyer claimed the 'experience of these novel surroundings' induced the student 'to raise his standard of living and culture'.[70]

The layout and design of the building followed the principles of a hospital or sanatorium, with central social and eating facilities and residential accommodation in three-storey blocks overlooking a clearing in the pine forest with a small lake and swimming pool and a sports field beyond. While the student rooms did not have individual balconies or terraces, a glazed veranda opened off the communal dining room and a sheltered terrace with a pergola covered with climbing plants shading garden chairs and tables adjoined the main lobby area. Spacious terrace-like balconies were provided in the accommodation for the staff.[71] The teaching building at the far end of the complex also incorporated a gymnasium, library, reading room and private study rooms. One of the most remarkable features of the complex was the long, glazed external corridor connecting the different parts of the campus. This provided a kind of 'promenade architecturale' during the course of which students could look out towards the pine forests, yet was wide enough for them to stop and talk to each other. The corridor was made deliberately long and the buildings spaced out through the grounds because 'the quickest way of getting together is not by building short corridors', but 'by creating the opportunity for establishing friendly contact'. The result was an extended linear layout 'not a concentric massing of buildings'.[72] According to Meyer, the three teaching rooms were located in the 'raised' storey above the gymnasium because the 'process of learning in the prime of one's life was an unusual posture for the ordinary "working man" too'.[73] The building (which also included many technologically advanced and ingenious facilities) was intended to give the trade unionist a very different experience from that of their typically run-down 19th-century industrial workplaces: a foretaste of the modernist utopia of the 'clean machine'. The experience must have been not totally dissimilar to that of the sick diamond workers who went as patients to the Zonnestraal Sanatorium. The Bundesschule was like a sanatorium for the healthy, where they learned new skills and ways of understanding the relationships of the workplace and the struggle between labour and capital.

A special issue of the French avant-garde architectural magazine *L'Architecture vivante* in 1933 was devoted to hospitals, clinics, old-peoples' homes and sanatoriums, and also included Richard Neutra's Lovell Health House, a Los Angeles doctor's private house designed to look like a hospital or clinic (see Chapter 6).[74] These and similar buildings were frequently published in medical and other specialist journals, as well as in national and international architectural and construction-trade magazines, reaching an influential audience of doctors, architects, designers, housing managers and other professionals across the world. In the introduction to his 1927 translation of Le Corbusier's *Vers une architecture* (*Towards a New Architecture*), the English architect Frederick Etchells illustrated a photograph of an operating theatre in a modern hospital. Etchells quotes from an advertisement in a special issue of the *Architects' Journal* of 1925 on hospital design:

> The modern hospital is a triumph of the elimination of the detrimental and the unessential. Because of its absolute fitness to purpose its operation theatre – like the engine room of an ocean liner – is one of the most perfect rooms in the world.[75]

Luxurious austerity

The austere and hygienic appearance of sanatorium buildings or hospitals also served as a model for the 'sober luxury' that became fashionable in the first decades of the 20th century. A luxurious interior might be hidden behind a plain modern exterior, within which ornament and decoration could flourish – controlled and quarantined, like a patient in a sanatorium or isolation hospital. Among the earliest of these were the series of villas for wealthy Viennese clients Adolf Loos designed shortly before the First World War, at the time when he was visiting Bessie Bruce in Swiss mountain sanatoriums. Despite Loos's many well-known attacks on ornament from 1897 onwards, his opposition was to uncontrolled and thoughtless ornament, rather than to ornament as such (see Chapter 4). The austere exteriors of the buildings he designed from 1910 to 1930 concealed a carefully articulated decorative programme, but little of this was visible from the outside. The sober undecorated elevations of Loos's best-known building, the Michaelerhaus in the centre of Vienna (1910–11), almost certainly owe something to the plain façades of Alpine sanatoriums and the whiteness of the snow around them. Loos's pupil Paul Engelmann described the Michaelerhaus shortly after it was completed in 1911 as shining with a glacier-like purity.[76] Built on a prime site in the centre of Vienna opposite the Hofburg (imperial palace) this up-market apartment building had an expensive men's outfitters on the ground and mezzanine floors, discreetly fitted out with luxurious woods and marbles. This combination of an austere outward appearance and refined luxury within was characteristic of many modernist buildings – especially if (like the Michaelerhaus) they were commissioned by Jewish clients.

Between 1926 and 1928, Ludwig Wittgenstein designed a large house for his millionairess sister Margarethe Stonborough in collaboration with Paul Engelmann, discreetly located in an unfashionable inner suburb of Vienna.[77] With its austere sanatorium-like exterior and richly furnished interior this 'modernist palace' was the ultimate 'clean machine': its institutional proportions and tall windows, wide terraces and balconies reminiscent of hospitals and sanatoriums. Wittgenstein had spent considerable time in military hospitals and prisoner-of-war camps during the First World War. One of his cousins, Paul Wittgenstein, was interned for long periods by his family in the Am Steinhof psychiatric hospital on the outskirts of Vienna and later became the subject of a well-known novel by Thomas Bernhard.[78] During the Second World War, the Stonborough-Wittgenstein House was employed by the Red Cross as an army hospital, a use to which it was easily adapted. In 1945, Russian soldiers moved into the building with their horses, where they would have been able to ride through its enormously tall metal doors and French windows without dismounting. Later it was used as a demobilization centre. Such institutional uses (it has more recently served as the Bulgarian Cultural Centre) are not out of keeping with the image of the building Wittgenstein conceived for Margarethe Stonborough.

As a trained engineer he ensured that the house would be a perfectly functioning piece of machinery, a domestic sanatorium where his sister's wealth would be shielded and protected from the angry and envious eyes of the poor – or the bureaucratic eyes of the Social Democrat town-hall officials. Austere and purist in form, the house was planned and overseen by Wittgenstein himself, who adapted and refined Engelmann's earlier designs. Jacques Groag, another of Loos's former pupils, acted as site architect and supervised the construction, while Wittgenstein himself controlled the whole enterprise with an extraordinary attention to details – especially in the interior. The contrast between Wittgenstein's perfectionist obsession with the functioning of the house as a clean and hygienic 'machine for living in' and his sister's sophisticated and 'aristocratic' decorative taste is an extreme example of what was characteristic of much modernist private housing of the inter-war period: the concealment of a comfortable and luxurious interior behind an austere and unassuming (almost 'industrial' or 'institutional') exterior. At night, the enormous glass windows were blacked out by metal shutters, which Wittgenstein had designed to sink silently into the floor during the day. These also provided security against burglars or marauding mobs. The removal of ornament from the exterior produces an effect of anonymity and ambiguity similar to that found in Loos's villas of the period, such as the Moller House in Vienna and the Müller House in Prague, and in the luxurious house Mies van der Rohe designed for the Tugendhat family in Brno.[79]

These houses looked extremely severe from the outside (particularly the side facing the street) but had interiors richly finished with the highest quality materials. Loos wrote that 'the building should be discreet on the outside and reveal its richness only on the inside'.[80] Many of those who commissioned modernist houses in Europe during the 1920s and early 1930s were Jewish – including the owners of the Moller, Tugendhat and Stonborough-Wittgenstein houses. The increasing anti-Semitism of the period was a further reason why they wished to mask their wealth behind the plain austere façades of the new architecture. Such houses performed a masquerade where a luxury product feigned the innocence of a standardized mass-produced one, and an appearance of hygiene and cleanliness was employed to veil the semblance of wealth, suggesting an institutional building like a sanatorium or clinic, rather than a large and expensive private villa. Yet such strategies proved useless once the Nazis had seized power. After the Germans invaded Czechoslovakia in 1938, the Tugendhats left for Switzerland, and eventually emigrated to Venezuela. In early 1940, Margarethe Stonborough moved to New York for the duration of the Second World War.[81]

Shortly after the war the Tugendhat House became a dance school, and during the communist period a children's hospital.[82] The vast living room – which had originally featured a floor-to-ceiling window that sank electrically into the floor – was ideal for dancing classes, and as a physiotherapy and rehabilitation gym for children who had problems with their motor skills. A photograph taken in the 1960s shows the sun-filled room with its huge walls of glass, empty except for gym mats laid out on the floor.[83] Although not Jewish himself, Mies van de Rohe also emigrated to the United States in 1938, where his practice flourished and his fame grew exponentially. In the late 1940s, he designed a spectacular single-storey glass-walled vacation house in the woods for Edith Farnsworth, a Chicago doctor, which (unlike the Tugendhat House) was wide open to the gaze of those who walked past it. Farnsworth eventually fell out with Mies over the design, which she believed exposed her to the stares of passers-by, prowlers, or voyeurs. She later wrote that this most minimal of modernist houses set in deep woods by a lake had been rumoured locally to be 'a tuberculosis sanitarium'.[84]

The sanatorium by the sea

In 1934, the seaside town of Bexhill-on-Sea in East Sussex commissioned a sparkling concrete, steel and glass modernist pavilion designed by Erich Mendelsohn and Serge Chermayeff. From the esplanade the pavilion resembled an ocean liner beached on the pebbled foreshore – or a 'sanatorium by the sea', contrasting dramatically with the red-brick Victorian and Edwardian buildings of the town's seafront. It provided regular relaxation for local residents (many of whom were retired) or a temporary 'cure' for the overworked and overstressed city dweller. The coast around Bexhill was popularly known between the world wars as 'the wealth of health' – trading on the association of bracing sea air and salt-water bathing with health, recuperation and relaxation that had successfully promoted seaside resorts in Britain for a hundred and fifty years.[85] Photographs of the period of holidaymakers in deck chairs enjoying the sun on the wide balconies and terraces of the pavilion resemble those of sanatorium patients taking the *Luft und Liegekur* outside their rooms (or passengers on a liner).

Among prominent features were south-facing solarium balconies overlooking the beach and sea, a dramatic glass-enclosed cantilevered spiral staircase, a 'sun parlour' shaded from the fiercer rays of the sun by the pavilion's roof slab, and a roof terrace where tennis or deck quoits and other games could be played.[86] A restaurant seating 200 people opened directly onto the south-facing ground-floor sun terrace, with panoramic views across the beach and out to sea through continuous plate-glass windows. Above this were a lounge bar and a small library or reading room – a 'model of modernist repose and calm'.[87] A combined theatre and concert hall with state-of-the-art acoustics could be converted into a full-size dance hall by taking out the moveable seating, and the lecture hall on the upper floor doubled as a conference room. The lightweight steel structure encased in a very thin coat of concrete faced with cream faience tiles helped to give the pavilion its lightness and airiness. Not previously used in Britain, this type of structure suggested positive associations with clean modern factories, open-air swimming baths, and sanatoriums such as the Zonnestraal which – although constructed with a reinforced-concrete frame – was so light and diaphanous it had the airy and transparent qualities of steel-frame construction. Mendelsohn had used steel-frame construction in Germany, but although striking and dramatic many of his public and commercial buildings had a heavy almost monumental character. The Bexhill pavilion has a freshness and airiness, perhaps influenced by the tradition of lightweight seaside structures, or may reflect Chermayeff's contribution to the design. Incorporating the direct enjoyment of the hygienic and health-giving effects of sun and fresh air as an integral part of its design, the pavilion quickly became a potent symbol of leisure, relaxation and enjoyment.

De La Warr Pavilion,
Bexhill-on-Sea, East Sussex, 1934–35,
photographed in the late 1930s
Erich Mendelsohn and **Serge Chermayeff**

That the pavilion was built in so conservative a seaside town was largely due to the support of Earl De La Warr, the socialist mayor of Bexhill who had been the first Labour peer in the House of Lords and served as a junior minister in Ramsay MacDonald's Labour government of the mid-1920s.[88] De La Warr had been responsible for the pavilion's specification with its ambitious range of facilities – combining relaxation and the culture of the body with provision for theatre, music and reading in a modern structure that took full advantage of the site's proximity to the beach and sea. Laying the commemorative plaque at the foot of the spectacular south staircase on 6 May 1935, De La Warr declared this marked 'a great day in the history of Bexhill' that would usher in a new era: 'A venture which is part of a great national movement, virtually to found a new industry – the industry of giving that relaxation, that pleasure, that culture, which hitherto the gloom and dreariness of British resorts have driven our fellow countrymen to risk in foreign lands.'[89] At Bexhill, relaxation and pleasure were to be 'industrialized' through the factory-like 'clean machine' of the dynamic steel-framed pavilion, bringing the new European culture of the body and the mind to Britain, without exposing its people to the 'risk' of travelling to 'foreign lands'. De La Warr's words were prophetic. The pavilion became a landmark in the creation of what came to be called 'the leisure industry' after the Second World War, and served as a model for many later 'leisure centres' built in Britain during the post-war period. But none recaptured its simple gracefulness and sense of style, except perhaps a few of the temporary buildings erected on the South Bank of the Thames in London for the Festival of Britain in 1951.

Although much altered internally, the pavilion remained popular among holiday-makers and local inhabitants in the years after the Second World War until package holidays and cheap charter flights in the 1960s took many of its potential clients abroad to guaranteed sunshine in Italy, Spain or Greece, and the building became increasingly run-down and decrepit. In the first years of the 21st century, the pavilion was restored, modernized and extended by the architects John McAslan & Partners as a national and international arts and entertainment venue. It continued to provide local and regional facilities, while preserving as many as possible of its original features and formal purity. Photographs from the pavilion's early years have the nostalgic and distanced quality of a collective and social 'mass' lifestyle that has largely been superseded today by more individual forms of leisure and entertainment. The way the majority of people enjoy leisure today has changed almost as much as the treatment of tuberculosis. When early 20th-century modernist buildings are restored, not only has the fabric to be renewed but new or changed uses also have to be imagined for them. This is as true of the Bexhill pavilion as of the Zonnestraal Sanatorium (see Conclusion).

3 Hygiene & cleanliness

Looking back towards the end of his life, the English architect Peter Smithson, who grew up between the two world wars, recalled that when he first read Walter Gropius's *The New Architecture and the Bauhaus* he noticed how 'everything in the images is so clean' and 'when you live in the North of England everything is dirty, and you think, modern architecture is wonderful'.[1] Hygiene and cleanliness had become major concerns of social reformers and medical professionals in western Europe and the United States by the end of the 19th century. The discovery of the microbial origin of typhoid and other infectious diseases in the latter part of the century fostered an awareness of the dangers of faecal contamination, which led to the general promotion of personal hygiene and cleanliness, and the hygienic construction and maintenance of housing and public buildings.[2] By the beginning of the 20th century, hygiene had become an issue of major international importance.[3] In 1904, the Congrès Internationaux d'Hygiène et de Démographie set up a permanent committee, followed by the establishment of the Office International d'Hygiène Publique in Rome in 1907. Dr Charlotte Olivier, the Swiss pioneer of tuberculosis treatment and health and hygiene education, declared at a congress on domestic education in 1908 that: 'Science teaches that rational nutrition provides the power of resistance, that in addition to correct nourishment man has need of air and light, that housing becomes unhealthy if this air and light does not penetrate it, that the rays of the sun purify the infected dwelling, and that a meticulous cleanliness prevents disease installing itself in the home.'[4]

Hygienic instruction and regulation was promoted through compulsory schooling and the provision of social housing by the state, by municipal authorities, by private employers, and by charities and trusts. Hygiene legislation was introduced in many western European countries in the early years of the 20th century, and public authorities promoted hygiene education.[5] In French primary schools, where education had been free of charge, secular and compulsory since 1881, 'lessons in the catechism were replaced by lessons on hygiene'.[6] Hygiene education was also disseminated through the work place – especially in factories – and through newspapers and illustrated magazines. In France, this was through the middle-class *L'Illustration* and more popular publications such as the *Petit Journal* with its illustrated supplement. In America, magazines such as *Health*, *Health Culture* and *Hygiene Gazette* had appeared at the turn of the century. From 1923, the American Medical Association published the popular magazine *Hygeia*, which dealt with issues of health, cleanliness and nutrition, and similar magazines appeared in Europe.

The traumas of death and destruction of the First World War, as well as the filth and disease, and the death of millions just after the war as the result of the so-called Spanish flu epidemic, produced a renewed preoccupation with the intimate relationship between health and hygiene. International hygiene exhibitions continued to be organized throughout Europe and North America during the 1920s and 1930s, and hygiene pavilions became familiar features of International Exhibitions or World Fairs – such as that commissioned by Léon Blum's Popular Front government for the Paris International Exhibition of 1937, designed by Robert Mallet-Stevens and René Coulon for a site on the Seine below the Pont d'Iéna.[7] The most famous hygiene exhibition of the inter-war period was the Internationale Hygiene-Ausstellung (International Hygiene Exhibition) which inaugurated the Deutsches Hygiene-Museum (German Hygiene Museum) in Dresden in 1930. The setting up of the museum is often mistakenly associated with the Nazis, who were later to exploit it for their own ideological ends after coming to power in 1933, when it became a centre for 'racial studies'. Nevertheless, the germs of some of these ideas had their origin in the pre-Nazi foundation. The founding of the museum dates back to 1912 following the success of an earlier International Hygiene Exhibition in Dresden in 1911, sponsored by Karl August Lingner, the multi-millionaire manufacturer of Odol mouthwash, to promote public and social hygiene. However, the First World War and the death of Lingner in 1916 delayed its opening until 1930. The museum building was designed in a monumentalist 'stripped classical' style by Wilhelm Kreis (who later worked extensively for the Nazis) but many of the displays for the 1930 exhibition (directed by the Dresden architect Paul Wolf) were in a more modernist style.

One of the most famous and popular exhibits in the museum was *Der gläserne Mensch* (The Glass Man) a transparent full-size representation of a naked male figure with hand-turned copper wires for veins:[8] 'Six feet tall, blond, with beautifully moulded muscles, well poised he rotates half a dozen times on a narrow table', according to a newspaper report. 'Twenty electric lights in sequence illuminate the main organs of the body, explained by a recorded lecture.'[9] The *gläserne Mensch* was modelled on a Greek statue, *Praying Boy* by Boedas (the son of Lysippus) from around 400 BC. The figure clearly embodied ideas about the implied relationship between transparency and hygiene and cleanliness. Unsuccessful attempts had been made to blow a transparent male figure from glass at the time of the first Dresden International Hygiene Exhibition in 1911 and the figure shown in the museum from 1930 was actually made of transparent plastic, not glass.[10] Also on display were wax models of body parts eaten away with cancers and other diseases. The Hygiene-Museum was largely destroyed in the

'Südbelichtung' (Lit from the South), show house,
International Hygiene Exhibition, Dresden, Germany, 1930
Helmut Lüdecke

bombing of Dresden, but was rebuilt and reopened in what was then East Germany – now featuring a transparent glass figure of a woman. A full-size horse and cow were added to the collection later.[11] Copies of these transparent figures for educational and medical use made in the museum workshop were among the most successful industries of the communist era. Since 1990 they have been made by a private company.[12]

The extent of the 1930 Hygiene exhibition was vast – 'in effect, a world's fair for hygiene'[13] – held on the same site as the earlier fair, immediately south of the city centre in a vast public park that also included the zoo and the botanic gardens. The pavilions and displays were connected by a miniature railway and organized around themes such as 'The Healthy City', 'Hygienic Clothing', 'Combating Vermin', 'Women: Family and Career', and 'The Hospital', where the latest medical instruments were exhibited and modern ideas about the care of patients demonstrated. A series of hygienic apartments and houses with 'hygienic furnishings' were also displayed.[14] The prototype 'hygienic houses' included a dwelling for a large family, for a patient suffering from a lung disease, and for a war invalid. A small house designed by Helmut Lüdecke with porthole windows for the bedrooms and larger rectangular windows for the living rooms was exhibited under the name 'Südbelichtung' (Lit from the South).[15] The Platz der Nationen

(Square of the Nations) included an international restaurant, open-air theatre, reception hall, police and fire departments, a modernistic tower, and the Halle der Völkerbundes (League of Nations Hall) with exhibition space for displays by nineteen countries – of which the most celebrated was that of the Soviet Union. A great deal of money, time and effort was put into representing the Soviet line on hygiene to the West. Designed by El Lissitzky, the display refined the bravura publicity and propaganda techniques he had developed for his famous Soviet pavilion at the 'Pressa' (International Press Exhibition) in Cologne in 1928, using the surface of the ceiling as well as the walls and internal spaces of the rooms. It included a full-sized model of the living room and bedroom of a Soviet existence-minimum flat that Lissitzky had designed for Moisei Ginzburg and Ignati Milinis's Narkomfin communal apartment building (1928–30) in Moscow (see Chapter 2).[16]

Hygiene had been energetically promoted in the Soviet Union in the 1920s, and hygiene propaganda reached a peak during the years of the first Five-Year Plan (1928–32). Hygiene became a metaphor for the rejection of the old bourgeois world, which was represented as unclean and unhealthy by Lenin and his successors. Lenin had attacked attempts immediately after the 1917 revolution to create socialism without fully rejecting the old 'unhygienic' world of the bourgeois past. He argued that the workers were 'building a new society without having first become New People cleansed of the dirt of the old world, still standing up to their knees in this filth'.[17] Not only the metaphorical filth of petit-bourgeois consciousness but also the literal dirt and dust that accumulated on petit-bourgeois *objets* had to be removed by banishing such objects themselves. In 1924, a guide for housewives, *Sovety Proletarskoia Khoziaike* (Advice for Proletarian Housewives), counselled: 'Let the proletarian house be light, spacious, decorated only with flowers and with objects which preserve the health of the body and the health of the revolutionary spirit.'

> [W]hile decorating her household the proletarian housewife must maintain one principle in particular: not to stuff the apartment with unnecessary extra furniture, nor hang useless rags for decoration. These not only significantly reduce the amount of light but also harbour dust containing all manner of parasites, and poison the home with throngs of tiny bacteria which are extremely harmful to one's health.[18]

Aesthetic ideas were closely linked to notions of hygiene, light, and openness in the reform movements in architecture and design of the early 20th century. The Austrian critic Joseph August Lux promoted suburban villas designed for prosperous clients by Secession architects such as Josef Hoffmann and Leopold Bauer with the aim of uniting 'hygiene, comfort and beauty', arguing that the 'principle of hygiene was also relevant to the layout of gardens which form a continuation of the house'.[19] Lux recommended the provision of washing facilities in every bedroom, and as many bathrooms as possible – at least three in a large middle-class villa, a novel idea at the time. After the First World War, which had destroyed the Austro-Hungarian empire and left a weak, small, defeated Austria, the Social Democrat municipal authorities of 'Red Vienna', although much concerned with questions of hygiene, could not afford to include even one bathroom per apartment in the social housing for which the city became famous. Instead, they embarked on an ambitious programme of public baths, swimming pools, health centres and laundries to provide communal services for tenants. Looking back on this time the Austrian architect and designer Friedrich Kiesler, who emigrated to the United States in the mid-1920s, compared the extreme austerity and near starvation of the post-war period in Vienna to the process of stripping down the forms of modernist architecture, which he described as 'architecture on a diet': 'As in our living habits, we started to clean off everything that was surplus in design – ornamentation, certain luxurious materials, mouldings, this and that. Everything became, over the years, simpler, cleaner, whiter [...].'[20]

In 1924, the editors of the Czechoslovakian architectural magazine *Stavba* (who included the influential architectural critic and theorist Karel Teige) declared that 'new architecture must be hygienic'. They demanded 'a maximum supply of air and natural light' in new buildings, which should be provided with 'smooth, easily cleanable walls, floors', and efficient artificial lighting, air-conditioning and heating systems.[21] These were typical of the concerns that dominated the thinking of modern architects in most European and North American countries between the wars. Although Teige's own position was combatively anti-bourgeois, the main (although undeclared) aim of health and hygiene legislation introduced in Europe and the United States in the early 20th century was to regulate social change by imposing ideas about public hygiene and private cleanliness that corresponded to middle-class values and standards, and by such means to control the lives and behaviour of the working classes.[22] Hygiene education, propaganda and promotion had similar objectives. Rules were drawn up and guiding principles laid down. Dirt and dust harboured germs that must be destroyed by fresh air and sunlight. Homes should be cleaned thoroughly every day and windows and doors opened each morning to let in the sun and air to destroy the germs. Heavy drapes and curtains, thick carpets and old furniture with decorative features that harboured dust and microbes should be thrown out and replaced with simple, easily cleaned modern furniture and light, easily washed curtains. Metal bedsteads made of brass or iron tubes (or later tubular steel) were recommended as preferable to wooden beds because they were relatively light and easily cleaned, and provided ventilation for the mattress and bed linen. Double beds – which in many working-class households ended up by being occupied not just by parents but children as well – were condemned as morally and hygienically unwholesome. This distaste for the double bed was also shared by the 'enlightened' sections of the professional middle classes and by many intellectuals, and found its way into modernist dogma. Most modernist houses were austerely equipped

with narrow single or twin beds, rarely with 'unhygienic' and 'unhealthy' double beds. Two single beds side by side (or preferably in separate rooms) were not only considered healthier and more hygienic than a double bed, but also suggested a different attitude towards sexuality. This signalled a belief that a cohabiting or married couple were linked in a looser and freer relationship – the social and sexual equivalent of the notion of light, air and openness. The 'open' marriage was the term typically used by the progressive middle classes. Karel Teige made such implicit condemnation of bourgeois sexual *mores* explicit, writing of the 'catafalque' of the traditional marriage bed. Teige considered the marital bedroom to be 'a hatching place of the most wretched forms of bourgeois sexual life, the stage of Strindbergian dramas, a roosting place of shocking erotic banality and decadence', which 'causes contagions and is the breeding place of quarrels as well as the source of family perturbances and thousands of neuroses'.[23]

In most western European countries these hygienic campaigns met with only moderate success among the lower middle and working classes. Simple wooden furniture seems to have generally found acceptance. Old-fashioned brass beds were more often bought because they were cheap second-hand, than because they were hygienic. But new modern steel beds never became popular, probably because of their association with hospitals, army barracks, and similarly regimented residential institutions.

Woman's bedroom, with single bed, in a house for the Werkbundsiedlung, Breslau, Germany (now Wrocław, Poland), 1929
Heinrich Lauterbach

In *Purity and Danger*, Mary Douglas has argued that in creating the modern clean and hygienic domestic environment we 'are not governed by anxiety to escape disease, but are positively re-ordering our environment, making it conform to an idea'. According to Douglas, there 'is nothing fearful or unreasoning in our dirt avoidance: it is a creative movement, an attempt to relate form to function, to make unity of experience'.[24] Statements by architects and designers in the latter part of the 19th and the first decades of the 20th century reveal this desire to achieve a creative unity of hygiene and wellbeing. In the mid-19th century, the architect and architectural theorist Gottfried Semper had maintained that a building should display 'maximum comfort and maximum cleanliness'. In 1896, Otto Wagner argued in *Moderne Architektur* that there were 'two conditions demanded by modern man that can be considered to be criteria' for 'the future design of architectureal works':

THE GREATEST POSSIBLE CONVENIENCE AND THE GREATEST POSSIBLE CLEANLINESS

Wagner maintained that 'artistic effect is inseparable from cleanliness',[25] and advocated: 'light, hygiene, plain surfaces, genuineness of material'.[26] Shortly after this he designed a bath made of plate glass and nickelled steel (see Chapter 10). Thirty years later Bruno Taut declared that:

> Rooms set aside for the preparation of food, such as kitchens and the like, or for the purposes of hygiene, such as bathrooms and water-closets, are no longer dissociable (from the standpoint of their hygienic value) from living or bed-rooms, because we recognize the importance of hygiene, just as we recognize that the requirements for comfort are more or less the same everywhere.[27]

Le Corbusier shared Taut's belief in the universal qualities of hygiene and comfort and the correspondence of the two. His obsession with air conditioning in the late 1920s seems to have been inspired as much by the desire to create sealed, 'hygienic' conditions as for climatic effect. He proposed a universal building with controlled ventilation, suitable for any climate:

> The building in Russia, Paris, Suez or Buenos Aires, the ocean liner crossing the equator, will be hermetically sealed. In winter warmed, in summer cooled, which means that pure controlled air at 18°C circulates inside at all times. The building is hermetic! No dust can enter, nor flies or mosquitoes. No sound![28]

Le Corbusier put his ideas into practice, incorporating sealed-glass façades in his Armée de Salut (Salvation Army) refuge in Paris (1930–32). The hermetically sealed south-facing glass wall of the Salvation Army hostel 'proved disastrous in summer due to thermal gain',[29] and Le Corbusier was forced by the Paris Préfecture to allow the installation of opening windows.[30]

Le Corbusier based many of his designs for villas and apartment blocks on the double-height artist's studio evolved in Paris and other European cities during the second half of the 19th century. This development had already created a fashion among prosperous upper middle-class clients for houses and apartments based on the studio model in the first years of the 20th century. The extra height of the 'live/work' studio space and its open-plan layout were associated not only with increased light, air and sunlight, but also with the openness of modern living in place of the closed individual rooms and claustrophobic arrangements of bourgeois domesticity.

After the First World War, the artist's studio, previously associated with an easy-going bohemianism and lax sexual morals, became identified with the hygienic cleanliness of a doctor's surgery. In the mid-1920s, a Dutch journalist wrote of the austere studio in which Piet Mondrian lived and worked in Montparnasse, where 'the atmosphere is so snowy, the air so glacially pristine'.[31] And in a manifesto written shortly before his death (published posthumously in 1932), Theo van Doesburg maintained that the modern artist's studio should be like a mountain sanatorium:

> Do not artists' studios usually smell like monkey houses? The studio of the modern painter must reflect the ambience of mountains which are nine thousand feet high and topped with an eternal cap of snow. There the cold kills the microbes.[32]

The studio should resemble 'a glass bell jar or a hollow crystal' – an environment of 'absolute cleanliness, constant light, a clear atmosphere'. Van Doesburg argued that there was 'much to learn from a medical laboratory'. The artist's palette 'must be of glass', his brush 'square and hard, dust-free and as immaculate as a surgical instrument', his paintings white. The studio house Van Doesburg designed for himself at Meudon just outside Paris was a 'white cell' where he could shut himself away from contamination, literal and metaphorical: 'The painter himself must be white, which is to say, without tragedy or sorrow.'[33] In a manifesto written six months earlier, he had declared:

> Looking around us, we see only manure, and it is in manure that filth and microbes live.
> Let them amuse themselves, down there in the depths: we want more, we want to mount the heights of truth where the air is pure and can be withstood only by metallic lungs.[34]

By 1930, Van Doesburg was critically ill with the acute asthma and was to die in Davos in early 1931.[35] The desire of many modernist artists to isolate their studio from the city outside, and to reconstruct this as an ideal hygienic and symbolically clean white cell can be seen as a longing for purity – a removal from the contagion of everyday life. This is apparent in many early modernist villas, based on the model of the artist's studio, such as those designed by Le Corbusier, who also worked as a painter.[36]

Raised on slender pilotis above a field at Poissy outside Paris, separated both physically and symbolically from the mire and filth of the city, Le Corbusier's Villa Savoye (see Chapter 10) was as spotlessly clean – at least in its ideal form photographed shortly after its completion – as the pure white 'medical laboratory' Van Doesburg demanded for the modern artist's studio. Today, no longer on the edge of the country but surrounded by factories and institutional buildings, the restored and pristine villa could easily be mistaken from a distance for a discreetly located medical laboratory.

Social hygiene

Middle-class obsessions with the health and hygiene of the working class were partly based on the assumption that a healthier proletariat would be more productive and cooperative, and perhaps also more contented and less prone to revolution. Ideas about health, the prevention of contagious diseases, and the cultivation of personal and social hygiene were applied in an authoritarian (or at least paternalistic) manner as measures of social control. Popular and scientific American journals of the 1930s made references to School Hygiene, Industrial Hygiene, Mental Hygiene, Sexual Hygiene, Social Hygiene, Emotional Hygiene and Moral Hygiene. These shaded off into more sinister preoccupations with eugenics and the survival of the fittest. Throughout the 1920s and 1930s hygienist and sometimes eugenicist objectives (along with aims of a more generalized social control) were advanced through the regulated provision of social housing, and healthcare and hygienic facilities. The advocates of modernist architecture represented it as better adapted to good hygiene and 'clean living' than traditional building. The language of hygienicism and of social reform of the period favoured modernist over non-modernist solutions, although in practice modernist designs remained in the minority.

In 1922, Dr Pierre Winter contributed an article on 'Le Corps nouveau' (The New Body) to *L'Esprit nouveau*, the magazine edited by Le Corbusier and Amédée Ozenfant, in which he contrasted the harmony of the body achieved by the Greeks and Romans with the 'modern' body sapped by overwork and dependence on drugs. Winter argued that modern science and sport had created renewed interest in the healthy body, and that artists and architects should devote themselves to its promotion.[37] Later Dr Winter presented Le Corbusier's Plan Voisin and his social housing at Pessac in the fascist magazine *Le Nouveau Siècle* in 1927, praising the way in which his designs prioritized health, hygiene, sunlight and fresh air.[38] Three years earlier, Le Corbusier had illustrated a 1924 article on 'Besoins types – meubles types' (Standard needs – Standard furniture) with a diagram showing the skeletal, circulatory and lymphatic system of the human body, reminiscent of the transparent models used in the teaching of medicine on which the oversized version at the Dresden Hygiene-Museum was based. After the Second World War he elaborated what he called the Modulor: a proportional system based on a caricatured over-muscled 1.75-metre-high male figure. This derived from Le Corbusier's experience of working on standardization systems for the Vichy government during the war,[39] although he later tried to disguise its origins by claiming that the Modulor was based on 'the 6-foot English detective' of Anglo-Saxon crime fiction.

While a stripped classical 'Roman' style was adopted for some (but not all) of the major public buildings in Mussolini's Italy, modernist architecture and design was also encouraged, or at least tolerated – especially in those areas that bordered on northern Europe such as Lombardy and Piedmont, which were geographically far from the Duce's increasingly imperial Roman capital. At a domestic level, hygiene, informality and absence of decoration were promoted. In a booklet aimed at young couples, *La casa che vorrei avere* (The Dwelling I Long to Have), a popular Italian writer on home economics and household management, Lidia Morelli, wrote in 1931:

> Better than in the past, the modern house reconciles the principles of wellbeing and economy. Without clutter, without formalities, without prejudices, without useless and flamboyant parlours, without out-of-place imitations of ancient styles, but with air, light, hygiene, a comfortable upkeep of simple and useful things.[40]

Similar ideas were the common intellectual property not only of fascist but also of socialist and libertarian reformers during the inter-war years – and of many whose political beliefs lay between these. Geneviève Heller has described how the Service d'hygiène in Lausanne (founded in 1917) had by 1924 established a complete programme for the promotion of health and hygiene in the old town area of the city. This was achieved by means of inspection, disinfestation, 'sanitary education' and, if necessary, the pulling down of whole quarters. The Service declared its mission to be 'the struggle against every recognized cause of the enfeeblement of the stock (*la race*)'.[41]

In The Netherlands, special estates were built by local authorities to be let at especially low rents to 'undesirable' families from slum areas who were moved into such temporary housing to be 'educated' into 'desirable' social practices before moving on to superior accommodation. In her well-known survey of inter-war European housing policy, *Europe Re-housed*, the British housing expert Elizabeth Denby wrote: 'These estates, which are meant to be educational, are, however, unpopular, as a definite social stigma attaches to those who go there, and in consequence they are not, and never have been, full.' Denby described the Asterdorp estate in Amsterdam built in 1926, where 132 houses had been constructed within an enclosing wall and the tenants were under strict control – although not as strict as similar estates in The Hague, where 'the great doors into the estate' were shut at 11 p.m., like a ghetto.[42] Designed to house displaced slum dwellers who could not afford average rents and 're-educated' families from transit centres, J. J. P. Oud's Oud Mathenesse (1923–24) estate in Rotterdam was known locally as 'Het Witte Dorp' (the White Village) because of its 'hygienic' whitewashed walls.

Like the estates in Amsterdam and The Hague described by Denby, these 343 tiny single-family houses with inside lavatories (but no bathrooms or showers) were intended as 'semi-permanent' accommodation, from which families would hopefully progress to more substantial municipally provided housing.[43] This village-like estate was designed to last twenty-five years – five years less than the Zonnestraal Sanatorium – presumably on the supposition that once the 'inadequate' sections of the working class had been educated into better ways such housing would no longer be needed. Built without proper foundations on thin concrete rafts, Het Witte Dorp survived for nearly seventy years, much loved by its original and subsequent inhabitants. It was finally pulled down in the early 1990s, and then only because after several renovations these temporary structures designed for a limited lifespan could no longer be adequately repaired and restored.[44]

'Social hygiene' – as much as physical hygiene – was central to social housing in Europe between the wars. Not only was each home to be provided with inside lavatories and baths, but also separate bedrooms for children of different sexes. Denby described how in The Netherlands (as in England) considerable importance was attached 'to the desirability of building working-class dwellings with three bedrooms, so that parents, boys and girls may have separate rooms'.[45] Earlier the priority had been to provide children with separate accommodation from parents. Then (as today) housing and social-service officials were concerned to prevent child abuse, which was very common at the time. Even Oud's tiny houses on the Oud Mathenesse estate were designed to provide separate bedrooms for children of different sexes. A 'moral modernism' characteristic of other Dutch architects of his generation like Jan Duiker marked Oud's designs for social housing, which aimed not only to shape the social and sexual habits of the inhabitants but also to educate their taste.[46] He wrote of the houses on their completion:

> The living rooms are papered up to the picture rail, above that white. The wall and floor where the stove or cooker will stand is finished with a layer of red, hard-baked tiles. In the middle of the rear wall, a shelf has been built out above which there is room for a mirror and on which portraits etc. can be placed: an interior so designed because experience has taught that residents are otherwise wont to arrange it in their own way.[47]

As well as attempting to control tenants' decorative taste, many of the features of Oud's housing were designed to enable parents to keep a careful watch over their young children. His five houses for the Weissenhofsiedlung model-housing exhibition in Stuttgart in 1927 were provided with glass doors to the serving hatches between kitchen and living room, so that the housewife could keep an eye on her children playing in the front garden. Each internal door was fitted with a peephole 'to see if lights were unnecessarily burning' at night, and to enable parents to keep a check on what their children were up to.[48] It is difficult to determine to what extent such design features were motivated by a response to tenants wishes, and how much by a desire to impose a restrictive bourgeois morality. (The specification of Oud's Weissenhof houses – which were generally considered by contemporary commentators to be the closest to realistic models for social housing in the exhibition – was more generous than those on his Rotterdam estates, with bathrooms and laundry rooms on the upper floor and relatively spacious kitchens.)[49] Oud's five houses were carefully planned as prototypes for a larger development on the scale of a whole estate, similar to the one he had recently designed for the workers' suburb of Kiefhoek in Rotterdam. Built as a complete estate, his Weissenhof houses would have had 'proper' streets in between each row, allowing what Oud described as 'ease of policing', by which he seems to have meant a system of informal 'neighbourhood watch' by the inhabitants.[50] From their kitchens the housewives would be able to see over the top of their back gates (which were designed deliberately low for this purpose) into the street behind, and across to the front gardens and front doors of the houses in the next row – to spot a potential prowler, child molester, or burglar. From the living room or kitchen they could keep an eye on their children playing in the long front garden, and keep watch on the street and the back gates of the row of houses opposite.

In The Netherlands, the elimination of the cupboard bed or sleeping alcove was one of the major aims of sanitary and hygienicist campaigns between the wars. The alcove bed had been imported into tenement housing in Dutch cities such as Rotterdam and Amsterdam in the late 19th century. This was based on long-established custom among peasant families in the Dutch countryside, from where the majority of the lowest-paid urban workers came.[51] (In a similar manner the bed alcove had been imported into 19th-century working-class tenements in Glasgow from rural housing in the west of Scotland.) The abolition of the 'unhygienic' and 'insanitary' bed alcove became a *cause célèbre* in Dutch social housing. Although only finally achieved by municipal legislation in Rotterdam in 1937 (and in Amsterdam much later), it had already been condemned in the Dutch Housing Act of 1902. By a curious irony, modernist designers reintroduced the bed alcove in a revised healthy and sanitary incarnation in other parts of Europe, in the United States, and even sometimes in The Netherlands itself.[52] The vogue for the sleeping porch on the balconies or roof terraces of modernist villas for 'healthy and hygienic sleeping' in the summer months (particularly in the South of France and Southern California) was essentially a hygienicist inversion of the traditional rural/urban working-class tradition of the bed alcove. A modified modernist version of the sleeping alcove was sometimes employed in social housing in the pursuit of the *Existenzminimum*. In his housing estates in Celle of the mid-1920s the German architect Otto Haesler reduced the bedrooms to a modern and hygienic version of the alcove. Owing to the pressure on resources (particularly during the dire economic straits of the late 1920s and early 1930s), the main room in European existence-minimum social housing was often designed as a living/dining/sleeping room and provided with fold-down beds. These were intended for parents or other adults living in the household, although there was no guarantee they would not be used for children.

Beds that folded down from the wall were used as a space-saving design in existence-minimum apartments for the Frankfurt *Siedlung* of Praunheim (1926–29) built under Ernst May, and the Bergpolder apartment block in Rotterdam by Brinkman, Van der Vlugt and Van Tijen (1933–34). In the middle-class Schröder House (1924) in Utrecht, Gerrit Rietveld had designed a tiny bedroom off the main living area for his client Truus Schröder, which was essentially a slightly more generous version of the traditional alcove bed. In 1933, Rietveld submitted an unsuccessful entry for a competition for inexpensive workers' apartments organized by the municipality of Amsterdam, where he attempted 'to make the limited floor space of the dwellings look as large as possible' by not splitting the space into small rooms and designing each apartment with a single living area.[53] The kitchen was in an alcove in the corner and there was a single sleeping space with beds separated by two-metre high partitions (which effectively made them alcove beds), with a shower and washbasins lined up along the centre of the room. In 1936, Rietveld designed an open-plan loft-style apartment above a cinema in the centre of Utrecht for himself and his wife and family, where his six children slept in bunks divided by a curtain – a system even closer to the traditional Dutch alcove bed. Donald Grinberg has argued that there seems 'to have been a deep psychological attachment to the dark and oppressive sleeping spaces' of the traditional alcove bed in The Netherlands.[54] In his housing designs Rietveld addressed the emotional needs embodied in this attachment, while providing functional basic sleeping accommodation for large families. Reworking the bed alcove in terms of well-lit and well-ventilated minimal modernist sleeping accommodation, he created enclosed and comforting spaces that still remained open to the light, air and openness of the modernist dream.

Concerns for health, hygiene and social control dominated the specifications of the two houses Walter Gropius designed for the Weissenhofsiedlung. Gropius wrote that: 'As a matter of principle, great emphasis has been laid on sanitation, and also on the provision of separate bedrooms for growing children.'[55] Gropius must have been horrified to learn that an 'extended family' of twelve people (including three adolescents and six small children) had occupied one of the houses, using the pantry downstairs and the laundry room upstairs as extra bedrooms with four children sleeping in the latter. When asked about this he replied: 'The house has irresponsibly been filled with twice the intended number of people, so that even I am quite unable to form any judgement of its performance in terms of home economics.' This extended family seems not to have been a working-class family but the bohemian ménage of a 'housewife, who is professionally active (craftswoman)'.[56] Later the house was more satisfactorily occupied – from a hygienic point of view – by a doctor and his wife.

Shortly afterwards, Gropius began to design hygienic living spaces for occupation by social groups other than the nuclear family. These were exhibited at the so-called

Werkbund Exhibition, in Paris at the Grand Palais in the summer of 1930, and at the 'Deutsche Bauausstellung' (Building Exhibition) in Berlin in 1931.[57] In Paris, Gropius exhibited a full-size mock-up model for the communal areas of a twelve-storey block of collective apartments. These were equipped with furniture by his former Bauhaus student and teaching colleague Marcel Breuer, who also designed a linked series of model rooms for single occupation with communal bathrooms and kitchenettes. As discussed in the previous chapter, communal living projects had been introduced in the Soviet Union in the 1920s, and similar ideas were energetically promoted in Czechoslovakia by Karel Teige and a number of left-wing Czech architects. Basing his ideas on the work of the sociologist Franz Müller-Lyer, Gropius had become convinced that the old forms of family and social life were breaking down as the result of the pressures of 20th-century modernity.[58] The hygienic austerity of Gropius and Breuer's designs aroused considerable comment in the French professional art and design press, most of it unfavourable. Pierre Lavedan claimed that Breuer's furniture had been devised in the belief 'that man is only a pair of buttocks'.[59] A more sympathetic discussion appeared in an article on the exhibition in the continental edition of the *Daily Mail* under the title 'Glass and Metal Furniture. Hygienic but not beautiful', arguing that such designs followed a 'primordial tendency' towards health and cleanliness: 'When one finds oneself in a kitchen or bar with a steel buffet, a table made up of a glass top and metal legs, and chairs that are most often made up of leather with metal backs and supports, one may well say that the maximum of hygiene has been attained.' The article concluded that: 'All this is extremely interesting as the demonstration of an attempt to create for the average person, at a reasonable price, a home where all modern necessities of hygiene and comfort are realized.'[60]

Health & biology

Apart from 'temporary' estates such as Oud's 'Witte Dorp', the majority of western European social housing between the wars – as in the late 19th century – was designed for the so-called deserving poor: the better paid and more 'socially stable' labour elites, such as artisans, craftsmen, and skilled engineering and printing workers. By encouraging the healthy and capable members of the proletariat to help themselves it was hoped they would better survive and reproduce, eliminating their less able fellows by 'natural selection' – and a little help from middle-class professionals. Similar approaches underlay the well-known social experiment run by Dr Innes H. Pearse and Dr G. Scott Williamson at the Pioneer Health Centre in Peckham in south London. Started as a birth-control centre, Peckham soon came to provide for families as a whole, and from 1935 was housed in a spectacular glass-and-concrete modernist building by the engineer architect Owen Williams, who had recently gained international renown as the designer of the Boots 'Wets' factory in Nottingham.[61] Standing in two acres of green space and built round a spectacular top-lit indoor swimming pool, this 'factory of health' served the immediate surrounding community on a day basis. It also contained a gymnasium, hot baths, nursery, a theatre which doubled as a dancehall, a licensed cafeteria, games rooms, work spaces for sewing and dress-making, and a series of medical and consultation rooms. Members were encouraged to help themselves and one another. Pearse and Williamson's ideas were heavily indebted to the Montessori theory of learning as a spontaneous process.[62] The emphasis was on 'self help', and the cafeteria and other facilities in the centre were consequently designed to be self-service – 'not an expedient but a principle'.[63] The only medical treatment dispensed at the centre was birth control. For other treatments the doctors referred members elsewhere. Williamson and Innes believed it was important that the families should be made to pay a (relatively) small fee for membership (2 shillings a week) as a guarrantee of their commitment.

As well as providing medical and social facilities, the team of doctors, researchers and health workers based at the Health Centre regarded this as 'a laboratory for the study of human biology'. The huge sheets of glass Williams employed for interior and exterior walls introduced abundant light, air and openness into the building and also allowed those who used the building to see the variety of activities going on around them, and the scientific and medical staff to observe this, 'looking through the glass walls of the Centre, as the cytologist may under his microscope watch living cells grow out in a culture medium'.[64] In *The Peckham Experiment*, the famous account of the centre and its work written with Lucy Crocker, one of the centre's researchers, Innes Pearse described how:

> The general visibility and continuity of flow throughout the building is a neces-
> sity for the scientist. In the biological laboratories of botany and zoology the
> microscope has been the main and requisite equipment. The human biologist
> also requires special 'sight' for his field of observation – the family. His new
> 'lens' is the transparency of all boundaries within his field of experiment.

Observation also depended on the continuous proximity of 'the human biologist' to the subjects of study: 'Sixteen steps down from the consulting room and he is engulfed in the action that is going forward, and which, by reason of the very design of the building, is visible and tangible to his observational faculties at all times'.[65] The transparency of Williams's building allowed the 'human biologists' to observe the members and the members to observe each other, enabling some to take inspiration from their fitter and more energetic fellows in the swimming pool or gym, it was hoped.

Membership of the centre was only available to families as a unit, and before joining each member had to undergo a 'health examination' – or 'biological overhaul as we prefer to call it'. This was followed by a 'family consultation', after which full membership was granted to the whole family.[66] The observation of 'each family acting in the social milieu of the Centre' continued the process of scrutiny: 'To see individuals at a social gathering, swimming, dancing, skating; at whist or billiards; at dramatic, musical, or other activity, provides us with essential data which serve to modify or enlarge observations made in the consulting room.'[67] Although there was a strong element of eugenicism (as well as voyeurism), in 'the Peckham experiment' it should perhaps be seen as an exemplar of the 'biologism' that dominated social theory at the time, manifested not only in the writings of health professionals but also of architects and designers such as Hannes Meyer, Ernst May, El Lissitzky and László Moholy-Nagy. Both Pearse and Williamson had medical degrees, but preferred to call themselves biologists.[68] At Peckham, this biologism seems to have been allied to a libertarian approach. It was observed that when medical and other advice was given in a paternalistic form this was often not acted upon, whereas when it was presented more informally and in a less authoritarian manner 'leaving it to spontaneity in the individual and to his own sense of responsibility', action was taken 'in the overwhelming majority of cases'.[69]

Such calculated (and paternalistic) non-intervention places the Peckham experiment close to other somewhat voyeuristic enterprises of British middle-class intellectuals of the late 1930s, such as the Mass Observation project – where middle-class observers were sent to observe and record surreptitiously 'ordinary life' in working-class cities such as Bolton in the industrial north of England. But the Peckham experiment was not just about observing individuals and families as biological specimens, it was also about trying to help the members of the centre lead fuller lives – and how such help might best be given. This humane and sympathetic approach was clearly closely attuned to the lives and needs of working people, however paternalistic certain aspects of the project may seem. Appointments were made at times that fitted in with the working and leisure hours of members, 'in such striking contrast

Pioneer Health Centre,
Peckham, London,
1934–5, (right) exterior,
(opposite) activities at
the Centre

Owen Williams

to the hospital and clinical services that it affords a matter for comment on the part of the members', as indeed it would today.[70] Clearly this approach was the social and institutional equivalent of the light, air and openness that was an intrinsic physical quality of Williams's concrete-and-glass building. Yet against this must be set patronizing comments, such as the following from the chapter on 'Social Poverty' in *The Peckham Experiment*: 'Every week', Pearse and Crocker claim, 'families in one stage or other of such dissolution join the Centre, many crossing its threshold only to quit – as quickly as they come – an atmosphere too strong, too vigorous for their ineptitude, their wilting strength or short-lived efforts'.[71]

The 'Peckham experiment' may have been tainted by eugenicism like many similar such schemes of the inter-war period. But with its sun balconies and swimming pools, sports and social facilities, the Health Centre was dedicated to achieving a state of positive health rather than the diagnosis and treatment of disease: its design closely related to the models of the sanatorium and the open-air school.[72] (The floor-to-ceiling bowed exterior windows of the south-facing front façade could be thrown back in summer to create a spectacular sensation of light, air and openness throughout the building.) Like the Cliostraat Open-Air School for Healthy Children in Amsterdam designed by Jan Duiker during the period he was working on the Zonnestraal Sanatorium (discussed in Chapter 7), the Peckham centre was intended to serve the healthy, rather than the diseased members of society.[73] 'The spread of health is as infectious as that of disease' Scott Williamson claimed.[74] The centre was aimed at the able-bodied and competent members of the working class who displayed initiative and were prepared to help themselves. Pearse and Crocker argued in 1943 that all other institutions which called themselves 'health centres' were in fact polyclinics, predominately concerned with the treatment of the sick, rather than with the study and maintenance of 'health'.[75] The group of doctors and researchers who worked at the Peckham centre were 'not clinicians seeking symptoms in a complaining patient, but biologists seeking evidence of health in an active non-complaining "man in the street"'. They claimed to have found that the great majority of families recognized – even if they did not fully understand – 'the value of the difference between these two points of view'.[76]

In an article in the *Spectator* in 1938, Frank Singleton had made a distinction between Peckham and the Finsbury Health Centre (1935–38), designed by Berthold Lubetkin and his Tecton partners as a clinic serving a densely populated and ill-housed area of inner-city London. 'Finsbury is not really a health centre in the same sense that Peckham is', Singleton maintained, clearly basing his arguments on those of Pearse and Williamson. 'It is a polyclinic, organized for disease.' He explained that 'Finsbury fights a magnificent rearguard action. Peckham, by contrast, is in the van, marching in front to guard against surprise, its object being not even the absence of disease, but positive health.'[77] John Allan – the architect who wrote the standard monograph on Lubetkin, and restored the Finsbury Health Centre in the late 1990s – has argued that: 'Such an amenity would have been something of a luxury in Finsbury, where less glamorous and more immediate problems needed to be tackled.'[78] And Jane Lewis claims that Peckham was chosen by Pearse and Williamson because it was a relatively prosperous working-class area.[79] Nevertheless, the difference between the two health centres was not as great as Singleton suggested. Finsbury had a solarium where children could receive artificial sunlight treatment for vitamin deficiency – as much a preventative as a curative measure. Glass blocks were used to create a 'sunny and airy effect' in the waiting hall, which was furnished with comfortable modern tables and chairs rather than the rows of benches found in most contemporary clinics. The therapeutic and preventative effects

of a healthy diet and plenty of fresh air and sunshine were invoked in two murals by Gordon Cullen. In the latter, slogans recommending 'Fresh air Night & Day' and 'Live Out of Doors as Much as You Can' were overlaid with a banner, 'Chest Diseases are Preventable and Curable'.[80] Lubetkin and Tecton had designed a tuberculosis and chest clinic for East Ham in the East End of London as an unrealized model project in the early 1930s, which was to form the basis for many aspects of the Finsbury centre.[81]

The Peckham Health Centre seems to have been hugely popular with the local inhabitants who enjoyed its facilities. It suspended its operations on the outbreak of the Second World War in 1939 and although it reopened in 1946, the welfarism of the first post-war Labour government was more attuned to identifying and curing disease than the analysis and encouragement of health. In 1950, the running of the centre was taken over by the LCC (London County Council) and operated under quite different principles, later the building was adapted for use as an adult education college.[82] In the late 1990s, it was converted into luxury 'loft apartments', the gymnasium, theatre and open-plan spaces subdivided, the swimming pool reduced in depth and its decommissioned diving boards festooned with indoor plants.[83] By contrast, Lubetkin and Tecton's Finsbury Health Centre has recently been restored and refurbished to a modern version of its original specification, dedicated mainly to curative rather than preventative medicine: to fighting already established disease, rather than promoting 'positive health' like the Peckham centre – an aspect of life today largely left to the profit-making 'private sector'.[84]

Finsbury Health Centre,
Finsbury, London, 1935–38
Lubetkin and **Tecton**

4 Dirt & decoration

In the literature of hygienicism, ornament and decoration were proscribed as the enemies of the hygienic and healthy home: harbouring dust, dirt, germs, infection and disease. The polemics against ornament by modernist architects and designers were carried on with a similar missionary zeal in the early 20th century. In *L'Art decoratif d'aujourd'hui* – published at the time of the Paris 1925 Arts Décoratifs exhibition, where luxury goods and products designed in a modern ornamental style were displayed – Le Corbusier advocated 'THE LAW OF RIPOLIN: A COAT OF WHITEWASH':

> Imagine the results of the Law of Ripolin. Every citizen is required to replace his hangings, his damasks, his wallpapers, his stencils, with a plain coat of Ripolin. His home is made clean. There are no more dirty, dark corners. Everything is shown as it is. Then comes inner cleanliness (...).[1]

Le Corbusier describes this as 'a moral act: to love purity!' – an act that 'leads to the joy of life: the pursuit of perfection'. Over two decades earlier, Adolf Loos had combined his attacks on unnecessary ornament and decoration with the celebration of efficient American plumbing, hygienic underwear and plain well-tailored English menswear. Loos's attacks on ornament were elaborated most forcefully in 'Ornament und Verbrechen' (Ornament and Crime), first written as a lecture in 1908. This appeared in French translation in 1913, but was not published in German until 1929 in the *Frankfurter Zeitung*, on the occasion of the CIAM conference on the *Existenzminimum* held in Frankfurt that autumn.[2] However, the substance of the essay was well known from hearsay, and from an earlier series of articles published at the turn of the century where Loos had rehearsed his arguments. 'Ornament und Verbrechen' did little more than summarize and emphasize in a dramatic and rhetorical form the most important points of his earlier essays.

Loos identified ornament with terms such as 'criminal' and 'degenerate', 'epidemic', 'backwardness' and (by implication) dirt and uncleanliness. Unnecessary ornament represented 'wasted labour' and was bad for the health of the worker who made it. In the past, the artist was a 'healthy vigorous figure, always at the head of humanity', whereas the 'modern ornamental artist' is a 'backward' and 'pathological case'. Loos argued that humanity as a whole is healthy and 'only a few are sick'. But the sick minority dictate to the healthy majority, compelling the worker ('who is so healthy he is incapable of inventing ornaments') to execute the ornaments they themselves have invented.[3] With the plethora of degenerate and unhealthy ornament, Loos had contrasted the work of the plumber in an earlier essay:

> One could well imagine our century without the cabinetmaker: we would have iron furniture instead. We could also abolish the stonemason: his work would be done by the cement specialist. But without the plumber the 19th century just would not exist. He has put his stamp on it, he has become indispensable.[4]

The penultimate sentence brings one up short. This was published in 1898, the year of the Emperor Franz Joseph's fiftieth jubilee – 'our century' was the 19th century. Fifty years later Sigfried Giedion was still celebrating modern plumbing for having banished ornament in *Mechanization Takes Command* (1948). For Giedion, the technological development of the standardized mass-produced white-enamelled bath had eliminated the proliferating decoration which 'disfigured' late 19th-century sanitary ware:

> All seems so simple in this plain, undecorated type. Yet the emergence of the standard form from the chaos of inadequate solutions was long delayed. The awareness that the mechanized bathtub cannot be a plaything for the ornamentalist was driven home only when the method of its manufacture – cast iron, enamel – raised a natural veto.[5]

For Giedion, the abolition of ornament is clearly (although subliminally) equated with the banishment of dirt. The decorated porcelain ware of the 19th century had concealed the dirt which the white enamelled bath made starkly apparent.

Loos believed the abolition of ornament would lead to a hygienic and pure new world of white-walled cities. In 'Ornament and Crime' he declared:

> Do you not see that the greatness of our age resides in our very inability to create new ornament? We have gone beyond ornament, we have achieved plain, undecorated simplicity. Behold, the time is at hand, fulfilment awaits us. Soon the streets of the town will shine like white walls. Like Zion, the Holy City, Heaven's capital. Then fulfilment shall be ours.[6]

Although dating from twenty or thirty years earlier, Loos's ideas continued to exert a powerful influence on architecture and design in the period between the wars, perhaps no more dramatically than in Tel Aviv (commonly known as the 'White City', and extensively developed in a modernist style during the 1930s and 1940s), of which the words quoted above read like a prophecy. While not Jewish himself, two of Loos's three wives were of Jewish origin – as were many of his clients and pupils, and he had toyed with the idea of moving to British-mandated Palestine to work as an architect at the invitation of one of his clients in the early 1920s.[7] In an Afterword to 'Ornament und Verbrechen', written in 1929 to accompany its publication in the *Frankfurter Zeitung*, Loos noted that although not previously published in German the essay had 'appeared in the languages of all advanced nations, even in Japanese and Hebrew'.[8]

The bombastic invective of Loos's polemic was to a large extent a journalistic or rhetorical device, reminiscent of the exaggeration and deliberate provocation of F. T. Marinetti's Futurist manifestos. Because of a failure to appreciate this, Loos's views have often been misunderstood and misinterpreted. He was not entirely consistent in argument or practice – the luxuriously figured fine woods and expensive marbles in his interiors assumed the role of the ornament he affected to abhor – and his ideas changed over the years. However, with some justification he could write in 1930:

> I have emerged victorious from a thirty-year battle: I have delivered humanity from superfluous ornament. It was a time where 'ornament' was synonymous with 'beauty'. Today, thanks to my life's work, this word is synonymous with 'mediocre'.[9]

Loos's attacks on ornament made a particularly strong impression in France. 'Ornament und Verbrechen' had appeared in translation in the magazine *Cahiers d'aujourd'hui* in 1913, probably on the initiative of the designer Francis Jourdain.[10] One of the circle of artists, designers and writers associated with the magazine, Jourdain was described in the issue in which 'Ornament et Crime' appeared as the French designer 'closest to the Great Viennese Adolf Loos'.[11] After the First World War, Le Corbusier republished the translation of Loos's essay in *L'Esprit nouveau*, the magazine he edited with Amedée Ozenfant, where it helped to give a renewed international currency to Loos's arguments during the inter-war period.[12]

The attacks on ornament by modernist architects and designers such as Loos and Le Corbusier paralleled those of hygienists and domestic reformers. Manuals of domestic economy from the last decades of the 19th century advised plain furnishings and paintwork. Simple uncluttered living and sleeping arrangements with bare and easily cleaned surfaces were recommended. Walls and furniture should be painted white or in light colours to reveal the dirt and dust, or (hopefully) their absence. Light-coloured walls and furniture demanded a meticulous cleanliness of the housewife (or her maid), and a determination to eradicate dirt at all cost. This did not make for an easy life, particularly for working-class and lower middle-class women on whom most of the burden of cleaning and cleanliness fell. A French manual of household management published a few years before the First World War claimed that:

> An object may be said to be clean when it is free from all stains and all dust. To struggle against dust, to remove it, whether from the surface of the body, from furniture or clothes, whether by cleaning the floors or renewing the atmosphere, is to do the work of the hygienist, fulfilling one of the most essential tasks of the housewife.[13]

Simple, light furnishings were equated not only with health and hygiene but also with moral rectitude, beauty and taste – the two last being middle-class values that were often difficult to instil into the working classes. Similar 'virtues' and aesthetic values were associated with 'dress reform' and the adoption of simple, hygienic and easily ventilated clothing. As with dress, movement and mobility were emphasized. Furniture should be light and easily moved as well as easy to clean, and open in its construction so that air could flow freely through it. Moral imperatives were frequently invoked. The purchase and display of luxurious and richly decorated artifacts or ornaments was condemned as inappropriate, and a misuse of household funds that needed to be carefully 'managed' by working-class families.

Simplicity was not only healthy and hygienic: it was also appropriate to the social station of the poor (as in medieval sumptuary laws). Health and housing reformers represented it as wrong to imitate those above one's social station, to 'give oneself airs' or to promote illusions of grandeur. A Swiss household manual of the 1890s addressed to the working and lower middle classes recommended: 'In every circumstance the best and most beautiful way of furnishing is where the different pieces harmonize with each other and, appropriate to and in perfect harmony with your income and social position, best fulfil their purpose.'[14] But simple and undecorated furniture was not necessarily cheap, and was more often purchased by middle-class professionals than workers. In the early years of the 20th century, art and taste were directly associated with cleanliness and hygiene, particularly in the campaign to educate the working classes in healthy and hygienic living. This was often described as 'aesthetic hygiene' in manuals and pamphlets published at the time. In 1912, the German architect and design reformer Hermann Muthesius declared in the *Jahrbuch des Deutschen Werkbundes* (German Werkbund Yearbook):

> Form is a higher intellectual need in the same way that cleanliness is a higher physical need, because the sight of crude forms will cause a really cultivated person something resembling bodily pain and the same uncomfortable sensation that is produced by dirt and foul smells. As long as educated people fail to experience as urgent a need for form as for clean clothes, we shall remain a very long way from conditions which can be even remotely compared with the great periods of artistic flowering.[15]

In western Europe, aesthetic hygiene was promoted through pamphlets, exhibitions, conferences, competitions, lectures and household manuals. After the First World War, the accumulation of trinkets and decorative objects by the working and lower middle classes was condemned in modernist texts such as Bruno Taut's *Die neue Wohnung* (The New Dwelling), first published in 1924 and provocatively subtitled *Die Frau als Schöpferin* (Woman as Creator). Taut argues that whereas 'previously, and to some extent today' people had 'turned up their noses at any dwelling that was not overflowing with all kinds of odds and ends', this will 'change entirely in no more than a decade'. By then 'everything in the way of knick-knacks, unnecessary items, and little pictures lying, standing, and hanging around the dwelling will be the reason for upturned noses and counsel against incautious contact with the peculiar inhabitants'.[16] A long sequence in Richter's film *Die neue Wohnung* is devoted to a satirical attack on the wasteful and unhygienic nature of the ornamental objects, heavy furniture and decorative trimmings of the working-class or lower middle-class 'front parlour' or *Salon*, which the housewife is shown endlessly dusting and cleaning.[17]

When first displayed during the summer of 1927, the model housing of the Weissenhofsiedlung had been accompanied by exhibitions of furniture and interiors in Stuttgart under the overall title of 'Die Wohnung' (The Dwelling, or The Home). Two posters designed by the painter and graphic designer Willi Baumeister showed old-fashioned ornate and dust-catching interiors cancelled with thick red crosses. Another poster by Karl Straub montaged photographs of models of the estate with some of the interiors – emphasizing the whiteness, light-catching and hygienic qualities of the Weissenhof project in contrast to the gloomy, unhygienic drapes and multitude of decorative objects of the two rooms shown in Baumeister's posters. At the time, a number of German critics and commentators pointed out that such modernist publicity strategies exaggerated the difference between what was shown at Weissenhof and the typical middle-class German interior.[18] Two English commentators, Howard Robertson and F. R. Yerbury, wrote of the 'warfare between romance and hygiene' evoked by such displays of stripped-down modernist architecture. They tried to take a distanced and more neutral stance, arguing that although hygiene 'suggests openness in everything: open windows, open minds, open spaces', the accumulation of personal objects evokes memory and continuity. 'Pictures and knick-knacks, to say nothing of hangings and carpets, especially in those pre-vacuum-cleaner days, were never particularly hygienic, but people cherished them [...].' Today, Robertson and Yerbury argue, 'we are apt to discard all objects which are dust-traps and germ-harbourers'. Slowly but surely 'the

Housewife dusting in the *Salon* (parlour). Still from Hans Richter's film *Die neue Wohnung* (The New Dwelling), 1930

death knell of these household gods has been sounded in a steady crescendo, rung by the growing popularity of modern notions of labour-saving as a reinforcement in the crusade against the microbe'.[19]

Campaigns against pictures and knick-knacks were also vigorously promoted in the Soviet Union, especially during the period of the so-called Cultural Revolution between 1928 and 1931. The constructivist architect Moisei Ginzburg described for a western European audience the emergence in the Soviet Union of a new group of clients, 'the working masses' whom he optimistically described as 'free of prejudices as far as taste is concerned, and not bound by tradition – factors that have in the past exerted a decisive, dominant influence on the thinking of the petty bourgeoisie'.

> Because of bare economic necessity the millions of workers have no love for the ornamental junk, the holy pictures, and all the thousands of useless articles that usually clutter up middle-class homes. These millions of workers must unquestionably be considered supporters of modern architecture.[20]

Readers of the organ of the Central Committee of the Union of Communist Youth, *Komsomolskaia Pravda*, were exhorted through metaphors of hygiene and cleanliness, to sweep away examples of 'domestic trash' such as overstuffed couches, bedsteads covered with 'playful decoration', floral-pattern wallpaper, and cheaply made ceramic or porcelain figurines of nude bathing beauties, kittens, butterflies, miniature elephants and entwined lovers.[21] The proliferation of these examples of kitsch 'bad taste' were blamed on the 'market forces' unleashed during the period of the New Economic Policy (NEP) when a certain amount of free enterprise was encouraged to 'regenerate' the battered Soviet economy after the Civil War. This had been initiated by Lenin in 1921, and was superseded when Stalin introduced the first Five-Year Plan in 1928. The Soviet campaign of 'aesthetic hygiene' came to an end in 1932 with the inauguration of the second Five-Year Plan, when the consumption of decorative artifacts was encouraged as an element of Stalin's consumerist domestic policies of the 1930s.[22]

Exhibitions of furniture specially designed for the working class had been organized in a number of countries in the years leading up to the First World War, and similar campaigns were promoted with renewed idealist vigour during the 1920s.[23] Social-housing architects furnished show houses or apartments to demonstrate the way they believed these should be inhabited – without the clutter and kitsch associated with working-class living in the early 20th century. In 1920, J. J. P. Oud exhibited a show apartment on his Spangen estate in Rotterdam, decorated in clear, bright colours by Theo van Doesburg and furnished with stripped-down wooden furniture designed by Gerrit Rietveld. Rietveld – who was himself from an artisanal background – wrote to Oud that his furniture was intended to be experimental, and should not be forced upon anyone against their will.[24] As far as is known, none of the Spangen tenants purchased any of the pieces. Fourteen years later a show flat with furniture by Rietveld was exhibited in the first high-rise block of workers' flats in The Netherlands at Bergpolder in Rotterdam, designed by Brinkman, Van der Vlugt and Van Tijen in 1934.[25]

In the early 1920s, Loos had furnished one of the houses he designed for an Austrian settlers' cooperative organization at the Friedenstadt Siedlung in Vienna with simple white-painted pine furniture.[26] This was put on show for a single day during which Loos and his second wife, the actress Elsie Altmann, received visitors, many of whom complained the rooms were too small for the traditional highly ornamented furniture they already owned (or coveted) – a standard complaint about social housing between the wars. Altmann described this in a patronizing account published many years later in her memoir of Loos, in which she claimed the show house was 'so enchantingly beautiful it made poverty seem like a privilege'.[27] Despite the largely unfavourable reactions to Loos's show house, the idea of displaying a furnished model-house became standard practice in social democratic Vienna during the 1920s and early 1930s, as it did elsewhere in Europe.[28] Regular exhibitions of model dwellings were shown in the gardens on the Ringstrasse outside the Vienna Town Hall in the centre of the city, initially organized by the settlers' cooperatives (for whom Loos had worked) and later by the Vienna municipal-housing department. In 1925, a Hygiene Exhibition dedicated to the theme of 'The New Household' was held at the Fair Pavilion in the Prater, Vienna's main park.[29] A mock-up of a typical Viennese municipal apartment demonstrated the lighter, brighter and more 'hygienic properties' of plain modern furniture as an alternative to the heavy, dark-stained and dust-harbouring traditional pieces typically found in the lower middle-class and working-class apartments of the period. Rather than architect-designed 'reform furniture', this was furnished with plain, simple, well-made wooden items readily available from furniture suppliers of a kind which tenants might well buy themselves.[30]

At the instigation of the architect and designer Margarete Schütte-Lihotzky – who also worked for the settlers' cooperative organizations at this time – the Warentreuband (Goods Trust) had been founded in 1922 to provide facilities for tenants to order well-made inexpensive furniture and other articles for their homes, and also clothing for themselves and their children, often at discounted prices. Schütte-Lihotzky described this as a 'poor man's Werkbund or Wiener Werkstätte': i.e. an attempt to 'improve' working-class taste rather as the Deutscher Werkbund and Wiener Werkstätte had tried to do for middle-class taste since the early years of the century. (In 1921, the German Werkbund had opened a Werkbund Haus on the Frankfurt International Fair site to display products that were judged worthy of Werkbund approval.)[31] The aim of the Vienna Warentreuband, Schütte-Lihotzky declared, was direct cooperation with industry to 'raise the general standard of living (*Wohnniveau*) of the working class', who had 'little tradition and therefore also fewer prejudices than the bourgeoisie'.[32] This was a view close to that of the Soviet architect Moisei Ginzburg quoted earlier, and was strongly contended by many of Schütte-Lihotzky's Social Democrat colleagues in Vienna. In 1925, she joined Ernst May's team of architects and designers at Frankfurt. Perhaps modelled on the Vienna scheme but more comprehensive, the *Frankfurter Register* was established in 1926 as a catalogue of selected furniture and household equipment judged by the neue Frankfurt staff to be well designed and well made – most of which was stocked in a municipally owned warehouse, ready for tenants to purchase.[33]

At the end of the decade, the Vienna municipal housing department replaced its exhibitions of model interiors with a more permanent institution, known by the acronym BEST.[34] Located on a prominent corner site at the enormous Karl Marx-Hof complex (which housed over 5,000 people), it was open to all the Vienna housing authority's tenants. Under the direction of the architect Ernst Lichtblau, from 1929 the BEST offered advice to tenants on organizing the interiors of their dwellings and where to find suitable reasonably priced furniture. It also held lectures and displayed approved 'well designed' furniture and other household artifacts in a permanent exhibition of a model apartment interior designed by Lichtblau and his Austrian Werkbund colleagues. The BEST was open on Friday and Saturday afternoons, Sunday mornings and most holidays, and advice and admission to lectures and other events were free. The furniture was lightweight and plain, made of tubular steel, wood or plywood, and designed to encourage 'domestic hygiene': easily cleaned, mobile and taking up little space. Although the advice bureau was well used, most of the furniture displayed was beyond the means of most tenants, partly because of the Europe-wide economic recession, but also because manufacturers were unwilling to produce designs in sufficient quantities to keep down the prices. Such paternalistic attempts to persuade the working classes to buy simple 'well designed' furniture were rarely successful. One of the few that were – and by virtue of necessity rather than choice – was the marketing of inexpensive Utility furniture in Britain during the Second World War, at a time when only 'hygienic' plain and unornamented furniture was allowed to be manufactured in order to save materials for essential war production (such as wooden frames for aircraft bodies). After the war, those who had purchased Utility furniture eagerly sought out more decorated and traditional pieces once these were again available.[35]

The hygienic home

In *Vers une architecture* (1923), Le Corbusier gently mocked hygienist campaigns and their publications, while at the same time promoting even more extreme advice to the middle-class public at whom his books and articles were aimed. Written in what would have been instantly recognized as a parody of the campaigning style of the hygienist and household management publications of the period, 'The MANUAL OF THE DWELLING' recommended readers to demand a south-facing bathroom [*en plein soleil*]: 'one of the largest rooms in the house or flat, the old drawing room for instance'.

One wall to be entirely glazed, opening if possible on to a balcony for sun baths; the most up-to-date fittings with a shower bath and gymnastic appliances.

An adjoining room to be a dressing room in which you can dress and undress. Never undress in your bedroom. It is not a clean thing to do and makes the room horribly untidy.

'If you can' – Le Corbusier advised – 'put the kitchen at the top of the house to avoid smells.' He recommended 'one really large living room instead of a number of small ones' with 'bare walls in your bedroom, your living room and your dining-room'. Readers were urged to buy 'only practical furniture', never 'decorative "pieces"': 'If you want to see bad taste, go into the houses of the rich.' A vacuum cleaner was a 'necessity', while clutter was prohibited: 'Keep your odds and ends in drawers or cabinets.' There should be ventilating panes in the windows of every room and children should be taught that 'a house is only habitable when it is full of light and air, and when the floors and walls are clear'. Heavy furniture and thick carpets must be eliminated. 'Bear in mind economy in your actions, your household management and in your thoughts.'[36] Despite the quasi-ironic introduction and tone, this apparently satirical 'manual' was intended to be taken seriously. Le Corbusier was to apply these principles in earnest to his own designs for middle-class villas in the 1920s.

An enthusiasm for large bathrooms and bare hospital-like rooms dated from shortly before the First World War, when hygienic minimalism or 'luxurious austerity' became fashionable among the more sophisticated European upper middle classes. Le Corbusier's comment that if one wanted to see bad taste one should go into the houses of the rich was true only of the unfashionable and 'vulgar' rich. In a novel published in 1913, purporting to be the diary of the multi-millionaire Arthur Olson Barnabooth, Valery Larbaud has his fictional protagonist reflect upon setting up a permanent establishment in London or Paris. Barnabooth decides his bathroom will be 'twice as large as the bedroom' which is to be 'a mere hospital cubicle, white, tiled, with no corners', and speculates about having the whole of his house furnished in a deliberately 'functional' and un-aesthetic manner:

> Most often I incline towards purely practical, almost scientific, furniture, carefully avoiding every artistic consideration. A roll-top American desk, a special armchair for work, and bare wood table and chairs: glass, marble, china, surfaces easily washed: as much air and light as possible.[37]

Larbaud was a close friend of Marcel Ray, the French writer and journalist (and later diplomat) who had translated Loos's essays 'Architektur' and 'Ornament und Verbrechen' into French, and was a subscriber to *Les Cahiers d'aujourd'hui* where Ray's translations had appeared in 1912 and 1913. He was almost certainly aware of Loos's writings when he described Barnabooth's deliberations on how to design the interior of his house.[38] Larbaud was himself a millionaire, if not quite as rich as his fictional protagonist. He was a noted linguist, translator and traveller, and his ceaseless travels across Europe in *trains de luxe* and *wagons lit* were the subject of many of his writings. *Wagons lit* sleeping and restaurant cars were admired for their efficiency, compactness and economic use of space by many modernist designers of the period, including Le Corbusier and Schütte-Lihotzky. (The restaurant-car kitchen was one of the models for the Frankfurt Kitchen and other experimental kitchens of the 1920s.) After the social and economic upheavals which followed the First World War, wealthy Europeans were even more inclined to mask extravagant lifestyles under a semblance of hygiene, austerity and 'plain living' (as we have seen in Chapter 2). This was partly to distinguish their homes from the over-elaborate houses and apartments of the petty bourgeoisie or *nouveaux riches*, but also so as not to flaunt their wealth too obviously in the social climate of the immediate post-war years, when many feared a Soviet-style revolution.

In Barnabooth's fictional diary, Larbaud has his multi-millionaire protagonist outline plans for his projected house in Kensington or Passy, declaring: 'I am also thinking of asking Francis Jourdain for furniture for the winter garden.'[39] At this time Jourdain was well known for his '*meubles interchangeables*' – standardized designs for cheap and simple whitewood furniture that could be configured in different ways to suit different needs. These had been discussed in a front-page article in the socialist newspaper *L'Humanité* in 1913, which characterized Jourdain as one of the first French designers to design cheap furniture for the working class.[40] Yet like William Morris before him, Jourdain was plagued by the necessity of pandering to 'the swinish luxury of the rich' (or in this case the 'swinish austerity' of the rich) in order to make a living. After the First World War, he began to work for Innovation,[41] the luxury travel goods company whose products Le Corbusier much admired and illustrated in his writings.[42] But Jourdain also continued to develop standardized and cheaply produced furniture, now sponsored by *L'Humanité*.[43] He designed a new series of *meubles interchangeables* aimed at working-class customers, manufactured by a company that had made aircraft components during the war.[44] This was described in a publicity notice as:

> Sober in form, of harmonious proportions, conceived in a resolutely modern spirit of rationalism which takes into account the demands of hygiene and of taste as much as of daily necessity, our interchangeable furniture meets your every requirement, suits every pocket, and is not out of place in any interior.[45]

Yet these designs did not sell well, and more often to middle-class professionals than to working-class customers. Many of the private commissions Jourdain received during the early 1920s were from multi-millionaire clients such as the Rothschilds, for whom he designed a white, hygienic nursery. Based on a geometric module that gave it a formal and rational unity, it also provided a clean and hygienic environment for children. Much of the furniture was built in. Jourdain exhibited a fussier and more

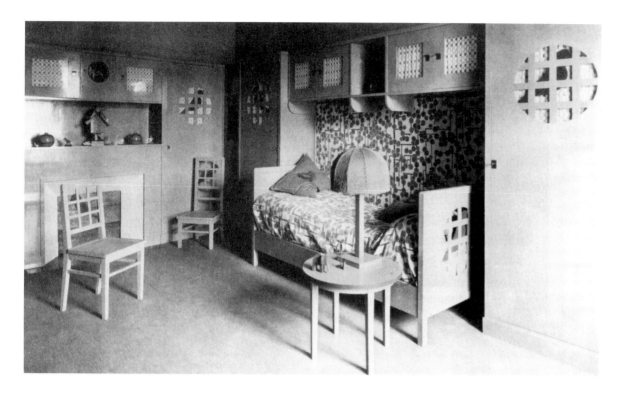

elaborately decorated version for the middle-class audience of the Salon d'Automne in 1920.[46] The simpler and more austere design realized for the Rothschilds more closely resembled the *meubles interchangeables*.

Furniture for the fit

During the 1920s and 1930s, furniture originally manufactured for sanatoriums and hospitals became fashionable for domestic use among the more sophisticated of the European and American middle classes. Perhaps the best known was Alvar Aalto's reclining bent-plywood Scroll chair (1931–33), designed for the Paimio sanatorium. Many of the materials used in the manufacture of modernist furniture – such as canvas, bentwood, bent cane, chromed steel tube, and steamed plywood – were employed for sanatorium and hospital furniture because of their ease of cleaning, resistance to dirt, and general hygienic qualities.[47] 'Hygienic' materials replaced traditional materials such as upholstery and carved wood, which harboured germs, insects and vermin, and provided breeding grounds for them. Dust containing tubercles and other bacilli lodged in upholstery, in crevices, and especially in decorative features, and was regarded as a particular enemy of hygiene to be eradicated at all costs. From the mid-19th century, manufacturers of multiply produced furniture such as Gebruder Thonet and Jacob & Josef Kohn made reclining chairs and day beds of bentwood and cane (regarded as

Nursery for the Rothschilds,
Paris, 1920
Francis Jourdain

more hygienic than traditional wood) both for use in hospitals and sanatoriums, and for the home.[48] The reclining couches (*Schlafsofas*) manufactured by Thonet from 1866 can frequently be seen in photographs of sanatorium rest halls (*Liegehallen*) and were popular for domestic use as well.[49] Local firms also produced furniture specifically designed for sanatoriums, such as the *Davoser Liegestuhl* (Davos Couch). Made from heavy cane and fitted with a mattress consisting of three thick cushions covered in natural cotton, and with an adjustable head roll, this recliner is still manufactured today by the same family firm of Graf in Davos.[50] In *The Magic Mountain*, the protagonist Hans Castorp reclines on a *Davoser Liegestuhl* reading a copy of *Ocean Steamships* under its 'little sunshade'. While the heat 'became unbearable' Castorp remained 'uncommonly comfortable', and 'did not recall in all his experience so acceptable an easy chair'.[51] Davos recliners are used for relaxation today by holidaymakers and hotel guests at the Berghotel Schatzalp in Davos Platz, a converted sanatorium which also contains the Blauer Heinrich Museum where original examples of the reclining chair are exhibited, along with a sleeping bag lined with black bear fur for use on cold days.

Many of the new designs of the 1920s and 1930s were updated versions of such vernacular originals, made of tubular steel or aluminium rather than cane or bentwood. With the development of nickelled and chromed tubular steel after the First World War many of the companies that manufactured bentwood and cane furniture, such as Thonet and Kohn, began to produce furniture in these new materials, both for home and medical use. A number of Marcel Breuer's earlier tubular-steel furniture designs of the late 1920s were directly derived from sanatorium recliners,[52] and his aluminium reclining chairs manufactured by the Swiss Embru company in the early 1930s were essentially more sophisticated versions of those employed in the *Liegehallen* and sun-terraces of sanatoriums.[53] Breuer developed these designs in Britain as the bent-beech plywood 'Long Chair', which was made and marketed by the Isokon company from 1935.[54] Also close in conception to medical chairs and sanatorium recliners were the *chaise lounge* Charlotte Perriand and Pierre Jeanneret designed in the late 1920s in Le Corbusier's architectural office, and Mies van der Rohe's minimalist chrome-plated tubular-steel *chaise longue* (c. 1930).[55]

These and similar designs were introduced into professional middle-class homes between the wars for reasons of 'optical hygiene' (or fashion) rather than to serve genuine medical needs, although tubular-steel and aluminium furniture was widely promoted as easily cleaned, hygienic, light and easy to move, so that it would not harbour dust and dirt. In a polemic article entitled 'Wood or Metal', Charlotte Perriand advocated the hygienic, functional and aesthetic qualities of metal over wood, arguing that 'Hygiene must be considered first: soap and water', and concluding that 'WE MUST KEEP MORALLY AND PHYSICALLY FIT'.[56] Mies van der Rohe wrote of one of his tubular-steel chair designs that it could be 'easily moved by anyone, and because of its sled-like base it can simply be pushed across the floor without damaging the carpets'.

It therefore promotes comfortable, practical living. It facilitates the cleaning of rooms and avoids inaccessible dusty corners. It offers no hiding place for dust and insects and therefore there is no furniture that meets modern sanitary demands better than tubular-steel furniture.[57]

By 1930, even the more conservative of the European middle classes had begun to accept such views. In the *Daily Telegraph*, an English establishment newspaper, Martha House wrote in the context of a display of designs by Jeanneret and Perriand:

First and foremost, metal and glass are taking the place of wood, as being at once cleaner, and as having the clean-cut, clipped look of modernness. If the surgery is clean and the kitchen is clean, there is no reason, says the modernist, why the rest of the house should not be clean, too, and with the same means which have been found satisfactory, even if they are used with a different suggestion.[58]

The promotion of tubular-steel furniture as hygienic and easily cleaned tended to give it a utilitarian aura, and its association with institutional buildings in the late 1930s and during the Second World War made it unpopular for many decades until there was a revival in the 1960s, and again at the end of the 20th century. But when first introduced during the late 1920s it was often identified with glamour and sexuality (also at the time frequently linked to hygiene and cleanliness). The young and attractive Perriand was photographed in seductive positions lying in the *chaise longue* she designed with Jeanneret, while lithe young women posed in model apartments designed by Breuer in photographs in fashionable German illustrated magazines. Visual parallels were suggested between the toned and exercised bodies of the young women (often represented as gymnasts or athletes) and the hard shiny surfaces of tubular steel and glass, signalling a clean and hygienic sexuality, intimately linked to health and fitness. Consequently, Breuer's apparently ascetic tubular-steel furniture became associated with the slim and attractive youthful female body. Once such associations were established, the furniture and 'equipment' continued to evoke a hygienic and athletic sexuality in public perceptions.

The fashion for hygienic austerity (particularly in Germany and central Europe) was the subject of a good deal of critical comment and satire. Modernist buildings and furniture were frequently attacked as sterile, clinical, surgical, or hospital-like by architectural critics – not all hostile to modernism – and sometimes savagely mocked by literary commentators. Citing a maxim 'formulated by a leading architect', the hero of Robert Musil's novel, *The Man Without Qualities*, declares: 'Modern man is born in a hospital and dies in a hospital – hence he should also live in a place like a hospital.'[59] Walter Riezler (the editor of the German Werkbund magazine *Die Form*) found Gropius's two houses designed for the Weissenhof housing exhibition over-hygienic and lacking in 'homely' qualities. Riezler claimed the austerity and hygienic appearance of the rooms in Gropius's model houses 'suggested to so many visitors a comparison with a hotel or a nursing-home (or even a surgical clinic)'.[60] The critic Karl Konrad Düssel wrote of Breuer's tubular-steel furniture that it was 'easy to imagine that a person might want this Constructivist objectivity [*Sachlichkeit*] in a room; but then he must not shudder at recollections of dentists and operating theatres'.[61] When similar furniture was shown in austere interiors designed by Breuer and Gropius at the Werkbund Exhibition at the Grand Palais in Paris in the summer of 1930 many French commentators and critics reacted in a similar manner. Pierre Lavedan described Breuer's two bedsitting rooms as 'cells as hygienic, as clean and as attractive as a dentist's surgery'.[62] The terms commentators used to ridicule modernist designs were often identical to those that the practioners and propagandists of modernism employed to promote them. In *L'Art décoratif d'aujourd'hui* (The Decorative Art of Today), his attack on the ornamental and luxurious 'art deco' tendencies of the Paris 1925 exhibition, Le Corbusier illustrated a dentist's surgery as a positive example of the 'rational' use of plain surfaces and simple unornamented forms.[63]

A satirical short story written by Bertolt Brecht, in collaboration with Elizabeth Hauptmann, 'Nordseekrabben oder Die moderne Bauhauswohnung' (North Sea Prawns, or the Modern Bauhaus Apartment) is set in the up-to-the-minute modernist Berlin apartment of an AEG engineer named Kampert. The main model seems to have been the apartment designed by Marcel Breuer for the theatre director Ernst Piscator and his actress wife Hildegard (Jurezyss) Piscator in 1927, photographs of which appeared in a number of illustrated magazines. Some of these featured Hildegard Piscator sitting on her own in the enormous high bare living room looking bored and lonely, or filing her nails seated at her spare, narrow Breuer dressing-table on a chromed-steel stool.[64] As in most modernist middle-class apartments there were separate bedrooms, and apart from a narrow single bed and a built-in cupboard Piscator's own minimal and ascetic bedroom appears to have been furnished only with elaborate gymnastic and exercise equipment – to provide him with what Breuer termed the 'healthy body culture'.[65] In Brecht and Hauptmann's story, Kampert is having a 'liquid reunion' with two friends who like him had served in the mire and filth of the trenches in the First World War, their reminiscences of which form a vivid contrast with the hygienic sterility of the apartment. After his wife has retired to bed and Kampert has gone out to buy a take-away carton of North Sea prawns, his two drunken friends 'work over' the apartment, reducing its fashionable hygienic austerity to a more 'homely' disorder.[66]

Two years later, in an article published in the *Münchner Illustrierte Presse* in 1929, the Austrian novelist and essayist Joseph Roth similarly satirized the modernist interior. Roth wrote of how clean and hygienic modernist interiors made him 'hanker for the mild and soothing and tasteless red velvet interiors in which people lived so undiscriminatingly no more than twenty years ago':

> It was unhygienic, dark, cool, probably stuffed full of dangerous bacteria, and
> pleasant. The amassing of small, useless, fragile, cheap, but tenderly bred

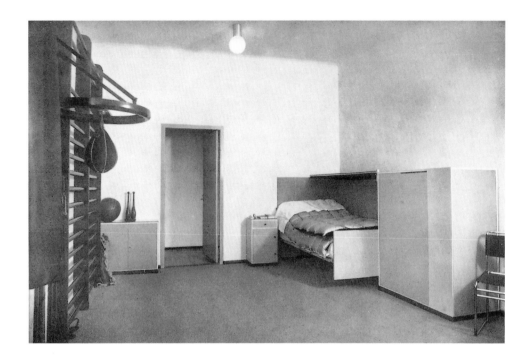

knick-knacks on the fireplaces and sideboards produced an agreeable contempt that made one feel at home right away.

Where the lives of an older generation had been 'lived in such poor taste', their children and grandchildren 'live in strenuously bracing conditions':

> Not even nature itself affords as much light and air as some of the new dwellings. For a bedroom there is a glass-walled studio. They dine in gyms. Rooms you would have sworn were tennis courts serve them as libraries and music rooms. Water whooshes in thousands of pipes. They do Swedish exercises in vast aquariums. They relax after meals on white operating tables. And in the evening concealed fluorescent tubes light the room so evenly that it is no longer illuminated, it is a pool of luminosity.[67]

The Soviet novelist and journalist Ilya Ehrenburg (who in the early 1920s had co-edited the international avant-garde magazine *Gegenstand/Objekt/Objet* with El Lissitzky in Berlin) published an article in the *Frankfurter Zeitung* after visiting the Dessau Bauhaus in 1927. Ehrenburg also toured the houses Gropius designed for the Bauhaus 'masters' and visited his social housing at the Törten Siedlung, on the outskirts of the city. Ehrenburg was impressed by the new Bauhaus building but criticized the application of the same design principles to housing, which he compared to barracks, 'rooms for sleep cleaned of dreams, for universal washing, for gymnastics and for some procedure which contributes to population increase'. He claimed that 'the imagination of a plumber is a very limited one', which could 'bring forth a new pipe system, but not a new cosmogony'.[68]

Ernst Piscator's bedroom,
Berlin, 1927
Marcel Breuer

5 The domestic clinic

By the late 1920s, the influence of hygienicist ideas was felt even in the modest interiors of the lower middle classes. But while the principles of hygiene and cleanliness had become generally accepted as appropriate for kitchen equipment and bathroom fittings, only a fashionable and sophisticated – or professionally committed – minority wanted their living rooms also to resemble hospitals or sanatoriums. Many early patrons of modernism were doctors, dentists, or in some way associated with the medical and healthcare professions. They identified their personal lifestyles with the latest 'progressive' ideas about health and hygiene by having their homes – as well as their surgeries, hospitals, or offices – designed in modernist style with white walls and large areas of glass in order to reinforce their professional standing among their colleagues, or to reassure their patients or clients. An unusually imaginative example was the house and surgery Adolf Rading designed in 1930 for Dr Rabe in the small German village of Zwenkau near Leipzig, which featured a large relief mural by Oskar Schlemmer.

Reminiscent of some of Loos's late villas, such as the Moller House of 1927–28 (although on a smaller scale), the white cubic structure was quite different in character to the low-lying house Rading had designed for the Weissenhofsiedlung (discussed in Chapter 7). The house and surgery were planned around a double-height combined entrance hall and living room through which patients passed on the way to the surgery, with a shaded balcony terrace at the back and steps leading down to a long garden.[1] Constructed from different types of bent metal rods, Schlemmer's relief sculpture was mounted on the high olive-green wall above the doors that led to the doctor's surgery and the children's playroom.[2] To the left above the playroom door a large male figure balanced a smaller female figure on his outstretched hand. Like many of Schlemmer's relief sculptures of this period, the larger figure appears to have articulated joints, which although they do not actually move seem to offer the possibility of movement. Above the surgery door was a small construction of concentric circular and orthogonal elements resembling a stylized representation of a star. To the right, an enormous 4.5-metre-high metal profile of a human face projected 8 centimetres from the wall, reaching to the ceiling and dominating the space. The changing light from the large

windows that lit the double-height entrance hall moving across the reliefs on the walls created subtly shifting shadows 'on the sundial principle'.[3] Schlemmer's metal reliefs visually echo the spare metal furniture and fittings Rading specified, which allow the space in the large airy room to flow through and around them: a circular tubular-steel dining table and tubular-steel chairs, a horizontal construction of metal struts suspended from the ceiling and supporting rows of strip lights, and a standard industrial

Dr Rabe's house, Zwenkau,
near Leipzig, Germany, 1930
Adolf Rading

iron radiator immediately to the right of the flush-fitting surgery door. The calm and austere space evokes notions of cleanliness and hygiene while avoiding sterility and anonymity. Schlemmer's sculpture with its combination of abstract and stylized figurative forms blends subtly with Rading's humanly scaled architecture to create a serene yet exhilarating impression that would have had a beneficial and calming effect on the patients as they waited to enter the surgery, or those who lived and worked in the house.

Doctor in the house

Perhaps the most spectacular and celebrated modernist house for a doctor was the Maison de Verre (Glass House), designed for a fashionable left-wing Paris gynaecologist, Dr Jean Dalsace and his wife Annie, at the end of the 1920s. Hidden from prying eyes in the courtyard of a *hôtel particulier* in an otherwise unremarkable street on the Left Bank, this building combined an austerely luxurious private residence with Dr Dalsace's consultation rooms – evoking both hygiene and discretion.[4] The house was a collaboration between the furniture designer and architect Pierre Chareau, the metal craftsman Louis Dalbet (who made most of the furniture and equipment) and Jan Duiker's former partner Bernard Bijvoet, who had moved to Paris in 1925.[5]

Unlike most modernist houses between the wars (and despite its name), the Maison de Verre did not feature white walls and large areas of transparent plate glass, but was constructed on a steel frame with walls of St Gobain Nevada glass lenses set in slim panels of lightweight reinforced concrete. Together with such discreet and austerely luxurious houses as the Stonborough-Wittgenstein House, Loos's Moller House and Mies van der Rohe's Tugendhat House, the Maison de Verre masked wealth and opulence behind an anonymous façade – in this case evoking an almost industrial modernity. In his book on glass in architecture, Michael Wiggington has argued that while Le Corbusier's 'machine for living in' (*machine à habiter*) was 'more metaphorical than literal', the Maison de Verre was 'a real machine': fitted out with specially designed technical equipment, hot-air central heating, and an industrial air-conditioning system.[6] Intended to link a well-known consultant's domestic life with his professional practice (and vice versa) through a modernist idiom that evoked the hospital, the sanatorium and the clinic, the building directly and intimately connected the living quarters with the suite of gynaecological rooms used by Dr Dalsace for his practice. The two zones were designed together as inseparable parts of a single structure; professional and private areas and functions closely integrated, with a minimal separation between them. The arrangement of functions followed the conventions of traditional live/work buildings, where the living quarters were placed above the areas designed for professional use.[7] Dr Dalsace's gynaecological suite was on the ground floor, the semi-public entertaining area of salon, study, living room and dining room on the floor above, with the private zone of bedrooms and bathrooms on the uppermost floor. The kitchen and maid's quarters were located in a separate linked wing at a 45-degree angle to the main building.

Much of the power and originality of the Maison de Verre is derived from the way the building embodies a number of interlinked elements that relate to the joint functions of domestic dwelling and professional consulting rooms. In a thought-provoking essay on the house, Sarah Wigglesworth has drawn attention to the metamorphosis of domestic equipment in the gynaecological suite: to the way 'the bed becomes a couch, the side table becomes a stainless steel trolley, and the table lamp becomes a light and speculum'.[8] But this also operates in reverse. In the living areas of the house the couch becomes a bed, the medical trolley a side table, the light and speculum a table lamp. As Dr Dalsace's patients arrived for their consultations they passed the main staircase that led to the domestic part of the house screened by a partition of perforated metal, which allowed them to catch tantalizing glimpses of the Dalsace family's living space, apparently designed as precisely and as hygienically as the gynaecological suite they were about to enter and in similar 'modern' materials. Wigglesworth argues that although 'there is no functional necessity to bring the two realms (doctor's suite and home) into contact', Chareau chooses to, 'as it were, flaunt the privacy of the domestic interior to the passing patient'.[9] Yet the purpose here seems rather to signal the continuity of the private and the public, the professional and the personal, and their mutual location in the principles of hygiene, health and cleanliness. The half-transparent half-opaque glass-lens and concrete skin becomes translucent at night when the interior is revealed – like the skeleton and internal organs of the human body in an X-ray.[10] Walter Benjamin, who came to know the Maison de Verre when he moved to Paris in the 1930s, described how modernist architecture with its enormous windows or glass walls displayed the interior like an X-ray.[11] The effect was rendered more spectacular and dramatic in the Maison de Verre by bathing the glass-lens walls with light from floodlights mounted on the forecourt and garden façades of the house. These were originally fitted with yellow and blue bulbs, to approximate daylight as closely as possible.[12] This created an arena lit by diffused floodlighting for performances and events in the double-height first-floor salon, where lectures and poetry readings were held and Mme Dalsace gave recitals on the grand piano placed against the glass-lens façade.[13]

Wigglesworth maintains that light is primarily an image of hygiene in the Maison de Verre: 'In modernist ideology, light is cleanliness. A clear skin indicates a clean body, a sanitized house. The medical suite is made of white walls and light. Within the house, the "sterilization" of the medical rooms also "disinfects" the other parts of the building.'[14] She sees the en-suite bathrooms of the house as hygienic cleansing stations which echo the layout of the gynaecological suite, arguing that 'the order of the medical suite infects the house'. Wigglesworth argues that: 'The surfaces are shiny, reflective, permanently bright, ageless. In place of the real, secreting body is a clinically clean, fetishized trope.'[15] Yet this would also be true of most mass-produced early 20th-century middle-class bathrooms with their standardized porcelain suites, white enamelled baths and unframed mirrors – although the high-quality machine-like surfaces of the sanitary ware and bathroom fitments in the Maison de Verre take this to extremes. Wigglesworth sees this as the substitution of 'a controllable, predictable, perfected environment' in place of the 'sentimental, fickle interior', as the 'birth of the sanitized lifestyle, the architecturally photogenic interior, the home rationalized out of inhabitable existence', which she claims has become the norm of design and 'life-style' magazines today.[16]

The Maison de Verre was ingeniously inserted under the top floor of an existing *hôtel particulier* because the elderly tenant refused to move out – a constructional feat that has been compared to a surgical incision and the grafting of a new organ into the body of the city.[17] Le Corbusier frequently employed the analogy of the modernist architect as a surgeon cutting out the old diseased organs of the metropolis, to be replaced with clean and hygienic glass-and-concrete modern buildings.[18] Wigglesworth claims that the manner in which the Maison de Verre was inserted into the surgically invaded body of old Paris like an *in vitro* fertilized ovum is symptomatic of the mechanistic masculinism of inter-war modernist architecture – where the architect appropriates both the role of the technical expert and of the physician, or in this case the gynaecologist. By combining the image of the 'clean machine' with images of health, hygiene, light and air, 'architect-physicians' believed they could produce a model for a new way of living. The Maison de Verre is unlike the majority of modernist houses of the period between the wars in that glass is largely employed to let in light, rather than to allow those inside to look out or those outside to look in. This links it to the villas of Adolf Loos who argued that windows were for admitting light rather than to gaze out from.[19] It is in many ways the opposite of Richard Neutra's Health House designed for Dr Philip Lovell in Los Angeles in the late 1920s (discussed in Chapter 6) or the glass-walled houses designed in the United States after the Second World War, such as Mies van der Rohe's Farnsworth House, Philip Johnson's Glass House, and their Californian derivatives of the 1950s and 1960s. Although like other early modernist buildings, the Maison de Verre was inspired by the mechanistic and hygienist metaphors of medicine and hygienicism current in the early decades of the 20th century, here light *suffuses* (or is *diffused*) through the semi-opaque glass lenses rather than pouring in through floor to ceiling plate-glass windows. While other architects had already exploited the effects of diffused lighting through the use of glass bricks, blocks and lenses in non-domestic buildings, the Maison de Verre, designed in part, at least, as a domestic space, was unique when it was built. Shortly afterwards, in 1931, Le Corbusier was to employ similar effects in the Maison de Clarté (House of Light) in Geneva, almost certainly aware of Chareau and Bijvoet's experiments in Paris.[20] Whether Dalsace or his wife influenced the designers in their choice of the material is unclear, although we know of at least one reason why Mme Dalsace appreciated the translucent yet semi-opaque qualities of Nevada lenses. It was apparently at her suggestion that the strips of clear-glass window inserted into the semi-opaque glass-lens cladding of the waiting room were placed at a height where patients were unable to see the Dalsace children playing in the garden – so as not to distress those who were having difficulty in conceiving, or seeking terminations.[21]

The Maison de Verre in Paris is linked to the Zonnestraal Sanatorium in Hilversum through the rather shadowy figure of Bernard Bijvoet, the extent of whose participation in both ventures remains unclear. Interviewed towards the end of his life about his collaboration on the Maison de Verre, Bijvoet 'remained unspecific with a modesty as exemplary as it was frustrating for the interviewer', according to Bernard Bauchet, the architect in charge of restoring the Maison de Verre in the late 1980s.[22] The Zonnestraal was a sanatorium building with medical facilities and accommodation for a hundred patients plus support staff, with enormous areas of rolled glass to intensify and refract the rays of the sun and to allow fresh air to circulate freely. It was designed to shine forth brightly as a symbolic embodiment of health and hygiene, of physical and mental rehabilitation through rest, relaxation and fresh air. The Maison de Verre was a sheltered site of intimate family life, of semi-public social events and cultural meetings, of professional gynaecological consultations, treatments and terminations, where light was mysteriously diffused, and sight alternately permitted and blocked. The family home and professional practice of a well-known specialist, it was inserted into the very heart of the city like a transplanted organ glowing mysteriously from within and without, allowing veiled glimpses of the patients to the inhabitants and of the inhabitants to the patients. Its most innovative components, the Nevada glass lenses in their lightweight reinforced-concrete panels, failed after twenty years – much as did the lightweight reinforced-concrete structural system of the Zonnestraal – and had to be replaced with improved modern versions in the early 1960s, and restored again in the late 1980s.

The Zonnestraal was built as a charitably funded specialist medical facility publicly displaying and reinforcing the links between modernist architecture, medicine and social welfare. The Maison de Verre was the luxurious private establishment of a fashionable gynaecologist with a rich clientele, albeit left wing and anti-fascist in his political views.[23] For Bijvoet's former partner Jan Duiker, the Maison de Verre was a luxurious parody of functionalism: a snobbish indulgence of the imagery of machinism and hygienicism. Writing shortly after the house was completed, Duiker criticized its flaunting of luxury masquerading as technological innovation: 'a functionalist snobbery much in demand in Paris and elsewhere', a 'vulgar formalism' of 'steel, chrome and nickel'. He ridiculed the steel columns with riveted joints, 'standing sociably' in the salon amid a collection of luxurious and expensive *objets*.[24] For Duiker, the clean and hygienic *haute bourgeoise* machine for living in represented an affront to the social hygiene and collectivist ideals that he and Bijvoet had striven for in the Zonnestraal Sanatorium.

The hospital in the home

If the modern house was a clean and hygienic domestic factory (or a machine for living in) the kitchen was the engine or powerhouse at its heart. Much thought and ingenuity went into the design of the modern kitchen, which was largely dictated by the demands of hygiene. In 1933, the avant-garde architectural magazine *L'Architecture d'aujourd'hui* devoted a special issue to the kitchen. The architect Louis Faure-Dujarric wrote that this 'should be the cleanest place in the home, cleaner than the living room, than the bedroom, than the bathroom'. The light 'should be absolute, nothing must be left in shadow, there can be no dark corners, no space left under the kitchen furniture, no space left under the kitchen cupboard'.[25] The best-known kitchen design of the inter-war period, the Frankfurt Kitchen, was painstakingly planned by a team of designers and architects working for Ernst May's neue Frankfurt, led by the young Austrian architect Margarete Schütte-Lihotzky. Schütte-Lihotzky had been diagnosed with tuberculosis in 1924 while working as a social-housing architect in Vienna. The issues of health, hygiene and cleanliness and the adequate provision of light, air, openness and space were given particular emphasis in a city where housing conditions were so bad that tuberculosis was endemic. The disease was known as 'the Viennese illness' throughout Europe and was the cause of one in seven 'natural' deaths in the city before 1914, and one in four during the First World War. Although both her parents had recently died of the disease, Schütte-Lihotzky recovered and returned to work after spending some months in a sanatorium.[26] Twenty years later, after five years imprisonment by the Nazis during the Second World War, she was again found to have tuberculosis and spent two months in a sanatorium in the Tyrol.[27] Despite these bouts of tuberculosis, Schütte-Lihotzky lived to be two days short of her 103rd birthday. During her first period in a sanatorium she had made designs for a 'tuberculosis *Siedlung*' where patients could live and work while receiving treatment as a halfway house between confinement in a sanatorium and a return to normal life. Although never realized, the designs were exhibited at the 1925 Vienna Hygiene Exhibition on the theme of 'The New Household'.[28] In 1928, while working for the neue Frankfurt, she designed another unexecuted project for a tuberculosis sanatorium in Marburg, in collaboration with Wilhelm Schütte.[29]

Schütte-Lihotzky's personal experience of tuberculosis almost certainly affected her approach to planning the Frankfurt Kitchen, which she seems to have conceived as a home workstation similar to the nurses' workstations in a hospital or sanatorium – where the processes of food preparation could be carried out in an hygienic and easily cleaned germ-free environment. The Frankfurt Kitchen was to be a 'clean machine' at the centre of the home: its hygienic and antiseptic laboratory. (The walls were painted blue, a colour believed to repel flies.)[30] Rather than the social centre of the house as it had been in the past, this was designed to be a functional space where certain actions vital to the health and wellbeing of the household were performed as quickly and efficiently as possible. While partly based on existing compact kitchens, such as the galleys of railway restaurant cars and ships, and influenced by ideas about 'scientific' and 'rational' kitchen layout promoted by 'specialists' in household management such as the American Christine Frederick[31] and the German Erna Meyer,[32] Schütte-Lihotzky's kitchen design almost certainly owed as much to the organization of hygienic facilities in sanatoriums and hospitals. One of her main concerns was the housewife's health:

> The problem of finding a more rational organization of the housewife's work is of nearly equal significance for all levels of society. Both the middle-class woman, who often has to run the house without help of any kind, and the working-class woman, who frequently has to pursue an occupation outside the house, are so over-worked that over the long run it cannot but have a negative effect on the general health of the whole population.[33]

Schütte-Lihotzky had made her first experiments with kitchen design while working in Vienna in the early 1920s, grouping together domestic operations that required water (washing and preparing food, cooking, washing up, washing clothes, etc.) and separating such 'wet' activities from the traditional live-in kitchen (*Wohnküche*). For reasons of hygiene, cleanliness and convenience these activities were concentrated in a *Kochnische* (cooking niche) or *Spülküche* (scullery) directly off the *Wohnküche*.[34] These experiments were eventually to lead to the adoption of the galley-like *Arbeitküche* (Work Kitchen) which Schütte-Lihotzky developed more fully with May and his team in 1926–27 as the Frankfurt Kitchen. One of the main reasons for the replacement of the *Wohnküche* by the *Arbeitküche* was to separate food preparation from the washing of dirty laundry, which – following the principles of Christine Frederick – was deemed to be unhygienic. This view still prevails today in many countries. In Sweden, it is illegal to fit a washing machine in a kitchen. In most continental European countries the washing machine is kept in the bathroom or a separate washroom, while in American suburban dwellings the washing machine is often fitted in the garage rather than in the kitchen.

At Frankfurt, Schütte-Lihotzky designed *Arbeitküchen* or *Kochküchen* (cooking kitchens) that were not only smaller and more compact, but also long and narrow like a railway restaurant-car kitchen, enabling the housewife easily to reach cupboards and shelves on either side of the room without moving, or with the minimum of movements. This narrowing of the kitchen in contrast to the larger traditional *Wohnküche* also had the side effect of making it impossible to accommodate a table or chairs. Walter Gropius wrote to the novelist Alfred Döblin about the kitchen of the Haus am Horn, the model house designed for the 1923 Bauhaus exhibition by Georg Muche and Adolf Meyer, which was one of the earliest modern *Arbeitküchen*: 'In each room function is important, for example the kitchen is the most practical and simple of kitchens – but it is not possible to use it as a dining room as well.'[35] Not all modernist architects favoured the long narrow *Arbeitküche*. Some of them designed kitchens closer to the Haus am Horn

Frankfurt Kitchen,
Frankfurt am Main, Germany, 1927
Margarete Schütte-Lihotzky

model, which employed a squarer format than most examples of the Frankfurt Kitchen, yet also aimed to be a working rather than a live-in kitchen. Georg Muche wrote that: 'The table stands in front of the window and forms, together with the stove, the tops of the low kitchen cabinets, and the sink, a wide and continuous working counter of uniform height, so that the usable area of this small kitchen is equal to that of a conventional kitchen two to three times its size.'[36] J. J. P. Oud in The Netherlands, Bruno Taut in Germany and Josef Frank in Austria designed updated versions of the *Wohnküche* that

Wohnküche (live-in kitchen). Still from Hans Richter's film *Die neue Wohnung* (The New Dwelling), 1930

permitted some degree of 'living' in the kitchen, while remaining too small for the whole household to eat together.[37]

During the early 1920s, considerable debate had taken place between the architects involved with the Austrian settlers' movement, such as Loos, Frank, Franz Schuster and Schütte-Lihotzky, and the officials of the Vienna municipal-housing department about whether social housing should be provided with an *Arbeitküche*, or a modern version of the traditional *Wohnküche*. At that time Schütte-Lihotzky and the settlers' architects had favoured the *Wohnküche* as the most practical solution for the particular circumstances of immediately post-war Austria, a time of great upheaval and deprivation. But in the very different social and economic circumstances of Germany of the late 1920s, Schütte-Lihotzky and the neue Frankfurt team determined that the *Arbeitküche* should replace the *Wohnküche*, which they now considered to be socially regressive and unhygienic, a view widely held at the time by left-wing architects and housing professionals. In designing the Freidorf co-operative housing near Basel, Hannes Meyer had opted for galley-type kitchens. Writing shortly after the estate was completed in 1921, he justified this on grounds of health and hygiene, arguing that: 'In deciding upon its floor plan, the first thing the housing reformer had to remember was the enormous contribution he could make towards a healthier and better family life by the way he allotted floor space inside the house.' During the planning of the estate the future occupants were given a questionnaire about their requirements. Meyer claimed that only two out of 115 had opted for the traditional *Wohnküche*, and consequently he had separated the kitchen from the dining room 'to the great benefit of the family's health', designing it 'as a passage of such narrow width that there is no space for family meals in the housewife's laboratory'.[38]

The old-fashioned *Wohnküche* was a space where the family ate and congregated together on a daily basis, often by force of necessity as many poor families would not have had a separate living room. In better-off working-class and lower middle-class households the kitchen was used for everyday living, while the living room was kept as a *Salon* or 'best parlour' for when guests called or for special occasions. This combination was common in western European countries (as in Britain) during the first half of the 20th century, and the subject of frequent attacks by modernist architects and housing reformers.[39] The *Wohnküche* was considered unhealthy and unhygienic due to the condensation caused by cooking and washing, as socially undesirable because women would be constrained to spend most of their day in it 'servicing' the family, and as both socially undesirable and unhygienic because it was sometimes used for sleeping by very poor and numerous families. By contrast, the Frankfurt-type *Arbeitküche* was intended to be solely a 'functional workspace', far too small for family gatherings, eating, or sleeping. It was the unhygienic nature of the *Wohnküche* – rather than the 'scientific' superiority of the *Arbeitküche* in terms of time-and-motion analyses – that seems to have been the deciding factor in the eyes of reforming modernist architects and designers. The 'labour-saving' qualities of the modernist kitchen were often emphasized in its promotion, presumably because it was thought this would appeal more directly to the housewife. This can be seen in a short documentary film *Neues Bauen in Frankfurt am Main* (New Building in Frankfurt) of 1926–27, where animated floor-plans demonstrated the superiority of the compact and carefully designed Frankfurt kitchen over the traditional *Wohnküche*.[40] But in Richter's *Die neue Wohnung* the extended attack on the traditional live-in kitchen and *Salon* draws particular attention to their dirt-attracting and unhygienic qualities. A sequence set in a *Wohnküche* shows a pipe-smoking father in braces and shirtsleeves reading the paper at the kitchen table; two bored-looking children sit opposite him, while the mother irons a mountain of freshly laundered washing. This is contrasted with the *Salon* or front parlour, which has elaborate dust-gathering furniture, kitsch ornaments and heavy drapes and curtains that need continual dusting and polishing.[41] In another long sequence, the preparation of coffee in an old-fashioned coffee pot in a traditional *Wohnküche* is compared with the speed and hygiene of making coffee in the compact *Arbeitküche* of one of Max Ernst Haefeli's model Rotachhäuser in Zurich, using a Cona machine that resembles a scientific laboratory retort – and which serves as a metonymic image of the 'clean machine' of the 'scientific' modernist household.[42]

Most modernist architects and designers believed in the application of 'scientific' methodology to the design of housing and the layout of the interior. Like their colleagues in other professions they favoured the intervention of 'experts' at every level of society, from attempts to restructure industry on the basis of work-study and time-and-motion studies to the reform of women's work in the home (household management). However, May and his colleagues approached projects like the design of the Frankfurt Kitchen with a belief in a methodology based on humanistic values as well as the professional or expert view. In the autumn of 1929, the neue Frankfurt hosted the second

CIAM conference devoted to the problems of existence-minimum housing, on which May's neue Frankfurt team had concentrated a great deal of research and experiment. May declared at the conference that the architect could not 'be solely responsible for solving the hundreds of issues' relevant to the problem of providing affordable accommodation for low-paid workers, arguing that 'we shall not be able to do without the help of hygiene experts, engineers and physicists'. Nevertheless, May insisted that 'man himself is the measure of the importance of this issue'. He maintained that 'respect for the biological and social status' of man – rather than 'fruitless theorization' – was necessary to build houses and apartments which 'although let at reasonable rents, will satisfy the material and spiritual needs of their inhabitants'.[43]

The Frankfurt Kitchen was not a single design but rather a series of variants intended for different types of dwelling, although this is not always apparent from photographs, or preserved or reconstructed versions in museums, which have helped to produce the kitchen's particular renown. The most famous example is installed in the basement of the MAK (Austrian Museum of Applied Arts) in Vienna, reconstructed in the last decade of the 20th century in collaboration with Schütte-Lihotzky, who was by then in her nineties.[44] But as well as the long narrow galley-type kitchen, there were also squarer versions and kitchens that fitted into a niche in a living room. More luxurious versions were developed, including two larger kitchens for middle-class dwellings with one or two servants.[45] Kitchens designed by other members of the neue Frankfurt team were also installed in some dwellings, such as Franz Schuster's alcove kitchen of 2.3 square metres and Anton Brenner's foldout kitchen, both designed for use in very small apartments by architects who like Schütte-Lihotzky had previously worked with the Austrian settlers' movement and the Vienna municipal-housing department.[46] Ferdinand Kramer also designed units that could be put together to make a 'non-fitted' kitchen.[47] As many as ten thousand dwellings are said to have been fitted with Frankfurt Kitchens, produced as a factory-assembled module delivered to the site and hoisted into place by a crane.[48] Individual units were also sold commercially through the *Frankfurter Register*, the catalogue of approved designs published by the neue Frankfurt.

The most common form of the Frankfurt Kitchen was 1.9 by 3.4 metres, nearly twice as long as it was wide. Cooker, sink and work surfaces were all approximately the same height to enable the 'average German housewife' to use them without bending, with standardized cabinets and containers above and below the work surfaces. (There were some slight variations in the height of work surfaces which were 'ironed out' in later derivatives, and in the ubiquitous post-1945 galley kitchen.) The units were positioned sequentially according to the notional progression of work processes involved in preparing a meal: chopping, washing, cooking, serving, washing up, etc. They were arranged not only to be 'rational' but also to be hygienic and easily cleaned. There were also built-in hygienic glass containers for loose food (relatively little food was pre-packaged in Germany at this time) and a folding ironing board.[49] Preparing food, ironing, and other kitchen tasks could be performed while sitting on a swivel stool so that the housewife could take the weight off her feet and avoid getting varicose veins. The central suspended electric light was positioned on a track so that it could be moved by a handle beneath its shade to illuminate the particular part of the kitchen where the housewife was working. The floor standing units were recessed a few centimetres at the bottom to allow ease of cleaning the floor and so that the housewife could stand close to them while she worked, and a built-in ironing board folded flat against the wall. Because many women who used the kitchen would be out at work, the kitchen was provided with a hay box where a preheated casserole could be placed to simmer slowly during the day (a precursor of the modern electric slow cooker).[50] In a newspaper article, May claimed: 'The perfection of our kitchen's interior is probably not matched anywhere else.'

> Our apartment kitchens are arranged in a way which completely separates kitchen work from the living area, therefore eliminating the unpleasant effects produced by smell, vapours and above all the psychological effect of seeing leftovers, plates, bowls, washing-up cloths and other such items lying around.[51]

However, the real agenda was ideological, as much a question of social as physical hygiene. By separating the living room from the kitchen people were forced to use the spaces provided for them in new and unfamiliar ways. (Demonstration kitchens were constructed in Frankfurt schools so that schoolgirls could be taught how to use the new *Arbeitküchen*.) This was an undisguised attack on traditional working-class and lower middle-class domestic customs, considered by those who worked on the neue Frankfurt project (and by many other radical architects and housing specialists) to be essentially *petit bourgeois*, i.e. aspiring to unprogressive lower middle-class values: a kind of social *un*hygiene. By carefully controlling the plan of the *neue Wohnung* it would be possible to produce the *neue Mensch* and the *neue Frau*. Freed from such *petit bourgeois* absurdities as the cramped and crowded *Wohnküche* and a *Salon* reserved for 'special' occasions, they would claim their social rights and fulfil their social responsibilities in the *neue Wohnkultur*.

It might at first seem contradictory that in a housing project supposedly devoted to the ideals of light, air and spatial openness the kitchen should be deliberately small and narrow. While the 'rational' reason for this was so that the work surfaces, sink and cooker could be reached with minimum movements, the 'ideological' reason was to prevent the kitchen from being used as a family living room, so that the housewife would not be tempted or constrained to spend too much time in it. Meals were to be prepared as efficiently, quickly and hygienically as possible in the galley-like kitchen and eaten in the living/dining room, leaving the housewife free to get on with her other activities in the more open and spacious parts of the house, in the garden, or on the terrace. Or away from the house altogether at her workplace, or enjoying the parks, playgrounds and open spaces in and around the city with her children. The kitchen was fitted with a wide (usually sliding) door linking it to the living room, so that even during the supposedly brief time spent preparing meals the housewife would not feel isolated from other members of the household and could keep an eye on the children.[52]

As a highly directed system of social control the Frankfurt Kitchen was bitterly opposed by conservative commentators at the time. It has also been condemned by some recent critics, including feminists who have challenged the idea that the redesign of the kitchen on the Frankfurt model could empower women, accusing Schütte-Lihotzky of collaborating with a male-centric modernist architectural profession to create a design inspired by the work processes of the factory which merely replaced one kind of drudgery with another.[53] Susan Henderson has argued that 'the professional dignity that the Frankfurt Kitchen was to confer on the role of housewife does not bear scrutiny. The workstation was not borrowed from the professional world, but from the factory, from labour characterized by single, repetitive, and mind-numbing opera-tions.'[54] But if we acknowledge (as I have argued) that the Frankfurt Kitchen was not so much based on the workstation of the Fordist factory production line as the workstation of a hospital or sanatorium, a different model emerges. The design was determined by careful attention to the movements and capabilities of the human body, with each area reduced to the smallest comfortable space a person could occupy.[55] But the *Arbeitküche* was not intended to be 'manned' (or 'womanned') for the whole of a working day, like a factory workstation. It was to be used quickly and efficiently to prepare meals and wash up, after which the housewife would be free to return to the living room, her bedroom, her work, or her own social, occupational or leisure pursuits.[56] It was also designed like a nurses' station in a hospital or sanatorium to be a vantage point from where the housewife could survey (and surveil) the family – and in particular her children – without having to be constantly moving around the house or apartment.

The Frankfurt team also designed a 'Frankfurt Bathroom', a tiny unit with a combination shower and 'Sitzbad' (sit-up bath), full-size washbasin and toilet, all fitted into an extraordinarily small space of 1.7 by 1.5 metres (see Chapter 10). But it was the kitchen that was given priority, symbolizing the way in which the New Architecture should be conceived from the inside out. The priorities of housing were to be 'first the kitchen – then the façade', according to the well-known slogan of Marie-Elisabeth Lüders,[57] an influential member of the BDF – the Bund deutscher Frauenvereine (League of German Women's Clubs), a powerful coalition of middle-class women's organiza-tions – and a FDP (German Democratic Party) member of the Reichstag with a special interest in housing.[58] Through the Frankfurt Kitchen the policy of the conservative BDF was realized in Social Democratic Frankfurt by Schütte-Lihotzky (who was later to become a member of the Communist party) in collaboration with other members of May's team, many of whom, like Schütte-Lihotzky, went on to work in the Soviet Union in the early 1930s. By another irony, such experiments in left-wing social engineering helped to produce an efficient military and civilian machine that could be put to use by an incoming Nazi government. As a critic observed as early as 1925: 'One of the reasons for the streamlining of the household was surely so that women could be moved into the factories at a moment's notice, just as the preoccupation with the health of workers had military implications.'[59]

In the design of the galley-type kitchens – as in many other aspects of design for social housing – modernist architects have been accused of insensitively applying middle-class standards and preoccupations to dwellings for predominantly working-class clients. But as has been argued, this was not so much the result of insensitivity as of ideological conviction: a deliberate onslaught on the traditional *mores* of working-class domestic life in an attempt to radicalize the proletariat. Leftist architects and housing managers saw the redesign of the kitchen as the key element in a process of 'social engineering' that would remove the social centre of the dwelling from the traditional *Wohnküche* to the modern living/dining room, while providing a separate adjoining *Arbeitküche* for the quick, efficient and hygienic preparation of food. The aim was to produce a new social role for the housewife by giving housework the aura of skilled work and the kitchen the ambience of the hospital clinic or the medical laboratory. By such means they hoped to change the traditional roles of working-class and lower middle-class women. This was not however intended to be the bourgeois 'professionalization' of the housewife demanded by the powerful and vociferous middle-class women's organizations of the period such as the BDF. By creating a communal living/dining area and a 'functional' *Arbeitküche* to replace the 'socially regressive' and matriarchal *Wohnküche*, the intention was rather to produce a collective space that could be negotiated by all members of the household.

Whether or not this campaign was successful, the galley-type working kitchen has almost certainly been the single most successful innovation of 20th-century modernism. Standardized kitchens and standardized kitchen units throughout the world have their origin in the experimental kitchen designs of the 1920s, and especially the Frankfurt Kitchen. Kitchens ultimately derived from the Frankfurt model are found today not only in social housing but also in luxury apartments and up-market housing, such as the converted or custom-built 'loft apartments' that became fashionable in western Europe and the United States in the 1990s and 2000s. With units based on a 60 cm module and work surfaces at a height of 90 cm (often too low for today's average heights), the 21st-century kitchen is clearly descended from ideas first tried out in the experimental standardized kitchens of the 1920s and 1930s in Germany, The Netherlands and Scandinavia: a model of the hygienic workstation, or clean machine.

6 Mountains & the sea

The idea that sun and fresh air were beneficial for general health and the treatment of disease has a history that predates the tuberculosis sanatoriums of the second half of the 19th century. While the preoccupation of modernist architects and designers with the principles of light, air and openness seems to have been directly based on ideas promoted by health and hygiene reformers in the late 19th and early 20th centuries, concerns about sunlight and the flow of fresh air in housing and the design of towns and cities go back at least to classical antiquity. (Aristotle drew up rules for the siting of cities, and Vitruvius wrote of light, air, sun, health and hygiene in his *Ten Books of Architecture*.) The modern belief in the curative and restorative properties of sunlight and fresh air originally derived from earlier medical beliefs about foul and stagnant air (miasma) as the cause of infection and disease. By the 1860s, such ideas were superseded by the theory of bacteria, based on the experiments of Louis Pasteur and Joseph Lister. But the bacterial theory did not destroy medical faith in the benefits of sunlight and fresh air. Pasteur also believed in the power of the sun to destroy microbes, and in the late 19th century manufacturers of 'hygienic products' such as soaps played on both bacterial theories and a belief in the benefits of sunlight. Lever Brothers called their best- selling soap 'Sunlight Soap', and named the company town – founded in 1888 and built in Arts and Crafts style for their employees in north-west England – Port Sunlight.

Paralleling the growth of the sanatorium movement in the second half of the 19th century, the more general benefits of sunlight and fresh air for human health and well-being had been widely adopted by medical reformers in Europe and America, by campaigners for dress and diet reform, and by housing professionals.[1] A report of the Amsterdamsche Woningraad (Amsterdam Housing Council) in 1909 typically argued that: 'Someone who is in the fresh air continually, who receives the beneficial effects of the sun, will have a much higher immunity against sickness than the person who has to live in stuffy, badly illuminated rooms.'[2] The deprivations of the First World War reinforced such arguments, and health, hygiene and the cult of sunlight and fresh air became dominant agendas in the 1920s and 1930s, especially in western Europe, North America and the new socialist republics of the Soviet Union.

Sunlight therapy, closely linked to the sanatorium movement and the cult of mountain resorts, had first become fashionable in the second half of the 19th century. In 1855, Arnold Rikli opened a nature-therapy sanatorium at Veldes in Upper Carniola, now Bled in Slovenia but at that time part of the Austro-Hungarian empire. Rikli had been born and brought up in Switzerland, and his 'atmosphere cure' was closely linked to the Alpine culture of the late 19th century. The basis of the treatment was the 'air bath' or 'atmospheric bath' (*Lichtluftbad*: literally 'light-air bath') where patients exposed their loosely clothed bodies to the fresh air. This was followed by short spells of controlled exposure to the rays of the sun, during which they lay on woollen blankets on inclined boards for twenty or thirty minutes with only their heads shaded. Finally they took a 'sweat bath', wrapping themselves in the loosely woven blankets on which they had been lying to induce perspiration.[3] Rikli popularized the beneficial effects of the radiation of air and sunlight through publications such as *Let There Be Light, or The Atmospheric Cure* (first published in 1869), which went through many editions in several languages. In his exhaustive study of the influence of technology on design, *Mechanization Takes Command* (1948), Sigfried Giedion traces these treatments back through the ideas of Jean-Jacques Rousseau to the bathing customs of the ancient world. As a fellow Swiss who had also spent part of his life in Austria, Giedion's enthusiasm for Rikli's methods is clearly based on personal experience. (Although Rikli died in 1906 and the Veldes sanatorium closed at the time of the First World War, treatments based on the 'atmospheric cure' continued to be available in his native Switzerland.)[4]

Rikli had arrived at his ideas as a boy while walking in the wooded foothills of the Alps near Berne, removing more and more of his clothing until completely naked.[5] Rikli made his patients at Veldes wear shorts, sandals and open-necked short-sleeved shirts, and was photographed wearing this 'hygienic walking costume' in 1869, posed bare headed and bare foot against a painted Alpine backdrop in the photographer's studio with his right foot on a cardboard rock. Holding his alpenstock in his left hand, and with his sandals slung round his waist, he gestures forcefully with his right towards the painted mountain peaks. He used an engraved reproduction of this with a more convincingly drawn-in Alpine background of lake, castle, mountains and shining sun as the frontispiece to *Let There Be Light*.[6] By the end of the 19th century, the exposure of the naked skin to the rays of the sun and sunbathing as a health treatment or as a preventive or prophylactic measure had become increasingly popular. In the 20th century, Rikli's 'hygienic walking costume' was to become universal for walkers and hikers, and eventually for holidaymakers in general.

For Le Corbusier (who also grew up in the Swiss Alps), sunlight, purity, cleanliness, hygiene and clothing were closely linked: 'Every man to-day realizes his need of sun, of warmth, of pure air and clean floors', he wrote in 'Architecture or Revolution', the final chapter of *Vers une architecture* (1923). 'He has been taught to wear a shiny white collar, and women love fine white linen.'[7] Health and dress reformers tried to extend the supposed benefits of sunlight from the upper and middle classes to the less receptive lower middle and working classes. The efficiency expert Herbert N. Casson maintained that the thick and impervious-to-light European male clothing of the period was partly responsible for the high rate of illness among working men: 90 million lost working days in 1927 – twelve times more than lost through strikes. Casson claimed the benefits of sunlight were more important even than sanitary hygiene.[8]

During the first decade of the 20th century, sun therapy began to achieve scientific and medical respectability. In 1903, Niels Ryberg Finsen, a former lecturer in anatomy at the University of Copenhagen, was awarded the Nobel Prize for Medicine for demonstrating the beneficial effects of light on diseases of the skin and his development of the ultra-violet lamp, which successfully cured cases of lupus (tuberculosis of the skin).[9] Also in 1903, Dr Auguste Rollier introduced sunlight therapy at his clinic in Leysin in Switzerland, and it was soon adopted by other physicians at Davos and Samedan. Rollier's sanatorium was built on a plateau high above the upper Rhône. This was at a considerably higher level (and exposed to more intense sunlight) than had previously been thought beneficial as a treatment for tuberculosis. Patients were administered carefully regulated doses of mountain sunlight combined with occupational therapy, educational classes and workshops in the open air.[10] This came to supersede more conventional open-air treatment for non-pulmonary tuberculosis (particularly tuberculosis of the bones and joints) in the early decades of the 20th century.[11] Many new sanatoriums were built at Leysin, all with open balconies facing south where patients 'clad in loin cloths or short shifts spent most of the day'.

> Arriving in Leysin by funicular from Aigle was indeed an awesome experience for anyone not familiar with the combination of brilliant sunshine and glittering snow, the air pure, the silence almost palpable. Here under Rollier's aegis row upon row of sanatoria dedicated to sun worship sprang up, their white cliff-like simplicity hardly disturbing the starkness and stillness of the landscape.[12]

A drawback of the high altitude of Leysin was that once patients were acclimatized they found returning to anywhere near sea level difficult. This was a problem even with sanatoriums situated at lower altitudes, such as those at Davos described by Thomas Mann.

It was at a sanatorium in Leysin that Loos and Kokoschka visited Bessie Bruce in the winter of 1909–10. Loos shared the late 19th-century Austrian obsession with health, fresh air and mountains, frequenting fashionable mountain resorts like Semmering with literary friends from Vienna such as Karl Kraus and Peter Altenberg. In 1912, he made designs for an enormous grand hotel at Semmering and a special school for girls for the educationist Eugenie Schwarzwald, located on the Pinkenkogel mountain high above the resort. Schwarzwald was married to a leading administrator at the Ministry of Finance and ran a progressive school for girls in Vienna where Loos, Schoenberg and Kokoschka taught. Loos had designed the study for her Josefstädterstrasse apartment and the project for the school at Semmering progressed to the point where 120 pupils from the Schwarzwald school in Vienna went to visit the proposed site, where they were shown the plans and model and heard Loos talk about them.[13] Although neither school nor hotel was built, the Alpine hotel remained one of his favourite projects. A model was shown at the Salon d'Automne in Paris in 1923 and was displayed again in the exhibition of his work that toured Germany in 1930 on the occasion of his sixtieth birthday.[14] In 1925, Loos was elected a committee member of the 'Das Haus in der Sonne' (The House in the Sun), an organization, of which Schwarzwald was president, dedicated to the free housing and education of deserving young women.[15]

One of Loos's last realized commissions was the Landhaus Khuner, a 'modernist' Alpine chalet (1929–30) for the vegetable-oil manufacturer Paul Khuner, built on a panoramic site a few miles from Semmering at Kreuzberg near Payerbach, overlooking pine and beech woods, high Alpine meadows and the mountains beyond. Loos regarded the traditional plain Alpine farmhouse or chalet as a functional solution to particular climatic conditions and cultural needs. But he deplored the kitsch decoration generally applied to 19th- and early 20th-century Alpine villas, believing such decoration should be stripped away rather as Arnold Rikli had stripped away his clothing in the Alpine sunlight. The Khuner house was a 'stripped down' version of a traditional Alpine farmhouse, with a low-pitched zinc roof and a large double-height living space surrounded by rooms on three sides and a gallery on the first floor. The end wall had a spectacular two-storey window with a breathtaking view across the valley to the Schneeberg and the Rax Alps, which led out onto a wide terrace where meals or drinks could be served in summer. There was also a small terrace above the roof with a shower, where *Licht-* or *Luftbad* could be taken. Since the 1950s, the Khuner House has been a small hotel and restaurant, retaining many of its original features.

In 1919, Bruno Taut published *Alpine Architecture*, which he had begun to write during the First World War. The book consisted of a series of thirty illustrations with hand-written captions of expressionist Alpine architectural fantasies depicting mountain tops glazed with glass vaults, and huge crystalline or stepped structures set in an Alpine landscape of mountains and lakes.[16] Here the diamond-like crystal motif Taut employed in his Glass Pavilion at the Werkbund Exhibition in Cologne in 1914 is transformed into the crystalline peaks of the mountains themselves and the faceted structures they harbour. His elaborate and unbuildable fantasies exerted a strong imaginative and conceptual hold on his generation of German architects. They were an inspiration for many of the (largely unbuilt) expressionist architectural designs of the early 1920s. But they were also to exert a powerful influence on how in the modernist buildings they designed in the later 1920s and early 1930s German and central European architects were to employ materials such as steel, reinforced concrete, and glass – emphasizing their crystalline and hygienic qualities. Modernist in its social commitment and utopian ideology, Taut's own social housing and public buildings of

the mid- and late 1920s demonstrated a pragmatic attention to the principles of light, air and openness, health and hygiene. By comparison, many of his contemporaries were too often tempted to indulge formal and structural acrobatics for their own sake in attempting to realize such principles through the use of 'modern' materials.

As a child and adolescent growing up in Switzerland, Le Corbusier was deeply affected by the Swiss tradition of alpinism and the mystique of mountains. As soon as he and his brother were old enough, the whole family began to climb across glaciers and slopes still covered with snow. As a boy he often spent the whole of the summer holidays in the Alps with his mother, brother and father, or with his friends. 'Sundays often found us together at the top of the highest hill. It had pinnacles as well as grandly sweeping slopes: pastures, herds of large cattle, uninterrupted horizons, flights of rooks. We were preparing the future.' Le Corbusier derived his alpinism from his father who was 'passionately devoted to the mountains and rivers which made up our landscape', and for whom it was of great importance that his sons shared his fascination for the

Landhaus Khuner,
Kreuzberg, near Payerbach, Austria, 1929–30

Adolf Loos

high-mountain culture of the Valais region. 'We were constantly on the mountain tops: the vast horizons were familiar. When there was a sea of mist, its infinite expanse was like the real sea – which I had never seen.'[17] An enthusiastic mountain climber with a particular preference for 'the highest region of the high Alps of Valais', Le Corbusier's father led annual group tours every summer with local guides and wrote enthusiastic and detailed reports of these in the magazine of the La Chaux-de-Fonds section of the Swiss Alpine Club. He also designed prefabricated wooden mountain huts constructed by carpenters in the valleys and hauled up the mountains by pack animals, to provide shelter for climbers under extreme weather conditions in the highest Alpine regions.[18] The fascination with the high open spaces of the Alps that Le Corbusier shared with his father almost certainly had a direct effect on his architectural designs in his preoccupation with tall buildings, elevated viewpoints, fresh air and open horizons. Charlotte Perriand, who worked in Le Corbusier's office as a young woman, had spent her childhood holidays with her grandparents in the mountainous French region of Savoie. Perriand produced many ingenious prefabricated designs for mountain chalets and ski-huts in the 1930s, and a series of projects for large-scale accommodation for winter sports at Les Arcs in Savoie that were built between 1967 and 1985.[19] 'I love the mountains deeply', she wrote. 'I love them because they are essential for me. They have always been the barometer of my physical and moral equilibrium.'[20]

An appetite for sunshine

Although mountain resorts remained fashionable, throughout the 1920s the Côte d'Azur and other parts of the Mediterranean coast became increasingly popular among wealthy north Europeans and Americans, who in the late 19th century had gone to the South of France to avoid the cold damp winters of northern Europe and the mid-west and eastern seaboard of the United States. F. Scott Fitzgerald's *Tender is the Night* opens with a description of a hotel near Cannes that has recently become 'a summer resort of notable and fashionable people' – while 'a decade ago it was almost deserted after its English clientele went north in April'.[21] By the mid-1920s, the Anglo-American and European smart set was beginning to visit the Mediterranean in the summer, or to stay there all the year round. This prompted the development of modernist forms of Riviera architecture designed for a leisured life of sun and fresh air in proximity to the sea, with flat roofs and terraces for sunbathing, large windows and white walls. The white walls, wide windows, sun terraces, flat roofs and balconies characteristic of modernist buildings seemed particularly appropriate to such leisured lifestyles in a Mediterranean climate. The white walls contrasted with and showed off the sunburnt skins of their occupants. Previously, the European middle and upper classes had favoured pale complexions. They had shaded their faces and bodies with hats and loose clothing against too much exposure from the sun in order to distinguish themselves from peasants and outdoor workers whose skins were dark and swarthy from labouring in the direct sunlight and open air.[22] The pale skin affected by the privileged classes prior to the First World War also signified cleanliness and hygiene. Unashamedly racialist advertisements for soaps and soap powders in the late 19th and early 20th centuries featured black children being 'cleansed' with soap, or exploited the contrast between black skins and sparkling white newly washed clothes.[23]

Once the skin of the fashion-conscious upper middle classes could be tanned by the sun, the whiteness or paleness of skin which had previously been the distinguishing mark of the non-manual worker was displaced onto the white, off-white or pastel coloured walls of the Mediterranean-style or modernist house, where the wealthy now spent much of their summers. The hygienic pallor of the villa walls served as a substitute for the former pallor of its inhabitants. Lightweight white clothes – such as cotton shirts, linen suits and tuxedos – were also adopted by the better-off in place of the darker colours they had formerly worn, as a further displacement of the once admired paleness of the refined European skin. As the emblem of modernity, the white wall was the displaced surface onto which is projected the whiteness of the European, who is not 'really' white but light hued – like the walls of many of the Weissenhof houses and apartments and other modernist buildings of the period (see Chapter 10).

In *Tender is the Night*, Fitzgerald has his wealthy American protagonists Dick and Nicole Diver virtually invent the Riviera summer season, or at least make it fashionable. Dick Diver is a psychiatrist married to Nicole Warren, a rich young Chicago heiress, who had been a patient at the Zurich sanatorium where he was a consultant, and of which he subsequently became co-owner with the help of Nicole's family money. After Dick begins to drink too much the couple leave the snowy Alpine sunshine and clear air of Switzerland for the summer sunshine of the Riviera coast, where they buy up half a village and rebuild it as a luxurious villa for themselves and their two children – making the nearby beach fashionable with wealthy American and European expatriates. At one point Dick appears on the beach in black lace swimming trunks which Nicole has made for him. But this garment designed to '*épater la bourgeoisie*' is a tease: the trunks are lined with flesh-coloured material. Eventually, however, the relatively pale Dick – the phallic first name is significant – cedes his wife to the French playboy Tommy Barban, whose sunburnt face is 'so dark as to have lost the pleasantness of deep tan without attaining the blue beauty of Negroes'.[24] Nicole marries Barban after divorcing Dick, who returns to the United States and is last heard of practising as a small-town GP in upper New York state.

Dick and Nicole Diver were partly based on Fitzgerald himself and his wife Zelda but mainly on his friends the American millionaire (and painter of a handful of astonishing proto-pop-art paintings) Gerald Murphy and his wife Sara.[25] Like the Divers, the Murphys had settled in Antibes – to which they had been invited by Cole Porter. Here they bought a nondescript pitch-roofed turn-of-the-century villa with a superb sheltered site and luxuriant garden full of exotic sub-tropical plants, the Chalet des Nielles.[26] The Murphys had the house remodelled and 'modernized' by two architects from Ohio, Hale Walker and Harold Heller. The small windows were opened up to form huge modern *pannes de verre*, the limestone walls covered with beige stucco, a third storey added, the pitched chalet roof replaced by a flat roof that served as a sun terrace, and a grey-and-white marble flagged terrace laid leading off the living rooms on the ground floor.[27] The interior was furnished with white-upholstered steel furniture, the terrace with wrought-iron café chairs which Murphy bought from a restaurant supplier and painted with silver radiator paint. The house was rechristened the 'Villa America', with a large, brightly coloured sign at the road entrance painted by Murphy in an ironic variant of the Stars and Stripes.[28] But this seemingly idyllic, moneyed modernist lifestyle was not to last. The Murphys' younger son Patrick was diagnosed with tuberculosis and – in a tragic reverse of the fictional Divers' trajectory – the Murphys spent eighteen months living close to him in Montana in Switzerland, where he was being treated in an Alpine sanatorium.[29] Murphy gave up painting in 1930 and a few years after the Wall Street crash the family returned to live in the United States, where Patrick died at the age of sixteen.

It was not only expatriate American multimillionaires like the Murphys who made the Riviera fashionable in summer during the 1920s, but also wealthy Europeans such as the French patrons of the avant-garde, the Vicomte and Vicomtesse de Noailles. Among the first modernist houses built in the South of France between the wars, the Villa Noailles at Hyères (1923–28), designed by Robert Mallet-Stevens, was undoubtedly the most discreetly sumptuous. With interiors and furnishings by a team of well-known interior and furniture designers, the villa was built to entertain a fashionable elite in a luxurious Mediterranean milieu of sun, fresh air, healthy exercise and aesthetic hygiene.[30] It was filled with works of art commissioned or purchased by the Noailles – including a painting by Piet Mondrian, and sculptures by Henri Laurens and Jacques Lipchitz. In his first letter to Mallet-Stevens concerning the villa, De Noailles wrote that the only constraint he would impose on the commission was 'the essential principle of all houses on the Côte d'Azur: the quest for sunshine'.[31] The Villa Noailles was carefully designed to produce a luxurious and aristocratic 'modernist austerity' in a Mediterranean setting where the restorative hygienic and health-giving properties of light, air and openness could be enjoyed to the full. Enormous glass windows sunk into the ground at the touch of an electric button, opening the covered swimming pool directly onto a large terrace fitted out with sports equipment and sunloungers specially designed by Mallet-Stevens.[32] A sleeping terrace with electrically operated mosquito curtains and a suspended bed by Pierre Chareau could be partially closed in with sliding glass doors, although this seems to have proved as impractical as the open-air sleeping arrangements in contemporary modernist houses in Southern California by Rudolf Schindler and Richard Neutra.[33] The villa was the subject of a short film directed by Man

Ray, *Les Mystères du Chateau du Dé* (1929), commissioned and financed by Charles de Noailles to display his house as a backdrop to Ray's surrealist fantasy.

The Irish interior decorator and furniture designer Eileen Gray (who had contributed a carpet, cushions and a dressing table for the Villa Noailles) planned the cryptically named E-1027 as a live/work space for herself and Jean Badovici, the editor of the avant-garde architectural magazine *Architecture d'aujourd'hui*. Perched on a rocky cliff site in a secluded and idyllic part of the Mediterranean corniche near Menton, the house was intended to make the most of the sunshine and sea air.[34] A few years later, Gray designed the nearby Tempe à Pailla as a vacation house for herself on a steep mountainside outside Castellar (1932–34), where terraces and living rooms were even more carefully oriented to receive the maximum sunshine in this most climatically favoured part of the French Riviera.[35] After Gray left E-1027, Le Corbusier frequently visited Badovici there, and in a notorious incident in 1938 painted brightly coloured murals on the white interior walls – as if wilfully tattooing the 'primitive' ornament proscribed by Loos onto the purist white body of Gray's modernist house.[36] To add insult to injury, Le Corbusier seems to have performed this desecration in the nude, and had himself photographed in the act. After the Second World War, he purchased a piece of land near the house and built a small *cabanon* or swimming hut on the cliffs. It was while swimming from there that he died of a heart attack in 1965.

With its Riviera-like climate Southern California provided an ideal location for the austerely luxurious modernist villas that catered to the fashionable sun-loving American upper middle classes of the 1920s. Two émigré Austrian architects, Rudolf Schindler and Richard Neutra, who had been strongly influence by the work of Adolf Loos (and who had been encouraged by Loos to work in the United States), eventually

Swimming pool, Villa Noailles,
Hyères, France, 1923–28
Robert Mallet-Stevens

found their way west to California, which seemed to offer ideal opportunities to produce a stripped architecture of light, air and openness.[37] Both designed innovative modernist houses for Dr Phillip Lovell, a well-known Californian naturopathic physician and advocate of healthy living and 'natural' diet. Lovell opposed the use of drugs and chemicals, promoting the physical and mental benefits of sunlight, fresh air and 'natural' unprocessed foods through his influential 'Care of the Body' column in the *Los Angeles Times*, and the Physical Culture Center he ran in Los Angeles. He also believed in permissive and progressive education and encouraged his own children to play in the nude.[38] Overlooking the Pacific Ocean at Newport Beach about an hour's drive south of Los Angeles, the Lovell Beach House (1925–26) was designed by Schindler so that Lovell and his family could get as near to the outdoors as possible while being able to sunbathe naked in privacy. The house was built with an exposed reinforced-concrete frame upon which the main living area – a single informal room to be used by the whole family – was raised above the beach and had dramatic views over the Pacific. The terrace on the flat roof provided space for physical exercises and sunbathing in private, open to the health-giving properties of the sun and sea air. The bathroom was provided with a 'Marathon' shower which produced needles of water that massaged and relaxed the body and could be used by two people at the same time. In 1926, the year the Beach House was completed, Schindler contributed six articles to Dr Lovell's column in the *Los Angeles Times* on architecture and its relation to health and hygiene, including one on 'Plumbing and Health'.[39] The house had no bedrooms as such but small dressing rooms on the top floor, which opened onto balconies or sleeping porches with long horizontal slits in the concrete providing spectacular views of the ocean from the beds on the open porches. However, these faced into the prevailing winds, and rain and sea-spray persistently blew onto the sleepers through the slits, which were later filled in and the porches glazed over.

Schindler had also been commissioned to design a house for the Lovells in Los Angeles but faults in the construction of the Beach House greatly increased its initial cost, while a mountain cabin he designed for Lovell in 1926 had been a disaster after two metres of snow fell on its flat roof in the first winter. Lovell transferred the commission for his Los Angeles house to Neutra, who had been in partnership with Schindler – resulting in a break between the two men that lasted twenty years. Neutra had served as an officer in the Austro-Hungarian army in the Balkans during the First World War where he was hospitalized with malaria and an early form of tuberculosis, and spent some time convalescing in a sanatorium in Stäfa near Zurich in 1919. This experience almost certainly had a lasting influence on both his designs and his writings, in which he emphasized the role of architecture in promoting mental and physical wellbeing.[40] Designed between 1927 and 1929, Neutra's Lovell Health House (as it came to be known) was built on a steeply sloping site in a hilly area of Los Angeles, oriented to the sun like an Alpine sanatorium. A lightweight prefabricated steel frame enabled the house to be very freely planned with enormous areas of glass for indoor sunbathing, rising two storeys above the swimming pool (which has been described as 'the real "living" room') with the main communal areas on the first floor and the family sleeping areas above.[41] The large, tray-like terrace balconies are suspended from the roof frame by slender steel cables. The main entrance is on the upper floor, and stairs lead down to the living areas below, a similar layout to that employed in many of the Davos-type sanatoriums built on steeply sloping mountain sites in Europe. The windows provided cross draughts from four directions.

Neutra also incorporated exterior space for relaxation and games, a small open-air theatre and a court for gymnastics. The swimming pool with its surrounding terraces is partly in the undercroft of the house with ultra-slender steel pilotis rising above it, while the other half juts out over the valley – so that one half is shaded and sheltered, the other open to the sun and air. The pool was filled with non-chlorinated water that was changed every two weeks and the old water used to water the garden. Neutra designed much of the furniture for the house, but ordered as many fittings as he could from catalogues of standardized products. A Ford Model T headlight served as a light fitting in the living room, embedded into a low wall that screened the staircase which led down from the main entrance where the family or their visitors arrived by car. One of the upstairs sinks was a dentist's basin. Lovell cultivated a similar public profile to the Hollywood film stars who consulted him, promoting his progressive views on health and education through his own lifestyle and the houses in which he lived. The Health House was open to the public on certain days and 15,000 people turned up over two weekends in 1929.[42] Although visually stunning and as photogenic as a Hollywood film star, the building was not without its faults. The tray-like roof and balconies provided shade but these were not always well oriented, so that the glazed corner of the main living area faced south-west and caught the full heat of the afternoon sun – roasting the family and their guests. The open-air sleeping porches on the roof terrace were no more successful than those in Schindler's Beach House or Mallet-Stevens's Villa Noailles, and were later closed in with glass. Given the publicity the house received at the time and its claims to produce a healthy lifestyle, it is ironic that seventy years later it featured in the Hollywood movie *LA Confidential* (1997) as the home of the gangster and drug addict Pierce Patchett – who runs an up-market prostitution racket where clients pay for women who look like film stars. The Lovell Health House had a more sympathetic role in Richter's *Die neue Wohnung*, where it features in a montage of modernist buildings with open-air terraces and roof gardens, wide windows and white walls to show the openness of the new architecture to light, air and sun.[43]

Neutra toured Europe and Asia in 1930 promoting the house. He attended the CIAM congress in Brussels, and visited the Van Nelle factory in Rotterdam. He had earlier met Kees van der Leeuw, the philanthropic Dutch industrialist responsible for commissioning the factory. Van der Leeuw had also commissioned the architects of the

factory, Brinkman and Van der Vlugt, to design an austerely luxurious modernist house for himself overlooking a lake in the outer suburbs of Rotterdam, in which he invited Neutra to stay.[44] While in the United States the following year, Van der Leeuw visited the Lovell Health House and agreed to help finance Neutra to build an experimental house for himself and his family, where new design ideas could be tested. This became known as the VDL (Van der Leeuw) Research House.[45] Neutra went on to develop the crisp, clean, hygienic lines of the Health House in a series of spectacular and luxurious houses in prime locations for rich Californians of the kind who consulted Dr Lovell. In particular, the bathrooms of these houses for wealthy film directors and industrialists disclosed a luxury that was emphasized rather than masked by their formal and 'hygienic' austerity. Yet in the small detached house he designed for the Vienna Werk-bundsiedlung model-housing exhibition in 1932, Neutra demonstrated that he could also design low-cost housing with some of the 'health-conscious' features of his luxurious Californian commissions. In this tiny single-storey house the whole of the flat roof was devoted to a terraced roof garden which occupied the same area as the rather cramped and austere single-storey living accommodation on the ground floor (see p. 147). This must be the greatest ratio of roof garden to living space of any modernist house in Europe – matched perhaps only by the luxurious guest pavilion for August and Hilda Heriot (also in Vienna) designed by the former Bauhaus students Franz Singer and Friedl Dicker between 1932 and 1934.[46]

Three years before the commission for the Lovell Beach House, Rudolf Schindler had designed Kings Road Studios in West Hollywood (1922) as a single-storey two-family house for himself and his wife Pauline and the construction engineer Clyde

Lovell Health House,
Los Angeles, 1927–29
Richard Neutra

Chace and his wife Marian, using lightweight preformed concrete 'tilt-slab' construction. Built around two patios surrounded by a lush garden, the house was planned with no living rooms as such but four 'studios' for each of the inhabitants, with a bathroom for each pair of studios and a kitchen shared by both couples. The studios were grouped so that each pair opened onto a patio, with sliding glazed doors and removable canvas screens. This combined privacy with a maximum openness to the sun and mild air of Southern California – although once again features such as the 'sleeping baskets' on the roof proved to be over optimistic about the Los Angeles climate. These open terraces protected by small roof canopies and canvas awnings were eventually glazed in, like the sleeping porches in the Lovell Beach House and Health House.[47] The experiment in shared communal living did not last long. The Chaces moved out after two years and were succeeded by Neutra and his wife Dione. In 1930, the Neutras also left after Schindler and Neutra had fallen out over the Lovell Health House commission. The Schindlers had separated in 1927, but Pauline Schindler returned to the house in the late 1930s after the couple had finally divorced – living in the part originally designed for the Chaces. Schindler used one of the studios in his section of the house as his architectural office until his death in 1953, while Pauline had custody of the kitchen for her own use. The arrangement of the studio house – where the principles of light, air and openness were intended to generate a new openness in living and more flexible human relationships – seems to have successfully accommodated the domestic pattern of a divorced couple living together but apart. Henry-Russell Hitchcock and Philip Johnson refused to illustrate Kings Road Studios in their seminal 'Modern Architecture: International Exhibition' at the Museum of Modern Art in New York in 1932 – or in their accompanying text, *The International Style* – although Johnson had visited the house in 1931. It seems that the house did not conform to Johnson's standards of hygiene.

Kings Road Studios,
West Hollywood, Los Angeles, 1922
Rudolf Schindler

Architect's own house,
Sandycove, Dublin, 1937–39
Michael Scott

Thirty years later he recalled: 'I went to see Schindler at his house. I didn't like the house, it looked cheap and the housekeeping wasn't good.'[48] Neutra's far glossier high-tech Health House was, however, included in the exhibition and its accompanying texts.

While the Côte d'Azur and Southern California provided ideal climates, the mild air of certain coastal areas of Britain and Ireland close to the Gulf Stream seemed to offer conditions suited to the open features of modernist architecture. Michael Scott's house near Dublin (1937–39), designed for himself and his family, was the first major modernist private house to be built in Ireland.[49] Dramatically sited at Sandycove on Dublin Bay, a few miles south of the city centre, the house is next to the Martello Tower where James Joyce lived for a short time in September 1904 – and which he used as the setting for the famous opening chapter of *Ulysses*.[50] The suburbs and small towns that line the coast of Dublin Bay to the south of the city have a balmy microclimate. Hardy palms and fuchsias grow in abundance in the gardens of the Victorian seaside terraces. Prominently sited on its wilder headland, Scott's austere white villa stands out against this lushness, although not without its own subtle and restrained sensuality – the sleekness of the curving white forms contrasting with the rugged roughness of the rocks. The house gains added drama from this spectacular site and its proximity to Joyce's Tower. Built on the site of a small quarry at Sandycove Point, the rocky headland that shelters the tiny almost totally enclosed beach against the blustering winds of the Irish Sea, the house curves protectively round its own enclosed garden – repeating the enfolding curve of the sheltered cove. The sweeping rounded bays of the glazed north-west façade visually echo the circular form of the Martello Tower, affording panoramic views from the high-ceilinged living room and the main bedroom on the upper floor across the shallow waters of the bay towards Dun Laoghaire, with distant views of Dublin and the Wicklow mountains beyond. Like many continental European and American

modernist houses, the living room had built-in facilities for film projection, providing a *representational* spectacle when the curtains around the huge bay windows were drawn.[51] With its curving façade and tall living-room windows overlooking the sheltered garden and the cove, the house turns its back on the Irish Sea. Only a few small windows and portholes punched through the pure white-painted concrete skin look onto the seaward side, where a rock path skirts behind the otherwise blank and defensive sea façade. This leads to the 'Gentlemen's Bathing Place, Forty Foot' into which 'stately, plump Buck Mulligan' plunges at the end of the first chapter of *Ulysses* as Stephen Dedalus walks away from the Tower.[52]

Many of the relatively few modernist houses built in Britain between the wars were situated in southern England or near the coast in order to get the maximum fresh air, if not sunshine. But whatever the location, their design was usually predicated on an optimistic view of the English summer climate. In the late 1930s, Maxwell Fry designed the Sun House, a luxurious white villa with spectacular roof terraces and balconies in the prosperous north London suburb of Hampstead, which appropriately enough has become the residence of the Indian High Commissioner. By contrast, Wells Coates's 'Sunspan Houses' were a series of relatively inexpensive off-the-peg 'standard' modernist dwellings, with the main living rooms facing south and long horizontal wrap-round windows to catch the sun throughout the day.[53] Designed in collaboration with David Pleydell-Bouverie, a prototype was shown at the *Daily Mail* Ideal Home Exhibition in April 1932 – advertised as 'the Home of Tomorrow with sunshine laid on', and the house with an 'appetite for sunshine'.[54] The sun had an almost universal currency as a popular symbol between the wars, perhaps because it was so often in short supply in many northern European countries. While white-walled modernist houses with promi-

Modernist and traditional detached houses,
Walton-on-the-Naze, Essex, 1930s

nent balconies or sun terraces such as those designed by Fry and Coates were most directly identified with the sun and sunlight, the image of the rising sun appears as a recurrent motif in the decorative stained glass in the doors and windows of speculative semi-detatched and detached housing built throughout Britain in the 1920s and 1930s. If these lacked the 'appetite for sunshine' of the modernist Sunspan houses with their white walls and long windows, they were spaciously laid out compared to the inner-city terrace houses of the 1900s – with plenty of light and air flowing through the interiors, balconies, and long gardens with lawns, flower beds, greenhouses and garden sheds.

Light, air & sun

Critics and commentators of the period frequently complained that although suitable for Mediterranean or Southern Californian climates, modernist features such as white walls, roof gardens, sun terraces and cantilevered balconies were inappropriate in northern or even central Europe. Reviewing the 1927 Stuttgart Weissenhofsiedlung, the left-wing Swiss architect Hans Schmidt had argued that many of the houses would be more suitable as holiday homes in southern Europe.[55] The critic Walter Riezler commented on the impracticality in Germany of Le Corbusier's Weissenhof houses with their roof gardens and double-height living rooms lit by enormous windows, which would overheat in summer and be extremely cold in winter.[56] Nevertheless, modernist architects persisted in the belief that open and transparent structures of glass, steel and concrete would demonstrate the benefits of sunlight and fresh air even in northern European climates such as those of Britain, Germany or the Nordic countries. In Sweden, a tradition of building summer holiday houses on islands or by the sea opened the way for a relaxed modernism geared to leisure and enjoyment in the sun – a tradition celebrated in the lightweight airy steel-and-glass buildings of the Stockholm Exhibition, which took place in the summer of 1930. Many Nordic modernist architects employed 'natural' materials such as brick and wood instead of steel and concrete to create softer forms that blended rather than contrasted with the landscape.[57]

While sunlight could not always be guaranteed in northern Europe, fresh air usually could – provided buildings were sited in areas free from environmental pollution – although this was not easy in cities still largely dependent on coal for energy and heating during the years between the wars. The idea of the *Luftbad* (air bath) where the body was exposed to fresh air rather than direct sunshine became increasingly popular in the first decades of the 20th century, especially in German-speaking and Nordic countries, inspired by similar ideas to those of the sanatorium movement and following the example of naturists such as Rikli. The cult of *Freikörperkultur* (Naturism) dates from the last decades of the 19th century in Germany, and the first nudist *Freilichtpark* (open-air park) opened in Hamburg in 1903. Following the traumatic horrors of the First World War, there was a renewed interest in the whole and healthy human body, and it has been estimated that about three million people in Germany belonged to nudist organizations in 1930. But the preoccupation with the beneficial effects of fresh air and sunlight was far more widespread than naturist or nudist cults, and was not only the preserve of strict modernists.

The early 20th-century *Lebensreform* movement – which encompassed nudism, vegetarianism, reform dress, and a cult of the outdoors – had become widely accepted in German-speaking countries, and similar movements were popular in England, The Netherlands and Scandinavia. In Germany, this formed the basis for a number of exhibitions aimed at a wider public who had come to enjoy the benefits of *Lebensreform* through gardening, the cultivation of allotments, and the building of small weekend houses or cabins on the outskirts of the city – a lower middle-class or working-class response to the impact of the English Garden City movement in the first decades of the 20th century. The most important of these exhibitions was the 'Sonne, Luft und Haus für Alle' (Sun, Fresh Air and a House for Everyone) exhibition held in Berlin in 1932. Organized by the director of the city's central building administration, Martin Wagner, in collaboration with the landscape designer and garden expert Leberecht Migge, the exhibition was devoted to a display of extendable ('growing') houses, allotments and weekend living. Wagner had been the architect and planner in charge of the neue Berlin, a project similar in scope and scale to May's neue Frankfurt. The exhibition took place at a time when as a result of the economic slump that followed the Wall Street crash of 1929 *Selbsthilfe* (self-help) and self-build housing were being promoted once more in central Europe. (The architects associated with the settlers' movements in Austria such as Loos and Schütte-Lihotzky had advocated similar ideas immediately after the First World War.) Extendable dwelling units were displayed at the exhibition designed by some of the best-known German architects, including Otto Bartning, Hugo Häring, Ludwig Hilberseimer, Paul Mebes, Erich Mendelsohn, Hans Poelzig, Hans Scharoun, Bruno Taut, Max Taut and Wagner himself.[58]

A long-term supporter of the SPD (German Social Democratic Party), Wagner had recently become highly critical of its policy, and particularly its housing policy – resigning from the party that year. In *Das wachsende Haus* (The Extendable House), published in connection with the exhibition, he advocated the utopian ideal of a single-

family house with a garden constructed from standardized parts – which could grow according to the needs of its inhabitants, and in which the outside and inside were closely integrated to realize the healthy and hygienic ideals of light, air and openness:[59] 'I can already see the day when the new customer will give the architect his order: build me a "Fresh Air and Gymnastic Bath" in the garden as a continuation of my bathroom! Build me a sleeping space in the garden, as an extension to my bedroom, so I can have views of the stars!' Wagner had come to believe that in the aftermath of the world-wide recession capitalism had entered a new phase in which the modern metropolis (or *Grossstadt*) would be replaced by more flexible communities, responsive to the new mobility made possible by modern transport. Through the extendable house Wagner believed a new communion of the city dweller with nature would be achieved in a modernist version of the Garden City:

> And thus the house grows in all its parts, within the garden. We of the big city will commune again with nature and with the land, we will entrust ourselves again to our senses, which now seem to be dead among the heaps of stone and asphalt. We will begin again to live with plants and animals, and from this communal life, we will attain a life that surpasses all technologies.[60]

The principles of sunlight, fresh air, health and hygiene were not exclusively the preserve of modernists. In 1928, an open-air display 'Wohnen im Grünen' (Open-Air Living) for the conservative Gagfah Housing Association demonstrated the benefits of more traditional house designs which enabled the inhabitants to live outdoors as much as possible in good weather.[61] Shown as part of a model-housing exhibition, 'Bauen und Wohnen' (Building & Dwelling), held in the leafy Berlin suburb of Zehlendorf, the display was somewhat surprisingly designed by Walter Gropius and László Moholy-Nagy.[62] (Hans Richter made a film for the exhibition, although unfortunately no copies seem to have survived.)[63] The Gagfah houses designed by Heinrich Tessenow and Hans Poelzig also had their sun terraces and 'outside rooms' – defined by wooden pergolas rather than the lightweight tubular-steel frames and canvas employed by modernist architects (see Chapter 8). Gropius and Moholy-Nagy perhaps felt able to justify the commission because many of the principles of light, air and openness upheld by modernists were incorporated in the balconies, verandas and terraces of the Gagfah houses.[64] Even though these remained relatively traditional in form, they shared a common origin with much modernist housing in the English and European Arts and Crafts and Garden City movements of the first decades of the 20th century.[65] The Gagfah development directly confronted a flat-roofed modernist *Siedlung* designed for the left-wing Gehag housing association by Bruno Taut. The standoff between the pitched-roofed detached houses of the Gagfah Siedlung and the flat roofs of the Gehag row houses and low-rise apartment blocks was considered a major ideological confrontation at the time.

Extendable house for 'Sonne, Luft und Haus für Alle'
(Sun, Fresh Air and a House for Everyone) exhibition, Berlin, 1932
Martin Wagner

The concerns with sunshine and the open air which had been a major feature of the social-democratic lifestyle of the 1920s and early 1930s also played an important role in the *Wohnkultur* of Nazi Germany, as they had earlier in fascist Italy, and in the ideology of the Soviet Union. Sanatoriums for tuberculosis and other diseases, and rest resorts for favoured workers and party officials were constructed in the Soviet Union in the late 1920s and 1930s, many of them located on the Riviera-like Black Sea coast. Sunlight and the beneficial effects of the sun's rays had a prime place in Soviet imagery, particularly during the Stalinist years. A healing and enlightening sunlight suffused the propaganda photographs and the socialist-realist paintings of the period. Painted, photographic and graphic representations of workers enjoying the health-giving rays of the sun appeared frequently during the 1930s, at the darkest period of the Stalin era. As well as the power and importance attached to sunlight, images of artificial light and of the electric light bulb in particular – known as *lampa Ilyicha* (Lenin's lamp) – often featured in Soviet propaganda: the 'spearhead of the great electrification campaign of the 1920s,' which 'brought electricity and artificial light to thousands of rural villages', dispelling 'darkness, vermin and the spectre of petit-bourgeois consciousness by the purifying and illuminating effects of its rays'.[66] But more light also meant that more dirt was revealed, as in Mikhail Zoshchenko's short story 'Electrification' (1924), where the narrator's landlady has the supply cut off and he comments: 'So you see comrades, light's good, but even light has its problems.'[67]

Extreme versions of the cult of the fit and healthy body were common to totalitarian ideologies: the fit body of the human subject tuned like an engine to produce a perfect 'fit' within the 'body politic'. Glimpses of such body fanaticism can be discerned in the writings and works of modernists such as Le Corbusier, who flirted with fascism in the 1930s and attempted to interest the French Vichy government in some of his proposals during the Second World War. In Italy, the culture of the sound and healthy body had played an important part in the fascist ideology since the early 1920s. Colonies (or holiday camps) in modernist style were built for Italian children to spend vacations by the seaside, and sun-therapy centres were opened in the countryside for children thought by school doctors to need such treatment. During the holidays they were sent to the seaside, the mountains, or a sun-therapy centre like that at Legnano about 17 miles from Milan, designed by the well-known modernist partnership BBPR (Gian Luigi Banfi, Lodovico Belgiojoso, Enrico Peressutti and Ernesto Rogers). Treatment was free for most children, although those who could afford it paid a small fee. Here for a fortnight they were given a special diet and took the sun on the first-floor sundecks and solariums, or in the grounds of the centre. Built by a private benefactor and donated to the Fascist Party, it was named after the Italian victory at Gondar during the Ethiopian war (1935–36). Lucio Fontana – who was to become well known internationally as a modernist abstract artist after the Second World War – decorated the walls of the canteen with relief sculptures celebrating Mussolini's 'Victory over the Lion of Judah'.[68]

7 Built into the sun

While gleaming white modernist villas on the Mediterranean or Californian coast had become the fashion accessories of the European and North American upper and upper middle classes, housing reformers also represented white walls, balconies, terraces and large windows as the essential elements of the healthy and hygienic modern house. The long lyrical series of shots of sunroofs, terraces, balconies, verandas and roof gardens, which opened the German version of Richter's *Die neue Wohnung*, included a sequence of people enjoying the sun on the terraced balconies of Max Ernst Haefeli's Rotachhäuser model housing in Zurich.[1] These were probably inspired by the Queen Alexandra Sanatorium at Davos, designed by Haefeli's father and Otto Pfleghard in 1907 with wide cantilevered terraces onto which the patients' rooms opened. The terraced balconies of the Rotachhäuser featured prominently in the illustrations to *Befreites Wohnen* as well as on the cover. Extensive terraces that resembled 'outdoor rooms' – often the size of a bedroom or living room – could be seen at the Weissenhofsiedlung in the summer of 1927, and at the model-housing exhibitions that succeeded it in Brno (1928), Breslau (1929), Basel (1930), Zurich (1931), Prague (1932) and Vienna (1932).[2]

Sun balconies or sun terraces – sometimes leading directly off the bathroom or bedroom – were a conspicuous feature of the modernist house of the late 1920s and early 1930s and architects often introduced terraces or balconies for formal and symbolic effects as much as for reasons of health and hygiene. Yet although the function of the small balcony in much modernist social housing was largely representational, it offered direct access, of however limited a kind, to light, air and openness, providing a space where a pot or window box with plants could be placed, and perhaps a chair for sitting in the sun. Larger middle-class modernist villas generally offered something more like the sanatorium terrace where it was possible to lie out on recliners and take the sun, or even sleep on warm nights. In the most luxurious upper middle-class houses the provision of light, air and openness was often taken to an extreme, with enormous terraces, sun decks, roof gardens and built-in swimming pools geared to leisured relaxation and indulgent regimes of physical exercise and body culture. But in the promotion of modernist architecture and design more modest versions of these features

were represented as within the economic range of ordinary middle-class people, or even better-paid workers.

The Davos-type sanatorium with its tiers of terraces had first provided a model for social housing when terraced apartment buildings were proposed at the turn of the 19th and 20th centuries in response to attacks by the hygienist movement on the insanitary character of the modern city. Tony Garnier advocated stepped-terrace housing and apartments in his utopian designs for Lyons, made in 1905 although not published until later. Occupying a central place in Garnier's utopian city was a stepped-terrace sanatorium or clinic for heliotherapy (sun therapy), providing the patients with individual balconies where they could receive the benefits of the sun while resting on recliners. The influential German architectural critic Adolf Behne argued that probably more than any other French architect Garnier 'respected and liberated healthy function, as his plan for the sanatorium in particular demonstrates'.[3] Stepped-terrace buildings were seen as a new and dynamic means of opening out and revitalizing the *rue corridor* – the insalubrious corridor-like street of the 19th-century city condemned by the hygienicist movement – without destroying the urban street pattern as did Le Corbusier's projects for tall tower blocks surrounded by green open spaces after the First World War. In their patent registration of a system for stepped-terrace construction (*construction en gradins*) in 1912, the architect Henri Sauvage and the entrepreneur Charles Sarazin described how a street with terrace apartment blocks on both sides created an 'open cone of air and light' (a term popularized by the architect and hygienist Augustin Rey) that would render the apartments more hygienic.[4]

Terrace of house, Werkbundsiedlung,
Breslau, Germany (now Wrocław, Poland), 1929

Theo Essenberger

Sauvage and Sarazin had been among the founders of the Société anonyme des logements hygièniques à Bon Marché (the Inexpensive Hygienic Dwellings Company) set up in 1903 to provide reasonably priced well-lit and well-ventilated accommodation for working-class families.[5] In 1912-13, Sauvage designed a stepped-terrace apartment block in the rue Vavin in Paris, popularly known as 'the Metro building' because its white-tiled façade resembled the interiors of the stations of the recently built Paris underground railway system. Intended for the middle rather than the working class, the rue Vavin building provided tenants with the air, sunlight and greenery that hygienists regarded as essential, while giving them direct access to the street, and preserving the integrity and vitality of the urban fabric. This was less easy to achieve in social housing because of the loss of accommodation due to the stepping back of the apartments. Sauvage proposed a large complex of terraced apartments for working-class tenants in the rue Admiraux in the northern industrial suburbs of Paris in 1913, which was not finally realized until 1926.[6] Its more economical design was less satisfactory in so far as it did not provide terrace facilities and direct sunlight for all the tenants, although its stepped structure enabled a heated, public swimming pool to be inserted at the bottom of the internal light well.[7]

Oriented to the sun

Since the 1880s, hygiene and sanitary reformers had been concerned with the provision of sunlight in buildings.[8] In the early 20th century, the growing preoccupation with health, hygiene, sunlight and fresh air had led housing professionals and architects to give priority to orientation towards the best light and maximum sunshine in designs for housing, and social housing in particular. Augustin Rey appears to have been the first to insist (at the International Tuberculosis Congress in Washington in 1908) that orientation towards the sun be one of the basic requirements of any town-planning programme, and that the direct rays of the sun should penetrate every apartment or house.[9] Modernist architects frequently cited such criteria as underlying their designs, as in Oud's description of his Weissenhof houses: 'A fundamental starting point for the creation of this type of house was, in the first place, the situation of the houses in relation to the sun. The living areas should face towards the south, the service areas towards the north.'[10] Before deciding the orientation of the villa E-1027, Eileen Gray calculated 'the precise passage of the sun'.[11] Working together on the design of the Schröder House in 1924, Rietveld and his client and collaborator Truus Schröder 'found it essential to begin with the plan', and to ask 'what's the best view, where does the sun rise?'[12]

In the later 1920s in Germany (and a few years later in The Netherlands), an obsession with ensuring equal amounts of sunlight for every dwelling led to increasingly rigid layouts for social housing, according to the principles of *Zeilenbau* (line building) – in Dutch *strokenbouw* (strip building) – where identical blocks of standardized apartment housing were aligned in parallel rows for maximum orientation to the sun.[13] The blocks were usually aligned north south, so that the windows faced east west and all rooms would get either the morning or the afternoon sun. This was probably derived from the layout of barracks, hospitals and sanatoriums in the late 19th and early 20th centuries. It also had roots in the Garden City movement. In 1902, the English Garden City architect Raymond Unwin maintained that: 'The essential thing is that every house should turn its face to the sun, whence comes light, sweetness and health. The direction of roads and the fronting to streets are details which must be made to fall with this condition, or give way to it.'[14] In 1909, the commission report of the Amsterdamsche Woningraad (Amsterdam Housing Department) argued for housing in blocks aligned north south with public gardens between them, and the short ends unbuilt 'which is important for air circulation': essentially a prescription for *Zeilenbau* or *strokenbouw*.[15] A tenement estate designed by J. E. van der Pek for the Rochdale housing association in Amsterdam was based on the Woningraad commission's recommendation, with the short ends of the block left open, although this type of layout was not generally adopted in housing in The Netherlands for nearly thirty years, a decade later than in Germany.[16] Introduced by modernist architects and planners such as Walter Gropius and Otto Haesler during the late 1920s, the principle was widely accepted, but not without considerable opposition. Rows of houses or apartments were laid out in straight parallel rows without regard to the topography of the landscape, aligned to provide maximum sunlight, fresh air, quiet and privacy for each dwelling.[17] Apartments were planned so that the morning sun penetrated the bedrooms and the living rooms enjoyed the after-noon sun. One of the first estates designed in this way was Haesler's Georgsgarten Siedlung in Celle of 1925. Here he adopted the 'finger' plan where blocks of apartments or houses were set at right angles to the streets.[18] This gave a more open and spacious appearance to the dwellings and 'introduced a suburban feeling into urban housing', following the aims of the pre-First World War Garden City movement.

The competition held for the design of the Dammerstock Siedlung model-housing exhibition in Karlsruhe in 1928 specified that dwellings were laid out according to the system of *Zeilenbau*. The winning scheme was by Gropius, with Haesler in second place. The two were asked to collaborate with a number of other architects on the final design and execution of the *Siedlung* under Gropius's direction. The Dammerstock Siedlung served to create a new orthodoxy within the modernist housing movement in Europe, and gave particular focus to the controversy over how social housing should be sited.[19] A number of architects and critics challenged this, condemning the rigid rows of housing at Dammerstock as mechanistic and impoverished. In a review in the Deutscher Werkbund magazine *Die Form*, Adolf Behne attacked the rigid adherence to the princi-ple of *Zeilenbau*, maintaining that there was no good reason why the kitchen, bathroom and WC should face east and the living room face west. He maintained that the living room could face south, where it would receive even more sunlight than if it faced west, and the kitchen, bathroom and WC (which did not need sunlight) could face north. Behne claimed that the sunlight from the south was far more intense than that from east or west – strong enough to penetrate through to the service rooms of the apartments and keep them 'disinfected and healthy'. He argued that too much emphasis was put on the morning sun. While it was 'certainly valuable to let the sun into the bedrooms', was the early morning 'the only opportunity to come into contact with the sun'? Behne maintained that: 'On good days, it shines another few hours on the way to work, to school and from school, and even working in the garden family members encounter the sun. For after all, man is mobile and does not live twenty-four hours a day in the house.' He claimed that adherence to the principle of *Zeilenbau* was based on a rigid hygienicism where human beings were thought of as concepts rather than living bodies, forcing the inhabitants to 'go to bed facing east, eat and answer Mother's letter facing west'. Apartments were organized so that it was not possible to live in any other way than that dictated by the architects.[20]

Behne argued that housing should be integrated into the fabric of the city, not laid out in long lines in suburban *Siedlungen*, however this might be thought to promote healthy and hygienic conditions. He attacked the hygienicist approach, arguing that: 'Medical research has shown that the inhabitants of houses which are considered to be unhygienic are healthier than the inhabitants of hygienic houses.'[21] This comes close to current medical thinking. (Improvements in hygiene are now thought to have been responsible for the polio epidemics of the 1950s, causing a drastic reduction in natural immunity previously acquired through unhygienic conditions.)[22] Behne maintained that true hygiene depends on a balance of factors, not rigid rules and formulae, an approach remarkably similar to that favoured today. Replying to a rejoinder to his criticisms by the leftist Swiss architect Hans Schmidt, Behne argued (again anticipating a view currently in favour) that the new architecture must secure its bases among the working classes by transforming itself from a 'passive system' imposed on the clients of social housing 'into one of consumer product and demand'.[23] In another article published in *Die Form*, Heinrich de Fries (who had collaborated with Peter Behrens on social housing) criticized the monotony of the layouts on the Dammerstock estate, claiming that the wide uniform spaces between the rows of housing increased the sense of alienation. De Fries had designed the Reichsheimstätten Siedlung in Düsseldorf, which he cited as an example of a less rigid layout, arguing that staggering the rows would have made the Dammerstock housing appear more open to natural light and fresh air.[24] In a paper delivered at the International Housing Conference in Berlin in June 1931, Josef Frank, who had wide experience of designing social housing in Austria, attacked the adoption of 'universalist' solutions to social housing. Frank pointed out that: 'The positioning of the windows of living rooms, bedrooms, kitchens, etc. in relation to the compass is always undertaken on the assumption that the rooms will be used for the purposes for which the architect intended them, but experience has shown that in practice this assumption is usually wrong.' He maintained that 'the question of direction is not by any means so important' although arguing that it was more important that the main living areas should be oriented to the south to receive direct sunlight all year round.[25]

A less rigid approach to orientation was taken in low-rise apartment housing for the workers from the Siemens electrical factory, constructed as part of Martin Wagner's neue Berlin programme and largely funded through the housing association set up by the Siemens company.[26] The commission was shared between six members of the Berlin avant-garde architects' association Der Ring. Hans Scharoun was responsible for the overall layout of the estate, which had a combined district central-heating plant and communal laundry. Scharoun planned this as a combination of rows of apartment blocks in north–south orientation, set at right angles to the main streets designed by Hugo Häring, Paul Rudolf Henning and Fred Forbat, with long blocks aligned along the streets with shops underneath by Gropius, Otto Bartning and Scharoun himself. This mixed layout created much greater variety and flexibility than earlier *Siedlungen* laid out strictly according to the principles of *Zeilenbau*, such as the Dammerstock Siedlung. All the architects included generous balconies and loggias at Siemensstadt to give as many of the apartments as possible direct access to sunlight, fresh air and openness. Scharoun moved with his wife into a two-bedroom apartment in one of his blocks where he lived for over thirty years – a rare example of a modernist architect permanently occupying a standard apartment in a social-housing block of their own design.[27]

In single-family detached houses designed for the Weissenhofsiedlung in 1927, both Scharoun and Adolf Rading – who were to collaborate on the organization of the next German Werkbund model-housing exhibition in Breslau in 1929 – had emphasized the close relationship of the interior spaces with the gardens and ground-floor terrace areas that extended directly from the large sliding windows and glass doors of the living rooms. In these prototype middle-class dwellings, the qualities of light, air and openness were particularly apparent, which was rarely possible in social housing without compromising other facilities. Rading declared in *Die Form* that he had decided to create something 'that would represent a deliverance from the stuffiness and the timorous, inhibited, petit-bourgeois atmosphere of our ordinary housing developments'. He designed the living rooms so that they could be converted from three rooms to one and vice-versa by means of folding partitions, and to be outward looking in their aspect:

> Life faces outward: the occupant does not find himself retreating, in the usual way, into his cave. The bedrooms, on the other hand, are accessible only by walking through the entire house. Here one has the feeling of being protected by the whole fabric of the house (by the distance one has walked); and yet the link with 'outside' has not entirely been lost, because from the main bedroom there is direct access to the garden.

Rading claimed that the whole house was characterized by 'this same longitudinal emphasis throughout, so that one no longer feels shut in within one's own "four walls", but has a feeling of wide open spaces, as on the promenade deck of a ship'. He described how: 'The long landing at the top of the stairs serves in conjunction with the sun terrace as a play space for the children. The children remain within earshot of the kitchen, and the space unfolds lengthwise, to give the children somewhere to run'. The terrace was provided with a high railing of closely spaced horizontal bars to protect the running children from falling through – a thoughtful touch absent from many modernist terraces of the period where the railings were inadequate by present-day safety standards, although aesthetically satisfying with their minimalist profiles and widely spaced bars. The utility room for laundry and ironing was placed on the upper floor of the house instead of relegated to 'its usual place in the cellar'. Its window looked across the terrace so the maid or housewife could keep an eye on the playing children as she worked and enjoy the view across the terrace, which could also be used for drying clothes. Rading pointed out that such a room 'is among the most used in the whole house', and was placed where 'the housewife or the maid will be grateful to have her often monotonous work cheered by doing it in beautiful surroundings'.[28]

The ground floor was designed so that when the folding partitions were opened and the whole of the downstairs space used as a single space, the inhabitants had to pass through the kitchen area to go upstairs. Rading intended this – and the fact that the maid had to pass through the living room from the kitchen to go out of the house – '*pour épater les bourgeois*'. These arrangements he adds 'might have been avoided by a few minor modifications, but in contemporary circumstances, and in view of the way of life implied by the size and layout of the house, such a sharp division seemed to me unthinkable and incongruous'. Rading argued that 'the routines and the needs of some great household with a position to maintain, or those of a hotel, have no application to middle-class circumstances – whatever people in this country may do for the sake of feeling grand and important'.[29] The critic Edgar Wedepohl commented sarcastically on the openness and lack of privacy in Rading's house, which was 'interesting by virtue of its unusual relationship between living and transit areas'.

> It almost seems as though the whole house has been designed for the sake of the hall which is produced by sliding back the doors of the living rooms. The direct approach to the kitchen is not the shortest, but even an unathletic person can step from the street into the bedroom through the window.[30]

Rading believed it was imperative 'to loosen up the house and bring it into relation with the garden', adding that this was 'an essential feature of all the houses' on the Weissenhof estate.[31] His house – which won praise for this from Giedion in a review of the exhibition in *L'Architecture vivante* – was destroyed during the Second World War and has not been rebuilt as were some of the other houses in the *Siedlung*.[32]

Like Rading, Scharoun aimed to produce a symbiosis between his Weissenhof house and its garden to emphasize the uninterrupted flow of space from the living rooms into the ground-floor terrace areas, producing 'a sensation of space extending far beyond the confines of the walls' by creating intermediate indoor/outdoor zones that could be enjoyed in hot summer weather.[33] Scharoun's initial design for the garden had included a children's play space with a tree to give shade, a swimming pool and gymnastics area protected by a 1.8-metre-high wall with an arbour containing a bench that overlooked the pool – in addition to a carefully designed lawn, herbaceous borders and planting areas directly accessible from the terrace outside the living room. Successive designs increasingly unified the indoor and outdoor spaces, although the swimming pool had to be omitted from the final design for reasons of cost. Karin Kirsch, the historian of the Weissenhofsiedlung, quotes a recent occupant of the house who observed that: 'Scharoun did not just plan the house; he dreamed it; he built it into the sun.'[34]

Scharoun, Rading and Richard Döcker seem to have achieved an integration of their houses with the landscape and terrain more effectively and unobtrusively than most of the other architects at Weissenhof.[35] By contrast, Le Corbusier's single- and two-family houses (see p. 136) straddle the falling terrain in a dramatic and bravura manner, defining and producing this as 'public' rather than 'private' space to be enjoyed by spectators (at the exhibition and subsequently) rather than by the inhabitants, as was to be the case with so many post-Second World War blocks influenced by Le Corbusier's example. His houses do not relate organically to the terrain, as do those of Scharoun

Single-family house, Weissenhofsiedlung,
Stuttgart, Germany, 1927
Adolf Rading

Apartments, Werkbundsiedlung, Breslau,
Germany (now Wrocław, Poland), 1929
Hans Scharoun

and Rading, and Döcker's two low-built ground-hugging houses. This was hardly surprising as Le Corbusier visited the site only once before drawing up plans, and badly miscalculated the fall of the land so that he had to shift the entrance of the single-family house into the basement. This meant that the inhabitants and their visitors had to enter through the boiler room: an apt embodiment of the idea of the house as 'a machine for living in', although the result of a design error rather than the architect's intention.

Even more 'built into the sun' than Scharoun's Weissenhof house was the villa he designed between 1932 and 1933 for the industrialist Fritz Schminke. On a plot next to Schminke's factory, the balconies, external staircases and sun terraces loop, cross and penetrate the asymmetric façades to create a house that was 'more balcony than house'.[36] Such generous provision of light, air and openness was not confined to Scharoun's work for the affluent. The apartment building with common eating and social facilities which he designed for the Werkbund housing exhibition he organized with Rading at Breslau in 1929 was intended to house single and childless married low-paid white-collar workers such as schoolteachers. This had communal terraces, patios and roof gardens as well as individual balconies – maximizing the openness of the building to sunlight and fresh air. In 1928, Scharoun wrote: 'One wishes to see something of the boldness of modern ship structures transferred to the design of houses and

thus hope to overcome the fussiness and narrowness of today's housing'.[37] At Breslau, he created an ambience closer to the decks of a liner than that of almost any other inter-war apartment building, except perhaps Wells Coates's Isokon Flats, which also incorporated communal facilities such as a restaurant. The crime writer and early Isokon resident Agatha Christie wrote: 'Coming up the street the flats looked just like a giant liner which ought to have had a couple of funnels, and then you went up the stairs and through the door of one's flat and there were the trees tapping on the window.'[38]

Other writers mocked such fashionable nautical features. The vogue for port-hole shaped windows, large areas of glass, and rooms opening directly onto balconies, terraces and gardens was slyly satirized by Joseph Roth in his 1929 novel *Rechts und Links* (Right and Left). A young Berlin businessman, Paul Bernheim, commissions a modernist house liberally equipped with these features, according to the specification of his powerful father-in-law Carl Enders:

> The house resembled a ship without a keel. Only the windows, which reached down to the ground, so that one might go in and out through them, suggested that it might be a dwelling. Otherwise it was painted white all over and seemed to be steaming along. A semi-circular redoubt, inside which one could – or should – eat breakfast in summer, seemed from the outside to contain the first-class cabins. The roof over the redoubt was like a spacious ship's bridge.

Roth also mocked the modernist obsession with sunshine and fresh air:

> The few transplanted trees clustered round the house, as though afraid of the barren expanse of the garden. Of the three elements of 'light, air and sunshine' that were sacred to Herr Enders and to modern architecture in general, Bernheim's house seemed at times to have more than the whole world, and one often had the impression when it was overcast outside and the air was a thick mist, that the rooms were full of their own private sunshine.[39]

A similar but darker critique of modernist architecture by the Frankfurt School philosopher and cultural commentator Ernst Bloch appears in *The Principle of Hope*, published after the Second World War, but begun before it:

> These days houses in many places look as if they are ready to leave. Although they are unadorned or for this very reason, they express departure. On the inside they are bright and bare like sickrooms, on the outside they seem like boxes on movable rods, but also like ships. They have a flat deck, portholes, a gangway, a deck rail, they have a white and southern glow, as ships they have a mind to disappear.

Bloch claims that from the beginning modern architecture was 'orientated towards the outdoors, towards sunlight and public life'. The 'essential feature with which the new architecture began was openness; it broke the dark stone caves, it opened up fields of vision through light glass walls'. But Bloch argues, 'this will towards an adjustment with the outside world was undoubtedly premature'. The 'southern pleasure in the outside world' did not result in happiness: 'For nothing good happens here in the street, in the sun; the open door, the enormously opened windows are threatening in the age of growing fascism [...].'[40]

> The wide window, full of the outside world, requires an outside world that is full of attractive strangers, not full of Nazis. A glass door, stretching down to floor level, really does presuppose that, if there is going to be anything peeping in, or pouring in, it will be the sunshine and not the Gestapo.[41]

Quite apart from the political and social considerations that Bloch refers to, the preoccupation with fresh air and sunlight of early 20th-century modernist architects often resulted in environments that were far from ideal. Roof terraces proved too cold for unreliable northern European summers, huge expanses of glass could prove unbearably hot when the sun shone, as in Le Corbusier's Armée de Salut (Salvation Army) hostel in Paris with its enormous sealed windows. Critics maintained that in their obsession with the restorative powers of fresh air and sunlight modernist architects frequently incorporated too much glass.[42]

The open-air school

Yet at a time when many people still lived in overcrowded, dark and insanitary housing conditions, light, air and openness were regarded as the main priorities in educational as well as hospital or sanatorium buildings, considered to be a means of compensating for the lack of these elements in the children's own homes. Schools were built with enormous areas of glass that could be opened up to the sun (or at least the fresh air) in summer, and even in winter, and with generous balconies or roof terraces where classes might be held outdoors in fine weather. Special open-air schools were designed to be used throughout the year with outdoor classrooms so that children received the maximum of light and fresh air. By 1937, there were ninety-six open-air day schools and fifty-three open-air residential schools in England alone.[43] Although some were specially designed for children who suffered from tuberculosis or similar diseases, others were intended for the education of healthy children. Like other institutions inspired by the ideals of light, air and openness, open-air schools predated inter-war modernism and had sometimes featured in early 20th-century Garden Cities.[44] Between the wars architects enthusiastically adopted the latest ideas about the hygienic benefits of light and fresh air in educational buildings, eager to exploit the newly developed structural techniques and materials which made it possible to employ very large areas of glass, cantilevered concrete balconies, and flat roofs that could support roof terraces.

While still working on the Zonnestraal Sanatorium, Jan Duiker designed the most famous of all modernist open-air schools: the Cliostraat Openluchtschool voor het Gezonde Kind (Cliostraat Open-Air School for the Healthy Child) in Amsterdam (1927–30). He also planned an open-air school for young patients at Zonnestraal with six classrooms grouped round a circular pool like the spokes of a wheel – although this was never built. The Cliostraat primary school was a highly sophisticated design for girls and boys aged from six to twelve, with classrooms that opened out on two sides onto open-sided terraces. The concrete roof and floor slabs shaded these terraces from direct sunlight and provided some protection from rain. Overhead radiant heating elements were incorporated into the concrete slabs so that the classrooms could be opened to the terraces even during the winter. Duiker was particularly proud of this feature and wrote in some detail about his heating system as part of the 'hygienic installation of the building' in an article on 'The New Functionalism in Summer and Winter', published after the school had been successfully in operation for several years.[45] When first built, the school stood in its own grounds free of buildings on all sides, but later blocks of three-storey brick pitched-roof flats were constructed around the site – hemming in the school that had been specially designed to be open to the sun and fresh air, and drastically reducing the playground area.[46]

As at the Zonnestraal Sanatorium, Duiker and Jan Gerko Wiebenga (who once again acted as structural engineer) wished to achieve a 'spiritual economy', creating a disembodied and almost weightless effect through the way materials were used. They glazed the windows of the classrooms so that the longer leg of the T-section steel glazing bars was inside the glass – instead of outside as intended by the manufacturers. This extended the glass membrane forward to the leading edge of the walls, creating an extraordinarily dematerialized effect: as though the whole building was literally open to light, air, sunshine and space. Unfortunately it also caused the metal frames to corrode over the years and when the school was restored the renewed metal glazing sections were reversed, largely negating the intended effect of dematerialization.

Duiker had first become involved in the hygiene movement when he and Bernard Bijvoet won a competition for an old people's home in Alkmaar in 1917.[47] He believed such facilities should be available to everyone, campaigning for healthier housing for the poor and the deprived with the slogan 'health rather than wealth'. In his own numerous writings and through his position as editor of the leading Dutch modernist architectural magazine *De 8 en Opbouw*, Duiker promoted the idea of 'a functional society', which he believed had been made possible by modern technology.[48] In an article entitled 'What About Our Clothes?' he compared 'the new functionalism in architecture' with the wearing of light hygienic clothing such as T-shirts, 'popular among young people'.[49] Duiker insisted that open-air schools were not just for sick children, but also for the healthy – strengthening their constitutions and making them more resistant to disease.

Cliostraat Open-Air School,
Amsterdam, 1927–30

Jan Duiker

The Cliostraat Open-Air School was built in a prosperous inner-city area of Amsterdam where most of its pupils would have come from relatively well-off homes. But it was intended to be a model that could equally well serve less privileged neighbourhoods. In an article entitled 'A Healthy School for the Healthy Child', Duiker emphasized the necessity of providing children with 'sunlight, ultra-violet rays, rest after exercise, ample fresh air for poisoned lungs, toughening up, in short, hygienic conditions'. Duiker claimed open-air schools specifically designed for children suffering from tuberculosis and other respiratory diseases were often cold and damp in winter, causing the children as much harm as good, and requiring them to wrap up in unhealthy and unhygienic layers of clothing. He maintained that:

> Our approach towards life in the fresh air will be on a different plane. Modern techniques enable us to keep the material used in the building to a minimum and to heat these almost entirely open spaces without any difficulty so that children need only wear light clothing, as is medically recommended.

Duiker praised experimental techniques of education such as the Montessori method, but argued that pedagogical systems could not in themselves have as strong an influence on the architecture of school buildings as 'hygienic factors'. Referring to the trend towards greater hygiene in the home, Duiker declared that 'a strong hygienic power [...] is influencing our life; one which will develop into a style, a hygienic style!' Citing housing built by 'progressive municipalities' for tubercular families, he argued that the standards of hygiene set by these should provide the standard for the provision of

housing for 'normal' healthy families. By admitting as much sunshine and fresh air as possible and providing hygienic and sanitary conditions, Duiker argued, modern housing would act as a prophylactic measure to prevent healthy families becoming sick families.[50]

The idea of providing maximum sunlight and fresh air were equally crucial in the design of the ULO school at Aalsmeer (1931–32) designed by Wiebenga, who had been responsible for one of the earliest glass-and-reinforced-concrete modernist school buildings in Groningen in 1923, in collaboration with Leen van der Vlugt, with whom he was later to work on the Van Nelle factory (1925–31). In the Aalsmeer school he incorporated elements drawn from his experience as structural engineer for both the Cliostraat school and the Zonnestraal. So closely did Wiebenga's school resemble a sanatorium with its airy skeletal decks, terraces and balconies that photographs of it have been confused with and reproduced as images of the Zonnestraal.[51] As in the Cliostraat school, Wiebenga's intention was 'to use architecture to express a new culture based on technology, hygiene and openness'.[52] At least one commentator doubted so much glass was really necessary for the health of the pupils, and wondered 'whether they will be able to concentrate in such surroundings with glass everywhere'.[53] 'Solar gain' – or overheating in summer – proved to be an issue with many modernist buildings of the period and may also have been a problem at Zonnestraal.[54] Even though the windows of the pavilions opened onto the balconies overlooking the pine woods, the enormous sheets of glass in the central-services building almost certainly overheated in hot weather.

Yet Duiker claimed that the huge windows of his Open-Air School which opened directly onto wide terraces for outdoor classes had proved to be 'airy' even during periods of great heat. He pointed out that this required a certain commonsense understanding of how such a building should be used:

> An airy room should be a room with a well-insulated roof with little mass and many open windows. Glass on the sunny side does not let through heat rays, only light rays. The energy of the light rays forms the source of heat, therefore the windows on this side should be closed and the curtains drawn, and so the light rays will remain outside. All the other windows should be open.

He argued that 'official science' was gradually becoming 'reconciled to glass architecture', and pointed out that the head of the heat and sound technical laboratory of the Technische Hochschule in Stuttgart lived in one of Le Corbusier's Weissenhof houses.[55] Duiker published a fake reader's letter in *De 8 en Opbouw*, complaining that he had refused to face up to 'the impossibility of keeping a glass wall or window open the whole year round in this climate'. In reply he claimed his Cliostraat school had already shown that 'open-air' housing would be possible too, but the problem was how to realize such housing within the framework of municipal provision. Duiker concluded:

'Though this is not an easy task, the objective has been defined and will be attained. Whether we live to see it is another question.'[56]

Unlike the Cliostraat Open-Air School for the Healthy Child, Eugène Beaudouin and Marcel Lods's Open-Air School at Surèsnes near Paris (1935–36) was designed for children who for health reasons could not go to ordinary schools. The classrooms were set individually in the grounds like the pavilions of a sanatorium and had three of their four walls entirely glazed with floor-to-ceiling folding windows, so that when opened each classroom was surrounded by fresh air and greenery.[57] External canvas blinds gave protection from the sun in summer and heating pipes were embedded in the floor, which was surfaced with slabs of natural stone. Warm-air ducts were laid along the length of the folding windows. Each child was supplied with a specially designed desk of cantilevered aluminium tube and plywood. The cupboards containing books and teaching equipment were on wheels so that they could be moved around the classrooms and into the outdoor teaching areas.

Outside each classroom there was a gravelled space shaded by trees for lessons in the open air. A glazed indoor restroom was furnished with specially designed tubular-steel and canvas recliners for the children to take their afternoon rest. The classrooms were linked by covered walkways to the main block in which were offices, dining room, workshops and a gym. On top of the main block was a large roof terrace where children could play or rest outdoors in the fresh air, when the weather allowed. There were indoor and outdoor playpools separated by glass windows which could be folded back, joining the two pools together. All parts of the school were linked by ramps so that children would not have to endanger themselves by climbing steps. A large globe with the countries of the world shown in relief was sited outside the school near the boys' entrance. This was encircled by a spiral ramp enabling the boys to explore the geography of the globe in detail, and perhaps to orientate themselves as young French-men towards a perception of their place in the world. (The school was built only five years after the Paris Exposition Coloniale of 1931.)

Situated high in the hills of the Solothurn Jura in Switzerland, Hannes Meyer's Pestalozzi school (1939) was designed to provide convalescent and rehabilitation facilities for physically debilitated children of all social classes. Based on the Pestalozzi method, a 'sound diet, good modern living conditions, and plenty of healthy games and sport', the school was funded through a trust set up with his wife by Dr Bernhard Jäggi – one of the founders of the Swiss co-operative movement and head of the Swiss Co-operative Union. Meyer had produced a number of designs for the co-op movement in the early 1920s, before leaving Switzerland to work at the Dessau Bauhaus in the late 1920s and in the Soviet Union in the early 1930s. With accommodation for twenty to twenty-five children and five or six supervisory staff, the home was built on a two-acre site above the centre of the old village of Mümliswil on rising ground that formed part of the south-facing slopes of the Passwang hills.

Two linked low blocks at right angles to one another created an L-shaped plan with a circular fully glazed solarium (or 'Round Hall') in the outward-facing angle of the two wings, with a spectacular view across the valley. This was used for the children to take their meals, and also for recitations, singing and other communal activities. On the roof of the hall was an open terrace for early morning exercises. Meyer's aim was to give architectural form to Pestalozzi's notion of the 'family circle', the educational aims of which were mutual aid and co-operation within a community. The children sat down at the horseshoe-shaped table with their adult supervisors so that 'by virtue of this democratic arrangement, all can share in the distant view'. At mealtimes children and staff sat round the outside of the table and the food was served from the inside. On social occasions, the space inside the table became the centre of activities such as recitation and singing. The angle between the two wings of the building was 'determined by the strict segregation of adults and children in two sleeping zones on the second floor'. (As today, there were anxieties about child abuse in children's homes.) Meyer was also concerned to provide both private and communal spaces:

> The home is deliberately laid out so that the zone of the child as an individual can be separated from that of the community when required, while still allowing a natural balance between the two. Each child should be able to 'retire within themselves' even when living in a community of twenty to twenty-five other children. They should be able to keep their things in a cupboard of their own and write a letter to their parents in a quiet corner.[58]

Thirteen years earlier, Meyer had designed an unrealized project for a primary school for girls on what he described as a 'highly unsuitable traditional school site in the old part of Basle'. 'Overshadowed by tall surrounding buildings and badly ventilated', this was the kind of dark and unhealthy inner-city area deprived of adequate light, air and openness represented in the opening sequences of Hans Richter's *Die neue Wohnung*. In their ambitious and justly renowned high-tech project for the Petersschule (published in detail with dramatic isometric projections in the *bauhaus* magazine in 1927), Meyer and his architectural partner Hans Wittwer demonstrated how the deficiencies of the site could be overcome by modern construction methods. Meyer argued that this was possible despite the fact that the total area assigned for the school was 'far too small for the ambitious building programme envisaged', and the 'usual over-development of the site leaves 500 sq. metres at the most for the playground, i.e. 1 sq. metre per child to play on'. While ideally a new site should be set aside 'as part of a planned development of the town', Meyer and Wittwer's proposed solution was a compromise that daringly employed new structural techniques to raise the classrooms and playgrounds as far as possible above the cramped site 'to a level where there is sunlight and fresh air'. The ground floor was used to house a swimming bath and gymnasium, while two enormous platforms suspended from the building by steel cables formed wide sun terraces that acted as playgrounds. Further play space was provided by roof terraces on the flat roofs above the classrooms, creating 'a total area of 1250 sq. metres of sunny space' raised above the miasma of the old town.[59] Along with the detailed plans and elevations, Meyer published complex calculations for ensuring correct levels of light.[60]

The design of modernist schools was intended not only to facilitate a hygienic and healthy environment for both sick and healthy children, but also to mediate between the individual and society. Open learning and informal relationships between teachers and pupils were to be enabled and encouraged by the design of new school buildings. In *Modern Architecture* (1929), Bruno Taut included an illustration of a classroom he had designed for the projected Municipal Secondary School in Berlin-Britz of 1927.[61] This comprehensive school for 3,000 students from sixth year to matriculation was to be run on the principle of pupils moving from classroom to classroom for different subjects, according to the project-centred educational ideas of Fritz Karsen based on the teachings of the American philosopher John Dewey.[62] Taut reproduces a photograph of a classroom for senior boys with its fully glazed outside wall slid back so that the room opens directly onto a terrace, with additional top lighting provided by clerestory windows. The boys are shown quietly studying individually or in small groups while the teacher stands ready to offer help when needed. Taut comments somewhat matter-of-factly on this illustration: 'Classroom with sectional door, and upper [clerestory] windows all round the room which can be easily covered and darkened (on right): although the boys are sitting with their backs to the window, they are not in their own light.'[63]

Sigfried Giedion reproduced photographs of Taut's classroom in *Befreites Wohnen* to demonstrate the importance of ideas about 'light, air and movement' in the design of modern educational buildings. One illustration is almost identical to that used by Taut, the other shows the tables and chairs moved out of the classroom onto the covered terrace where the boys continue to work both together and individually in the fresh air, informally overseen by their teacher.[64] In the campaigning style Giedion adopted in his pamphlet, he declares: 'The SCHOOLROOM becomes as much as possible opened up. One WALL is reduced to sheets of GLASS that can be lowered or slid together.' A canvas blind can be seen rolled against the canopy that shelters the terrace, which could presumably be lowered to provide shade from excessive sunlight in high summer and also perhaps give protection from wind or rain. The incorporation of clerestory windows as well as floor-to-ceiling 'sliding glass walls' enabled 'tables and chairs to be placed in every possible orientation without too glaring a light'.[65] Taut's romantic alpinism of the immediate post-war years had metamorphosed into a more pragmatic approach. Through an architecture employing modern techniques and materials that maximized the benefits of fresh air, sunlight, openness and circulation, he believed it was possible to break down the traditional structures and divisions of society and establish the basis for new and more flexible personal and social relationships. The classroom was also reproduced in detail in Richard Döcker's *Terrassentyp*, with a lengthy quotation from

Taut on the educational philosophy behind the school.[66] It is somewhat disappointing to learn that these frequently reproduced photographs were in fact of a full-scale model classroom with carefully posed teacher and pupils that Taut built to demonstrate the design and educational philosophy of the 'Karsten school' – which for various reasons (financial and political) was never realized.[67]

Today, most open-air facilities in schools built between the wars in northern Europe have fallen into disuse. This is generally put down to the unreliability of the summers and the deterioration of the buildings, particularly during the Second World War when there was not sufficient money, materials or labour available for proper maintenance and repairs. In reality, this was as much due to changes in social circumstances and conditions. Great improvements in the home conditions of pupils were made during the post-war decades in terms of the elimination of insanitary and unhealthy housing. In the very different educational climate immediately after the war outdoor classes were thought to be too distracting and uncontrollable. Despite the renewed emphasis on healthy bodies, fitness and physical exercise today, such features are still often regarded as inappropriate in educational circles. However, in the early 21st century new school buildings have begun to incorporate similar features to the modernist designs of the 1920s and 1930s, based on a more sophisticated and tried building technology.[68]

Mock-up of classroom for Municipal Secondary School, Berlin-Britz, Germany, 1927

Bruno Taut

8 The outdoor room

The design of balconies, terraces and roof gardens is perhaps the clearest demonstration of how modernist architects addressed the issues of light, air and openness between the wars. It was also a terrain over which differences and debates were hotly fought. Many of those who were primarily interested in the design of social housing considered such features a waste of valuable space – and impossible to provide in a dwelling whose specifications were cut down to an *Existenzminimum*. Others believed that they served an important representational, as well as a practical function: signifying the right of working-class tenants to a 'ration' of open space and fresh air in the modern city. Often underused, glazed, or walled in, or otherwise altered (sometimes beyond recognition), such features are frequently today the saddest aspects of inter-war modernist housing, where once they were among its proudest features.

Since the early 1920s, Le Corbusier had been a powerful advocate of the terrace and the roof garden. The roof garden made possible by modern means of construction was one of his 'Five Points of a New Architecture' – published on the occasion of the Weissenhof model-housing exhibition. The roof gardens of the single- and two-family houses he designed for the *Siedlung* were intended to demonstrate the principles of his manifesto.[1] Le Corbusier had been able to develop his ideas without undue financial restraint in the mid-1920s in a series of luxurious villas for private clients, culminating in the Villa Stein–De Monzie near Paris with its complex system of terraces and roof gardens – often known by the appropriate name of 'Les Terrasses' (The Terraces).[2] Reviewing the house in 1928, Sigfried Giedion described the uplifting sensation of stepping out onto the terraces 'stretched out like a membrane', and feeling oneself 'flooded with air as if from floodlights [...] watched by the eyes of the thousands of surrounding windows'. While Giedion considered the luxurious interactions of the spaces of the villa and its terraces almost excessive, he implied that this might be redeemed 'as a productive force' by its power to inspire the introduction of light, air and openness into more economical types of housing.[3]

Shortly after leaving Peter Behrens's office in Berlin, Le Corbusier had made what he was to call his 'Journey to the East' – a voyage through the Balkans and along the

north coast of the Mediterranean to Istanbul in the summer of 1911, where he had been deeply impressed by the white walls, flat roofs, balconies and roof terraces of Mediterranean and near-eastern vernacular architecture.[4] Earlier, Le Corbusier had worked for the French pioneer of reinforced concrete Auguste Perret, one of the first French architects to incorporate terraces into his buildings.[5] Employing the reinforced-concrete system he had developed with his brothers and exploited through the Perret Frères construction company, Perret constructed roof terraces featuring concrete pergolas, flowerbeds and pots.[6]

In the 1920s, Le Corbusier argued for the incorporation of roof gardens and terraces on the basis of health, hygiene, fresh air and sunlight, proposing exercise on the roof garden or terrace as the antidote to the diseases that bred in the modern city, and claiming in the *Almanach d'architecture moderne* that 'the United States is winning the battle against tuberculosis through solariums'.[7] A film made in collaboration with Pierre Chenal in 1929, *L'Architecture d'aujourd'hui*, culminated in a tour of Le Corbusier's austerely luxurious Parisian villas of the 1920s, focusing particularly on their terraces and roof gardens and concluding with final close-ups of a man and two women doing gymnastic exercises on the roof terrace of the Villa Church.[8] At the beginning of the decade he had proposed roof terraces or solariums for the *immeuble-villas*, a system of duplex apartment housing based on his standardized Maison Citrohan 'type house', each of which was provided with a deep covered balcony or loggia. Although these were never built, some of the major features were incorporated in Le Corbusier's post-Second World War Unités d'Habitation. In these enormous slab-like concrete apartment blocks, each double-height apartment had its own balcony, while the sculpted roof terrace of the first Unité in Marseilles was designed to accommodate a children's pool and kindergarten with views towards the Alps and the Mediterranean.

Single- and two-family houses,
Weissenhofsiedlung, Stuttgart, Germany, 1927

Le Corbusier

At Weissenhof, only Le Corbusier's houses featured roof gardens as such, although many of the single-family houses incorporated large sun terraces or substantial balconies. These often employed a 'one-and-a-half-storey' layout where the upper rooms occupied only part of the floor area, with the remaining part forming a terrace that resembled an open-air room.[9] This created the dramatic visual impression of the *Siedlung* as a series of stepped terraces spilling down the slopes of the hilly terrain, growing 'organically' from it according to one view – or contrasting 'alienly' with it, like an 'oriental' or Arab village, according to the opposing viewpoint.[10] These stepped profiles produced a more natural integration with the other buildings and the landscape at Weissenhof than the formally more self-contained forms of Le Corbusier's houses, each topped with its own roof garden. Facing south and protected from north winds by the main body of the houses, these 'open-air rooms' are among the most striking aspects of the estate, designed to promote the hygienic and health-promoting activities of sun-bathing and gymnastics. Most featured a cubic or rectangular frame of metal tubing which provided supports for protective canvas sunscreens and served to 'sketch in' or define the volume of a virtual room in space, as in the houses designed by Walter Gropius, Richard Döcker, Bruno Taut and Adolf Schneck – while the house designed by the veteran German architect Hans Poelzig had a more substantial wooden framework resembling a pergola. These terraces provided domestic leisure and sports facilities and were often fitted with open-air showers. In one of Döcker's houses, the partly roofed-over terrace was accessible from both living room and bathroom and had wall bars for gymnastics and a shower. The bathroom was large and spacious and could 'also serve as

Terrace of house,
Weissenhofsiedlung,
Stuttgart, Germany,
1927
Richard Döcker

a gymnasium'.[11] In a second house by Döcker access was through a three-leaved glazed door opening from the living room onto the terrace. This formed a large open-air room that could be completely curtained off and also had a shower with hot and cold water.[12]

Although unusual in middle-class housing of the type provided at Weissenhof, such facilities were common in the more luxurious modernist houses of the later 1920s. Sigfried Giedion illustrated a relatively spartan example in *Befreites Wohnen*: a terrace equipped with shower and gymnastic equipment on the roof of André Lurçat's Villa Guggenbühl in Paris.[13] Robert Mallet-Stevens had written in 1924 of how reinforced concrete had made possible 'terraces laid out as open-air rooms', and incorporated roof terraces luxuriously set up for outdoor entertaining in the series of substantial villas he designed in the rue Mallet-Stevens.[14] In *Bauen in Frankreich*, Giedion described one of these as 'the most comfortably arranged roof [terrace] that we have ever seen'. Served by a dumb waiter running up from the kitchen, it had a roof-top pantry and a 'flat concrete baldachin cleverly suspended from broad chimneys' which protected the table linen 'from every last particle of soot!' Giedion comments disapprovingly: 'Le Corbusier's astringency reinterpreted for the *gourmand-élégant*.'[15] In Loos's equally luxurious (if perhaps more astringent-looking) Müller House in Prague, a second 'summer' dining room opened onto an extensive rooftop terrace with a built-in shower, although this was not as lavishly fitted out as the Mallet-Stevens's house.[16]

An earlier and more modest middle-class example was the house Ernst May designed for himself and his family in 1925, immediately after his appointment as director of the Frankfurt Municipal Building Department. This had a large *Sonnendach* (roof terrace) reached by an outside staircase that led up from the mezzanine gallery of the living room. Like the terraces that appeared two years later at Weissenhof, this could be closed off with canvas curtains mounted on a metal framework to provide privacy and shade. Outdoor rooms like this were generally too expensive to include in social housing, but May and his colleagues managed to provide substantial terraces in some of the earlier Frankfurt estates such as the Niederad (Bruchfeldstrasse) Siedlung built between 1926 and1927, before the existence-minimum 'ration' of dwelling space had become further reduced during the final years of the decade. Some houses in the Praunheim Siedlung had a *Dachgarten*, a roof terrace where clothes could be dried or aired after being washed in the communal self-service laundries provided in the larger Frankfurt *Siedlungen*. The terrace could also be used for sunbathing in the hot central European summer, or for growing tomatoes, shrubs or flowers in pots.

Le Corbusier incorporated very extensive terraces and roof gardens in the company estate he built for the French industrialist Henri Frugès at Pessac near Bordeaux in 1926, although these seem to have been problematic from the beginning. In his first account of modernist architecture, published in 1929, the American architectural historian Henry-Russell Hitchcock condemned Pessac as a failure, arguing that Le Corbusier had paid excessive attention to the principles of light, air and openness.

Hitchcock claimed he 'had done too much work for millionaires and artists ready and able to afford the expenses of aesthetic research' to realize effectively 'the practical principles of his earlier housing schemes':

> Considering the fact that so large a part of the site was given over to gardens it was senseless extravagance to devote nearly half the cubic content of the houses to the luxury of open entrances and terraces. The extraordinary planning which was forgivable in a large villa, made the interiors of these houses particularly uncomfortable for the small-salaried employés for whom they were designed.[17]

Hitchcock's view was confirmed by the later history of the Pressac estate. Most of the terraces and some of the roof gardens were subsequently walled in or glassed over by their inhabitants, although recently these have been restored to their original aspect.[18] This has been a frequent occurrence with early modernist social housing and may be as much to do with changing lifestyles in the later decades of the 20th century as the need for more indoor space – with ownership of cars providing easier access to week-end chalets and second homes and the availability of cheap package holidays in the sun. Many of those who lived on the Pessac estate also reduced the width of the windows in their houses.[19] The same thing happened on Gropius's Törten estate in Dessau. Presumably, the inhabitants felt that these windows provided 'too much light' or left them overexposed to the eyes of neighbours or passers-by.

In the 'Manual of the Dwelling' in *Vers une architecture* (1923), Le Corbusier had demanded a large south-facing bathroom with a glazed wall opening onto a terrace for sunbathing, supplied with 'the most up-to-date fittings' and 'a shower bath and gymnastic appliances'. While this reads like a description of the terraces incorporated by

Architect's own house,
Frankfurt am Main, Germany, 1925
Ernst May

many architects at Weissenhof and may well have inspired their design, Le Corbusier himself preferred to demonstrate the roof garden as described in his 'Five Points of a New Architecture'.[20] Yet for all the virtues claimed for this in his programme – mainly preventing the roof slab from drying out and leaking – at Weissenhof he seems merely to have attempted to recreate the ground-level garden on the roof. In the semi-detached houses the roof terrace occupied the whole of the top floor, apart from a small study reached by steps from the floor below. Although the single-family house had two bedrooms at the level of the roof terrace, both here and in the semi-detatched houses there is little direct interpenetration between inside and outside of the kind found in many of the houses designed by other architects at Weissenhof.

A more flexible and less programmatic system of terraces and roof gardens (as at Pessac) might have been more appropriate for what was after all a suburban estate, but in the high-profile international context offered by the model-housing exhibition Le Corbusier seems to have wanted to present in realized form some of his best-known and as yet unbuilt designs. The detached single-family house at Weissenhof was the first and virtually the only effective realization of the standardized Citrohan house first designed in the early 1920s, based on the double-height live/work space of the Parisian artist's studio.[21] The double-family house was an updated version of the earlier Maison Domino, a building type Le Corbusier had derived from the grid-like structure of the standard reinforced-concrete frame – so named because of the six dots by which the six columns were represented on a plan.[22] The rooftop garden was a prominent feature of both these types, which were designed for narrow inner-city sites, whereas the Weissenhofsiedlung was a suburban estate on a hillside overlooking the city, although Le Corbusier claimed they could be built on any site in the world. At the end of the section on roof gardens in 'Five Points of a New Architecture' he wrote that 'the roof garden means that a city can win back for itself the whole built-up area'.[23]

Many of the features displayed at Weissenhof, such as flat roofs, terraces and wide windows, were represented by the promoters and protagonists of the new architecture as the components of a healthier way of living: a modern lifestyle that would enable people to be more in touch with their own bodies through a direct contact with sunlight, fresh air and the natural world. But not all of the housing in the Weissenhofsiedlung had all these features. Often seen as the closest to prototypes for social housing, J. J. P. Oud's row of four single-family houses had neither roof gardens nor terraces. Instead Oud included an enclosed drying and ironing room on the upper floor, providing what were then considered essential facilities for a working-class or lower middle-class family. While the small metal-railed cantilevered concrete 'Juliet' balconies, which opened off the landing at the top of the stairs, might seem to be little more than token representational symbols of light, air and openness, these were specifically designed to air bedding – still a common 'hygienic' practice today among all social classes in continental Europe, although almost unknown in Anglo-Saxon cultures.

Row of three houses, Weissenhofsiedlung, Stuttgart, Germany, 1927
Mart Stam

After Oud's row of single-family dwellings, the Dutch architect Mart Stam's three austere and economical row houses are generally considered to be the nearest to viable low-cost social housing types at Weissenhof. Two have no balconies, with little inter-penetration between the interior and the exterior. Exceptionally, the third house was provided with a substantial roof terrace that had facilities for gymnastics. Sheltered by glass screens that matched the long horizontal windows of the bedrooms in the other houses, this created the somewhat surrealist effect of an apparently half-built room open to the air and sky. Reached by a spiral staircase rising up two floors from the garden, this resembled the upper deck or bridge of a ship rather than the 'outside rooms' with direct access from bathroom or living room designed by many of the German architects – and was closer in conception to Le Corbusier's roof gardens.

While Le Corbusier's Weissenhof houses were criticized as more appropriate to a Mediterranean than a northern or central European climate by both traditionalist and some modernist critics, the terraces of other architects found more general approval. The differences between Le Corbusier's roof gardens and the open-air rooms of the German architects were perhaps as much cultural as the product of different architectural agendas. Although he was born and grew up in Alpine Switzerland, Le Corbusier had been strongly affected both by his early travels as a young man in the Mediterranean area and a decade of working in France. While his ideas about roof gardens were clearly related to southern European and Mediterranean traditions, the German and central European conception of the outside room seems closer to that of the terrace or balcony of the Alpine sanatorium which Peter Behrens had attempted to incorporate into his Weissenhof apartment block (see Chapter 2).

Light & shade

At various points in his career Le Corbusier was strongly attracted and influenced by the architecture and way of life of the Mediterranean littoral of southern Europe and North Africa. As a young man he had been involved in an entrepreneurial project in North Africa that celebrated French colonial power, European control of the Arab city, and the domination of Catholicism over Islam. While employed as a draughtsman in the Perrets' office in 1908 and 1909 he had worked on the project for the Catholic Cathedral in Oran, for which Perret Frères were the engineers and constructors.[24] Although Le Corbusier did not go to Oran himself, the design and method of construction for the project (reinforced concrete) made a powerful impact on his later development as an architect.[25] Two years later, after having worked in Peter Behrens's office in Berlin, he set off in the summer of 1911 on his 'Journey to the East'. He recorded his impressions in a travel journal, the early chapters of which were published in a local newspaper in his hometown of La Chaux-de-Fonds in Switzerland – although the majority of the original text only appeared posthumously.[26] The predilection for smooth whitewashed surfaces and cubic forms in Le Corbusier's architecture of the 1920s seems to have owed a good deal to his memory of the vernacular and monastic Mediterranean architecture he saw during this journey, and on an earlier visit to Italy in 1907.

In the second volume of his *Oeuvre complète*, he traced back his notion of the *promenade architecturale* to Arab architecture. Le Corbusier argued that architecture was not static, but should be experienced by walking through it – rather than viewed from a single viewpoint, as in the perspective systems of representation that had dominated European architectural design since the Renaissance.[27] If the unfolding of the interior was intended by Le Corbusier to be perceived by the individual moving through it on foot, the exteriors of his buildings were designed to be experienced from the moving car as the owner or visitor drew up to the house. If the slower 'oriental' pace of the Arab walking on foot controlled the form of the interior, the modern European and North American mode of perception of 'seeing at speed' – or what László Moholy-Nagy called 'vision in motion'[28] – defined and produced the exterior. This can be seen at its most spectacular in Le Corbusier's designs for the Villa Savoye where the smooth, sleek, industrial horizontals of the exterior both produce and are the product of the experience of arriving at the villa by car, driving up to and under its seemingly floating or hovering volumes and continuing between the pilotis and the ground-floor retaining wall until the main entrance is reached. Once inside the house however, the pace and formal development is determined by the act of walking up the long sloping ramps from ground floor through the first floor accommodation to the roof terrace that dominates the house.[29]

Despite his declared respect for Arab architecture, Le Corbusier's first (and only) realized North African commission did not turn out entirely happily, although the building that resulted is one of his most fascinating works. The Tunisian contractor

Lucien Baizeau had been impressed by Le Corbusier's three houses at Weissenhof, which as we have seen many critics argued were more appropriate to a Mediterranean climate. Baizeau commissioned a villa for his family on the North African coast near Carthage (1928–29). Le Corbusier did not visit the site but based his design on photographs and detailed descriptions of the terrain and the local climate provided by Baizeau. The first scheme was an adaptation of the Citrohan-type house he had employed for his detached single-family house at Weissenhof. This incorporated three glass-sheathed interlocking double-height spaces to provide air circulation, with a flat concrete roof raised on thin pilotis to shade the roof terrace. Baizeau was critical of this design because he claimed it could not cope with the climatic conditions of the site, which was subject to the *sirocco* – the hot dry wind that blows off the Sahara. After a number of attempts to revise the original design to accommodate these criticisms, Le Corbusier accepted his client's demands for a house with wide terraces on each floor. The solution (following Baizeau's suggestions) was a radical adaptation of his basic Maison Domino structural frame of regularly spaced pilotis and reinforced-concrete floor slabs that also took into account the principles of natural climate control used in traditional Arab architecture.

With his architectural partner Pierre Jeanneret, Le Corbusier designed a concrete structural frame for the house where the floor slabs consisted of a continuous concrete tray with up-turned edges – providing the parapets for wide terraces at each floor level. This technique had been introduced to Europe by Wiebenga, notably in his early Technical School in Groningen (1922–23), designed with Leen van der Vlugt. Wiebenga also used the system when he collaborated with Duiker on the design of the Cliostraat Open-Air School, which has many similarities to Le Corbusier's slightly later Villa Baizeau. By employing a reinforced-concrete frame of square-section pillars with up-turned floor trays, Duiker and Wiebenga were able to provide open-air classrooms on terraces that were shaded from direct sunlight and protected from rain by the floor slab above. Wiebenga was born and brought up in the Dutch East Indies and many of the buildings of the 1920s and 1930s on which he worked as structural engineer or designed himself as architect are marked by an attempt to devise a structural and sheathing system that allowed as much direct exposure to fresh air as possible while providing shade and protection from the direct rays of the sun.[30]

In the final design for the Villa Baizeau the accommodation on each floor was enclosed in different ways to suit the client's particular requirements, while keeping the outer walls well within the pilotis so as to create wide terraces at each level – affording extensive outdoor shade and natural circulation of air. There is 'no façade in the traditional sense'.[31] The naked cast-concrete frame is displayed on the outside of the house in a manner closer to the work of Perret than the taut glass-and-stucco skin of Le Corbusier's recent purist villas near Paris, anticipating his later post-Second World War designs such as the Unités d'Habitation in France and Germany, and his work in India.

The 'free plan' was one of Le Corbusier's 'Five Points of a New Architecture' and the structural frame of the villa allowed this to a greater extent than any of his earlier designs, exploiting to the full the possibilities envisaged in the Maison Domino-type house while at the same time providing a natural non-mechanical air-cooling and climate-control system. The introduction of mechanical air conditioning in modern buildings essentially negates the ideals of light, air and openness that inspired early modernism, destroying the delicate balance of sunshine, fresh air and spatial openness created by carefully linked combinations of windows, balconies and terraces.[32]

Le Corbusier seems not to have been particularly happy with the final version of the Villa Baizeau, and gave more space to the first project in the 1910–29 volume of his *Oeuvre complète*. However, he illustrated the executed version as one of the Four Compositions published in 1929 to demonstrate the four major ways in which the Maison Domino and Maison Citrohan models could be developed as complex spatial compositions. The three other examples were the Villa La Roche-Jeanneret, the Villa Stein–De Monzie and the Villa Savoye. Tim Benton has seen the Villa Baizeau as providing a model for the spatial complexity of the Villa Savoye, and its extensive *promenade architecturale*.[33] Le Corbusier's own comments on the illustrations of the Villa Baizeau were terse and unenthusiastic, revealing the 'disappointment dogging the entire proceedings'.[34] Nevertheless, the villa can be seen as one of Le Corbusier's most original and intriguing early modernist designs, not only for its anticipations of later schemes for tropical climates but also because of his (albeit somewhat reluctant) development of the Domino model to its logical conclusion.

Owing to the failure of his sealed system of controlled ventilation or *respiration exacte* (literally, 'correct breathing') for the Salvation Army Hostel in Paris, Le Corbusier was eventually compelled to allow the installation of opening windows in the building.[35] After the Second World War a *brise-soleil* was added to protect the glass windows from sunlight in the summer. This was essentially the solution Baizeau had advocated – and which Le Corbusier had reluctantly accepted – for shading the windows of his house from the fierce North African sun with the projecting horizontal floor slabs that also formed the terraces.[36] Le Corbusier developed the idea of the *brise-soleil* in his own projects for tropical or sub-tropical climates from the early 1930s.[37] This solution was employed for the Ministry of Education and Health building in Rio de Janeiro designed in the late 1930s by a team of Brazilian architects led by Lucio Costa, with Le Corbusier acting as consultant.[38] The building displayed the 'Five Points of a New Architecture' (and many other of Le Corbusier's ideas) more spectacularly than any of his own executed works up to this time.[39] It is still frequently misattributed to Le Corbusier.[40]

When he designed the stepped-terrace villa for the lawyer Gustav Scheu in the prosperous Vienna suburb of Hietzing in 1912, Adolf Loos was probably influenced by the flat-roofed vernacular architecture he had recently seen in Algeria. (He visited Biskra twice during the previous two years, while searching for marble to clad the

Michaelerhaus, and when accompanying Bessie Bruce on a 'winter cure'.)[41] Loos later denied any 'oriental' influence, although acknowledging that until recently flat roofs and roof terraces had been practical only in southern climates. When he designed the Scheu villa over a decade before, the general response had been 'a shaking of heads':

> People thought that type of building might be appropriate for Algiers, but not for Vienna. When designing the house I did not have the Orient in mind at all. I just thought it would be very convenient to be able to step out from the bedrooms, which were on the second floor, onto a large, communal terrace. Anywhere, in Algiers as well as Vienna. This terrace, then, which was repeated on the third floor (an apartment that was rented out), was the unusual, exceptional feature.

Loos pointed out that terraces have been usual in the Middle East 'for thousands of years', but had not been used in central or northern Europe, because with 'the construction methods available until now flat roofs and roof terraces could only be built in frost-free regions'. But the introduction of asphalt and 'Hausler-type roof cladding' had made possible their construction in climates subject to frost and even snow.[42]

It was Gustav Scheu who as a Social Democrat city councillor had been responsible for Loos becoming involved with the settlers' housing cooperatives after the First World War. Scheu and Loos opposed the building of enormous inner-city apartment blocks by the Vienna municipal-housing authority. Many of these were provided with balconies, loggias and terraces, 'so that the poorer tenants, who can rarely afford a summer's holiday, have at least an opportunity to enjoy the open air'.[43] But frequently these were more symbolic than practical – often small, awkwardly shaped, and ill-oriented towards the sun. The apartments themselves were often cramped, badly ventilated and dark – and usually did not have their own bathrooms. Tenants had access to communal open space in the *Höfe* (central courtyards) or gardens around which the blocks were built, and to communal facilities such as laundries, kindergartens, baths and showers.[44] Some of the larger complexes, such as the Karl-Marx-Hof (or 'superblocks' as they were sometimes called), were provided with an even greater variety of social amenities, such as tuberculosis clinics, kindergartens, advice centres and youth hostels.[45] But these had to serve large numbers of tenants and were often regimented and authoritarian, supervised by insensitive officials appointed by the municipality rather than elected by the tenants themselves. Architects working for the self-help settlers' movement, such as Loos, Josef Frank, Franz Schuster and Schütte-Lihotzky, argued that single-family row houses with long 'productive' gardens on the periphery of the city provided better access to light, air and openness. Here tenants could grow fresh vegetables at minimal cost and benefit from healthy exercise in the unpolluted fresh air of the outer suburban areas on the edge of the Vienna Woods, or similar unspoilt tracts of green space surrounding the city.

Although accepting some commissions for inner-city apartment blocks, Frank continued to believe like Loos that the *Siedlung* of single-family row houses with gardens offered the best solution to the housing problem in Vienna. He argued that this type of housing established a direct link between people and nature, creating a community with an equality between its inhabitants.[46] Frank was able to put such ideas into practice in the early 1930s as director of the Vienna Werkbundsiedlung model-housing exhibition, where he commissioned a variety of model dwellings suitable for adoption as social housing 'to give as many examples as possible of the arrangement of one-family houses of the smallest type', arguing that 'different types of people need different types of houses'.[47] Built on a pleasant sloping south-facing site, not dissimilar to that of Weissenhof, in the outer western suburb of Lainz, the Vienna Werkbundsiedlung was originally planned to coincide with the Werkbund Congress held in Vienna in the summer of 1930, but was postponed for two years due to financial and other problems. The estate consisted of relatively low-cost housing, which nonetheless provided the maximum of 'bourgeois culture' Frank believed lower middle-class and working-class tenants were entitled to expect, in opposition to the views of many of his fellow-socialist contemporaries.[48] Originally projected within the municipal building programme, the *Siedlung* was to have been located on a more central and urban site with small apartment blocks as well as single-family houses. As realized in suburban Lainz, the estate comprised one- and two-storey detached and semi-detached houses, three-storey row houses, and a series of very small existence-minimum two-storey row houses – each dwelling provided with a 200-square-metre garden. The costs were 18 per cent higher than for similar speculative housing and Frank justified this as 'offset by the better adjustment to new standards of life, and the higher aesthetic, hygienic and social values'.[49] But at a time of high unemployment and political and financial crisis few people were able to afford to buy the houses and the municipality took over the remainder and rented them to tenants.

Frank asked his architects to design single-family housing types (or prototypes) which could be repeated to produce a whole *Siedlung* of identical dwellings. He commissioned short rows of houses, pairs of semi-detached houses, and occasionally single detached houses like that by Hans Vetter, which had an ingeniously asymmetric arrangement of window openings and distinctive porthole windows lighting the bathroom and front door. In a poster advertising and promoting the exhibition, Vetter's small detached house was replicated by photomontage techniques as a row of three, and Ernst Plischke's pair of semi-detached houses were shown forming a continuous row. In the foreground, two tramcars are represented in schematic graphic form, their rectangular shape and repeated abstract forms echoing those of the Vetter and Plischke houses – suggesting that the houses could be built in quantity, just like trams. Behind Vetter's 'row houses' can be seen an unmodified image of Richard Neutra's single-storey detached house with its roof entirely given over to a garden. This was the one design that did not really conform to Frank's directive for houses that could be replicated in rows. It was perhaps included on the poster to show that the individual

Werkbundsiedlung, Vienna, Austria, 1932. Richard Neutra's single-storey house with roof terrace is clearly visible (centre)

detached house surrounded by a garden – in addition to the garden it bore on its roof – remained a possibility on the outskirts of the city. But also perhaps because (more dramatically than any of the other designs) it displayed the interaction between house, garden and terrace according to the principles of light, air and openness: a small piece of Southern California transposed to a Vienna suburb.[50]

Frank was opposed to what he considered overly functionalist and reductive modernist developments in Germany and had attacked these in a paper delivered at the 1930 Vienna Werkbund congress, attended by Gropius and Mies van der Rohe among others.[51] In commissioning architects for the Werkbundsiedlung he invited those whose contribution he believed had not been sufficiently recognized, such as Rietveld and Neutra.[52] Frank urged his architects to exploit space to the maximum, providing 'the greatest comfort possible in accordance with a strict observance of the principle of minimum wastage of space' – essentially a less dogmatic restatement of the principle of *Existenzminimum*.[53] He encouraged them to emphasize the relationship between inside and outside areas in order to maximize the amount of light, space and openness in their designs. Particular attention was paid to the gardens, which were intended to interact with the inhabited space of the house and to provide the residents with the pleasure of contact with nature and the open air – an interaction that in almost every dwelling was mediated by means of a patio, courtyard, veranda, terrace, balcony, or pergola, and often several of these features together. Frank believed a dynamic relationship between house and garden was an essential element of modern living, which applied to lower middle-class and working-class housing as much as to the luxurious bourgeois villa.

In the smallest existence-minimum houses like those designed by Margarete Schütte-Lihotzky (who by this time was working in the Soviet Union), based on her work with the settlers' movement in Vienna and for the neue Frankfurt, the

specifications were too minimal for much more than a patio and pergola linking house to garden, and it was mainly in the larger houses on the estate that more generous terrace-type features were found. Oskar Strnad's elegant pair of semi-detached houses had sheltered loggias opening off the curving garden façades of the living rooms with generous south-facing terraces on the upper floor onto which the children's bedrooms opened.[54] Frank's own externally austere detached studio house was planned with the living/dining room and two bedrooms on the ground floor, and an upper floor entirely taken up by a second living room that opened directly onto a large terrace running the whole width of the house. An elegant arched pergola created a shaded entrance patio, linking the house to what was originally the electrical substation for the *Siedlung* – now a small display devoted to the Werkbundsiedlung organized by the local museum. As in Neutra's tiny single-storey house, the whole of the flat roofs of Josef Hoffmann's row of four single-storey houses were designed as roof terraces, reached by internal staircases lit by huge vertical windows that dominate the exterior. Loos designed two pairs of semi-detached houses with his pupil Heinrich Kulka which featured generous windows, sheltered terraces and balconies on the south-facing façades. He also introduced subtle variations of level in the interiors, in a simplified version of the complex spatial planning according to the principle of *Raumplan* (literally: 'space plan') which he had first tried out in his austerely opulent middle-class villas of the 1920s. Two courtyard houses designed by Anton Brenner – who like Schütte-Lihotzky had joined the neue Frankfurt after designing social housing in Vienna – were remarkable for their compact dimensions and the ingenious way each was built around a large sheltered courtyard (*Wohnhof*) for outdoor living during the hot Viennese summers.[55]

The architects of the Vienna Werkbundsiedlung directly addressed the principles of light, air and openness that lay at the centre of the modernist project, providing the 'maximum openness to nature: balconies, terraces, gardens' within the restrictions of relatively small budgets.[56] Although Frank was highly critical of the Stuttgart Weissenhofsiedlung and its over emphasis on experimentation with new materials, in many ways the Werkbundsiedlung had more in common with Weissenhof than the other model-housing exhibitions held in Europe in the five years between 1927 and 1932. Many commentators have seen the Stuttgart model-housing exhibition as constituting the first major demonstration of an international modernist style of architecture. Rather (as Tim Benton has argued) it should be seen as displaying a significant moment when a number of modernist stylistic variations still appeared possible, with no single style predominating.[57] Like Weissenhof, the Vienna Werkbundsiedlung displayed a variety of different solutions within what might otherwise have seemed to be a restricted modernist vocabulary. It strongly signalled that the essential principles of modernist design remained a concern with hygiene and health, openness to nature, and the provision of the maximum light, air and space possible within the means available, however limited.

'A place in the sun'

In the early 1930s, the Baedeker guide to Germany described the Stuttgart Weissenhof-siedlung as 'an interesting colony of ultra-modern flat-roofed houses with wide windows, large verandas and roof gardens'.[58] White walls, flat roofs, wide windows, terraces and roof gardens were commonly seen as the distinguishing characteristics of the modernist house – features that identified the modernist style as 'international' rather than indigenous. Yet these features were characteristic of Mediterranean or North African vernacular domestic architecture, and in employing them modernist architects consciously evoked such associations. For northern Europeans (even modernists) the Mediterranean was regarded nostalgically as a kind of utopia – the southern European paradise where, in Goethe's words, 'die Zitronen blühn' (the lemon trees bloom).[59]

This association of the white walls, flat roofs, terraces and roof gardens of inter-war modernist buildings with Mediterranean or North African architecture was presented as both negative (in the racially loaded attacks and smears of those who opposed them) and as positive (in the writings of modernist practioners and apologists). As discussed in Chapter 6, some commentators and practioners sympathetic to modernism criticized the adoption of such features as inappropriate to buildings designed for northern or central European climates, while Ernö Goldfinger, a second-generation modernist architect whose early work was produced in the late 1930s, could dismiss the 'white' architecture of a few years earlier as 'casbah' architecture.[60] But the real opposition came in the form of right-wing racialist attacks. A notorious photomontaged postcard depicted a panoramic view of the Weissenhofsiedlung as an Arab casbah. This was based on a well-known black-and-white photograph of the estate which typically rendered the exterior walls of the houses and apartment buildings as pure white – giving no tonal indication of the different pastel colours in which a large number were painted.[61] Alfred H. Barr, the first director of the Museum of Modern Art in New York, who spent three months on sabbatical in Stuttgart in the spring of 1933, recalled that 'a cleverly faked postcard of the Weissenhof appeared showing camels and Arabs wandering through the white-walled flat-roofed houses of "Stuttgart's Moroccan Village"'.[62] Many of the neue Frankfurt estates were referred to popularly as the 'new Morocco', and similar racist nicknames were given to J. J. P. Oud's housing block at Hook of Holland. Le Corbusier's social housing of 1926 at Pessac was referred to locally as 'the Moroccan or Algerian district' or 'the casbah'.[63]

Undoubtedly, many of the influences of traditional and vernacular modes of building from other cultures on European architecture of the early 20th century can be traced to the legacy of European imperialism. The declining but still powerful colonial systems of Britain, France and The Netherlands had a significant impact on the development of modernist architecture in these countries between the wars. And despite the loss in 1918 of the colonies Germany had acquired in sub-Saharan Africa during the 19th century, colonial attitudes continued to influence German modernist architectural thinking and practice between the wars. The generation of architects who embraced modernism in the 1920s had grown up in a Germany that had briefly possessed 'a place in the sun'. Much of the building between the wars in what was then British-mandated Palestine – and which in 1948 was to become the new state of Israel – was in a purist white modernist style mainly designed by Jewish architects who had left Germany and central Europe in 1933, or shortly before. Although adapted to provide coolness and shade in the intense heat of the middle-eastern climate, this was (and continues to be) generally known in Israel as 'Bauhaus style'.[64] Tel Aviv in particular was developed as a model modernist Mediterranean metropolis, popularly known as 'the White City'.[65] The development of a modernist style of architecture in mandate Palestine was the direct result of anti-Semitism in Germany and central Europe between the wars. Yet the transplantation of what – for all its claims to be 'international' – was essentially a European style, imposed a western mode of architecture that served to reinforce the dominant position of the Jews in mandate Palestine and Israel. The 'white' architecture of the Jewish settlers formed a clear ideological contrast with the buildings of the indigenous Arab population, built in a middle-eastern or Mediterranean vernacular of the kind that had itself strongly influenced European and North American modernist architecture.

Not all German-Jewish architects went to Palestine after 1933. When the world-wide recession and a new right-wing local government curtailed the neue Frankfurt housing project, Ernst May had gone with several members of his team to work in the Soviet Union in 1930. On leaving Russia in 1934, May could not return to what was now Nazi Germany on three counts. He was Jewish, he had been a member of the proscribed SPD, and he had worked in the Soviet Union for the Soviet government. May emigrated to colonial British East Africa (parts of which had been German colonies before the First World War), basing himself from 1937 in Nairobi, but working throughout what is now Kenya, Uganda and Tanzania until the end of 1953, when he returned to Germany. Unlike many architects with whom he had worked in the Soviet Union in the 1930s, such as Mart Stam and Hans Schmidt, who went to the GDR after the war, May worked in social housing in Hamburg in West Germany after his return to Europe.[66]

Initially, May's commissions in East Africa were for houses for white farmers and low-rise city apartment blocks for middle-class whites, although he also designed a hotel and a cigarette factory. Later, he received a number of commissions for public buildings for non-whites: a school for girls and a maternity hospital – both commissioned by the Aga Khan, for whom he designed a luxurious seaside residence in Dar es Salaam – and a cultural centre for an African coffee planters' cooperative in Moshi at the foot of Mount Kilimanjaro.[67] May also applied his experience of existence-minimum housing to the design of a minimal concrete one-family single-storey house for Africans, intended as temporary accommodation which could be erected in a single day. This was based on the form of traditional Africa dwellings, but instead of using indigenous materials prefabricated concrete slabs were hung from reinforced-concrete standards spaced at 3-foot centres.[68] Two prototypes were built: one with a pitched roof, the other with rounded parabolic sides. Neither model for existence-minimum concrete huts was realized beyond the prototype stage, although May's designs for more conventionally constructed one-family minimum housing for Africans at Kampala in Uganda and low-rise blocks at Mombasa in Kenya were built between 1952 and 1956.[69] These were very similar in specification to the accommodation May and his colleagues had designed to house the homeless and unemployed at Mammolshainer Strasse, the most basic of the neue Frankfurt apartment blocks – provided only with communal kitchens and baths, and intended as temporary accommodation (although not demolished until 1981).

May's work in East Africa was paralleled by a number of British architects who began to work in British West Africa immediately after the Second World War, during the final years of the British empire. In 1945, Maxwell Fry and Jane Drew were appointed town-planning advisers to the British West African colonies of Nigeria, the Gold Coast (now Ghana), Sierra Leone and the Gambia, and later designed the University of Ibadan in Nigeria. In the 1950s, a number of other firms of British architects established practices in the region.[70] The most celebrated modernist architectural scheme to be realized in a former European colony was for the regional capital of Punjab at Chandigarh in post-British India, designed by Le Corbusier in collaboration with Maxwell Fry and Jane Drew.[71] Detailed discussion of this project lies outside the scope of this book, but it is clear that in this enormous project Le Corbusier incorporated lessons learned from his major inter-war colonial design for the city of Algiers – and its failure to be realized. Le Corbusier's plans for the radical restructuring of Algiers date from early 1931.[72] The project was to obsess him for the next decade, and was given

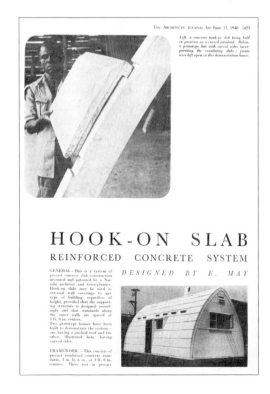

Prototype concrete temporary house, Kenya, as illustrated in the *Architects' Journal*, 1946

Ernst May

renewed impetus with his appointment in the early 1940s to a number of government committees under the collaborationist Vichy regime.[73] Although there was never any possibility of these proposals being implemented by the French authorities in Algiers, Le Corbusier's plans entailed 'the most far-reaching interference by France in any of its colonial dominions'.[74]

Altogether he made six plans for the city (known as the Plans Obus) in just over ten years.[75] These were all essentially variations on the same theme. A huge raised motorway following the curve of the harbour joined the European suburbs of Saint-Eugène and Hussein-Dey to a series of vast apartment blocks of about twenty-three storeys situated on the heights above the city centre at Fort-l'Empereur, which could house around 220,000 middle-class Europeans. These were linked by the viaduct above the casbah – where Le Corbusier had spent much of his time during his two-week stay in Algiers in 1931, and which was to be preserved in his plans as a sanitized and 'picturesque' tourist attraction – to a huge thirty-one-storey slab block forming a business-centre complex, intended to revitalize the rundown dockland area of the Quartier de la Marine. Among the most admired aspects of Le Corbusier's plans was his proposal for the housing at Fort-l'Empereur. This consisted of a honeycomb structure of double-height or duplex units, where the concrete frame of the block defined each unit, the arrangement and exterior cladding of which could be left to the taste of the occupants.[76] In one sketch Le Corbusier depicted duplex units with Moorish façades next to others reminiscent of his 1925 Pavillon de l'Esprit Nouveau.[77] Had these been designed for Algerians rather than French settlers it would have had a quite different significance. But the Fort-l'Empereur blocks were to house the French colonists, whose choice of a Moorish façade would not so much have expressed their 'own bad taste', as Manfredo Tafuri claims, but rather have indulged a nostalgic orientalism within a framework of up-to-the minute modernity.[78]

A direct development of Le Corbusier's Algiers project was his design for the Unités d'Habitation, the most famous of which was erected between 1947 and 1952 in the suburbs of Marseilles on the Mediterranean coast. Like the Plans Obus housing, this was based on the 'unit' or cell ultimately derived from the traditional double-height Parisian artist's studio, which Le Corbusier had first projected in the early 1920s and presented publicly in prototype form at the 1925 exhibition in Paris as the Pavillon de l'Esprit Nouveau. The units could be employed either as individual dwellings as a series of Citrohan-type houses, or slotted together to form a block of individual apartments (or *immeubles-villas*) like a gigantic honeycomb. But unlike Le Corbusier's proposals for the housing at Fort-l'Empereur, the Unité did not allow the residents to choose the façades of their apartments like a set of curtains.

It was perhaps appropriate that the first and most famous Unité should have been built in Marseilles, 'a city intimately connected with the French empire'.[79] A particular symbiosis seemed to exist between Marseilles and Algiers, the major French North

African colonial city. The film historian Ginette Vincendeau has argued that in the 1930s Algiers, 'the most "Frenchified" colonial capital, with modern quarters built in the style of late 19th-century French provincial architecture', was seen as an extension of Marseilles – 'the two cities sharing a number of features'.[80] In a mirror image, Marseilles was perceived as an extension of North Africa: the archetypal French Mediterranean metropolis, the main port for passenger and freight traffic to Algiers, and a colonial capital. After the Second World War it was regarded as almost a part of the Maghrib itself – a perception that North African immigration to the city since independence has done much to perpetuate. With its *brises-soleil* and dramatic roof terrace with spectacular views across the Mediterranean and towards the Alps, the Unité preserves something of the colonialist utopianism of Le Corbusier's Algiers project.[81]

Originally, the Unité was intended to house the port workers who had lived close to their work in the *vieux port*, which was blown up by the retreating Germans at the end of the war. However, when completed it proved too expensive for social housing and was eventually let to middle-class tenants. Equipped with a nursery, crèche, shops, hotel, bar-restaurant, youth clubs, and rooftop paddling pool, the liner-like megastructure was designed to supply every necessity for its inhabitants.[82] Planned as a prototype for social housing anywhere in France or abroad – examples were built at Nantes, Firminy, Briey-en-Fôret and in Berlin – the Unité seems best suited to the Mediterranean climate of a middle-class Marseilles suburb. Some of its present-day inhabitants are almost certainly *pieds noir* – the French colonists whom Le Corbusier's Obus project had been intended to house and who left Algeria after independence, often settling in Marseilles and other parts of the French Mediterranean coast. Rising above the coastal suburbs of the city, the Marseilles Unité bristles with the imagery of liners and steamships Le Corbusier so often evoked in his early writings. It stands like a huge beached relic of the ferries that plied between Marseilles and the North African colonies – a sun-baked grey-white emblem of former French expansionism and colonial control. Lucio Costa, the architect of the Ministry of Health building in Rio de Janiero, recalled that when he was going to visit the Unité in Marseilles he suddenly saw it rising out of the early morning mist like a great liner.[83]

In the Marseilles Unité, Le Corbusier's ideas on social housing were perhaps most successfully and spectacularly realized within the terms – and limitations – of those ideas. But in the decades immediately after the Second World War the Unité was to be a dangerous and often disastrous model for social housing in the very different climatic and social conditions of northern Europe. While Morocco and Algeria were still French colonies the French authorities made experiments with megastructural housing in the 1950s.[84] Similar solutions were adapted for housing in France in the 1960s. Today, it is immigrants from North Africa who mainly live in these now run-down and dangerous housing estates, built to far less generous specifications than Le Corbusier's Unités, in the outer suburbs of Paris and other major French cities.

9 Water & bathing

Water was as central as sun, light, air and openness to the representation of modernist architecture in the years between the wars. Baths, bidets, washbasins and lavatories were key elements (and symbolic forms) of the new architecture. Water was a direct element of many modernist buildings – like the waterfall and stream that flowed under and through Falling Water, Frank Lloyd Wright's house for Edgar J. Kaufmann in western Pennsylvania (1935–39). In Mies van der Rohe's Barcelona Pavilion (1929), the limpid reflective sheet of water against which the vertical planes of the pavilion were set was as vital an element in its formal composition as the plates of marble and plate glass that formed its walls. But the modernist building where water was the predominant feature which caught the public imagination was the Penguin Pool at the London Zoo (1933–34), designed by Lubetkin with his Tecton partners.

Familiar to those who have visited the zoo and anyone with even a passing interest in the modern movement, the Penguin Pool is one of the most popular and internationally famous examples of 20th-century architecture. (Thomas Leeuwen compares the pool with the Barcelona Pavilion as 'the other single great monument of modernism'.)[1] It still thrills visitors with its spectacular design, which until 2004 continued to function as a display device for promoting some of the Zoo's most popular inmates. When first built in the mid-1930s it instantly became a runaway tourist attraction. The pool focused international attention on the development of modern architecture in England – putting this as much on show as the penguins themselves – and exposing it to a wide public in a context close to popular culture.[2] The pool displayed the penguins in a setting of dazzlingly white reinforced concrete and sparkling blue water – or rather water that *appeared* to be blue. This illusion was created by the blue mosaic tiles that lined the pool's bottom and sides like the outdoor swimming baths of the time, which it consciously evoked and closely resembled in its construction and imagery.[3] As in swimming pools where continuously flowing water lubricated the metal slides provided for swimmers to enter the water, the concrete ramps of the Penguin Pool were designed to be kept permanently wet by a revolving fountain.

Penguins had caught the popular imagination at the beginning of the 20th century through the Antarctic expeditions of the time.[4] This fascination was probably related to the mystique of mountains and alpinism discussed in earlier chapters. Both fixated on notions of purity, cleanliness and whiteness. The success of the Penguin Pool as a show-case for the birds further promoted their popularity and encouraged the public to view them as amiable and anthropomorphic creatures. The adoption of the Penguin name and symbol for the highly successful series of paperback books published in England by Allen Lane from the mid-1930s was certainly related to the success of the Penguin Pool. The first version of the Penguin symbol was drawn by Edward Young (who designed the early covers) based on sketches made at the Penguin Pool.[5] Lane asked Lubetkin to build a replica model of the pool in the forecourt of the new premises for Penguin Books, but Lubetkin declined, claiming this would 'devalue the original'.[6] As a display device the pool was cleverly conceived to demonstrate the contrast between the penguins' comic clumsiness on land and their sleek speed and manœuvrability in the water. This was achieved by manipulating the material in ways that paralleled the characteristics of

The Penguin Pool,
London Zoo, 1933–34
Lubetkin and **Tecton**

155

the birds themselves. Penguins are unable to fly more than a few feet, but are very efficiently adapted to fast and skilful swimming. Seen standing or waddling around on land or ice they appear clumsy and slightly ludicrous, if lovable and attractive to the anthropomorphically disposed viewer. But as soon as they launch themselves into the water they become like streamlined torpedoes. (The caption to a poster for the London Zoo in 2002 claimed: 'A penguin can only "fly" underwater.')[7] Concrete is a heavy inert constructional material, which by means of careful calculation and reinforcement can be made to perform space-defying feats like a ballet dancer. Material and subjects were thus perfectly matched. In the pool's double-spiral rampways, reinforced concrete's spectacular leap into structural sublimity presented a dramatic and unforgettable visual equivalent to the penguins' sudden metamorphosis into sleek agility as they nose-dived into the water.

It is clear that Lubetkin's intent was as much to 'stage' and present the penguins to the public as to provide them with an environment suitable to their needs.[8] This was in line with the views of the more radical fellows of the Zoological Society such as Julian Huxley, the scientist, socialist and eugenicist (and adviser to the Peckham Health Centre) who negotiated the commissioning of the pool, and the zoo's director Sir Peter Chalmers Mitchell who was preoccupied with the idea of pavilions as 'showcases' for animals and birds.[9] Lubetkin argued that the Penguin Pool had to be a union of the swimming pool and the circus, of active and passive entertainment. The pool and Lubetkin and Tecton's other designs for the London Zoo, such as the Gorilla House, clearly reveal Lubetkin's interest in theatre and performance. These zoo pavilions represent an architecture of 'staging' derived from the Russian Constructivist designs of the 1920s with which Lubetkin was familiar, and a fascination with the notion of spectatorship and spectacle that was a particular cultural phenomenon of the years between the wars.[10] This was a period when the mass spectacles of cinema, gymnastics and sport, and the public political rally made possible by the new technology of amplification, became dominant popular media. It was a time when leisure was taken *en masse*, as can be seen in early photographs of the Bexhill Pavilion.

The Penguin Pool was popular not only with the public, but also with the zoo authorities and staff – at least when first built. Its 'streamlined uncluttered form' made it easy to clean. It gave the sparkling impression of a hygienic modern environment, free from the more pungent animal smells of most zoo buildings. Nevertheless, the pool seems to have been a less-than-ideal habitat for the Antarctic penguins for whom it was designed. The ramps were left in the original concrete while the surrounds to the pool were surfaced alternately with slate and rubber 'to provide stimuli to the birds' sensitive feet'.[11] But the black-footed penguins that latterly inhabited the pool suffered aching joints from having to walk on hard surfaces all day, and doubts have been cast on how well adapted this 'model home' was even to the original Antarctic birds' needs.[12] It is now widely believed that the pool's spectacular ramps did not provide the ideal habitat for penguins – anymore than the concrete surfaces of much post-Second World War housing afforded a suitable habitat for working-class tenants. The penguins were finally withdrawn from the Penguin Pool in 2004, after they appeared to be happier in the duck pond to which they had been temporarily moved while the pool was being cleaned. The water has now been drained from the Grade I listed structure and the penguins replaced by porcupines.[13]

If by current standards for the housing of animals and birds in zoos the Penguin Pool seems to have catered less than perfectly to the needs of the penguins, and even arguably caricatured and sentimentalized them, it may nevertheless have contributed something to their protection and conservation in the wild by helping to make them among the most popular and most frequently anthropomorphized of creatures in captivity. By anthropomorphizing penguins it projected them as models for human behaviour and human society. According to the architectural historian Thomas Leeuwen, the pool 'could be regarded as a modernist laboratory for a future hydro-dynamic society of men, since the new architectural configuration is here tested on penguins, long known for their abilities to simulate human bipedal propulsion and to excite sympathetic responses in their human observers'. Its location in one of the world's best-known zoological gardens meant that 'humans interested in the experiment could have ready access to this desirable model home'.[14] As a journalist wrote in 1938 in a magazine aimed at women with young children: 'How many citizens of London have brooded over the railings of that pool envying the penguins as they streak through the blue water or plod up the exquisite incline of the ramp – and have wondered sadly why human beings cannot be provided, like the penguins, with an environment so well adapted to their needs.'[15] Even if the pool eventually proved not to be so well adapted to the penguins' needs, it nonetheless provided a powerful utopian model of social change.

Pools of light

In a report on the sanitary conditions of the working-class population of Great Britain in 1842, the English sanitary reformer Edwin Chadwick projected the modern city as a social body through which water must constantly circulate, ceaselessly flushing out and washing away its bodily fluids, excrement and wastes. Without water constantly pumped in and channelled out, circulating through the intestines of the city, its interior fabric – its flesh – could only stagnate and rot. The faster the flow the fewer stagnant pockets to breed disease and pestilence, and the healthier (and wealthier) the city would be. Chadwick's papers were published in 1887 as *The Health of Nations*, probably to evoke the title of the 18th-century economist Adam Smith's *The Wealth of Nations*. 'Just as Harvey redefined the body by postulating the circulation of the blood', Ivan Illich has argued, 'so Chadwick redefined the city by "discovering" its need to be constantly washed.'[16] And within the city the individual bodies of its citizens needed constant washing and bathing. Previously the prerogative of the wealthy, in the late 19th century washing and bathing became the obsession of the middle classes, who attempted – successfully, eventually – to impose their obsessions on the population of Europe and North America as a whole. When Alfred H. Barr wanted to illustrate a modernist model of the development of 20th-century art and design in the catalogue for the seminal 'Cubism and Abstract Art' exhibition he curated at the Museum of Modern Art, New York, in 1936, he used the model of the 'flow chart'. Barr's 'flow chart' alluded to a model commonly employed in scientific and management writings between the wars – which was itself derived from the image of the circulation of water through the modern house and the modern city.[17]

Legislation on the provision of inside toilets and showers or baths for each household coincided with a period when the middle classes were finding it increasingly difficult to afford servants, and no longer had direct control over the lives and personal hygiene of those who served or serviced them. Such legislation provided a close substitute: indirect control over the hygienic aspect of other peoples' lives.[18] Health and housing authorities often favoured showers rather than baths, arguing that these were healthier and more hygienic and less likely to be 'misused' by householders. Apocryphal stories and jokes about working-class householders keeping coals in their baths were common in Britain between the wars, while in Switzerland not only coal but also rabbits were reputedly housed in bathtubs.[19] Such middle-class misrepresentations masked the real reasons for the specification of showers in social housing: they were cheaper to install, required less space, used less water and 'wasted' less time – unlike 'lounging' in a bath. Left-wing commentators such as Karel Teige also argued in favour of showers in social housing for virtually identical reasons. These were greater hygiene, the extra space needed for bathrooms and the added cost of installation, the price of hot water to the tenants (expensive at the time, even when provided by rubbish-burning district-heating systems) and the time saved by taking a shower rather than a bath: 'a factor very important for a person working outside of the home and for a home without a servant or a maid'.[20] Teige assumes that the members of a working-class family will bath only once a week. But this presumed that when tenants had a bathroom in their new house or apartment they would continue the practice of the weekly bath as formerly taken in a public bathing establishment. In practice, the acquisition of a bathroom effected a change in the traditional pattern of personal hygiene to more frequent bathing, particularly among the younger generation who grew up from childhood with a plumbed-in bath.

Even after indoor lavatories and baths or showers were provided for new social housing, local municipalities continued to provide communal baths for those who were still without such facilities – as they had done in the second half of the 19th century.[21] As earlier, facilities were often combined with swimming baths, designed to encourage healthy exercise as much as cleanliness, and to keep the working classes out of the pubs and gambling shops, or from indulging in other leisure activities of which the middle classes morally disapproved. Since the second half of the 19th century swimming baths had been constructed by municipal authorities to regulate both the hygienic conditions where people bathed – many 'natural' swimming and bathing places used by the working classes were insanitary and polluted – and to enforce 'decency' and 'morality'. (Bathing naked in lakes and rivers was common among both sexes before the advent of municipal swimming pools.)

In Switzerland, municipal bathing establishments were constructed alongside Alpine lakes. In cities such as Paris, Frankfurt and Vienna, floating bathing establishments had been established on the Seine, Main and Danube since the late 17th century, although these were generally privately run.[22] The best known was probably the Piscine Deligny in Paris, moored at the quai d'Orsay since Napoleonic times. It was reconstructed in 1953 and continued in use until it sank in 1993.[23] Similar 'floating baths' were moored in the Giudecca Canal in Venice at the point where it meets the Grand Canal, and in Amsterdam where the city's canal system meets the Amstel river and seaport. Floating baths were also situated directly in the sea. One of the largest was the colossal Bagno Maria in the bay of Trieste, built in 1858 with separate pools for men and women. Today, one of the few surviving floating baths is the Frauenbad in central Zurich, moored where the river Limmat enters the lake.[24] When floating baths had appeared in Boston in the 1860s they were criticized as 'floating sewers'.[25] However, by 1889 there were fifteen moored on the East River in New York serving tenement dwellers. In the 20th century most of the floating pools that survived were rebuilt or adapted so that they were filled with 'clean' mains water rather than filtered river water, creating 'an enclave of purity in contaminated surroundings', as in Rem Koolhaas's fable, 'The Story of the Pool'.[26]

In Russia, the public bath had a very specific character, that of the steam bath. This was typical even of the most rural villages, which according to El Lissitzky 'traditionally solved the problem in a very simple way: usually a small hut with a large stove was placed next to the village well'. Russian cities on the other hand 'developed the public bathhouse with its large communal steam room', while floating swimming pools in the rivers were used during the summer. Writing in 1930, Lissitzky described this tradition of communal bathing, and how in the Soviet era 'the large bathing facilities on the Russian Riviera, which take up one third of the whole Black Sea coast from the Crimea to Batum, are used by the Russian population as open-air bathing establishments'. Since the Revolution these had become open to all. Lissitzky illustrated an unbuilt design for a bath and swimming-bath complex in Leningrad by A. Nikolzki, 'planned as a large garden'. The layout was circular with a round swimming bath in the centre surrounded by ranks of individual baths located in a sunken basement. On top was an enormous sundeck surrounding the pool, covered by a glass dome that could be opened in summer.[27]

Before the First World War most municipal swimming baths in northern and central Europe had been heated indoor pools. After the war the emphasis changed to open-air baths, although some indoor pools continued to be built such as the Amalienbad in Vienna (described in Chapter 10) and the municipal baths at Roubaix near Lille (1927–32). Commissioned by the socialist town council of this northern French textile-manufacturing city, the Roubaix Piscine was designed by Albert Baert in a monastic rather than modernist style embellished with masonic imagery. The pool was housed in a space like an enormous basilica, with two huge stained-glass windows at either end of the pool in the form of the rising and setting sun – oriented so that the light of the 'real' rising and setting sun would stream through the appropriate window at morning and evening. Closed for safety reasons in 1985, it reopened in 2001 as the city's municipal museum with statues flanking the pool and applied art exhibited in the shower cubicles.

With the renewed emphasis on fresh air and sunlight that characterized the period between the wars, open-air unheated swimming baths were built throughout Europe – although often used for only two or three months a year – because it was believed that Vitamin D received through exposure to sunlight would help to lessen the incidence of diseases such as tuberculosis and rickets. As Elizabeth Wright has argued: 'It required a public "leap of faith" to believe that the climate had become more like that of southern Europe. There was no literal change in the climate, a psychological change had taken place.'[28] Many of these pools were designed in modernist style and some became world famous. A particularly fine series of baths and bathing resorts were built along the Swiss lakes in the late 1920s and 1930s. Adolf Steger and Karl Egender's Strandbad at Küsnacht on Lake Zurich (1929–30) features in a sequence at the end of Richter's *Die neue Wohnung* (1930)[29] and is illustrated in Hitchcock and Johnson's *The International Style* (1932).[30] The Swiss architect, artist and designer Max Bill – who had recently graduated from the Bauhaus – designed the lettering on the entrance pavilion.

In the period between the wars and during the first decades after the Second World War, open-air swimming pools were enormously popular.[31] Favoured sites of physical culture and the cult of the healthy and well-cared-for body beautiful, these were celebrated and recorded in numerous amateur and professional photographs and ciné films of the period. Perhaps because central heating and constant hot water in domestic homes were less general than today and people were used to cold water and cold rooms, they seem to have been able to tolerate lower water temperatures. In the later decades of the 20th century most of these open-air baths have been replaced by heated open-air or glassed-in pools, at least in northern Europe. Some of the most famous of the great modernist pools, such as J. B. Van Loghem's swimming baths at Haarlem in The Netherlands, have been demolished.[32] But a number of others survive, such as the Freibad Allenmoos open-air baths in Zurich (1938–39) designed by Werner Moser and Max Ernst Haefeli, and Marc Piccard's spectacular Swiss lakeside bath of Belle-Rive Plage near Lausanne (1937), which has recently been restored.[33] Another spectacular survivor is the Opel-Bad designed by Franz Schuster and Edmund Fabry in collaboration with the landscape architect Wilhelm Hirsch in Wiesbaden in Germany. Situated on a wooded hilltop with spectacular views overlooking the city, from which it can be reached by tram or on foot up a steep incline, the bath complex is sheltered from the prevailing winds by woods to the north and east, while the 'absolutely hygienic naturally heated water' is pumped up from a deep spring in the Taunus mountains.[34] With an open-air swimming pool, sports facilities and a restaurant, the Opel-Bad was intended to attract visitors away from the historic spa in the centre of the city, providing more up-to-date and democratic facilities.[35] Designed in the Weimar era, the bath complex was not completed until 1934 after the Nazis had come to power in Germany.

Special areas were provided at swimming pools for spectators and other non-participants (such as those accompanying young children) to sit and watch. In this respect the pools of the 1920s and 1930s were quite different from 19th-century outdoor bathing establishments. These were specifically designed to *prevent* spectators or passers-by from seeing the bathers, who were segregated into separate pools or swimming areas for the different sexes – often with special facilities for young children,

Opel-Bad, Wiesbaden, Germany, 1932–34
Franz Schuster and Edmund Fabry,
and Wilhelm Hirsch (landscape architect)

so that they should not see adult bodies unclothed.[36] In particular, the provision of separate and carefully policed and patrolled bathing establishments for women (where they could bathe and swim unobserved by male eyes) were regarded as of utmost moral importance. During earlier periods, bathing and swimming had been regarded as a kind of medical treatment (hydrotherapy). Immersion of the body in the water – rather than the exercise provided by swimming or water sports – was what was considered to be important. The notion of the actual physical enjoyment of the experience itself (or the enjoyment of the spectacle of watching others participate) was not officially recognized, although no doubt this played a surreptitious role in the popularity of such establishments. By the 1920s and 1930s, the moral climate had changed. The cult of the body demanded spectatorship: looking as well as direct participation.[37]

Pools built between the wars in Europe and the United States were not segregated according to sex, although there were different changing areas for men and women, and shallow paddling pools were provided for very young children, but these were generally not visually separated from the main pool by screens, as in the past. Swimming and sunbathing were regarded as not merely therapeutic but as a fulfilment of the self and of the individual within a mass society. The fit and healthy should provide a praiseworthy spectacle for others to admire and strive after. Children and adolescents were encouraged to watch and take example from the healthy, fit (and perhaps beautiful) bodies of their elders, and vice versa.[38] Notions of cleanliness and hygiene were instilled by the spectacle of the healthy well-formed and well-used body set against the sparkling clear chlorinated water of the artificial pools or the carefully regulated and tested waters of an Alpine lake – or glimpsed in the constantly running hot-and-cold showers against the scintillating white walls and hygienically tiled floors of the changing areas. The German abstract painter and designer Willi Baumeister – who worked as a graphic designer for the neue Frankfurt, and designed posters for the Weissenhofsiedlung model-housing exhibition and colour schemes for many of the interiors – wrote in the Swiss avant-garde architectural magazine *ABC* in 1926: 'Appreciation of the forces of nature through light, air, sport will decrease the demand for physicians and pharmacies. Swimming in the nude will counteract dismal eroticism. The new generation is a new species.'[39] Swimming pools and the culture of the healthy and fit nude or semi-nude body provided an essential element of the mass culture of the inter-war decades. This was related to what the German cultural critic Siegfried Kracauer dubbed the 'mass ornament': the dance routines of young female troupes such as the Tiller Girls, and the spectacular mass gymnastic displays characteristic of the period promoted by social-democratic regimes between the wars as well as by the totalitarian regimes of the Soviet Union, Fascist Italy, or Nazi Germany. Kracauer considered the 'mass ornament' as a passive acceptance of the repetition and replication of industrial production. But it is possible to take a more positive view: to see the enjoyment of and participation in such spectacle as an affirmative and life-enhancing activity.[40]

In 1930, the French sculptor Aristide Maillol was taken by his German patron, the collector and aesthete Count Harry Kessler, to see the new *Siedlungen* designed by Ernst May and his team of architects and designers for the neue Frankfurt. As well as the housing estates and schools of the suburban and inner-city estates, Maillol and Kessler visited an open-air swimming bath and stadium where they saw naked young men and women diving and swimming. Kessler recorded in his diaries how they sat together on the terrace overlooking the swimming pool watching the bathing and sunbathers. 'Maillol was in raptures about the unabashed nudity. He continually drew my attention to the splendid bodies of girls, young men and boys. "If I lived in Frankfurt, I would spend my days here drawing [...].'" Kessler assured Maillol that this was indicative of 'only a part of a new vitality, a fresh outlook on life', which since the First World War had been successfully promoted in Germany: 'People really want to *live* in the sense of enjoying light, the sun, happiness and the health of their bodies. It is not restricted to a small and exclusive circle, but is a mass movement which has stirred all of German youth.'[41] In hindsight, Kessler's language appears to anticipate the kind of views associated with the Nazis, but his politics were of the left. Less than three years later, in March 1933 – shortly after the Nazis had come to power – he was to leave Germany for Paris, never to return.[42] Not only did Kessler have left-wing sympathies, he was also homosexual; Maillol was not. From innumerable testimonies of the period it is clear that enthusiasm for sport, gymnastics and light, air and sunshine were not the prerogative of proto-Nazis.[43] The cult of hygiene, sport and the body could appeal to the homosexual and the heterosexual alike, to the upper-class aesthete and the sculptor from a peasant background, to the factory worker as well as the bank clerk, the social democrat as well as the clerical conservative, the Soviet worker as well as the Nazi stormtrooper.

The English poet Stephen Spender wrote after his first visit to Germany as a young man in 1929: 'It was easy to be advanced. You had only to take off your clothes.'[44]

> The sun – symbol of the great wealth of nature within the poverty of man – was a primary social force in this Germany. Thousands of people went to the open-air swimming bath or lay down on the shores of the rivers and lakes, almost nude, and sometimes quite nude, and the boys who had turned the deepest mahogany walked amongst those people with paler skins, like kings among their courtiers.[45]

Nudism had been promoted throughout the 1920s in Germany. In 1923, Adolf Koch, a teacher in a working-class area of Berlin, had started to run nude gymnastic classes, on the principle that nudity conferred social equality on people. He was prosecuted for the corruption of minors, but responded by founding a private gymnastics school in Berlin where he promoted *Freikörperkultur* and published several books in which he traced nudism back to its roots in the classical world of Greece.[46] Koch claimed that a 'healthy body' was the goal of his teaching: 'Working against tuberculosis, dipsomania, venereal diseases, etc, is an obvious extension of the cultivation of the body.' He advocated the classical ideal of *mens sana in corpore sano* (a healthy mind in a health body), maintaining that: 'We strive for the unity of body and spirit.' Koch argued that the cultivation of the body should be the antidote to war, 'based on respect for the body of the other'.[47] The culture of the body was not just the preserve of minority groups, but an important and influential part of Weimar culture. It was promoted in *Weg zur Kraft und Schönheit* (The Path to Strength and Beauty), a spectacular documentary film produced in 1924 by the mainstream UFA studios, featuring dancers and gymnasts and the advocates of *Lebensreform* and body culture, 'the representatives of a new generation' who 'take advantage of light, air and water'.[48] Among the dancers in the film was the young Leni Riefenstahl, who ten years later directed the *Triumph of the Will* which celebrated the Nazis' Nuremberg rally through 'masses of bodies in constant motion'.[49]

Nudism in the 1920s 'promised to reclaim the body that was mercilessly pressed into service at the assembly line and functionalized by the industrial process'.[50] But some of its advocates in Germany were less libertarian than Koch. Hans Surén (previously head of the German Army School for Physical Exercise) had served in the former German colonies in Africa and promoted the idea that the cult of nudity endorsed feelings of national and racial superiority.

> If physical strength is allowed to decay, even the highest achievements of the spirit and the most profound scientific knowledge will not avert national decline and death. Using every means possible with unflagging energy, a nation should be united in the will to promote the strength of its people.[51]

First published in 1924, Surén's *Der Mensch und die Sonne* (Man and Sunlight) went through sixty-one editions in little over a year, and appeared from 1936, the year of the Berlin Olympic Games, with the subtitle *Arisch-Olympischer Geist* (The Aryan-Olympic Spirit). It was illustrated with photographs of oiled and tanned naked or scantily clothed men and women exercising or posing in full sunlight. Surén wrote in his preface to the sixty-first edition that: 'The astonishing success of my book shows how aptly it reflects the aspirations of the true German race.'[52] Yet although *Der Mesch und die Sonne* was one of Hitler's favourite books, nudism was banned in Germany after the Nazis came to power.

The nudity or semi-nudity of the bodies of the patrons was matched by the nudity or semi-nudity of the architectural forms of swimming baths. Open-air pools were among the most dynamic of the new building types evolved between the wars that made dramatic use of modern materials and construction techniques. Their functional specifications and symbolic forms were particularly suited to 'modern' materials and structural elements such as reinforced-concrete columns and pilotis, cantilevers, steel girders, lightweight spiral staircases, plate-glass windows, and white-painted concrete or rendered walls. The design of swimming pools and lakeside bathing establishments required the strong horizontal forms that many critics and practioners regarded as an essential component of the modernist style. Circular or semi-circular elements were often employed in the spectator or café areas of inter-war swimming baths, providing almost panoptical viewing positions with sweeping vistas of the pools and the surrounding concrete or grassed areas designed for sunbathing and relaxation. The bright synthetic blue of the chlorinated water (an illusion created by the blue tiles often used for the underwater parts of the pools, as in the Penguin Pool at the London Zoo) contrasted with the white or off-white tiled surrounds, and the reinforced-concrete canopies and cantilevered diving towers. The heavy-gauge chromed-steel and aluminium-painted tubing of railings and the supports for the diving boards gleamed and glittered in the summer sunlight. The filtration plant was prominently displayed like a robotic mechanical sculpture: the 'clean machine' which guaranteed the hygiene and purity of the water, aerated by fountains that formed a decorative (as well as functional) feature at one end, or sometimes both ends of the pool. Some municipal baths included facilities for dancing as well as swimming, and these activities were combined in the holiday camps (often built round a spectacular pool) which became popular in Britain during this period. Bravura displays of modern constructional techniques, the many-tiered diving boards often resembled the elaborate structures of the Russian Constructivists, one of whom, Alexander Rodchenko, went on to produce spectacular photographs of young men and women diving into pools during the Stalinist years of the 1930s.[53]

Originally introduced in the early 19th century as part of military training in Prussia, diving had been extensively developed in Sweden and became an Olympic sport in 1904 – after which diving boards attained 'dizzying heights'.[54] The vogue for elaborate diving towers reached a peak between the wars, although since the late 1950s safety regulations have meant that these have largely become defunct, reduced to decorative features or removed. Diving combined water, air and sun, symbolizing man's (and woman's) mastery over space and gravity. It was perhaps no coincidence that it reached its apogee in the era of speed, the 'record', and organized sport: an era when the aeroplane was rapidly being developed both as a weapon of war and as a means of travel, and preparations were already being made for space travel. As well as emulating the 'clean-machine-like' form of the modern stressed-metal-skinned monoplane, swimming and diving gave human beings the sensation of oneness with nature – and of a close kinship with those creatures that were natural aquatic exhibitionists. The keen swimmer and diver in skin-hugging swimsuit and latex diving cap became almost as sleek and projectile-like as penguins or seals as they cleaved the clear blue water: the soft human body apparently adopting the stressed-skin carapace of 'the clean machine'.

While inland pools tended to emphasize the sporting and athletic aspects of swimming, those built beside the sea or mountain lakes aimed to create an atmosphere of leisure and relaxation. The designers of the famous and beautifully equipped Swiss baths sited on the banks of the country's large Alpine lakes in the late 1920s and 1930s devoted special care and attention to landscaping the immediate surroundings of the pools and keeping their modernist concrete-and-glass buildings low, light and airy to blend in with the natural lakeside scenery which patrons could enjoy while swimming or sunbathing. In Vienna, the 19th-century tradition of bathing in the Danube continued into the 20th century. Between 1919 and 1934, the Social Democrat city administration renovated many of the river baths and constructed new swimming pools in heavily crowded working-class areas and in the outer suburbs. Some were indoor pools like the Amalienbad, but many were outdoor summer pools such as the enormous Kongressbad bathing complex designed in 1928 by Erich Leischner, with a 100-metre long Olympic-size swimming pool, separate children's pool, *Zonnenbad* (sunbathing area), and a large café complex set amid sloping lawns shaded by trees.[55] With its long low buildings painted in bright crimson and white (the municipal colours) the Kongressbad advertised (and still advertises) itself in large letters above its main entrance as 'Schwimm- Sonnen- und Luftbad Gemeinde Wien' (Vienna Municipal Swimming, Sun and Air Bath).

Situated along the Alte Donau (Old Danube) – an oxbow arm of the river bypassed in the 19th century to form a long winding lake – were communal bathing establishments like the Angelibad and the Arbeiterstrandbad (Workers' Beach Bath). Here also were the baths of the various unions and professional associations such as the Police Bath, the Tram Drivers' Bath and the Railway Workers' Bath – still in operation today. Several miles up the Danube beyond the small town of Klosterneuburg was the Kritzendorf Strombad (Kritzendorf River Bath), set amid willows on a straight stretch of the river, surrounded by a colony of summerhouses or weekend houses favoured by artists, designers and writers (many of them Jewish).[56] Following the *Anschluss* (union of Austria with Nazi Germany) in 1938, the weekend houses at Kritzendorf belonging to Jewish owners were confiscated and redistributed, many to Nazi party members. After the Second World War, some attempt was made to return these to their surviving original owners or their heirs. But the majority had either emigrated before the war or been murdered by the Nazis, and their houses were sold on to new owners at knockdown prices. Although the central Strombad complex (erected in 1928–29 to replace earlier *ad hoc* structures) and many of the original summerhouses still survive, Kritzendorf has a rather forlorn air today: a sad shadow of its prime when in high summer trains left for the resort every ten minutes from Vienna's Franz-Josef Bahnhof, and crowded steamers brought bathers and holidaymakers up the Danube for a day by the river.

Communal baths

At the German Werkbund exhibition organized by Walter Gropius at the Grand Palais in Paris in the summer of 1930, the main display that greeted visitors as they entered was a full-size mock-up of the interior of a communal apartment designed by Gropius and

Marcel Breuer.[57] This bravura modernist structure of steel-and-glass blocks built round a swimming pool and gymnasium was accompanied by examples of modernist artefacts, and photographs and slides of 'The New Germany'. Reviewing the exhibition in a Swiss newspaper, Sigfried Giedion described how:

> On approaching the exhibit, one's eye is at once caught by the glass walls of a swimming bath and gymnasium. It seems at first sight astonishing to have a swimming bath right in the foreground; but later one realizes that this first impression is thoroughly right, since it at once gives the French a sensation that this exhibit touches on fundamentals [...].[58]

The communal facility of the municipal swimming bath – so potent a modernist architectural phenomenon between the wars – can perhaps be seen as a revival of the cultural tradition of communal bathing as practised by the Greeks and Romans, in Europe during the Middle Ages, and in Islamic and Slavic cultures today. In the final section of *Mechanization Takes Command*, Giedion characterized this as 'total regeneration' bathing, contrasting it with the isolated modern individual who bathes alone and

Kritzendorf Strombad (River Bath), Kritzendorf,
Klosterneuburg, near Vienna, 1928–29, photographed in 2004
Heinz Rollig

in private in the five-foot (1.5-metre) standardized 20th-century bathtub. In the former (where bathing is seen as a regular and total regeneration of body and spirit), Giedion argues that hygiene is combined with rich symbolic and social functions, while in the latter it is reduced to a hygienic routine which the individual performs secretly and privately in the isolation of the bathroom.[59] Some of the most spectacular public swimming baths were built in Giedion's native Switzerland between the wars, and it is curious that he seems not to have regarded these as 'total regeneration' bathing.[60] For they appear much closer to the types of social bathing he describes and admires than the solitary hygienic bathtub installed in the individual home. In *Befreites Wohnen*, Giedion had illustrated the Zurich Strandbad with the caption: 'Today people instinctively demand sunshine, light, mobility. They want to relax in green spaces rather than "city parks".'[61] But two decades later in *Mechanization Takes Command* he comments disdainfully:

> Civic authorities pride themselves when, after many struggles, they have succeeded in wresting a stretch of beach for the recreation of the masses. Establishments of this sort record all the ineptitude and helplessness of our period when faced with the problem of regeneration.

With the ignorance of the city-dwelling sunbather who seeks 'to make up in a few hours, weeks, or months of starvation of sun and air' by leaving 'their bodies to roast in the sun', Giedion contrasts Arnold Rikli's 'prudent dosage of the rays' at his nature-therapy sanatorium in Veldes and those who continued this tradition in Switzerland.[62] As in 'Red Vienna', the socialist municipality in Zurich (known at the time as 'Red Zurich') had taken up the building of swimming baths as part of their electoral campaign in the 1930s, creating an environment where people could enjoy their leisure in healthy and pleasant surroundings while also providing work for the city's unemployed. The radical architects of the Swiss neues Bauen saw the design of open-air swimming baths as one of the most challenging and exciting of new building forms. New structural methods could be combined with the latest 'hygienic' materials and 'clean' machinery and equipment, to produce a social facility that was both formally spectacular and aesthetically satisfying – and immensely popular. While in hindsight Giedion's condemnation of incautious sunbathing may seem medically prudent, his disdain for the attempts of 'the masses' to enjoy fresh air and sunlight can be explained only by his increasing conservativism during the 1930s and 1940s.

Preoccupations with hygiene and cleanliness in the home and leisure facilities were paralleled by concerns with hygiene and cleanliness in the workplace. Pithead baths were built – mostly to modernist designs – between the wars in coal-mining areas of Europe to provide showers and washing facilities for miners when they returned to the surface from their shift at the coalface, and hygienic facilities for storing clean and dirty clothing.[63] Work-based communal baths of this type could be seen to be as much about social bathing and 'total regeneration' as about cleanliness and hygiene. In the, past miners had to return home in their soiled work clothes and wash in portable zinc baths, filled with water from the kitchen range by their wives – or their mothers if they were unmarried. It was customary for the women to wash those parts of the miner's body he could not reach himself. This ritual was deeply rooted in the folk memories of mining communities and has often been represented in literature, for example in Emile Zola's *Germinal* (1884–85) and the novels, plays and short stories of D. H. Lawrence (the son of a miner), and in painted, filmed and photographic representations.[64] For a few decades in the first half of the 20th century the private ritual of washing in a zinc tub in the domestic kitchen was replaced by a communal rite where miners showered together, often washing each other's backs. This came to be regarded by the miners themselves not just as a hygienic process but also as a relaxation from the tensions and dangers of the workplace: a 'safe' masculine space for joking, horseplay and male comradeship – a 'half-way house' between the dangerous male sphere of the mine and their return to the familial space of the home.

Pressure for the provision of pithead baths had originally come not from the miners themselves or their representatives, but from middle-class professionals inspired by a zeal for hygienicist reforms and ideas about 'morality' and social control. The aim was to provide efficient washing facilities so that the miners would not have to walk home unwashed (which was regarded as unseemly and unhygienic), or soil public transport with their dirty clothing, as they began to live further from their work. It was also believed that the provision of pithead baths would relieve women of an unnecessary burden, and 'protect' young children from seeing their fathers or elder brothers bathing naked in the family kitchen. (Most miners lived in 19th-century housing without indoor bathrooms until after the Second World War.) Earlier pithead baths in continental Europe had usually consisted of a large hall with a high ceiling, and showers provided in the wings. The miners' clean 'home' clothes were stored while they were underground (and their dirty work clothes when they were off-shift) by hauling these into the upper part of the hall through a system of hooks and pulleys. But this meant that the miners' wet and dirty work clothes were mixed with their own dry clothes, and was inefficient and unhygienic. In Britain, the Miners' Welfare Commission developed a rationalized system of twin locker rooms, based on Taylorist and Gilbrethian principles.[65] Heated lockers to store and dry wet work clothes were placed on one side of the shower area, and lockers for the miners' home clothes on the other, so that soiled and clean clothes could be kept entirely separate.

The passage of the miners through the baths was like a ritual of cleanliness where they symbolically shed their work personas with their work clothes, passing from the subterranean zone of the pit via the 'waterlock' of the pithead baths to the outside (and above-ground) realm of family and leisure. The baths were a 'clean machine' through which the miners were processed, like the coal they mined. In most pithead baths the water tower – an important functional feature of the building – was given central importance to create an impressive symbolic form: representing the head of water that would cleanse and revive the miners after they had ascended from their subterranean workplace on their way back to home, rest, relaxation and leisure. The importance of natural light was regarded as essential so as to make it easier to keep the bathhouses clean and hygienic, and in order to create an atmosphere of 'health and brightness' in contrast to the subterranean darkness of the miners' workplace. The 'emphasis on health' was an essential element in the design of pithead baths, in the belief that their function was 'not simply to clean and dry miners', but also to 'improve their health and welfare'.[66] This had the additional advantage for the coal owners that miners would be healthier as a result and (hopefully) take fewer days off due to sickness.

The baths also had the effect of introducing miners to a standard of hygiene and comfort they had not known before and could not match in their frequently inadequate and substandard housing, which was often rented from the coal owners. After the end of the Second World War this came to create an expectation of – and later a demand for – proper bathing and washing facilities in the miners' own homes. In its annual report of 1933 the Miners' Welfare Commission argued that: 'We do not feel justified in allowing expenditure on ornament and decoration, but our architects are able to achieve results of architectural worth relying solely upon line and well-proportioned surfaces.'[67] However, this did not mean that the miners wished to replicate this austere hygienic style in their homes, where the choice of decoration and furniture would anyway have largely been left to their wives. With the closing of coal mines throughout Europe in the last decades of the 20th century and the provision of private bathrooms in the homes of the few miners still working, such establishments no longer survive. With the demise of pithead baths (along with the decline of many of the open-air swimming baths of the 1920s and 1930s) 'total regeneration' bathing has increasingly given way to the isolated individual rituals of the private bathroom that Giedion deplored.

10 Washing & watching

In the late 19th and early 20th centuries, the process of washing became intimately connected with that of watching. This was not merely a question of sexual voyeurism, but also of surveillance over the hygiene and cleanliness of others. In 1898, Otto Wagner designed a glass bath for the model interior of a block of low-cost middle-class apartments, one of which he is thought to have occupied himself for a time. Constructed from four rectangular plate-glass panels set in a nickelled-metal frame, the bath was like a huge glass coffin (or gigantic fish tank) in which the bather would have been clearly displayed for inspection by any other member of the household who came into the bathroom: naked and clean – or at least in the process of being washed.[1] The technique of construction was similar to the glass vitrines for displaying china and other objects that Wagner had recently designed. The glass bath was like a vitrine for the display of the naked and cleansed human body: a spectacle of hygiene. It also resembled a glass sarcophagus in which the living (rather than the dead) body was contained and displayed – a 'monument to hygiene', as Paul Asenbaum and Reiner Zettl have argued.[2] Wagner's metal-and-glass bath might be compared with the diamond-shaped metal-and-glass hanging lamps (c. 1900) which Adolf Loos employed in his designs for apartments and shops from the early 1900s to the early 1930s. For Loos, light symbolized both nakedness and cleanliness, and he frequently employed bare light bulbs in his interiors without any shade or bowl. In the early years of the 20th century, the 'indecent nakedness' of buildings such as Loos's Michaelerhaus in central Vienna was linked to the 'scandalous' nudity of the painted and drawn figures of Klimt, Schiele and Kokoschka.[3] In a memorable description, the poet and aesthete Richard Schaukal described Loos's building as a provocatively semi-nude figure. Schaukal saw the 'naked' upper storeys (which housed apartments) emerging from the richly figured marble 'fabric' of the ground floor and mezzanine (which housed Goldman & Salatsch's up-market men's tailoring establishment) as like a nude stepping out of its clothing: 'The naked body of the building rises up from out of the rich robe that appears to have slid from its hips.'[4] In a variation of this image, Loos's pupil – and Ludwig Wittgenstein's future architectural collaborator – Paul Engelmann contrasted the 'tender and virginal' upper part of the building with the luxuriant and lascivious lower part, which he described as 'almost like a harlot'.[5] Loos himself seems to have favoured Raoul Auernheimer's characterization of the upper part of the building as a 'smooth façade' like a 'clean-shaven face'.[6] For Loos, cleanliness and nudity were always closely linked.[7] Yet a caricaturist at the time compared the Michaelerhaus with an open geometric sewer grating.[8]

Like Le Corbusier, Loos considered the plumber the most important agent of civilization and culture. He saw plumbing not merely as the convenient provision of water for washing. It was a cultural symbol, as well as the means to cleanliness and bodily hygiene. For Loos, the plumber was 'the pioneer of cleanliness', 'the state's chief craftsman', the 'quartermaster of civilization'.[9] Writing in 1898, he claimed that there would have been 'no 19th century without the plumber' who had 'become indispensable to us'. He identified plumbing and the plumber with England and America, claiming that Austria and Germany – which in medieval times were at the forefront of hygiene – had now become backward. In the Middle Ages, Germany was 'famous for its water use', the 'great public baths were always crowded', and 'everyone took at least one bath a day'. Loos claimed that 'in the house of the German burgher the bathroom was the most splendid and sumptuous room', while 'the famous bathrooms in the Fugger House in Augsburg' were the 'crowning jewel of the German Renaissance!' But in the late 19th century the Germans and Austrians had fallen behind and become backward compared to the English and Americans, with many middle-class homes still lacking a bathroom:

> An apartment without its own bathroom! In America an impossibility. The idea that at the end of the 19th century there is a country with a population of millions whose inhabitants did not have the opportunity of taking a bath every day would seem outrageous to Americans.[10]

Loos's recollections of his stay in the United States in the mid-1890s were somewhat rose-tinted and unreliable.[11] In 1897, over 90 per cent of the families in the working-class tenement areas of America's four largest cities had no baths, and a contemporary account estimated that the inhabitants bathed on average less than six times a year.[12] Nevertheless, England and America were a useful stick with which to beat the Austrians and Germans for their lack of personal hygiene at the end of the 19th century. (At this period water closets were known and advertised by plumbing contractors in Austria as 'englische Aborte'.) And if not necessarily true at the time, Loos's words were prophetic – because the development of bathroom and lavatory facilities in the United States and England was to take off dramatically in the early decades of the 20th century.

According to Loos, Germans (by which he also meant Austrians and other German-speaking central Europeans) avoided dirt because they disliked washing. He claimed the upper-class German believed that only the working class get dirty and needed to wash, citing a cartoon from the Munich satirical magazine *Die Fliegende*

Blätter where a young boy who has been told by his schoolteacher he should wash daily is reproved by his father with the comment: 'A man must be a filthy swine if he has to wash every day.'[13] By contrast, the (upper-class) Englishman 'is unacquainted with the fear of getting dirty'. Loos quotes 'a great statement' from a novel by Heinrich Laube, one of the radical group of *Junge Deutschland* (Young Germany) writers of the 1830s: 'Germany needs a bath.'[14] Austria and Germany do not need art, Loos argues. First they need a proper culture: the culture of freely flowing water, the culture of the plumber. 'Alongside academies, they should build swimming baths, alongside professors they should appoint swimming-bath attendants.' Twenty years later, the Social Democrat municipal council in Vienna inaugurated a policy of building a series of open-air and indoor swimming pools and hot baths throughout the city, and especially in working-class areas.

A higher standard of hygiene, Loos argued, will produce better art. The state should have an interest in 'increasing the desire for cleanliness' among its people: 'For only *that* people which approaches the English in water use can keep step with them economically; only *that* people which surpasses the English in water use is destined to wrest from them the sovereignty of the world.'[15] The answer to Loos's quasi-rhetorical question is of course the United States: an interesting anticipation of the rise to power of what was to become by the beginning of the 21st century 'the world's only super-power'. Loos's remarks on bathing and his belief that Germany and Austria needed 'a good bath' is reminiscent of F. T. Marinetti's declarations in his early Futurist manifestos that Italy needed to be cleansed and refreshed by a 'bath of blood', a common belief in the late 19th century among Italian irredentists and nationalists (and also among anarchists and socialists of the period). The symbolism of Loos's 'good bath' is itself not wholly innocent, and can be very easily elided into the 'bath of blood' – as it was during the Nazi era in Germany and Austria. The gas chambers at Auschwitz were disguised as showers.

In his views on bathing, water, cleanliness and plumbing, Loos anticipates the obsessions of Le Corbusier, and the discourses of health, cleanliness and purity of the inter-war years central to the international development of modernism. By the first decades of the 20th century, his 1898 assertion that plumbing was the signifier of civilization had become a commonplace among commentators on English and American domestic arrangements. In the early 1900s, Hermann Muthesius praised the plain and utilitarian English bathroom as a model for Germany to adopt: 'Such a modern bathroom is like a piece of scientific apparatus in which ingenious technology celebrates its triumph and any imported "art" can only have a disturbing effect.'

> Here we have an entirely new art that requires no propaganda to win acceptance, an art based on actual modern conditions and modern achievements which perhaps one day, when all the fashions that parade as modern movements in art have passed away, will be regarded as the most eloquent expression of our age.[16]

In America, similar views were promoted. The bathroom was described in *House and Garden* in 1917 as 'an index to civilization': 'Time was when it sufficed for a man to be civilized in his mind. We now require a civilization of the body. And in no line of house building has there been so great progress in recent years as in bathroom civilization.'[17] A promotional booklet published by the Standard Sanitary Manufacturing Company in 1931 declared that 'with one exception, every room in the American home of today has a history that stretches back to feudal times'. That exception was the bathroom: 'This room is modern – it is American.'[18] Such ideas also found a voice in Britain, although by this time it was far behind America in the provision of built-in domestic baths. In a government report on *The Working Class Home: Its Furnishing and Equipment* of 1937, a witness is quoted as declaring that 'the fitted washbasin was the most civilizing influence of which she could think'.[19]

As late as 1948, in *Mechanization Takes Command* (which was first published in the United States), Giedion was claiming the white standardized bathtub as a cultural symbol in terms reminiscent of Loos and Le Corbusier:

> The concise line of this white bathtub will perhaps bear witness to later periods for the outlook of ours as much as the amphora for the outlook of 5th-century Greece. It is a luxury article, which the combination of refined metallurgical and technical skills transformed into a democratic utensil.

Giedion argued that the double-shell standardized white bathtub which in Europe 'still smacks of luxury' stood 'among the symbols of our time'.[20] Many of the ideas developed in detail in *Space, Time and Architecture* and *Mechanization Takes Command* were first formulated during the 1930s when Giedion was working in his native Switzerland, where he was active not only as an architectural historian but also as general secretary of CIAM, promoting modernist architecture and design and running a furniture retailing company, Wohnbedarf. In 1935, he had been one of the organizers of the exhibition 'Das Bad von Heute und Gestern' (The Bath of Today and Yesterday) at the Zurich Kunstgewerbemuseum (Zurich Applied Art Museum) and designed the historical section.[21] Much of the research on baths and bathing that Giedion later incorporated into *Mechanization Takes Command* dates from this period.[22]

In the United States, standards in the provision of washing and sanitary facilities in middle-class housing had been set by hotels, where large establishments first introduced rooms with en-suite bathrooms and WCs from about 1870.[23] Even in the early decades of the 20th century most European hotels still only provided washbasins with hot and cold running water in each room, and a communal bathroom at the end of the corridor. Notable exceptions were the hotels of the Côte d'Azur,[24] where the new practices of prolonged exposure of the naked or semi-naked body to sunlight were matched by the provision of proper hygienic facilities for washing and purifying bodies darkened by the sun. The carefully washed and cleansed sunburnt bodies of the middle and upper classes distinguished them from the dark but unwashed bodies of peasants who had acquired their suntans through their work and going about their everyday lives. Only after the First World War did bathrooms cease to be luxuries. In the United States between 1921 and 1924 the number of households with bathrooms doubled. By the late 1920s, 71 per cent of urban and 33 per cent of rural households had installed bathrooms, and by 1934 89 per cent of housing units in New York City had a bath or shower.[25] The majority of well-to-do European middle-class dwellings had begun to be equipped with at least one bathroom with running water from the beginning of the 20th century.[26] As a novel facility in the majority of households the bathroom constituted a new kind of room, without a pre-history. (In the past, portable baths would have been set up in the dressing room, living room, or kitchen – depending on the class of the bather.) Modernists believed that this meant that the bathroom could be designed without preconceptions. The enforced plainness of mass-produced porcelain and cast-iron ware and the increasing obsession with hygiene meant that the bathroom could be a quasi-functional 'pure' undecorated space: a 'hospital within the home'. This would later (they hoped) set a model for other parts of the house or apartment, becoming 'the laboratory' from which 'the modernization of the rest of the home would eventually follow'.[27]

The one-piece double-shelled enamelled-steel bath had been introduced in the United States around the time of the First World War, and mass production began in the 1920s. The 5-foot norm became standard in the United States and England.[28] Owing to lack of space, baths were frequently much smaller in continental Europe. This was often a half-length *Sitzbad* (sit-up bath) of thick white porcelain-ware with a ledge on which the bather sat while bathing, usually combined with a shower fitment – like the extremely compact 'Belco Camera Bad', included in the *Frankfurter Register*. To cut costs and space in the Frankfurt estates a special model bathroom was designed, known as the Frankfurt Bathroom. Although less well known than the Frankfurt Kitchen, this tiny unit was exemplary: with a washbasin, a toilet and a combination shower and *Sitzbad* fitted into an extraordinarily small space of 1.7 by 1.5 metres.[29] The components could be combined in different configurations and were installed in many Frankfurt houses and apartments. 'The smallest bath in the smallest space' and 'a bath for every dwelling' were the slogans used to promote the units.[30] Most of the dwellings built by the neue Frankfurt had fitted bathrooms, with the notable exception of the Mammolshainer Strasse estate for the homeless, where communal baths were provided instead, along with communal kitchens. Many of the bathrooms of the model dwellings at Weissenhof were fitted with pairs of basins so that two members of the family could wash at the same time. Some modernist bathrooms were fitted with three basins, the third being placed over the end of the bath – useful if all members of the family were getting up and going out at the same time, and perhaps coming close in a small way to Giedion's ideal of communal ablution. At the insistence of Truus Schröder, Gerrit Rietveld equipped the Schröder House (1924) with small washbasins in each room or partionable space.

Frankfurt Bathroom,
as shown in the
Frankfurter Register,
late 1920s
Ferdinand Kramer and
Karl Gutmann

It was not possible to make such generous hygienic provision in social housing for the working classes in most European countries, although providing proper facilities for personal hygiene – ideally baths or showers, and at least separate lavatories for each household – were among the main aims of architects and housing officials between the wars. Of equal importance was the provision of adequate facilities for washing and drying clothes both in single-family houses and in apartment blocks, where communal drying rooms were usually situated on the top floor – as in Mies van der Rohe's Weissenhof block. The provision of individual bathrooms or showers for each household became standard practice in newly built social housing during the 1920s in some (but by no means all) western European countries. Although legislation on the provision of baths in all new municipal housing in England dates from 1919, a bath or shower was not made compulsory in new housing until as late as 1965 in The Netherlands.[31] In his first designs for the Kiefhoek estate in Rotterdam (1925–30), which consisted of rows of single-family houses for large families of up to eight people (typically, two parents and six children of different sexes), J. J. P. Oud had included a shower under the stairs, with running water on the first floor. But cost restrictions forced him to omit these in the final designs, providing only an inside WC and running water downstairs. In an article about the estate published in the English art-and-design magazine the *Studio* in 1931, Oud wrote that it was 'highly desirable that the margin of costs should be increased, to allow of these being included, on the score of the great importance of health and cleanliness'.[32]

In many central European countries, such as Austria, individual bathrooms were not provided in newly built social housing between the wars – only separate WCs with washing facilities in the scullery, or *Waschküche* (laundry room: literally 'wash kitchen'). This was itself a considerable advance on earlier tenement buildings, where communal WCs were grouped together on each floor at the back of the building by the light well. In the 'superblocks' constructed in Vienna by the Social Democrats from the mid-1920s to the early 1930s, the individual WCs in each apartment were generally located at the front of the building, with their small windows arranged together on the façade so as to be clearly visible from the street. In one block designed by the Secessionist architect Josef Hoffmann, the windows were in the shape of portholes. This signalled their function and symbolism (and association with water) on the stripped austere façade of Hoffmann's building even more clearly than the customary small rectangular windows.[33] The display of lavatory windows on the façades of the Vienna *Gemeindebauten* (municipal housing) was considered an object of civic and individual pride by the city authorities, and by many of the tenants. They were also the 'butt' of scatological comments and jokes, particularly from those opposed to the Social Democrat administration – and rumoured to be covert gun emplacements in the event of proletarian revolution.[34]

While the Vienna municipal apartments lacked their own bathrooms, there was sometimes a built-in washtub in which either clothes or people could be washed. Or occasionally even a plumbed-in bath in the kitchen or scullery with a wooden lid so that it could double as a table or work surface when not in use. In the largest of the *Gemeindebauten*, centrally located communal baths and laundries were provided, along with shops, public libraries and kindergartens – communal services which were also a source of considerable civic pride. In addition to such facilities within the superblocks themselves and the outdoor swimming baths in the inner suburbs and on the outskirts of the city described in the last chapter, the Vienna municipal council built a number of enormous indoor bathing and swimming complexes, some of which even outdid the superblocks in splendour. The most famous and grandest is the Amalienbad (1923–26), which has been described as a 'stone manifesto' of the Social Democrats' endeavours 'to raise public hygiene awareness': a public monument which would 'promote the health and wellbeing of the working classes'.[35] Designed by Otto Nadel and Karl Schmalhofer to accommodate 1,300 people at a time, the baths were the largest in Europe: 'a veritable cathedral of hygiene and the cult of the body'.[36] Laid out like a Roman bath, the complex provided hot baths, steam and therapeutic baths, and a huge heated swimming pool in the shape of a basilica, with a ten-metre high diving board and a vast sliding glass roof which could be opened in warm weather – all sumptuously decorated with ornamental ceramic tiles. Two storeys of galleries around the bath housed the changing

Amalienbad, Vienna, 1923–26,
photographed in 2005

Otto Nadel and Karl Schmalhofer

booths, and there was a restaurant and a hairdressing salon. At the centre of the bath complex was a huge water column with a clock indicating *die neue Zeit*: the 'new time' of social-democratic paternalism.[37] It was as if the municipal authorities had taken heed of Loos's exhortation of over twenty-five years earlier to build swimming baths in addition to academies – and appoint swimming-bath attendants as well as professors.[38]

Nevertheless, Loos continued to criticize the Vienna municipal authorities, with whom he had fallen out after many bureaucratic frustrations encountered while working as chief architect of one of the settler's organizations in the early 1920s.[39] In 1930, he attacked 'the new tenements built by the city council which have no running hot water, no central heating or bathrooms'.[40] Loos argued that the city housing authorities should have tried to provide more than minimal sanitary and hygienic facilities in the outwardly grandiose and sometimes luxuriously ornamented apartment blocks they had been building in Vienna since the early 1920s.

Pilotis & plumbing

One of the main reasons the first skyscrapers were constructed in Chicago in the 1880s was to raise the business quarter of The Loop above the insanitary marshes and sewers of the hinterland of Lake Michigan. Soon Chicago architects were building tall apartment blocks as well as offices. While raising office workers and apartment dwellers above the insanitary street level, these buildings also had to be equipped with 'sanitary fittings' (including garbage disposal as well as plumbing) to drain off the filth, waste water and excrement produced by the vast numbers of people who used them. In Giedion's words: 'the skyscrapers and their sanitary equipment grew up together.'[41] It was no coincidence that Chicago should have indulged in the hygienist fantasy of 'The White City', the ephemeral display of white plaster constructions surrounded by water and fountains at the Chicago Columbian Centenary Exposition of 1893, which Adolf Loos had visited on his trip to the United States. Although impressed by the early American skyscrapers of Chicago and New York, most European modernists rejected their vertical configuration and extolled the virtues of the horizontal, emphasizing the quality of appearing to 'hover' above the ground as one of the key elements of the new architecture, as if fearing direct contact with the surface of the earth. However, Le Corbusier's early obsession with the tall building, and his impassioned championing of the piloti – the reinforced-concrete columns which could raise a building visibly, structurally and symbolically above the level of the ground – seems essentially to have been a desire to lift the ideal human habitation above the shit, detritus and bacteria of the early 20th-century city. (He referred to 'tubercular Paris'.)[42] The pilotis on which his Villa Savoye (1928–31) is raised resemble the down pipes of a drainage system that voids filth and excrement away from the house into the earth, leaving the upper floors in a pristine state of cleanliness.[43] Pilotis served to make visually apparent the actual separation between the corrupted and poisoned earth of the city and the pure fresh air and sunlight of the atmosphere above it. They also enabled a detached 'gaze from above'. Raised on pilotis above the field in which it was built, the Villa Savoye resembles a giraffe-like 'seeing machine' perched high above the sordid everyday world at ground level.[44]

Among the most distinctive features of the interior of the Villa Savoye is a freestanding washbasin, placed in the middle of the entrance vestibule as if guarding the threshold. Rising like a porcelain column from the floor, the washbasin announces its function both symbolically and literally: to wash away the corruption and contagion at ground level before the inhabitants or guests ascend the stairs or ramp to the living areas on the first floor. The freestanding washbasin is a symbol of a higher spiritual hygiene, and has been compared to a statue or fountain in a Renaissance vestibule or 'nymphaeum'. Its presence commands visitors – like a manual of hygiene and household management – to wash away the pollution of the ground, and the city from which they have arrived, before ascending to the raised living areas that are physically removed from the contamination below. (The Villa Savoye was designed as a weekend or vacation house, within easy motoring distance from Paris.) It also symbolically commands the visitor to wash the filth of the city from their eyes as well as their hands.[45] Arguing that the vestibule is 'a place of ritual purification, the equivalent of a holy-water stoop', the architectural theorist Colin Rowe has observed that 'any details which one might associate with the act of washing (towels and soap) are conspicuously absent and would surely damage the pristine impact of this very obsessive little statement'.[46] While this is true of the carefully arranged contemporary photographs Le Corbusier had taken of the villa, towel and soap might well have been present when no photographer was around. In one of the early photographs of the entrance hall of the Villa Savoye, a vase of flowers can be seen placed on the plain hall table attached to one of the pilotis. Flowers and plants as 'real' – rather than representational elements – were one of the few forms of ornament or decoration admitted into the modernist interior, and their placing and care was regarded as of crucial importance. At Robert Mallet-Stevens's villa for the De Noailles at Hyères, Theo van Doesburg was commissioned to design a small flower-arranging room for Marie-Laure de Noailles to cut and arrange flowers.[47] The washbasin at the Villa Savoye may have served a similar function for Madame Savoye or one of her servants to cut and arrange the flowers that guests brought for her as they arrived by car from Paris.

Characteristically, Le Corbusier chose an *objet-type* for the 'nymphaeum' of the villa – a standardized off-the-peg porcelain washbasin equipped with hot and cold taps. Such a functional 'found object' was equipped to serve more than one purpose: to provide water for arranging flowers perhaps, as well as the ritual purification of washing hands (and the symbolic washing of eyes). Rowe argues that there was always the greatest anxiety for Le Corbusier positively to 'celebrate the triumph of running water', citing the bidet illustrated at the head of the chapter 'Other Icons: The Museums' in *L'Art décoratif d'aujourd'hui* (The Decorative Art of Today).[48] Le Corbusier also placed a bidet next to the marital bed in the apartment in Paris at rue Nungesser et Coli which he designed for himself and his wife, who is said to have concealed it beneath a knitted cover.[49] Le Corbusier's bidet has sometimes been compared with Marcel Duchamp's *Fountain*: an upturned urinal signed 'R. Mutt', submitted for an exhibition of the American Society of Independent Artists in New York in 1917. A work of art that only has any meaning in the context of early 20th-century obsessions with whiteness and hygiene, Duchamp's *objet trouvé* was intended to be as transgressive as Le Corbusier's *objet-type* (the bidet) was supposed to be reassuring. In a kind of parody of Loos's views on American plumbing, Duchamp once declared that: 'The only works of art America has given are her plumbing and her bridges.'[50] *Fountain* was never displayed publicly in the 1917 exhibition, but remained hidden behind a partition so visitors could not see it.[51] In the only photograph that exists of the original, taken by Alfred Stieglitz, the urinal is hung upside down. The dark gaping hole where the flush pipe would normally be connected to the plumbing system appears as if about to pour urine onto the floor.[52] The hygienic apparatus whereby the (male) body's waste fluid is carefully caught in a white porcelain tray and flushed out of sight is represented as cut off from the essential circulation of water. Like the human body itself, its pure white porcelain form *leaks* and has become an object of abjection.[53] The Villa Savoye went through an abject period of neglect after the Second World War. The French architect Bernard Tschumi has described the villa at this period, derelict: 'the squalid walls of the small service rooms on the ground floor, stinking of urine, smeared with excrement, and covered with obscene graffiti'.[54]

Around 1927, the Dutch photographer Paul Citroen (who studied at the Bauhaus) photographed the WC of the Rietveld Schröder House in Utrecht. Rather than represented as a symbolic site of purity and hygiene, the lavatory of this iconic modernist house is shown as rather grubby and well used – jolting our expectations and calling to mind Duchamp's *Fountain*. The seat is missing and a roll of toilet paper lies casually as if left after use beside the lavatory bowl, which is fitted sideways, perhaps to make it easier for Schröder's children to use. It is difficult to know quite how to interpret this apparently unposed photograph of a WC that has clearly been given good use by a family with three young children. Is it a deconstructive gesture, questioning and mocking the hygienicist tenets of modernism, or is it a 'realistic' representation of 'the way things are' in an imperfect world? Either way, it remains a compelling and somewhat mysterious image, perhaps unique in the documents of modernist architecture and design.[55] It also signals the differences between the two houses. Where the Villa Savoye hovers ethereally above the ground, a pristine classical form raised hygienically and spiritually on its pilotis above the fields, the Schröder House is firmly sited in the heavy soil of the Dutch polders. (Rietveld once described the liminal edge-of-city site where the Schröder House was to be built as 'somewhere where one would go to have a piss'.)[56] The one a weekend retreat for the Savoyes to escape the heat, tedium and filth of the city, the other a family house for a widow with three children sited at the earthy interface between city and countryside.

In the Hildebrand House in Blaricum, which Rietveld designed in 1935, there is a WC off the main ground-floor entrance hall. As was normal practice at the time there are no washing facilities inside the WC, but there is a standard washbasin in the entrance hall fitted under the window which looks out across the spacious front garden, the front drive, and the trees that separate the garden from the neighbouring houses. The positioning of the basin directly below the window signifies even more clearly than the free-standing basin in the vestibule of the Villa Savoye that it is eyes as much as hands that are being cleansed. Yet as always with Rietveld's designs, function and ritual are closely interlocked. (An unexecuted design for a holiday house for himself and his family on a slope overlooking a river has a single living and sleeping area with a circular washbasin forming its central focal and functional point.)[57] In his single-family house at Weissenhof, Le Corbusier also placed a washbasin in a vestibule. This was not freestanding as in the Villa Savoye, but sited against a wall adjacent to (but outside) a downstairs WC, like that in Rietveld's Hildebrand House. As described earlier, Le Corbusier apparently miscalculated the fall of the land on the site, so that the entrance to the house had to be rerouted through the boiler room in the basement. Thus not by design but by serendipity, washbasin and central-heating boiler stand guard over the vestibule – the *lars* and *penates* of the clean modernist 'machine for living in'.

Electrical wiring as well as plumbing was frequently displayed in the modernist buildings of the late 1920s and early 1930s, some decades before the deliberate exposure of services in late 20th-century 'high-tech' architecture (often known as 'bowelism'). Adolf Rading had run the plumbing and electrical wiring along the inside surfaces of the walls and ceilings of his Weissenhof house with no attempt to mask or conceal them.[58] Like architects seventy years later, Rading painted the pipes in bright colours and mounted the wiring on wooden brackets so that it stood several centimetres proud of the walls. The effect must have been a little like the transparent figure at the Hygiene-Museum, Dresden, with its web of veins, nerves and bowels. The critic Edgar Wedepohl commented sarcastically that the effect was both 'positively ornamental' and 'rather like varicose veins'. Arguing that it 'certainly does not make the house any simpler to keep clean' – i.e. it was 'unhygienic' – he wondered whether 'the obtrusive colouring of the gas, water and heating pipes actually does anything to make the house more like a home'.[59] With subtler irony, Kurt Schwitters claimed that 'Rading has built his entire house for the sake of the electrical wiring' which 'really does look terrific', adding: 'I hope the idea will catch on; then we shall soon have in our own houses those beautiful overhead wires that so pleasantly adorn the urban scene.'[60] In his Törten Siedlung social housing in Dessau (still under construction when the Weissenhof exhibition opened), Walter Gropius incorporated the 'beautiful overhead wires' of electricity pylons into the townscaping of the estate.

From the beginning of the 20th century, modernist architects and designers had regarded plumbing fixtures as a model for their designs. Loos and Le Corbusier had extolled bathroom fittings as '*objets-types*': the gradually evolved product of a line of anonymous designers. In his review of the Weissenhofsiedlung, Siegfried Kracauer (who had trained and practised as an architect in Berlin) argued that architecture had now finally caught up with plumbing. At last it had found the same level of 'quality' as the design of modern bathroom fittings: 'The precise little tap, which was far ahead of the world it was made for, now finds houses that live up to it; and bathtubs no longer put dining rooms to shame.'[61] Of Mies van der Rohe's block of apartments, which had been built with a steel-frame – known in German as *skeletonbau* or 'skeleton construction' – Kracauer commented: 'Hygiene; no fuss. A skeleton, thin and agile like a person in sport shirt and slacks.'[62] A similar image of stripped-down skeletal sportiness was suggested by the new tubular-metal furniture. Evoking the hospital and the sanatorium, and the functional and hygienic qualities of mobility and ease of cleaning, placed in the interior of the modernist house this furniture also served as an emblematic incorporation of abstracted signs for the human body and the circulation of body fluids. In contemporary architectural photographs of modernist interiors of the late 1920s and early 1930s, tubular-steel furniture frequently acts as a substitute (a 'sit in' rather than a 'stand in') for the human body, representing it in schematic and abstracted form. In the modernist interior, plumbing also functioned as a metaphor for the alimentary system and the circulation of the blood. The snaking iron or copper pipes and gleaming chromed taps were emblems of the process of circulation. (Water was the 'life blood' of the modern(ist) house.)

The chrome-plated piping of tubular-steel furniture was like a symbolic representation of the plumbing systems that serviced the modernist house and kept it clean and hygienic. Chrome plating was liberally used in bathrooms for taps, spouts and handles – the visible parts of the plumbing that were in direct contact with (or in close proximity to) the human body. Because designers such as Stam and Rietveld did not have access to pipe-bending equipment, the early prototypes of their tubular-steel furniture were made from water or gas piping, using plumber's 'elbow joints' to join straight lengths of pipe. These looked clumsy and awkward, qualities that these two Dutch designers consciously exploited in their furniture designs. By contrast, later more developed models were manufactured with sophisticated industrial equipment, elegantly curved and sleekly chromed. (Stam dismissed the more extravagant and baroque of these as 'steel macaroni monsters'.) They gleamingly evoked the flow of water through the pipes of the domestic plumbing systems, promising assurance of the cleanliness and hygiene of the modern home. Their smooth glinting sophistication was a metaphoric substitute for the plumbing that so often failed to function satisfactorily in the modernist house.[63]

White wash

Water and whiteness were closely linked in late 19th-century and early 20th-century discourses about hygiene and health. Where water represented circulation and the washing away of dirt and germs, whiteness was identified with the pristine surfaces washed by the flow of water – rendered pure, clean, 'as new'. The commonest form of applying white paint to an exterior or interior surface until the middle of the 20th century was whitewash. The name is significant: white symbolically washes clean what it covers. Yet whitewash actually obliterates what it covers up. In this sense its qualities are the opposite of water, which is transparent (although of course it can also be reflective). In the chapter in *L'Art décoratif d'aujourd'hui* (The Decorative Art of Today) entitled 'A Coat of Whitewash: The Law of Ripolin', Le Corbusier argued that white is like a *tabula rasa* against which can be set the apparatus of the new life, the new way of living.[64] Unlike coloured paint or unpainted woodwork, a white-painted or white-tiled surface exposed the dirt and demanded to be wiped clean. Loos wrote in 1898: 'Instead of cladding the bathtub in white tiles, people in Austria prefer coloured ones, in order to hide the dirt, a manufacturer [...] naively assured me. Instead of being enamelled in white, the only suitable colour, tin tubs too are also covered in dark enamel.'[65]

Loos not only had the bathrooms he designed painted white, but also living rooms and bedrooms.[66] In 1903, he designed an all-white bedroom for his young first wife, the actress Lina Obertimpfler, in their apartment in central Vienna.[67] The bedroom was dominated by a low double bed consisting of two mattresses placed directly on the floor, one on top of the other, like a dais or altar.[68] The top mattress was covered with a white bedspread which seems to merge into the thick white angora rug that covers the lower mattress and part of the floor. The walls were painted white and the bed surrounded by white cambric curtains hung from a metal or wooden framework, which also ran in front of the windows and behind the dressing table, like the curtains that screen off beds in a hospital ward.[69] With its evocation of hospitals or sanatoriums, this undoubtedly alluded to hygiene, as well as to purity and holiness, sexuality and death. In the 19th century, tuberculosis was known as 'the White Death' from the pale complexion of those who suffered from the disease, and 'because of its long association with childhood, innocence and even holiness'. It was also (paradoxically) identified with febrile sexual desire and sexual activity.[70] In *L'Art décoratif d'aujourd'hui* Le Corbusier too associates white with hygiene and young women. He fantasizes about an idealized 'shop girl' immune to fashion and the taste for cheap ornament of her peers, who (he speculates) might decorate her room by painting it white. She would furnish this with a mass-produced wicker armchair or Thonet bentwood chair and a reproduction table, 'in the manner of Louis XIII' from the Bazaar de l'Hôtel de Ville. These would be painted with white Ripolin, rather as Mondrian applied a coat of white paint to the cheap second-hand furniture in his Paris studio to disguise any ornamental features and make it 'disappear' visually. In addition, Le Corbusier decreed that his shop girl is to have a 'good well-polished lamp', 'crockery or white porcelain', and 'three tulips in a vase' on the table.[71] (Mondrian went even further, and painted his tulips white.) As discussed earlier, the early white-walled villas of Loos were perceived as shockingly naked by contemporary commentators, in the same ways that the nude drawings and paintings of Gustav Klimt, Egon Schiele and Oskar Kokoschka were considered to be shocking at the time.[72] Just as tubular-steel furniture came to be identified with the smooth slim limbs of athletic young girls, the white modernist wall evoked the naked (female) body sunning itself on the terraces and verandas of the modernist house, although such associations between sexuality and the white wall were generally implied rather than made explicit. An exception to this were the surrealist photomontages of Karel Teige, where photographs of the nude or semi-nude bodies of young women were collaged onto photographs of white-walled modernist buildings such as Oud's Hook of Holland housing and Lurçat's Villa Guggenbühl in Paris.[73]

By the late 1920s and early 1930s, white had become the fashionable colour (or 'non colour' as Mondrian called it). In an article, 'Weiss, alles weiss' (White, Everything White) published in the Werkbund magazine *Die Form* in 1930, J. E. Hammann claimed that white 'gives our time its distinctive and clear colour note'.[74] Through their writings and by example since 1917 or 1918, Mondrian, Van Doesburg, and other artists and designers associated with De Stijl had promoted the use of pure colour in combination with the 'non colours' white, black and grey in painting, architecture and design. Largely through their influence and example, in the early 1920s pure (and often primary) colour had been employed extensively by modernist architects and designers, including those who taught or studied at the Bauhaus, and independent (although influential) architects such as Bruno Taut. This had been succeeded from the mid-1920s by an increasing tendency towards the use of neutral tones of grey, and pastel or ochre colours – but especially white – in place of primary colours, which were now considered brash and outdated. In 1926, Oskar Schlemmer had helped organize 'The White Festival' in Gropius's new Bauhaus building at Dessau, which was 'four-fifths white and one-fifth colour' (red, blue and yellow).[75] Disappointed at the reception of the designs for the Aubette (1926–28) – a huge leisure complex in Strasbourg he had decorated with a spectacular series of brightly coloured abstract wall-paintings in collaboration with Sophie Taeuber-Arp and Hans Arp – Van Doesburg envisioned a pure-white display space that would be the opposite of the dynamic brightly coloured rooms of the Aubette:

> The space, containing autonomous sculptures and objects of great abstract reality, will only be visible from a gallery. Free baths will enable people to cleanse themselves of all filth, and identical colourless cloaks obtainable in the cloakroom will eliminate all annoying distinctions in attire. Visitors will be supplied with felt slippers, so that there will be no irritating footsteps.[76]

Van Doesburg's idea of a hygienic white gallery space is close to the pure-white space he was to advocate two years later for the artist's studio (discussed in Chapter 3). In the manifesto 'Towards white painting' (1929), published in April 1930 in *Art Concret* – the first and only issue of the new magazine Van Doesburg edited to promote his post-De Stijl ideas – he describes white as 'the spiritual colour of our times, the clarity that directs all our actions', arguing that it was 'the colour of the new era' of 'perfection, purity and certainty'. For Van Doesburg, white 'includes everything'. It is the purity that raises human beings above the material world of dirt and excrement.[77] His rejection of colour for the purity of white may have been related to his own acute medical condition at the time, but it paralleled shifts in architectural fashion at the end of the 1920s and the beginning of the 1930s.

Perhaps more than any other characteristic (the flat roof, the sun terrace, the wide window) whiteness and the white wall have become associated with modernist architecture – often referred to as 'white architecture', although by no means all of it was white. The association was reinforced by the high-quality reproduction of black-and-white photography in books and periodicals, which attained a technical peak in the years between the two world wars through the four-tone photogravure process. This emphasized (and sometimes falsified) the whiteness of the modernist architecture it was employed to reproduce. Although white was employed extensively in modern architecture in the 1920s and 1930s, its use was not as universal as modernist propagandists and historians (or contemporary photographs of modernist buildings) might lead one to believe. The crisply reproduced black-and-white photography of the period exaggerated the extent to which white walls were ubiquitous by reducing the subtle colour washes, greys and off whites often employed by modernist architects and designers to a bleached-out dazzling white. In an article published in the *Architectural Review* shortly after the Second World War, the artist and printmaker Michael Rothenstein pointed out that the sophisticated techniques developed between the wars for reproducing black-and-white architectural photographs had effectively eliminated colour from modern architecture. He argued this had been achieved through the monochromatic photographic representation of a distorted view of early 20th-century modernism, while at the same time prolonging this distortion by example.[78]

The photograph Sigfried Giedion had used for the cover of *Befreites Wohnen* gave the impression of brilliant sunlight streaming through the sliding windows of Max Ernst Haefeli's Rotach houses, limpidly rendered in black and white. In reality, the interior walls of Haefeli's houses were an 'indoor explosion of colour', with walls painted in 'radiant yellows, greens and oranges'.[79] The exteriors of many of the houses and apartment blocks at Weissenhof were painted in pale pastel colours. However, this was not apparent from black-and-white photographs taken at the time, the recycling of which in art-historical texts continues to confirm the impression that this demonstration piece of inter-war modernist architecture was painted white or off white.[80] The name of the

Siedlung no doubt helped further to identify the white wall with modernist architecture, although it was actually called after Philip and Sebastian Weiss, two baker brothers who once lived on the land where the estate was built.[81] As artistic director of the Weissenhofsiedlung Mies van der Rohe was undoubtedly aware that by specifying pastel-coloured or off-white walls the estate would appear a unified white when reproduced in black-and-white.[82] In the contemporary photographs and collective memories of the period, Weissenhof has assumed a permanent aura of austere whites and off whites. The bleached-out tints of the exteriors of the houses and apartment buildings as represented through black-and-white photography helped to create an overall sense of unity. Together with the ubiquitous flat roofs and sun terraces, this served to give the estate the 'Mediterranean' aspect so often remarked on by critics both sympathetic and hostile.[83]

Not all modernist architects and designers, however, welcomed the homogenous white coat with which modernism came to be associated in the late 1920s and early 1930s. In 1930, Bruno Taut, whose small house at Weissenhof had been painted in De Stijl-like primary colours (much to the scorn and mirth of the younger and more fashion-conscious architects), complained that white had 'become the password [...] the fortune bearer of the perfectly functional architect'.[84] Many leftist and socially conscious architects rejected the dogma of the pure-white wall, which they considered to be an aestheticized or formalist fad. Hannes Meyer argued that it was necessary to 'avoid a pure white finish for the house'.[85] As director of the Bauhaus from 1928 to 1930, Meyer encouraged the development of a series of austerely decorative Bauhaus wall-papers in muted tones and colours, which were commercially manufactured and marketed by a Hanover firm at moderate cost.[86] He believed these would satisfy a natural desire for decoration, while realizing the ideal of 'hygiene in the worker's home' as effectively as the modernist white wall.[87] Rather than facing the exteriors of his buildings with white-painted concrete (or plaster painted to look like concrete), Meyer employed brick, a standardized material that was tried and long lasting, although not 'new' – and therefore condemned by most modernists.[88] Meyer was a keen advocate of modern materials in architecture but nevertheless believed that tried and established means were appropriate if they best fulfilled the required function, and that these should not be disguised by plaster or coats of white paint.

The association of white with hygiene and purity in modernist architecture and design was not merely a matter of fashion. It cannot be separated from ideas about racial difference and white superiority that characterized the final years of European colonial domination. In 1919, Adolf Behne had identified a racialist element in the distaste for colour among the fashionable European middle classes, claiming sarcastically that 'colourlessness is the mark of education, white like the European's skin!' Behne claimed: 'Civilized people of our climes look down on chromatic art and chromatic architecture as they look down on coloured human bodies – with a kind of horrified shudder.'[89] Preoccupations with health, hygiene and cleanliness first emerged at a time when the dominant white races were differentiating themselves by social and cultural means from people of colour.[90]

In the second half of the 19th century, notions of hygiene had become a way of separating one race (or one class) from another, or of distinguishing sub-groups within a class system.[91] The ways in which modernist artists, architects and designers employed white in their work between the world wars must be seen in the context of an era when European colonial power was still dominant, although on the verge of the decline and collapse that took place after the Second World War. In modernist art, architecture and design, white and whiteness were employed in an awareness of white's corollary (and obverse) black. For Le Corbusier – as for many intellectuals of his generation – the celebration of white was combined with the exoticist (and erotic) fascination with the black skin of the African or the African-American, and with notions of the nobility, truth and honesty of the 'primitive'.[92] White was both 'primitive' and 'modern', as was its antithesis black, which Le Corbusier equated with 'primitive' nobility. Black and white 'frame' each other by their extreme tonal contrast, as demonstrated in the black-and-white ciné and still photography of the period. (The film historian Richard Dyer has argued in his thought-provoking study of early cinema, *White*, that the medium of film – predominantly black-and-white in its early days – was particularly attuned to privilege the representation of the white skin, and to disadvantage the black.)[93]

In 1927, Adolf Loos made his well-known designs for a house in Paris for the African-American singer and entertainer Josephine Baker, centred around a spectacular indoor swimming pool. Here Loos allowed his obsessions with plumbing and water full reign. However, the exact status of the project is unclear. The design appears to have been something of a fantasy project for Loos, who met Baker while he was living and working in Paris during the mid-1920s, and became obsessed with her.[94] Baker had come to France with the *Revue Nègre* in 1925 and was to remain there for the rest of her life.[95] She had previously lived in an apartment with an indoor swimming pool in the Champs Elysée (where she had been set up in 1926 by her then lover Marcel Ballot) – and was also in the habit of unabashedly receiving visitors in her bath. Loos was thirty-three years older than Baker and there seems to have been no overt sexual relationship between the two, although Le Corbusier (seventeen years his junior) is believed to have had an affair with her on a transatlantic liner at around this time.[96] Baker was apparently flattered by Loos's interest, but there seems to have been no commission as such, and it is not even certain whether he showed her the plans or model.[97] Shortly afterwards, Baker revealed her taste in architecture to be somewhat different, buying an eclectic-style 19th-century chateau in the Paris suburbs in 1929 where she lived until 1947. However, Loos considered the design to be one of his best projects, exhibiting a model of it in the retrospective of his work that celebrated his sixtieth birthday in 1930.[98]

In recent years, the Baker House has received considerable attention in the light of late 20th-century critical preoccupations with issues of race and gender.[99] Loos's views were probably no more (nor less) racist than those of the majority of the European intellectuals and artists born in the early 1870s who were his contemporaries, such as Piet Mondrian whom both Loos and Baker knew in Paris. Loos's fascination with Baker might be compared with Mondrian's enthusiasm for jazz and popular dances such as the Charleston.[100] Loos also learned the Charleston, apparently taught by Baker herself who – he claimed – considered him one of its best exponents in Paris.[101] The project for Baker's house linked two properties the singer already owned on a corner site at the junction of two streets. It had a flat roof with skylights above the swimming pool and a distinctive round tower rising over the entrance.[102] The private areas of the house were situated on the top floor; underneath was a social area or 'club' for professional entertaining with large and small *salons*, and a small circular café in the tower. The garage and services were on the ground floor. The swimming pool was on the top floor, around which the two bedrooms, dining room and a small circular sitting room were located. Only Baker and her personal friends and guests would have had physical access to it, but the volume of water extended down through the more public areas below. A series of thick water-resistant windows were located under the surface of the pool in the tunnel-like corridors connecting the two *salons*. Through these anyone using the pool could be observed 'swimming and diving in its crystal-clear water, flooded with light from above', like fish or sea mammals in an aquarium, or 'an underwater revue', according to Kurt Unger, Loos's assistant on the project.[103]

With its 'supernatural light effects', Loos apparently considered the pool as the most beautiful space in the house.[104] The centring of the house around it clearly relates the project to contemporary preoccupations with health, hygiene, cleanliness and water – and also with sexuality. Most recent critics have seen the project as embodying a voyeuristic desire to watch Baker through the underwater windows as she swam naked or semi-naked in the pool, maintaining that in Loos's design she was to be 'staged' swimming in her own pool for the delectation of her guests.[105] Yet Baker herself might also have gazed back at her guests as they peered at her through the glass windows, or watched them as *they* swam in the pool.[106] The house is a fantasy in which anxieties about race, gender, health and hygiene are played out in the context of Baker's role as a contemporary icon of black femininity and 'primitive' sexuality.

In Loos's design, the L-shaped façade of Baker's house was to be faced with plates of marble in alternating horizontal black-and-white stripes.[107] Some critics have seen this as directly evoking an image of Africa – the stripes of a zebra, or the strong pattern of light and shade in the forest or jungle.[108] (Although he never went to sub-Saharan Africa, Loos had visited the Maghreb on two occasions: in 1910 while looking for marble for the cladding of the Michaelerhaus, and in 1911 with Bessie Bruce.)[109] For others the black-and-white bands seem to evoke a tattooed skin, like that of the Papuan against whom Loos inveighed in 'Ornament und Verbrechen'.[110] By contrast with these banded façades, the best known of Loos's Viennese villas of the post-First World War period, the Moller House (1927), has a dazzling white cubic exterior.[111] Black-and-white banding or chequer boarding was a common motif in Viennese decorative art of the Secessionist period. But by employing such strongly emphasized bands of alternate black-and-white marbles in a design for an African-American entertainer in the late 1920s Loos was clearly signalling a rather different agenda. The house for Baker should be seen more specifically in the context of the position of black entertainers and performers working in Europe at the time, and especially in terms of the cult of 'negrophilia' in Paris during the 1920s. Baker was relatively light-skinned and probably of mixed race.[112] The banded façade for her house appears to produce a visual equality of white and black. The two 'non colours' are held in balance, while at the same time the starkly juxtaposed tones appear to shimmer and vibrate: creating an optically produced third tone of grey, ethereal and disembodied – the three tones perhaps alluding to the client's mixed ancestry.

In 1931, Baker published a novel entitled *Mon sang dans tes veines* (My Blood in Your Veins) co-written with her husband and business manager Giuseppe (Pepito) Abatino and a ghostwriter, Félix de la Camara. The novel directly addressed the issue of race. Its main protagonists are the black servant Joan and her white employer Fred who were raised together in New England. When Fred is injured in a riding accident Joan donates blood to him, so that he literally has 'her blood in his veins'. The 'fresh blood' of 'audacious immigrants who make America great' regenerates the country, 'giving new vigour to anaemic decadent civilizations'.[113] Although in this particular passage the reference seems to be to European immigrants, the argument of the novel was that a mixture of black and white blood could also achieve such a reinvigoration. *Mon sang dans tes veines* was published after Loos made his design, but he might well have been familiar with such ideas from conversations with Baker. Nevertheless, the Baker House remains as problematic in its racial as in its gender politics. By employing black-and-white surfaces, water, glass, and a seemingly voyeuristic system of display and spectatorship, Loos produced an iconic – although for many today a profoundly disturbing – design.

Model of house for
Josephine Baker,
Paris, 1927
Adolf Loos

11 The clean machine

In the early part of the 19th century, the factory was seen as dirty, insanitary and dark: a place of disease and dis-ease, of oppression and exploitation. Throughout the later 19th and early 20th centuries the majority of factories and workshops continued to be unhealthy and unhygienic sweatshops. But in more developed parts of Europe, industrial legislation, the evolution of paternalistic forms of capitalism and the growth of socialism and trades unionism served to advance the reformed or 'model' factory, promoted by their owners and architects as places of hygiene and health – indeed as healthier and cleaner than the homes of those who worked in them. New developments in manufacturing methods – and in particular multiple and mass production on the 'American system' – led to the development of new types of factory design, notably the two- or three-storey 'daylight factory'. Predominately horizontal in aspect, the American daylight factory was a standardized industrial building type specifically evolved for the production techniques of the late 19th and early 20th centuries. With wide steel-framed windows allowing natural light to penetrate into the centre of the building and long floor runs to accommodate assembly lines, its design served to provide healthier working conditions while at the same time increasing production.

Just as the building of pithead baths was a means of banishing the traditional pre-conception of the mine as a place of dirt and darkness, so manufacturing industries tried to rid themselves of the image of grime and filth that clung to the 19th-century factory. A clean factory would help to prevent sickness and absenteeism, but a factory designed to *look* clean and hygienic might do even more to project the appearance of purity and wholesomeness considered essential to sell so many consumer products in the first part of the 20th century. 'A clean well-lighted and well-ventilated factory', Henry Ford wrote in his bestselling autobiography, *My Life and Work* (1922), was 'absolutely essential to high capacity, as well as to humane production'. In the most recent Ford factory buildings, exhausted air was pumped out through the hollow structural columns and fresh air introduced, so that a 'nearly even temperature is kept everywhere the year round and, during daylight, there is nowhere the necessity for artificial light'. According to Ford: 'Something like seven hundred men are detailed exclusively to keeping the shops clean,

the windows washed, and all of the paint fresh. The dark corners which invited expecto-
ration are painted white.' He claimed: 'One cannot have morale without cleanliness. We
tolerate makeshift cleanliness no more than makeshift methods.'[1] Social control over
employees was introduced through a 'Sociological Department' to oversee their moral
and physical welfare. The Department published a pamphlet of *Helpful Hints and Advice
to Employe(e)s* recommending that they 'should use plenty of soap and water in the
home, and upon their children, bathing frequently'. In language reminiscent of Adolf
Loos, it claimed: 'Nothing makes for right living and health so much as cleanliness.
Notice that the most advanced people are the cleanest.'[2]

In his autobiography, Ford described how after the First World War he had taken
over the Detroit General Hospital, which had run out of funds before the buildings were
completed. From the end of 1919 this had become The Henry Ford Hospital, equipped
entirely with private rooms in groups of twenty-four.[3] There was no choice of rooms.
Each was identical in size, fittings and furnishings, with its own bath. 'It is planned that
there shall be no choice of anything within the hospital. Every patient is on an equal
footing with every other patient.' The building was designed to minimize the amount of
walking the nurses had to do, like a factory organized according to time-and-motion
studies: 'Each floor is complete in itself, and just as in the factories we have tried to
eliminate the necessity for waste motion, so have we also tried to eliminate waste
motion in the hospital.' Ford argued that:

> The same kind of management which permits a factory to give the fullest service
> will permit a hospital to give the fullest service, and at a price so low as to be
> within the reach of everyone. The only difference between hospital and factory
> accounting is that I do not expect the hospital to return a profit; we do expect it
> to cover depreciation.[4]

By the beginning of the 20th century, the image of the grimy and unhealthy industrial sweatshop had been challenged by that of an airy, light-filled workspace: a clean
and hygienic 'machine for working in', more like a hospital than a factory.[5] And the
perception of the machine itself had changed from that of a crude and filthy coal-fired
steam engine to that of a gleaming icon of modernity driven by internal combustion
or electricity – the image of 'the clean machine' that was to exert such a powerful influence on modernist design and architecture of the period.[6] In the final chapter of *Vers
une architecture* (1923), 'Architecture or Revolution', Le Corbusier wrote: 'Everywhere
can be seen machines which serve to produce something and produce it admirably, in a
clean sort of way.' By contrast, 'The machine that we live in is an old coach full of tuberculosis.' He argued that: 'There is no real link between our daily activities at the factory,
the office or the bank, which are healthy and useful and productive, and our activities
in the bosom of the family which are handicapped at every turn.'[7] Later in the chapter,
Le Corbusier describes the home of the modern professional as an 'uncleanly old snail

Fiat motorcar works,
Lingotto, Turin, Italy, 1914–21
Giacomo Mattè-Trucco

shell', as opposed to the ideal of 'a machine for living in', which he argues can be 'in all simplicity a *human* thing'.[8] Throughout the 20th century the clean hygienic appearance of modern factory and office architecture was employed to promote ideologies of health and hygiene, and to endorse commercial products that reinforced such ideologies. In 1952, Lever Brothers commissioned Skidmore, Owings & Merrill to design Lever House (the first major curtain-walled office block built in New York after the Second World War) to improve 'their post-war reputation amongst the American housewife and shop-keeper'. The construction of this steel-and-glass building for the multinational manufacturers 'of personal cleanliness and hygiene products', who in the 19th century had made a fortune from Sunlight soap and built Port Sunlight as a company town for their workers, 'became a widely reported spectacle'.[9]

The modern(ist) factory

In the first decades of the 20th century, European architects projected the modern American-style factory as a dynamic image of progressive modernity. Among European industrial buildings, mythic status was accorded to the Fiat Lingotto works in Turin (1914–21), designed by the company engineer Giacomo Mattè-Trucco and closely modelled on American daylight factories. The mile-long three-storey automotive production plant was given a dramatic and elegant European twist with its rooftop test track and spiral access ramps. But it was primarily the American factory itself that fascinated modernist architects and designers. Or rather it was photographic representations of

American industrial constructions – and especially reinforced-concrete daylight factories and concrete grain silos – which captured the European imagination. For few European architects had actually been to America and seen these buildings for themselves. In the early 1920s, when enthusiasm for 'Amerika' was at its height, among the better-known European modernists only Erich Mendelsohn had visited the United States and seen the originals.[10] Walter Gropius had written admiringly of American factories and grain silos as early as 1913 in an essay in the *Deutscher Werkbund Jahrbuch* (German Werkbund Yearbook), illustrated with a famous series of photographs that continued to be recycled again and again as icons of modernist admiration in architectural publications during the 1920s. Yet Gropius only went to the United States for the first time in 1928 after he had resigned as director of the Bauhaus, a trip apparently kindled by the enthusiasm of the Dutch industrialist responsible for commissioning the Van Nelle factory, Kees van der Leeuw.[11] Le Corbusier first visited New York in 1935.

Most American factories were designed not by architects but by structural engineers. While praising American engineers for the straightforward monumental simplicity and sobriety of their work, European modernists condemned American architects for their traditionalism and timidity in hiding innovative structures behind Beaux Arts façades and ornamentation. In *Vers une architecture*, Le Corbusier wrote: 'Let us listen to the counsel of American engineers. But let us beware of American architects.'[12] Already in the early 19th century, the German neoclassical architect Karl Friedrich Schinkel had promoted the factory as an important new building type. In the first two decades of the 20th century, architects such as Peter Behrens, Hermann Muthesius, Tony Garnier, Hans Poelzig, Erich Mendelsohn, Walter Gropius and Adolf Meyer had all sought commissions to design factories, much as their 19th-century predecessors had canvassed for commissions for public buildings and museums, and as did their successors in the final decades of the 20th century. In his famous designs for a series of specialized industrial buildings for the great electrical combine AEG, erected in Berlin between 1907 and 1914, Behrens gave the modern factory a sublime solemnity which raised it to the summit of modern building types. This undoubtedly had a powerful influence on the young architects then working in Behrens's Berlin office who included Gropius, his future partner Adolf Meyer, Le Corbusier and Mies van der Rohe, all of whom regarded the factory and related industrial buildings as prime exemplars in the production of the modern.

Not only did many modernist architects in Europe design factories, they also designed other types of building such as hospitals, schools and housing to look like factories, as was common in the United States.[13] Even sanatoriums such as Zonnestraal – built to care for those whose health had been ruined by years of working in unhygienic and dangerous industrial sweatshops – were designed to resemble the most up-to-date modern American factories. With its airy terraces and balconies, its gleaming pipes, and the proud display of the polished machinery of the laundry and heating system, Zonnestraal projected the image of 'the clean machine' bathed in healing and germ-destroying sunlight. The seemingly indeterminate spaces, the hovering and apparently gravity-defying lightweight structure, the sparkling white walls and huge rippling sheets of glass produced an almost mystical 'spiritual' aura. Evoking the modern hygienic factory, Zonnestraal was designed to shame and condemn the cramped and unhealthy working conditions of the dark and dirty diamond-polishing workshops where many of its patients had contacted the lung diseases for which they were being treated. The sanatorium elicited similar responses as American-style modernist industrial buildings built during the same period, such as Brinkman and Van der Vlugt's spectacular concrete-and-glass tea, coffee and tobacco Van Nelle factory (1926–31), which seemed to float like a white liner across the polders and canals of its green-fields site on the outskirts of Rotterdam.

The model of the multi-storey concrete-framed American 'daylight' factory provided a potent image that captivated a whole generation of European architects, who adapted its standardized modular form to the design of 'collectivized' social housing, schools and colleges, hospitals and sanatoriums. By the 1920s, this type of factory was already becoming obsolete in the United States, at least in the motorcar industry where it was being superseded by the infinitely adaptable single-storey steel-framed shed-type factory building developed by specialist industrial architects such as Albert Kahn Associates in close cooperation with Ford and General Motors automotive engineers. Multi-storey reinforced-concrete-framed daylight factories, such as Kahn Associates' Highland Park Original Building for the Ford Motor Company in Detroit, may have been obsolete in terms of motorcar production by the First World War.[14] Nevertheless, the building continued in use for the production of Model T Fords throughout the 1920s, in parallel with the new River Rouge plant, originally erected for the construction of motor-torpedo boats towards the end of the First World War. As a building type, the multi-storey daylight factory remained sustainable for other kinds of multiple-production process: in particular for the mass production and packaging of smaller and lighter consumer products as in the Van Nelle factory, the two pharmaceutical factories built in the 1930s for the Boots company at Beeston near Nottingham, the Wedgwood china factory (1936-8) at Barlaston in Staffordshire, and the Austrian State Tobacco Factory in Linz (1930–34; see Chapter 12).[15] The extensive use of large sheets of rolled glass in late 19th- and early 20th-century factories was not only adopted for economic reasons. The *American Architect and Building News* argued that while the extra expenditure on large steel-and-glass windows might not be immediately apparent, it was fully justified by 'the improved health, the improved moral, physical and aesthetic conditions' of the workforce.[16] A commentator in a German trade journal claimed that 'light, cleanliness and organization have a moral effect on the work ethic, which is of no small import for the profitability of the works'.[17] Nevertheless, the daylight factory was evolved as much to save the manufacturer money as to provide a healthy environment for the workforce. In restricted sites in great industrial cities such as Berlin, Liverpool, Glasgow and Chicago a large area of glass made the most of cramped or narrow lots, and reduced the cost of providing artificial light. Increased natural lighting also had the advantage of improved surveillance of the workforce by management. There would be no dark corners in which 'shirkers' could hide.

With its clearly articulated and unitized structure, the American daylight factory seemed to evoke the idea of productive labour, perhaps even the working-class solidarity it had so often effectively destroyed in the United States. The modular construction and long wide windows of the American daylight factory became models not only for European factories but also for austerely luxurious modernist villas and social housing, and for educational buildings. In 1922, Robert Mallet-Stevens wrote: 'Apartment blocks, public buildings, workers' housing, the wealthiest villas will in the future be designed in the same spirit as factories.'[18] During the 1920s, modernist architects concerned with the problems of housing design and production were convinced that the solution lay in rationalization, prefabrication and mass production. They were inspired in their belief by their admiration for modern industry and industrial forms, and by the writings of American industrial and management theorists such as Frederick Winslow Taylor and Frank B. Gilbreth. In 1924, the Russian architect Moisei Ginzburg claimed the factory 'already represents a kind of housing – true, a housing more for labour and machines than for man, but housing nevertheless'. He maintained that 'an analysis of such industrial structures should be of great importance' to the design of social housing.[19] Three years later, Ginzburg argued that: '*Productive or labour processes* are generally associated with images of the workshop or factory; *social processes*, with housing and collective buildings. There are no fundamental differences here.'[20] Like most Soviet intellectuals in the 1920s, Ginzburg was even more deeply under the spell of Americanization – and in particular Taylorism and Fordism – than his contemporaries in Germany. Although Lenin had initially viewed Taylorism as a rationalized technique for increasing the exploitation of labour, he later came to believe that its application could create the circumstances whereby the proletariat could take over the means of production.[21] Lenin's views had encouraged many western European as well as Soviet intellectuals to look favourably on Taylorism during the 1920s, including the first leader of the Italian communist party and marxist theorist Antonio Gramsci, who had been based in Turin during the time of the building of the Fiat Lingotto plant.

Walter Gropius, however, seems to have been more directly inspired by Henry Ford than by the theories of Taylor and Gilbreth. Fordist ideas had gained great popularity in Germany with the publication of a translation of *My Life and Work* in 1923.[22] This coincided with the stabilization of the Deutschmark, the adoption of the Dawes Plan to combat spiralling inflation, and subsequent American investment in Germany and other parts of the European economy. In 1924, the Ford Company of Germany inaugurated its first assembly line in its factory in Cologne. Between 1927 and 1932, the Dagenham plant was constructed down the Thames from London as a one-tenth replica of the River Rouge complex. Another plant was built in Amsterdam in the early 1930s, where parts manufactured in Dagenham and shipped to The Netherlands were assembled. Jan Duiker, the architect of the Zonnestraal Sanatorium and the Cliostraat Open-Air School for the Healthy Child, visited the Amsterdam assembly plant in 1933 and wrote about it in the modernist architectural magazine he edited, *De 8 en Opbouw*:

> The big pier receives from Dagenham all parts ready-made and packed.
> Cranes put everything in a great hall, which occupies the entire height of the plant.
> Then there is a division: a ground floor and a gallery.
> Heavy parts remain downstairs: motors and chassis; the light parts go upstairs: bodies.
> Both begin their trip through the plant on the conveyor belt simultaneously.
> The bodies are assembled upstairs, the chassis downstairs.
> Then as a buffer of stock, the body is taken downstairs and awaits its turn on small gliders in the company of its many brothers.
> The chassis comes gliding along on the belt and is pushed under the lifting rail along which like a cow in the slaughter house the body is rolled above the chassis on a rolling hook and is placed on the chassis.
> It is fixed, oil, petrol and water are put into the tanks and the new Ford leaves the plant.

Duiker was no doubt aware of Henry Ford's claim that the idea of the assembly line had come from the 'dis-assembly line' of Chicago slaughterhouses and meat packers, hence the simile of the car body as like a cow in the slaughter house.[23] He praised the organization of the assembly line ('There is much to see and much to learn for an architect') but observed that in practice 'the manufacturing is not as perfect as we thought'. When the two pieces of the body were welded together 'quite a few dents and bumps have to be soldered, smoothed out, polished and sanded', resulting in considerable loss of time. He noted that the contact points between the wooden framework and the steel carcass needed to be packed with soft cloth (swanskin) to prevent vibration, commenting that 'together with the mock-velvet lining' inside the body this does not say much for the 'interior hygiene' of the motorcar as a whole. Duiker admired the construction of the car's roof, which he argues could teach architects a thing or two about the construction of a modern leak-free flat roof, but criticized the disparity between the structural engineering of the assembly plant and the cosmetic additions of the architects, who had introduced unnecessary decorative features.[24]

The influence of the daylight factory can be seen in many early modernist educational buildings designed in the 1920s and 1930s – the best-known example of which is Gropius's Bauhaus building at Dessau – and also in numerous schools constructed after the Second World War, especially in Britain.[25] An early European example that predates the Dessau Bauhaus was the joint Senior Secondary Technical School and Industrial

School in the Dutch city of Groningen, designed by Jan Gerko Wiebenga and Leen van der Vlugt between 1922 and 1923.[26] Wiebenga had recently been appointed director of the schools, which were built on a single site in a similar manner to the Bauhaus complex at Dessau, which incorporated a trade school as well as the more famous design school.[27] A row of single-storey workshops used by both Groningen schools and lit by clerestory roof lights separated the two blocks of classrooms: one of three storeys, the other of two. This was a similar layout to early 20th-century European factories, such as Walter Gropius and Adolf Meyer's Fagus-Werk shoe-last factory in Alfeld an der Leine, where single-storey workshop buildings were fronted by two- or three-storey administration and office buildings, which although minimal in decorative detail were designed to have a more 'architectural' and imposing character. With prominent concrete sills running beneath the long horizontal strips of metal windows, the Groningen school buildings did not have the degree of transparency Gropius achieved later in the curtain wall he designed for the Bauhaus workshop block at Dessau – or of the glass-and-steel façades of Brinkman and Van der Vlugt's Van Nelle factory, for which Wiebenga acted as consultant structural engineer. Designed to produce effects of lightness of being and mental and physical exhilaration in those who worked in or visited them, these later buildings were intended to symbolize 'enlightenment' and the 'spiritualization' of work and industry. The inner and outward hygiene and cleanliness of the industrial (or quasi-industrial) building and the transcendent poetry of 'the clean machine' were evoked through an overwhelming and almost blinding physical sensation of light.

A perfect fit

Photographs of the Fagus administration building appear frequently in histories of 20th-century architecture, where it is customarily represented as one of the earliest examples of modernist architecture and nearly always misleadingly described in terms of its structural innovation.[28] Newly published research has helped to clarify the crucial relationship between the architects, their clients and the special nature of the product produced: shoe lasts designed for the manufacture of well-fitting, hygienic and healthy modern footwear.[29] The founder of the Fagus factory Carl Benscheidt had grown up as a sickly child in a large impoverished family and had become a lifelong nonsmoker and vegetarian. Inspired by the Lebensreform movement, Benscheidt aimed to employ the latest technological advances to counteract disease and bodily deformity. The Fagus factory was to be 'an agent for social change and new standards of hygiene, visibly preaching a gospel of reformed living'.[30] The declared goal of Carl Benscheidt and his son Karl – who had studied the latest American methods of manufacture and management in the United States – was to elevate the level of public health by making machine-made lasts that would produce naturally fitting but affordable shoes to counteract the deformation and discomfort caused by badly made footwear.[31] The

Benscheidts' beliefs were closely linked to ideas about health and improved education. In 1912, they asked Gropius and Meyer to draw up designs for a new hospital for Alfeld. Although never built, this was conceived like the Fagus-Werk as a combination of relatively traditional and 'proto-modernist' buildings with flat roofs and large steel-and-glass windows.[32] The block for the hospital administration and medical wards was designed as a plain but imposing two-storey pitched-roof structure. A flat-roofed wing housed the operating theatre, with floor-to-ceiling windows in projecting box frames closely related to the huge steel-and-glass windows of the Fagus administration building – features that were intended to 'draw attention to the special function of this wing: an ultramodern, hygienic workplace where science and technology were put in the service of health care'.[33]

The oldest of twelve children of a Sauerland farmer, the elder Benscheidt had been frustrated in his ambition to become a doctor and had found work at the naturopathic centres run by Arnold Rikli in what were then the southern parts of the Austro-Hungarian empire (see Chapter 6).[34] Many patients suffered from foot problems caused by ill-fitting footwear and one of Carl Benscheidt's responsibilities was to measure patients' feet for shoe lasts, which were made in Switzerland, in order to produce correctly fitting shoes for them. After working for a number of shoe and shoe-last manufacturing companies in Germany, Benscheidt had eventually set up the Fagus company in Alfeld in 1910 with American backing.[35] This was named after the tree that provided the raw material for shoe lasts: the common European beech *fagus sylvatica*. It was an appropriate name for the company whose factory was to become one of the icons of early 20th-century modernist architecture. For besides shoe lasts, beech wood was also the raw material for one of the earliest examples of batch or quantity production in Europe: bentwood furniture of the type manufactured by the multi-national Thonet company since the 1840s in virtually every continental European country where *fagus sylvatica* grew, and frequently used by modernist architects such as Loos and Le Corbusier in their interiors.

Although manufactured from a traditional and 'natural' material, the early 20th-century wooden last – 'the foot-shaped wooden form over which the parts of a shoe are shaped and joined'[36] – was a sophisticated man-made 'tool' designed for batch or quantity production. It was a highly evolved form, akin to the anonymously designed 'male accoutrements' such as pipes, walking sticks, cigarette cases and travel goods perfected by generations of skilled craftsmen that Loos and Le Corbusier admired – and which Le Corbusier called '*objets-types*' (type objects).[37] The wooden shoe last could also be considered a 'human-limb object', a phrase Le Corbusier coined for human artifacts such as clothes, crockery and cutlery which extended the functions and forms of human limbs.[38] These qualities are captured in Fagus photographs of carefully ranged shoe lasts, as smooth and elegant as a well-shaped human foot. The Neue Sachlichkeit photographer Albert Renger-Patzsch documented the process of production from the

Shoe lasts, Fagus factory,
Alfeld an der Leine,
Germany, c. 1930

rough beech logs to the finished last in a series of photographs in which the 'human-limb object' can be seen gradually and almost miraculously emerging from the material, like a sculpture carved from a block of wood or stone.[39] While Renger-Patzsch's pictures of the Fagus factory convey very little about the conditions of work, they do tell us a great deal about the way the Benscheidts wanted to represent the places and processes of manufacture to their customers (and to posterity) through images of light-filled hygienic buildings, pristine products and clean machines.[40]

In the early 20th century, shoe manufacture seems to have played an important role in discourses around health, hygiene, paternalistic social control, the alleviation of poverty, and the commissioning of modernist architecture. After the First World War, Tomáš Bat'a developed his multinational shoe empire from his headquarters in the Moravian town of Zlín, opening factories all over the world. Like the younger Benscheidt, Bat'a had worked in shoe factories in the United States before the war and in 1919 had visited the Ford works at River Rouge. In Zlín, he commissioned reinforced-concrete factories based on those he had seen in the United States, and imported the latest American machinery and Fordist production methods.[41] He built model housing for his workers and also provided a hospital, schools and adult education colleges, a department store, churches, a cinema, a community centre, an art museum, and an art and design college based on the model of the Bauhaus, and financed and constructed the town's electricity network. Bat'a declared: 'Our aim is to build a garden town, full of sunshine, water and green grass – a clean town with the highest of wages, prosperous crafts and business, a town with the best of schools.'[42] He considered himself responsible not only for his employees training but also for their moral welfare and that of their families, justifying this with hygienist rationales reminiscent of Henry Ford. 'People with dirty character', he maintained, 'cannot do clean work.'[43]

Memorial Pavilion to Tomáš Bat'a,
Zlín, Czechoslovakia (now Czech Republic), 1932–33
František Lydie Gahura

After Tomáš Bat'a's death in an air crash in 1932, his half brother Jan took over the running of the company. A monument to the founder was erected in Zlín town centre: a transparent plate-glass pavilion by František Lydie Gahura, where a replica of the Junkers plane in which Bat'a had died was suspended in an interior designed by the Bauhaus student Zdeněk Rossmann. (After the invasion of Czechoslovakia in 1938 the Nazis removed the plane, and the pavilion was later remodelled to become the Zlín art gallery.) While the spirit of the founder watched over the centre of the company town, the new director watched over the work force. The administrative building was designed by the Slovak architect Vladimír Karfík, who had worked with Le Corbusier in France and with Frank Lloyd Wright in the United States. Here Jan Bat'a had an office constructed inside a gigantic glass-walled lift provided with air conditioning and a washbasin, situated at one corner of the administration building (which was probably the tallest building in Europe at the time).[44] It rose through the building's seventeen storeys, enabling Bat'a to 'move vertically throughout the administrative block and meet his employees', and also served as a surveillance device – the equivalent of the video cameras fitted in the workplace today.[45] After 1948, Bat'a was nationalized and renamed Svit – which means 'light' in Czech – but since 1989 has reverted to its original name. Shoes are no longer manufactured there, but the town has been restored and refurbished and new buildings commissioned – including a concert hall and library designed by the Czech-born neo-modernist architect Eva Jiricna, who grew up in Zlín.

At the time when he was designing the new Bauhaus buildings at Dessau in 1925, Gropius began to draw renewed attention to the Fagus-Werk, in particular those elements of its design that could be represented as precursors of the new school buildings. The factory as a building type had been the focus for the most influential of his early writings and conference papers.[46] It was not entirely surprising that – although not a factory itself – Gropius's best-known and most influential post-war building was designed to *look* like one. The factory-like appearance of the Dessau Bauhaus distinguished it from the building the school had previously occupied in Weimar between 1919 and 1925, designed before the First World War by Henry van de Velde for the Weimar Arts and Crafts School. As a building type, Van der Velde's school was essentially an enlarged version of the late 19th-century artist's studio and clearly recognizable as a cultural and educational institution. Gropius's Dessau Bauhaus on the other hand spoke the language of the industrial factory and the production line: of hygiene, spiritual transcendence and 'the clean machine'. It was a building type that was to have an extraordinarily wide influence on modern architecture throughout the world, and especially on the design of schools, colleges, and other educational establishments.

The industrial imagery of the new Bauhaus building at Dessau – and of the spectacular glass-walled workshop block in particular – was especially important for Gropius in his aim of realigning and repositioning the Bauhaus in relation to industry. By employing a spectacular curtain wall constructed from standardized steel windows designed for industrial buildings, Gropius aimed to give the workshop block an appearance that would evoke a two- or three-storey 'daylight factory' on the American model. By specifying a reinforced-concrete frame set back about one metre behind this dramatic curtain wall of glass, he emphasized and exaggerated the industrial metaphors of light and transparency beyond what would have been usual in the context of an industrial building – at least until the construction of the Van Nelle factory in Rotterdam a year or two later.[47] The clean functional- and hygienic-looking industrial appearance of the new Bauhaus buildings signified the turn towards 'art and technology' that Gropius had adopted at the school since 1923, and especially after its move to Dessau in 1925. The workshop block with its steel-and-glass curtain wall was equipped with state-of-the-art modern woodworking and metalworking machinery.[48] It was this part of the school complex that was imbued with the most direct industrial imagery, as if to convey the impression that mass-production processes actually took place here, rather than, as Gropius proclaimed at the time, the development of *prototypes* for industrial production.[49] Although he argued that these prototypes were intended for mass production, most of the designs from the Dessau Bauhaus that went into production were manufactured commercially outside the Bauhaus by batch- or multiple-production methods. But the factory-like aspect of the new building (and the workshop block in particular) gave the new Bauhaus the industrial look that Gropius needed to attract sponsorship and support from manufacturers in the industrial city of Dessau, where the school had relocated the previous year.

12 Manufacturing enlightenment

Where Walter Gropius had incorporated references to American daylight factories in the design of the Dessau Bauhaus to signify the school's industrial orientation, in the Van Nelle factory Brinkman and Van der Vlugt inflected the American model with the educational imagery of the Dessau school complex, and the Groningen schools Wiebenga had designed with Van der Vlugt. By such means they promoted the educational (or enlightening) role of the factory in order to embody the paternalistic values of 'enlightened' Dutch capitalism. As the partner mainly responsible for commissioning the Van Nelle factory, Kees van der Leeuw visited the new Dessau Bauhaus a number of times. He was accompanied on at least one occasion by Van der Vlugt, and perhaps also by Wiebenga in his role as consultant structural engineer for the factory.[1] Van der Leeuw admired the Groningen schools, and this probably influenced his choice of Van der Vlugt as architect and perhaps also Wiebenga as consultant engineer.[2] The structure of the Van Nelle factory was a combination of American techniques of reinforced-concrete construction (mushroom columns and floor slabs) and a European curtain wall of steel and glass, similar to that of the Bauhaus workshop block. Undoubtedly, Van der Leeuw and his architects and engineers were impressed by the way Gropius had incorporated industrial imagery into the design school, and the similarities between the two buildings are not coincidental. Nevertheless, while the curtain wall of the main Van Nelle factory building seems to have been derived from that of the Bauhaus workshop block rather than from American examples, there were a number of obvious differences.[3] The Bauhaus curtain wall was entirely glazed, while that of the main Van Nelle factory building alternated steel plates from floor to workbench height with full glazing up to the ceilings which flooded the interior with light and allowed the workforce spectacular views across the surrounding polders.[4]

The proportions of the curtain wall of the factory were based on the 1 x 0.5-metre standard glass panels used in greenhouses in The Netherlands, which were cheap and readily available. These had even more rippling imperfections than the glass used for the Zonnestraal, and in sunlight produced sparkling reflections from the outside.[5] Where the Bauhaus workshop block had a rectangular-section reinforced-concrete frame, for the Van Nelle factory Wiebenga designed a structural system of reinforced-concrete mushroom columns based on American practice that did away with the necessity for reinforced-concrete crossbeams to support the floors.[6] The columns become progressively slimmer on the upper floors of the main factory building, where they have to carry less weight.[7] The mushroom-column construction allowed the full height of each storey to be used for windows, producing smooth ceilings which Van der Leeuw argued 'were pleasanter to look at and better for lighting than a concrete-frame floor'.[8] Despite the different structural systems, the set backs of the supports a metre or so behind the curtain walls of the two buildings are similar, increasing the apparent 'transparency' from the outside, and the amount of light that floods into the interiors. The light streaming through the tea, coffee and tobacco factory was intended to symbolize enlightenment, both spiritual and moral, while also evoking the clean hygienic spaces of the hospital and the sanatorium. Van der Leeuw was obsessed by cleanliness and hygiene at both a practical and a symbolic level. These were essential components of the theosophical doctrines, of which both he and his architect Van der Vlugt were adherents at the time. (Like many industrialists of the period, Van der Leeuw was also a freemason.) The new factory was to be a 'clean machine' representing progress and modernity, producing enlightenment as well as tea, coffee and tobacco.

Towards the light

Like the Benscheidts, Kees van der Leeuw exemplified a type of industrial patron not uncommon in the 19th and 20th centuries who combined ruthless business acumen and 'modernizing' instincts with 'philanthropic' interests – and in Van der Leeuw's case, esoteric theosophical beliefs. More unusually, he was also to undertake a professional training in psychoanalysis and medicine.[9] After the completion of the Van Nelle factory in 1932, Van der Leeuw went to Vienna where he was analysed by Freud's favoured pupil Ruth Mack Brunswick and possibly by Freud himself – qualifying as a medical doctor and psychoanalyst in 1939.[10] But at the time of the design and construction of the factory both he and his architects were deeply involved with theosophy. His brother J. J. van der Leeuw was a leading theosophical writer and theorist whose books are still in print today, while he himself was one of the main supporters and backers of the Order of the Star in the East, the theosophical sect founded by Annie Besant and C. W. Leadbetter in Benares in 1911.[11] Many of the Order's activities were concentrated in The Netherlands, and Van der Leeuw had become its secretary in 1923. He was also a leading member of the P. C. Meuleman Theosophical Foundation in Amsterdam, and was instrumental in the commissioning of a temple for the foundation from Brinkman and Van der Vlugt in 1925, the same year as the commission for the Van Nelle factory. For theosophists, light was invested with a powerful symbolism. Spiritual enlightenment was seen as 'moving towards the Light'.[12] In the great circular auditorium of the

P. C. Meuleman temple, Brinkman and Van der Vlugt incorporated theatrical effects of light descending mysteriously into the hall from hidden overhead sources in Wiebenga's spectacularly engineered reinforced-concrete roof.[13] Equally dramatic light effects were employed in the Van Nelle factory – far brighter than strict function (or the provision of better working conditions) required, creating an 'environment of enlightenment' in a modern 'cathedral of labour'.[14] Shortly after joining the Order of the Star in the East in 1914, Van der Leeuw had been assigned the task of investigating 'progress in the spirit of co-operation and profit sharing among the working classes, the relationship between employers and employees, the Higher Socialism, and Women's Labour'.[15]

In theosophical doctrine, Americans were revered as a 'new race'. Kees van der Leeuw had become fascinated by American ideas about scientific management, Taylorism, and marketing when he first visited the United States as a young man in 1911. After work had already begun on the foundations of the factory, he spent three weeks in the autumn of 1926 travelling from the East to the West Coast visiting the most modern factories, including those of Ford. He took note of the latest methods of mass production and industrial construction, and investigated and researched the most recent ideas on improving industrial working conditions through better lighting, ergonomics and the study of posture.[16] Many of these ideas were to be incorporated into the internal design of the Van Nelle factory, and items of equipment unobtainable in Europe were imported from the United States. As at the Fagus-Werk, American ideas were mediated through European sensibilities and adapted to very different European conditions of labour, production and marketing. The *aura* of 'Americanization' that appeared to emanate from these industrial buildings was as important as any directly imported ideas about mass production, work management, or factory construction.

The Van Nelle factory was built on reclaimed polder land the company had bought cheaply over a period of time since 1916, when plans for a new building had first been developed. The spacious green-fields site would have allowed plenty of room to lay out the manufacturing and warehouse complex as a series of low shed-type buildings on the model of the Ford River Rouge plant, which Van der Leeuw had visited on his research trip in 1926. But for the different operations involved in the processing and packaging of tea, coffee and tobacco a multi-storey building on the model of the American daylight factory combined with a series of low warehouses was probably the most rational solution. In 1923, Van der Leeuw had made a study trip to factories in Britain, where he had been greatly impressed by the Cadbury 'factory in a garden' at Bournville near Birmingham.[17] Occupying less ground space than a series of large single-storey buildings, the Van Nelle factory complex enabled the company to retain much of the surrounding greenery – part of which was later laid out as a garden – and provide sports fields for the workers and tennis courts for the executives.[18] The qualities of light, air and openness and the 'green fields' image of the complex were preserved, and employees further 'bound' to the workplace through recreational activities.

Although strictly less economical than a long low shed-type plant, what may have been lost in productive efficiency through the horizontal-vertical organization of the Van Nelle factory was balanced by enormous gains in terms of promoting a 'brand-image' for the company and marketing its products. In a lecture on the building of the factory for the Nederlands Instituut voor Efficiency (Dutch Institute for Efficiency) in 1930, Van der Leeuw claimed that the huge curtain wall of the factory was worthwhile 'if only for advertising reasons'.[19] The site on the Spangensche Polder at Overschie just outside Rotterdam was accessible from the navigable Delfhavensche Schie, and close to the main railway line and road to The Hague and Amsterdam. The long multi-storeyed factory with its glinting glass-and-steel curtain walls created a powerful image for passing travellers. (Most people in a small country like The Netherlands would have travelled past it at least once in their lives.) The words 'Van Nelle' appeared in large sans-serif letters on the top of the factory, so that the name of company was clearly visible from road and rail as at the Ford factories in Detroit, and the Fagus-Werk at Alfeld, which was sited close to the main railway line to Hanover.[20] The lights were left on in the building on Tuesday and Friday evenings to create a dramatic display visible from many parts of Rotterdam, as well as from the railway line and road. After visiting the factory in 1930, Howard Robertson and F. R. Yerbury wrote that from the train window at dusk 'it appears in its full blaze of glass and steel for one short moment', as the evening sun caught its wall of windows. After dark 'when the whole building is left with all its lamps aglow', it appeared as 'a huge rectangle of light, its transparency barred by the long tenuous lines of the solids between the dominating areas of glass'.[21] From its inception in the late 1920s to the cessation of production in the late 1990s, the Van Nelle factory did not merely produce tea, coffee and tobacco in neat colourful paper packages.[22] It also produced a corporate or brand image, as had Behrens's designs for AEG, and Gropius and Meyer's Fagus factory for the Benscheidts.

In a report Van der Leeuw had written for the Van Nelle board in 1915, he had already recommended a new factory on a 'green-fields' site at the edge of the city – arguing that the way its design and siting represented the company to the public and its clients was as important as how it functioned as a manufacturing plant:

> A factory on a large piece of ground planned with lots of space, visible from different sides on the important line between Rotterdam and Amsterdam, will present a single facade of 60 or 80 metres on the Oostzeedijk. Further modern provision, like housing for the workers, sports grounds, a garden, will certainly improve our 'standing' as manufacturers.[23]

As eventually built, the main façade of the three connected factories was not 60 or 80 metres, but an imposing 220 metres – and provided sports grounds and a garden (although not housing) for its workers. Van der Leeuw clearly did not agree with Henry Ford, who said that the Ford company 'would prefer to be advertised by our product, rather than where we make our product'.[24] Nevertheless, the displaying of the company's name in large letters on top of the clean-lined hygienic modern factory echoed Ford's own practice on his factory buildings, clearly identifying it with a brand of tea, coffee and tobacco that was already a household name in The Netherlands.

In the early years of the century, the Van Nelle company had become highly successful through the introduction of packaged products for the retail trade, based on American practice.[25] Van Nelle products were not of particularly high quality. What made them distinctive and attractive to the public was that they were pre-packed. This was their main selling point at a time when most tea, coffee and tobacco was sold loose, bagged by the retailer at the point of sale – a practice not particularly conducive to cleanliness and hygiene. Van Nelle had a rapidly growing trade among the Dutch

Van Nelle Factory,
Schiedam, Rotterdam, The Netherlands, 1925–31
Johannes Brinkman and **Leen van der Vlugt**

lower-middle and better-paid working classes, for whom the convenience of being able to buy pre-packaged goods of consistent if not outstanding quality had an obvious appeal. Pre-packed goods were promoted as cleaner and more hygienic. In 1931, the company commissioned the well-known French poster designer A. M. Cassandre to design a poster advertising Van Nelle coffee that featured a giant coffee bean in a transparent packet, 'to emphasize the hygienic and hermetically sealed packaging' of its products.[26] Like the transparent cellophane in Cassandre's advertisement, the steel-and-glass walls of the factory served as a silvery translucent see-through packaging for the clean modern machinery of the processing plants within.[27]

In the early decades of the 20th century, the drinking of tea and coffee and the smoking of tobacco were closely associated with modernity in The Netherlands, as elsewhere in Europe and America.[28] These products were also identified with cleanliness and health, something that is difficult to appreciate today, particularly with regard to smoking, the public perceptions of which have changed drastically over the last decades. During the 1920s and 1930s, this was associated with a positive modernity – and even perceived as hygienic, possessing sterilizing and 'fumigating' properties that could destroy germs and mask bad smells. At a time when people bathed or washed less frequently smoking was a means of concealing strong body odours. Tea and coffee were seen as healthy and wholesome alternatives to alcohol, which was considered to be a 'scourge': a corrupter of the working classes and the enemy of a well-regulated life. (Like Carl Benscheidt, Kees van der Leeuw was a life-long teetotaller and vegetarian.) Cafes and teashops were regarded as clean and respectable places where 'decent' people (and particularly women) could meet, unlike the sordid and ill-regulated bars and pubs where alcohol was consumed. The Van Nelle publicity department encouraged public perceptions of tea, coffee and tobacco as hygienic, wholesome and healthy, and organized promotional coffee and tea buffets and smoking contests in cafés throughout The Netherlands.[29]

All over Europe, tobacco factories were designed in modernist styles that reinforced associations between modernity and smoking, and emphasized the hygienic conditions under which tobacco and tobacco products were prepared. A striking example was the Austrian State Tobacco Factory in Linz, the first large-scale steel-framed industrial building in Austria, designed by Peter Behrens in collaboration with Alexander Popp between 1929 and 1935.[30] Close to the city's international river port on the Danube, the factory was carefully planned to produce a powerful impression. With its sweeping curve and long horizontal bands of steel-framed windows flush to the exterior, the 230-metre-long façade of the manufactory dramatically conveys the rhythm of the six storeys stacked above each other. Designed for production flow with 80 per cent humidity and constant lighting, the factory was equipped with the most up-to-date production lines. Sited diagonally opposite the Parkbad (an open-air swimming-pool complex built on the banks of the Danube in

Austrian State Tobacco Factory,
Linz, Austria, 1930–34, photographed in 2005
Peter Behrens and **Alexander Popp**

1930), it backed onto what was then the new city slaughterhouse – not inappropriately linking hygiene and cleanliness with the 'dis-assembly line' on which 'the American system' of mass production had been based.

By contrast with the smooth continuous façade of the Linz factory, the vertical staircase towers that separate the Van Nelle tea, coffee and tobacco manufactories and the diagonal conveyor bridges that link the factory block with the warehouses give the industrial complex a more varied emphasis and presence, signifying that this was a series of plants that produced several staples, rather than a single product. A number of curved elements were also introduced into the design at a relatively late stage. These included the low, bowed office wing near the entrance, and the round directors' hospitality suite (or 'tearoom') perched dramatically on top of the factory block like a ship's bridge or airport control tower, with a spectacular view of the whole city.[31] Because of the differences in height between the manufactories and the lower-lying warehouses on the other side of the 'factory street', the covered conveyor bridges through which the raw materials passed for processing were set at an angle. In combination with the curving elements of the building, these helped to create a hypnotic and enticing (almost voluptuous and exotic) effect appropriate to the products processed in the factory and the city in which it was located. At the time, Rotterdam was the world's largest commercial port, importing raw materials from distant parts of the non-European world. As in

Britain, commerce and industry in The Netherlands were closely linked to a dependence on colonial markets and sources of raw material. Tea, coffee and tobacco were the staples of the Dutch colonial trading system, although by the 20th century Van Nelle were importing supplies from sources far beyond the Dutch empire. The company's enterprise was deeply rooted within the colonial project that had brought about the rapid development and expansion of the cities of the western seaboard of The Netherlands since the 17th century, and of Rotterdam in particular during the later 19th century. In the first decades of the new century, the Dutch colonial empire was still a powerful commercial and cultural force, although (like Britain) The Netherlands was to undergo a rapid process of decolonization shortly after the Second World War.

Just as the business of the Van Nelle company was based predominantly on imported products of colonial origin, Kees van der Leeuw's theosophical beliefs were also a hybrid product of the European colonial project. As a young man, he travelled to many sites in Europe and the Far East that were considered important in both theosophy and freemasonry. (A file of photographs in the Van Nelle archives is labelled 'Occult Tourism'.)[32] As with other European colonial powers, at the end of the 19th century liberals in The Netherlands had constructed a myth of 'ethical colonialism' that denied that Dutch colonialism was actually imperialist.[33] Van der Leeuw's particular combination of esoteric spiritual beliefs with the promotion of an 'ethical' and paternalistic capitalism was closely linked to this. The adoption of a modernist style of architecture with white walls and large areas of glass for the Van Nelle factory buildings can be seen as consistent with the reinforcement of the myths of 'ethical colonialism' and 'enlightened capitalism'.[34] As a symbol of modernity and 'modern' products, the Van Nelle factory became associated in people's minds with the idea of a tolerant and respectable bourgeois democracy promoted from the early decades of the 20th century as the official image of modern Dutch society.

Like the Benscheidts, Van der Leeuw was well aware that a healthy and contented workforce was also a productive one, and believed that the new building would not only benefit the physical and mental health of his employees but also increase their productivity. He was an admirer of Walther Rathenau, the chairman of AEG who had become German foreign minister in the Weimar republic. Rathenau regarded industrial enlightenment as a prescription for defeating the radical left, and had prefaced his book *Von kommenden Dingen* (Of Things to Come) in 1917 with the invocation 'to hit doctrinaire socialism right in the heart!'[35] Nevertheless, Van der Leeuw also seems to have been on good terms with the left-wing architect Mart Stam, who worked in the Brinkman and Van der Vlugt office at the time of the design of the Van Nelle factory and has sometimes been credited with a major role in its conception.[36] While admitting that considerations of profit and economy were paramount, Van der Leeuw emphasized the necessity for light and harmonious working conditions for the workers in the factory, insisting that they should have unobstructed views across the fields and dykes around the building.[37] A special feature was made of the ultra-hygienic washing and lavatory facilities which were fitted with the latest suspended toilet bowls and high-pressure flushing mechanisms imported from the United States.[38] The toilet cubicles were 'well ventilated', with low door-height partitions (another American innovation) and 'drenched with light' from the windows that filled the upper part of the back wall.[39] These hygienic facilities were grouped in the staircase towers that gave access to the production floors and provided separate entrances and facilities for male and female workers.

Van der Leeuw had paid special attention to the needs of his women employees (who formed the major part of the Van Nelle workforce) and had consulted with the American Bureau of Women in Industry while in New York in 1926. The ultra-hygienic facilities, the spectacular illumination of the factory floors, and the fine views across the polders were in part at least intended to attract and keep happy his female workers. The green-leafed plants in metal planters attached to the tree-like mushroom columns which can be seen in many photographs of the factory interior seem to have been a further attempt to create an attractive environment for the women workers. (These large tropical houseplants added to the impression that the factory – with its windows based on those of the standard Dutch greenhouse – was an exotic hothouse.) There are many similarities between the Van Nelle and another important modernist European daylight factory whose workforce consisted largely of women. Owen Williams had designed the Boots 'Wets' factory at Beeston (1930–32) with a reinforced-concrete mushroom-column construction system and a spectacular steel-and-glass curtain wall allowing light to flood the factory floors.[40]

As with the Dessau Bauhaus and the Fagus administration building, claims that the transparency and lack of solid internal partitions in the Van Nelle factory rendered the organization 'transparent' and 'open' were something of an illusion. Van der Leeuw wrote that: 'We intended in this manner to promulgate the idea of mutual openness: the staff can see what's going on upstairs and know that anyone can see what's happening below – without this giving the feeling of being spied on.'[41] In reality, the structure of the company was hierarchical and paternalistic. A former Van Nelle coffee sorter recalled that: 'When the supervisor gave a sign, all the sorters went to the toilets at the same time.'[42] The layout of the factory was designed as much on principles of surveillance and social control as to provide improved conditions for the workforce. The penetrating light not only enabled the workers to see clearly the work they were allotted to do, and do it as quickly as possible, it also allowed them to be clearly seen by the management. The curving office block overlooking the entrance to the factory permitted the executives to observe the workers as they arrived or left. Van der Leeuw's own office was at the very end of the block nearest the access road so that he could keep an eye on all activity in the 'factory street', and allowed him to watch the arrival and departure of the workers and note those who were late.[43]

Transparency and open planning enabled both the workforce and office staff to be surveilled by the executives.[44] The emphasis on light, air and openness made 'the people inside the factory, from the worker on the conveyor belt to the office staff, totally visible'. The sports facilities and hygienic washrooms and toilets 'literally bound the workers to the factory area for a longer period', providing recreational and sanitary facilities at the place of production of a kind that had not yet been introduced by the state in social housing – 'the place of reproduction of the labour force'.[45] As noted earlier, J. J. P. Oud's Kiefhoek estate in Rotterdam was built (at the same time as the construction of the Van Nelle factory) with indoor toilets, but without the showers originally included in Oud's designs. However, the provision of such facilities in the workplace may have been problematic – at least when first experienced by workers unfamiliar with such hygienic luxury. As Jan Molenaar has pointed out, those accustomed to a weekly bath in an unplumbed washtub 'must have experienced the gleaming white American sanitary ware as alienating and sanatorium-like', while the 'cropped American-style doors to the cubicles may have made them feel uncomfortable as well'.[46] The sanitary facilities in the factory were also designed to ensure the quality of the products, which 'were produced in highly hygienic conditions from raw material to packaged product'. The health and wellbeing of the employees had direct benefits for the company. 'The healthier the employee, the fewer the absences through illness, the greater the production, and so forth.'[47] The segregation of the sexes by means of separate entrance staircase towers and washing and toilet facilities was not designed primarily for the benefit of the workers, but to discourage 'inappropriate sexual behaviour' which might reduce their productivity. Despite such precautions, when Van der Leeuw undertook an investigation into the workings of the company on his return to Rotterdam in 1940 after qualifying as a doctor and psychoanalyst in Vienna, he found large numbers of staff 'indulging in alcohol and the company of the opposite sex during working hours'.[48]

Van der Leeuw seems to have had more concern for his company's workers' wellbeing than many employers of the period, including Ford, whose industrial practices he criticized in a report of his 1926 American visit (couched in the jargon of American work management):

> When for instance a department is closed, for the time being or permanently, the workers are fired without any arbitration, which is not in line with modern business principles about continuity of employment and the avoidance of 'peaks'. There are no pension and social security systems.

He claimed the Ford factory buildings were so wide that workers in the middle of the factory floor had to work with artificial light the whole time, and that there were often too many workers crowded into the workspaces.[49] This had a deleterious effect on 'the quality of the air, something which the labour inspectorate in our country would not accept'.[50] But he seems to have disapproved of one of the directors of another American car manufacturer queuing up with his workforce in the works canteen.

Many who visited the factory shortly after its completion enthusiastically praised the design of the building and the working conditions there – among them Le Corbusier, and Robertson and Yerbury. Le Corbusier described it as 'the most beautiful spectacle of the modern era' he knew, claiming that it was 'the scintillating proof of life to come, so clean and of an implicit purity'.[51] Its glass-and-metal façade probably inspired the *refuge* he designed for the Armée du Salut in Paris in the early 1930s.[52] For Le Corbusier, his Salvation Army hostel was 'a factory of goodness'.[53] It resembled an industrial production line in which the destitute person (the raw material) is cleansed, refined and processed into a normal member of society, rather as tea, coffee and tobacco were refined and processed into finished products in the Van Nelle factory.[54] A few commentators took a more negative view of the enterprise. After visiting the factory, the Dutch socialist artist and writer R. N. Roland Holst (who painted murals celebrating the achievement of the 8-hour day in Berlage's Dutch Diamond Workers' Union building in Amsterdam)[55] described it as ' a building that depicts the modern era':

> A factory such as this is perfect, but it sickens me nonetheless to see the work done there; work is reduced to the most deathly monotony and the highest intensity, a perfected system of exploitation, but one that is more or less mechanized and which has a strong aesthetic character. A palace for mechanized exploitation.

Roland Holst also visited the house Van der Leeuw commissioned for himself from Brinkman and Van der Vlugt, commenting that it had 'the same glass-and-steel style, which can also provide the utmost in refined luxury and comfort'.[56] Such 'domestic factories' were intended to be demonstrations of their owners' devotion to the factory ethic and the factory aesthetic. These austerely luxurious houses were designed to evoke the image of 'the clean machine', of the hygienic modern factory and its interior, with enormous windows that let in as much light as possible. They featured the latest sanitary and bathroom appliances, cooking and laundering facilities, and incorporated furniture and fixtures in chromed steel or other modern materials similar (or sometimes identical to) those employed in the directors' office and company boardrooms. Van der Leeuw's discreetly sumptious white-walled modernist house (1928–29) overlooked a lake in the outer suburbs of Rotterdam and was tailor-made to its owner's refined minimalist taste: with a theosophical meditation room, a glass-walled winter garden, a gymnasium, and a sun terrace for nude sunbathing on the roof. The house was also equipped with an electrically driven pipe organ and a built-in sound system linked to loudspeakers in each room, electrically operated strip windows, internal climate control and a machine that produced ozone. Van der Leeuw – a large part of whose fortune was derived from tobacco – could not abide smoking and a small corner of the living area was curtained off for smokers, with a powerful extraction system to remove the fumes.

Two other directors of Van Nelle followed Van der Leeuw's lead and commissioned luxurious modernist villas from the firm: the head of the tobacco division A. H.

Sonneveld, and the head of the tea and coffee division M. de Bruyn.[57] Van der Leeuw's younger brother M. A. G. (Dick) van der Leeuw – also a Van Nelle partner, who was suspected of having tuberculosis, and had spent some time in Swiss sanatoriums – had the architects convert a cottage in the dunes at Rockanje (where he had been advised to take 'the healthy sea air') into a modernist home.[58] This was conveniently close to the Oostvoorne airstrip, from where he could pilot his own plane to the Van Nelle factory, landing on the company playing fields. As Jan Molenaar has commented: 'Only a rich, upper-class citizen could afford the life he enjoyed there with his wife and daughter: a free-and-easy outdoor existence, surrounded by nature, with a strong focus on health, modern comfort and hygiene.'[59] Dick van der Leeuw was killed while returning from a business trip to London when the light aeroplane he was flying crashed into the sea near Rotterdam in 1936. Two years earlier, his brother J. J. van der Leeuw had died piloting his own plane across Africa after delivering a lecture in Johannesburg while on a worldwide theosophical tour.

The light that failed

Notwithstanding its careful design incorporating the latest American ideas, the new Van Nelle factory was not a success in business terms, partly due to the worldwide slump which coincided with its opening, the deaths of several family board members, and Kees van der Leeuw's departure to Vienna. Nor did it succeed as a utopian industrial enterprise, and Van der Leeuw was unable to realize 'his ideal as a theosophist' to 'found a model society in which the workers would live healthier and happier lives'.[60] After the factory had been in operation for a time, he had the employees medically examined in order to demonstrate that they were healthier than in the company's old 19th-century factories and warehouses in the inner city. But contrary to expectation, the blinding light and open transparency of the new factory buildings did not produce a healthier and happier workforce dedicated to their work. There were also serious social problems and unrest among the workers.[61] Perhaps in anticipation of this, Van der Leeuw had ordered armour-plated steel shutters, to protect the immense expanses of steel-and-glass curtain wall, from the Gispen company, who also supplied the factory offices and directors' homes with hygienic and mobile tubular-steel furniture.[62]

Despite its shortcomings as a paternalistic and utopian project, the international renown of the factory building was widely disseminated through photographs reproduced in industrial and architectural magazines, documentary films, histories of architecture and commerce, and in exhibitions and books.[63] For the inter-war and immediately post-1945 generations in The Netherlands, the Van Nelle factory epitomized a progressive image of Dutch industry and industriousness, and an 'ethical' conduct of manufacture and commerce – an image based largely on the company's own promotional activities.[64] Through such representational means, the image of the

Van Nelle works as a model factory was employed to promote the idea of a modern architecture that could achieve a new industrial beauty through the celebration of hygiene, health and Taylorism.[65] 'The transparency of the façades, the pump room and the switch rooms on the factory street, the movements of the automatic packing machines on the ground floor of the factories, the constant stream of products on the conveyors through the air and in the halls [...] all breathed an industrial perfection.'[66] The image of the factory as a hygienic and light-filled 'clean machine', as an icon of international modernist architecture and modernizing industrial capitalism in the period between the wars, belies its utopian and commercial failure.

Van Nelle Factory,
Schiedam, Rotterdam, The Netherlands, 1925–31,
photographed in 1996
Johannes Brinkman and **Leen van der Vlugt**

Conclusion

By the 1980s, the multi-storey 'daylight' complex of the Van Nelle factory had become obsolete when horizontal single-storey plants were increasingly being adopted for the processing of staples such as tea, coffee and tobacco. Like the Zonnestraal, it had only a limited lifespan for the purpose for which it was originally designed. Its listing as a 'modernist monument' in the mid-1980s made it increasingly difficult to adapt to modern production methods.[1] When I visited the factory in 1996 production was being wound down. A few bales of tobacco lay scattered artfully like modernist sculptures on the tobacco-processing floor, scenting the air with a heavy old-fashioned smell. Shortly afterwards, the factory finally became redundant and production ceased. In the first years of the 21st century, the manufacturers and warehouses were skilfully restored as a complex of architectural and design offices under the supervision of Wessel de Jonge, who was also jointly responsible for the restoration of the Zonnestraal. This change of use was made possible by the mushroom-column and curtain-wall construction system, as Van der Leeuw had foreseen.[2] The factory was designed as a 'loose envelope' that could easily be adapted, unlike the tight functional specification of the Zonnestraal, which made it much more difficult to convert to a new use.[3]

Nevertheless, after many years as a partial ruin the Zonnestraal has also now been restored to a remarkable semblance of its original pristine state by De Jonge and Hubert-Jan Henket.[4] The earliest plans for restoration proposed new uses such as craft workshops, and the provision of 'alternative' spaces for artists and designers – a plan similar to that eventually adopted for the Van Nelle factory.[5] However, the restoration as undertaken aims to return the sanatorium to something closer to its original function: providing healthcare, rehabilitation and aftercare. The central-services pavilion is already completed and the Dresselhuys pavilion is in the process of being restored.[6] Later buildings are to be demolished and the natural environment around the sanatorium re-established, financed by modern housing which will be constructed in another part of the woods. Although the functions for which the two buildings were designed were very different, the former sanatorium and factory have much in common beyond

216

the fact that they are both in The Netherlands.[7] They were designed to embody the principles of light, air and openness, and the ideals of health, cleanliness and hygiene, and were considered by their architects and those who commissioned them to have a 'spiritual' as well as a material dimension. Like many modernist buildings of the inter-war years, they went through a period of decline – and virtual dereliction in the case of the Zonnestraal – followed eventually by restoration or reconstruction. Perhaps more than any other buildings of the period, they seem to embody the idealistic hopes and contradictions of the modernist adventure.

These two ambitious and complex modernist projects stand as exemplary testaments to the uneasy coexistence of paternalistic capitalism and utopian idealism that characterized the modern movement in architecture during the years between the two world wars. The Van Nelle complex was conceived as a clean machine: a healthy, hygienic and profitable model manufacturing plant through which enlightenment streamed. Zonnestraal was intended to be a factory of health that would process sick workers into fit and capable individuals. Both were products of the early 20th-century capitalist system: the one of an 'enlightened' paternalistic business ethic, the other of a militant trades unionism fighting antiquated, exploitative and unhealthy workshop practices. For political reasons during the Cold War decades following the Second World War, modernist architecture was represented as embodying and expressing social-democratic values. This was a fallacy. Modernist architectural forms were employed (often spectacularly) to promote the values of Mussolini's Italy and those of the Soviet Union in the early communist era, as well as of capitalist democracies in The Netherlands, Weimar Germany, Czechoslovakia, France, Britain, Scandinavia and the United States. However, the uneasy relationship between social democracy and paternalist capitalism seems to have found a particularly poignant form in some of the modernist buildings of the inter-war period – nowhere more so than in the Van Nelle factory and the Zonnestraal Sanatorium with their crisp orthogonal white walls and scintillating panes of glass, their brilliant and visually stunning exploitation of the imagery of hygiene and health, light, fresh air and openness.

The survival beyond their intended lifespan and the eventual deterioration of buildings such as Zonnestraal has meant that they have changed in ways their designers did not foresee (or did not wish to foresee). Modernist architects in the 1920s and 1930s believed their buildings should look pristine as on the day they were completed, or – perhaps more importantly – photographed. Hence their obsession with photographic images in which these buildings would look eternally young. In the first decades of the 20th century, writers, artists and architects were obsessed by youth, and what they saw as the characteristics of youth. This preoccupation became a symbol of regeneration in response to the destruction of a whole generation of European young men in the First World War. The obsession of early modernist architects with eternal newness and youth is almost certainly connected to this. Modernist buildings were not intended to grow old. Like those who age suddenly after appearing youthful beyond their time, unrestored modernist buildings now seem particularly ancient and decrepit. The photographs by which they are internationally known through reproduction remain pristine and young as on the day they were taken, while the buildings they represent have become streaked with damp and rust, scabrous with decay, and rotten within. We are used to the aging of our fellow human beings, yet it can come as a shock that this also happens to human artifacts and buildings, particularly since these have been designed in the past to age gracefully, to patinate and weather well.

Modernist buildings like Zonnestraal depended largely for their life as *architecture* (as opposed to *building*) on the circulation of reproduced images, photographs in books, exhibitions and magazines, slides, drawings and models. For most people today they remain simulacra: hypnotically compelling reproductions on the pages of architectural books or magazines – or film, TV, or computer screens. Modernist architects' preoccupation with photographic representations of their buildings was symptomatic of a desire to capture them as pristine and perfect, before the process of weathering and use had blurred and blunted these qualities.[8] The photographic representation of modernist architecture in magazines and books in the 1920s and 1930s was dominated by a formalist aesthetic typified by the work of Charles Sheeler in the United States and by Albert Renger-Patzsch in Germany, which served to efface and deny qualities of place, habitat, location and site, as well as weathering, and the marks of use. Such pristine aesthetizised images represented modern buildings as possessing universal (or international) qualities. This was achieved by their powerful evocation of abstract notions of space and plasticity, and their elimination of the presence and specificity of human beings – of the untidy edges and leakages associated with human life.

This process of sanitized representation paralleled the processes of hygiene, isolation and cleanliness that characterized medical and social thinking in the years between the wars, and in particular of the sanatorium movement of which the Zonnestraal was a part. Hygiene and hygienic discourses are essentially a system of control. The idealists of the modern movement such as Jan Duiker tried to suborn such dominant notions of hygiene and health to utopian ends. They succeeded, but they also failed. Zonnestraal became a ruin because tuberculosis and related lung diseases were (at least temporarily) eradicated. But also because the idealism that the sanatorium represented – both as an icon of international modernist architecture, and as an ideal championed by men like the leaders of the Dutch Diamond Workers' Union, Henri Polak and Jan van Zutphen – was eradicated too.

The modernist buildings of the years between the two world wars were designed to evoke images of a hygiene and cleanliness that was both literal and symbolic. These crisp, sparkling artifacts crumbled and decayed after a few decades of use. Their concrete façades became cracked and leprous as though they themselves were diseased,

218

as in a sense they were. Today, many of them have been restored to a state of health and cleanliness, cured of their 'sickness' and the depredations of time, rather as the human body is repaired and renewed with transplants, grafts, bypasses and other interventions of modern medicine. Yet in a few years they will require attention once more, like the human body itself, although (unlike the human body) they can probably be maintained almost indefinitely, given sufficient money and professional dedication. Not only have many of these buildings recently been restored to a pristine state, like the clean machines they once aspired to be, so also have the machines or equipment they originally housed. The long obsolete boilers of the Zonnestraal have been lovingly rebuilt by a central-heating company – gleaming in their boilerhouse as in a painting by Léger of the immediately post-First World War period. In Loos's Müller House in Prague, the old coal-fired Strebel boilers (now superseded by gas boilers) have been restored to non-operational glory. These were the boilers which in 1951 killed the owner and commissioner of the house Dr František Müller with carbon monoxide fumes while he tried to stoke them himself – no longer permitted (or able to afford) a servant in post-Second World War communist Czechoslovakia.[9]

Light, air and openness remain ideals today, albeit articulated differently from the inter-war years and tempered by changes that have taken place in society and in technology over the last eighty years. We are still concerned with health and hygiene. Our machines have got cleaner and smaller, and although our obsession with them has not diminished it is articulated differently. After several decades of censure as 'clinical', 'cold' and 'alienating', modernism has become fashionable again: both in public buildings and in types of housing that deliberately eschew the 'domestic' for the industrial look of the factory, office or hospital – although this is largely confined to housing for the privileged and wealthy. The recent taste for loft living and the conversion of factory, office, hospital and sanatorium spaces into domestic apartments reveals a continuing fascination with health and hygiene, openness and light, and the 'clean machine'.

While many modernist buildings from between the wars are still under threat, a considerable number have been restored or reconstructed over the past two decades. These include Rietveld's Schröder House and Erasmuslaan houses in Utrecht, Brinkman and Van der Vlugt's Sonneveld House in Rotterdam, Gropius's Bauhaus building in Dessau, Wells Coates's Isokon flats, Lubetkin and Tecton's Penguin Pool, Highpoint flats and Finsbury Health Centre (all in London), and Mendelsohn and Chermayeff's De La Warr Pavilion, Bexhill-on-Sea. Buildings that were totally destroyed during the Second World War such as J. J. P. Oud's Café Unie in Rotterdam, or designed as temporary exhibition structures and then dismantled, such as Mies van der Rohe's Barcelona Pavilion, have been reconstructed.[10] Theoretically, this process could be taken even further to realize buildings that were never built, and it is possible today to experience and move through both built and unbuilt buildings by means of computer-based techniques of virtual reality.

However, restoration has not been extended to all modern-movement buildings, even when these have been highly regarded. Oud's Oud-Mathenesse estate in Rotterdam (1922–24) was designed to last for only twenty-five years, and constructed without proper foundations. Although the estate became popular with its tenants, it was eventually demolished in the early 1990s after a prolonged debate about its preservation, having survived for seventy years. A modern pastiche was built to take its place. On the other hand, the small site hut Oud designed for use while the estate was being built (and then demolished) has been faithfully reconstructed. This more directly represented a formalist De Stijl aesthetic, and was painted in the De Stijl primary colours: red, yellow and blue. It is open to the public for two hours a week, with old photographs of the original displayed inside. 'Its primary colours are always fresh', Wouter Vanstiphout writes. 'Thanks to the regular defacements with graffiti, it gets repainted nearly every week.'[11] Oud's slightly later Rotterdam estate of single-family houses at Kiefhoek (1925–30) was so radically restored it was virtually rebuilt, with each pair of houses reconstructed as double-fronted single-family houses. The only problem was that this left the new houses with two front doors. The solution was to make one front door into a 'door-shaped window'. Otherwise, the reconstruction was 'fanatically precise', with obsolete building techniques being employed by the restoration architects and craftsmen.[12] Similar techniques have been employed in the reconstruction of the Zonnestraal, where the windows have been replaced with plate glass made in a factory in Estonia that still manufactures glass with the original ripple in it.

The decline and eventual rebirth of buildings such as the Zonnestraal draws attention to the contradictions of early modernist architecture, where a recognition of the need for buildings that would last only as long as they were needed coexisted with a desire to create a totally new kind of architecture in which similar formal and structural ideas were employed both in luxury houses and villas for the wealthy and in hospitals, sanatoriums, social housing and hostels for the working class. This has now become an architecture where excavation, rehabilitation, restoration and preservation have replaced ideas of the destruction of the old by the new, and of building temporary and replaceable structures for a utopian future. Jan Molema and Wessel de Jonge have argued that Jan Duiker 'trusted the notion of progress too much for the good of his own buildings' such as the Zonnestraal and Cliostraat Open-Air School.[13] This is true only if one believes these buildings should last longer than Duiker intended. Other architects and critics maintain that it might be better to allow such modernist ruins to be demolished. Mohsen Mostafavi and David Leatherbarrow have argued that: 'Is it not false to envisage the life of a building as something that extends in perpetuity, something that must indefinitely bear the burden of its history?'[14] This raises a number of important issues. Restoration, reconstruction, or re-creation blurs the relationship of modernist buildings with their particular historical moment. It is especially problematic for buildings whose original function has now been superseded. Many modernist buildings

De La Warr Pavilion, Bexhill-on-Sea, East Sussex, 1934–35, photographed after restoration in 2005
Erich Mendelsohn and **Serge Chermayeff**

of the 1920s and 1930s were, like Zonnestraal, designed to have a relatively short functional (as well as technical) life expectancy and are also in a sorry condition today – or have been altered beyond recognition. Duiker himself was opposed to the change of use of buildings designed for a particular purpose. Ostensibly on the basis of his views, a number of Dutch architects argued in the early 1980s against the restoration or reconstruction of Zonnestraal.[15]

However, the current restoration of the sanatorium complex to something quite close to its original function appears to respect Duiker's views and intentions. Writing of the recent restoration of Giuseppe Terragni's Sant'Elia's Infant School in Como, Maristella Casciato and Cristiana Marcosano Dell'Erba maintain that the architectural value we place upon such modernist icons is inseparable from their 'image of perfect integrity as artifacts', and this in turn is dependent on the most fragile of materials and constructional details. 'From top to bottom of their delicate plaster skins, their great areas of glass held in the slenderest of metal frames, their un-protected planar façades, the traces of human life and the work of the elements are immediately visible.'[16] And De Jonge has argued that in devising techniques for the conservation and repair of modernist buildings it is necessary to arrive at 'a new conceptual approach that will allow us to foster the spirit of modernity' without destroying this fragility and transparency. For if the characteristics of transitoriness are concealed in perpetuity by advanced restoration techniques, 'an artificial memento is all that will be left behind'.[17]

Sensitive restoration can allow us to gain more insight into the historical circumstances that produced modernist buildings, even as this promotes new fashions for 'retro' design and pastiche 'neo-modernism'. These architectural forms were originally inspired by a vision of human bodies and minds liberated and healed, yet such architecture was also a means of surveillance and constraint. We need to be aware that the ever more seductive and elegant images produced by new restoration techniques and new reproductive media are also the product of particular historical circumstances and ideologies – as were the originals.

Notes

Bibliographical references given in abbreviated form in the Notes are given in full in the Bibliography.

Introduction

1 Scheerbart, 1914, extracts translated in Benton and Benton, with Sharp, 1975, p. 73.
2 E. J. Jelles, 'Zonnestraal', in Jelles and Alberts, 1976, p. 22.
3 See Vickery, 1971, p. 147.
4 De Back, Berndsen and Berns, 1996, p. 25.
5 Richter, 1930. See Janser, 1997, passim; Andres Janser, 'New Living: A Model Film? Hans Richter's Werkbund Film: Between Commissioned Work and Poetry on Film', in Janser and Rüegg, 2001, pp. 16–35, and frame enlargements pp. 38–121. The English title of Richter's film appears as New Living in Janser and Rüegg, 2001, and Janser, 1997. It is better translated as The New Dwelling.
6 See Janser and Rüegg, 2001, pp. 38–40 translation of the intertitles slightly modified. The publicity brochure for the film which emphasized 'Licht und Luft' (Light and Air) is reproduced pp. 36–37.
7 For typophoto, see Ute Brüning, 'Typophoto' in Fiedler, 1990, pp. 205–37.
8 Janser and Rüegg, 2001, pp. 109–17; Giedion, 1929, pls 59–62. Giedion illustrated more photographs and plans of Zonnestraal than of any other building. (See also Taut, 1929a, pp. 181–82, where five photographs of the sanatorium are illustrated.)
9 Janser and Rüegg, 2001, pp. 118–19.
10 Döcker, 1929. On the first page Döcker invokes 'Light, Air and Sun' and the 'hygienic formation (Gestaltung)' of lives'. Chapters include 'The Hospital, the Essential "Healthy" Building Type' and 'Light, Sun, and Medicinal Waters in the Hospital' (by Dr Poehlmann).
11 Giedion, 1929, pls 4 & 5.
12 Giedion, 1941. Space, Time and Architecture was a revised and extended version of the Charles Eliot Norton lectures Giedion delivered at Harvard in 1938 and 1939.
13 For a succinct account of the Frankfurt notion of Existenzminimum, see Iain Borden, 'The Politics of the Plan', in Borden and Dunster, 1995, pp. 215–21. See also Steinmann, 1972; Bullock, 1978.
14 See Hirdina, 1984, which reprints many articles and illustrations from Das Neue Frankfurt, the magazine May issued (from October 1926) to promote the neue Frankfurt. Das Neue Frankfurt was edited for most of its run by Josef Gantner. It made dramatic use of the New Typography in its layout, photographic illustrations, and covers, designed by the graphic designer Hans Leistikow and his sister the photographer Grete Leistikow. A double issue in 1931 was devoted to hygiene (vol. 5, no. 4/5, April–May 1931).
15 Georgiadis, 1993, p. 77. Sigfried Giedion was the influential secretary general of CIAM, which had been founded the previous year in La Sarraz in Switzerland. (See Mumford, 2000, passim.)
16 Moholy-Nagy, 1925; English translation: Moholy-Nagy, 1967, p. 38.
17 For example Giedion, 1941; Hitchcock and Johnson, 1932, reprint, 1995; Pevsner, 1936, revised edition: Pevsner, 1960 (and subsequent editions); Banham, 1960. A year before Befreites Wohnen Giedion had published an analysis of the early development of modern architecture that emphasized new structural methods and building materials, see Giedion, 1928a, English translation: Giedion, 1995. More recent accounts include Frampton, 1985; Colquhoun, 2002.
18 Rietveld, 1932, translated as 'New functionalism in Dutch furniture' in Küper and Van Zijl, 1992, pp. 36–37, translation slightly modified.
19 Rietveld, 1948, translated as 'Interiors' in Küper and Van Zijl, 1992, p. 46.
20 Döcker, 1929, p. 1.
21 Some of these issues are raised in Forty, 1986; Colomina, 1997, pp. 60–71; and Worpole, 2000. For another discussion of the relationship between modernist architecture, race and colonialism, see Overy, 2005, pp. 50–67.

Chapter 1 The city in the country

1 For the ANDB (Algemeene Nederlandsche Diamantbewerkers Bond), see De Burcht van Berlage, 1991. The union was founded in 1894 and was one of the first in The Netherlands to introduce minimum wages, sickness, disability, unemployment and death insurance, paid holidays and an eight-hour day.
2 The headquarters building at 3–9 Henri Polaklaan, Amsterdam was completed in 1900. See De Burcht van Berlage, 1991, passim; Polano, 1988, pp. 152–53. The Beurs was built between 1898 and 1903.
3 The laundry was destroyed during the Second World War. See Jelles and Alberts, 1976, p. 20; Molema, 1989, pp. 54–57.
4 The Gooiland Hotel was completed by Bijvoet in collaboration with Piet Elling. See Jelles and Alberts, 1976, pp. 96–107; Molema, 1989, pp. 166–83.
5 After the new sanatorium was built the villa housed the nurses.
6 Workers in the diamond-polishing industry were all men. However, from the beginning the sanatorium was made available to some patients who were not members of the union as various outside bodies had contributed to financing it. See De Back, Berndsen and Berns, 1996, p. 19.
7 Patients were put on a high-calorie, high-fat diet to build up their strength.
8 The naming of the fund, and later the sanatorium, was derived from – and was a homage to – a Belgian anti-tuberculosis fund that had suffered during the German occupation in the First World War.
9 In restoring the sanatorium, glass was sourced from Lithuania where it is still made by the drawn-glass process – rather than the float-glass process invented by Pilkington in the 1950s and now generally adopted. (Information Wessel de Jonge, 2004.)
10 See for example J. Lambert, G. Saache and P. Bailly's Pavillon des Diamantaires (Diamond Merchants Pavillion) for the Arts décoratifs exhibition in Paris in 1925. (Illustrated in Charlotte Benton, 1975, pl. 11.)
11 See 'Het Bondsgebouw', in De Burcht van Berlage, 1991, pp. 13–28.
12 Although Mondrian occasionally employed the diamond format in his work, the rather different use of the diagonal in Van Doesburg's work became a point of confrontation between the two artists in the mid-1920s. See Blotkamp, 1994, pp. 185–99.
13 Illustrated in Overy (1991), 2000, p. 81 fig. 56.
14 Zonnestraal was designed around a pentagonal plan, which is also a theosophical plan. There are a number of references to theosophical ideas in Duiker's works, including the name of the apartment block 'Nirwana' which he designed in collaboration with Wiebenga in The Hague in 1927. See Derwig and Mattie, 1995, p. 31, p. 39 n. 1. Cf. the discussion of Kees van der Leeuw and the Van Nelle factory in Chapter 12.
15 'Many modern buildings weather very inelegantly and, in contrast to many older structures, a patina on their immaculate envelope rarely suits them.' (De Jonge, 1998, in Cunningham, 1998, p. 154.)
16 For the effect of time and the elements on modernist architecture, see Mostafavi and Leatherbarrow, 1993, passim.
17 The phrase was apparently coined by an American advertising agency, N. W. Ayer, in 1948 for the diamond company De Beers.
18 According to Walter Rathenau – the son of the founder of the company Emil Rathenau, and later managing director – AEG was in 1907 'undoubtedly the largest European combination of industrial units under a centralized control and with a centralized organization'. (Quoted in Wilson, 1981, p. 78.) In 1922, Rathenau became German Foreign Minister and was assassinated by anti-Semitic right-wingers shortly after signing the Treaty of Rapallo with the Soviet Union.
19 Lenin, 1970, p. 82.
20 See discussion of this in later chapters, see also Overy, 2005.
21 More than 2,000 members of the ANDB were murdered by the Nazis during the Second World War. (De Burcht van Berlage, 1991, p. 41.)
22 Peter Smithson, 'On Duiker', from the introduction to Forum, Special Issue on Duiker, no.1, 1962, reprinted in Smithson, 1981, p. 42.
23 De Jonge, 1998, in Cunningham, 1998, p. 150.
24 De Jonge, 1998, in Cunningham, 1998, p. 153. 'The lack of covering arose as much from poor control during construction rather than from design failure.' (De Jonge, 1998, in Cunningham, 1998,

p. 157 n. 12.) To fill the narrow and complicated formwork more easily the concrete mix was apparently watered down to make it more fluid. This and other errors of construction seriously compromised the strength of the structure.

25 Johannes Duiker, 'Dr Berlage en de "Niewe Zakelijkheid"', *De 8 en Obouw*, no. 5, 1932, pp. 43–51, cited in translation by De Jonge, 1998, in Cunningham, 1998, p. 151.

26 Wiebenga's contribution to the design and planning of the Zonnestraal sanatorium – as well as a number of other seminal modernist buildings in The Netherlands such as Duiker's Open-Air School in Amsterdam and Brinkman and Van der Vlugt's Van Nelle tea, coffee and tobacco factory near Rotterdam – went well beyond the normal involvement of a structural engineer. (De Jonge, 1998, in Cunningham, p. 157 n. 5.) For Wiebenga, see Molema and Bak, 1987.

27 De Jonge, 1998, in Cunningham, 1998, p. 150. See also Henket, 1998, in Cunningham, 1998, p. 16.

28 De Jonge, 1998, in Cunningham, 1998, p. 149, p. 157, n. 3. Owing to the decline in the Amsterdam diamond industry since the late 1920s as the result of competition from Antwerp, Zonnestraal increasingly treated patients who were unconnected with the diamond industry.

29 The murder of so many Dutch Jewish diamond workers in the Holocaust further exacerbated the industry's decline. The ANDB was wound up in 1958. Its Berlage-designed headquarters building in Amsterdam is now the Dutch National Trades Union Museum.

30 Sant'Elia and Marinetti, 1914, English translation, Conrads, 1970, p. 38. This part of the manifesto is now thought to have been added by Marinetti. (See Meyer, 1995, pp. 141–68.)

31 Van Doesburg, 1925, pp. 225–27; English translation, Van Doesburg, 1990, p. 61.

32 Henry Ford, from an interview with A. M. Smith (nd) quoted in Giedion, 1929, p. 3. This has been translated from the German text, as I have been unable to trace the original interview.

33 Giedion, 1929, p. 7. Hilde Heynen comments: 'Nowhere else in Giedion's work is this concept of deliberate transitoriness so emphatically stated as in *Befreites Wohnen*, a book that in terms of its rhetorical structure also has the character of a manifesto.' (Heynen, 1999, p. 36.)

34 Henket, 1998, in Cunningham, 1998, p. 14.

35 Tuberculosis was the single greatest killer of males in the United Kingdom. See Bryder, 1988, p. 11.

36 Susan Sontag has compared the use of disease as metaphor in attitudes to cancer and tuberculosis. See Sontag, 1991, passim.

37 The BCG (bacille Calmette-Guérin) vaccine had been discovered in 1921 but did not become generally available until after 1947. The antibiotic streptomycin (discovered in the United States in 1943) was combined with two non-antibiotic drugs – isoniazid (discovered in the US in 1952) and PAS (para-aminosalicylic acid, discovered in Sweden in 1943) – to form the 'triple drug' chemotherapy, which produced an effective cure for tuberculosis. See Wainwright, 1990.

38 Beatriz Colomina claims that subsequent research 'established that there was no scientific basis' to 'air and sun therapy'. (Colomina, 1997, p. 60.)

39 Professor Sir Maxwell Joseph and Dr R. T. D. Oliver have argued that exposure to sunshine and confinement in sanatoriums 'were so successful' in the treatment of tuberculosis in the days before antibiotics because vitamin D induced by the sun activates the phagocytes to convert TB from a lethal to a non-lethal infection – as long as the diet contains sufficient zinc and vitamin A, provided for example by fat in milk. Joseph and Oliver claim that the recent rise in the incidence in tuberculosis is because people who have arrived in western Europe from countries where the sunlight is very strong are at higher risk of TB in cold, non-sunny climates like Great Britain, 'particularly if they wear clothing so that no skin is exposed'. (Letter from Professor Sir Maxwell Joseph and Dr R. T. D. Oliver of St Bartholomew's and the London Hospitals, *Guardian*, 27 November 2003.)

40 See Dormandy, 1999, pp. 129ff.

41 Brehmer argued this in his doctoral dissertation, 'De legibus ab initium atque progressum tuberculosis pulmonum spectatibus' (The Laws concerning the Beginning and Progress of Tuberculosis of the Lungs) in 1853, published in book form in 1857. Brehmer's book remained a bestseller for many decades. (Dormandy, 1999, p. 150.)

42 Dormandy, 1999, pp. 150–51.

43 Dettweiler's regime became the basis for the treatment introduced by Professor Robert Philip at the Royal Victoria Hospital for Consumption in Edinburgh from 1899. (Dormandy, 1999, pp. 152–53.) See also Porter, 1997, p. 422; Campbell, 1999, p. 340 n. 11.

44 Davos had been a centre for the treatment of scrofula (tuberculosis of the lymphatic glands) since 1841. (Dubos and Dubos, 1953, p. 176.)

45 Mann, 1996, passim (originally published as *Der Zauberberg*, 1924). From May to September 1912 Mann's wife Katia was in the Waldsanatorium (Valbella clinic) in Davos, founded in 1898, where she was treated for acute bronchitis. A surviving X-ray of her lungs taken there shows no sign of tuberculosis. (Kurzke, 2002, p. 278, p. 298.) Mann visited his wife for three weeks shortly after she arrived at the sanatorium, in May 1912.

46 These included *The Sacred Mountain* (1926) directed by Arnold Fanck (in which Leni Riefenstahl made her acting debut), Fanck's *The White Hell of the Piz Palü* (1929) and *The White Frenzy* (1931), Ernst Lubitsch's *Romeo and Julia in the Snow* (1920) and *Eternal Love* (1929) – and Riefenstahl's own directorial debut *The Blue Light*, in 1932.

47 See Miller, 1992, pp. 16–19, illustration p. 19.

48 Heller, 1979, p. 124; Campbell, 1999, p. 332. The North of England Furnishing Company Ltd (now Amdega Ltd) manufactured a revolving summerhouse known as the Darlington Shelter from 1913, which was used by tuberculosis patients. (Campbell, 1999, p. 341 n. 35.) George Bernard Shaw had a rotating summerhouse in his garden at Ayot St Lawrence in Hertfordshire where he wrote in the afternoons.

49 Giedion, 1929, pls 63–65; Döcker, 1929, p. 70 pls 109–10. It is described in both as a 'Volksheilstätte' (Public Sanatorium).

50 Giedion, 1941, pp. 248–49 (illustration p. 249, where it is captioned 'Queen Alexandra Sanatorium, Davos, 1907').

51 Mann, 1996, p. 8. The Queen Alexandra Sanatorium had been established 'for the special treatment of an intermediate class of consumptive patients between the rich and the poor'. (British Journal of Nursing, 20 May 1905, p. 388.)

52 See A[rthur] R[üegg], 'Bella Lui Sanatorium', in Janser and Rüegg, 2001, p. 123.

53 Illustrated in Janser and Rüegg, 2001, p. 112. According to Rüegg the recliners were produced by the Basler Eisenmöbelfabrik Breunlin in Sissach. (Janser and Rüegg, 2001, p. 113).

54 Duiker visited Britain twice between 1919 and 1925 as a member of a study committee. Among other institutions, he went to Sir Robert Philips's aftercare colony in Edinburgh. (Molema and De Jonge, 1985, p. 51.)

55 By 1938, Papworth had a population of 1,000 including 360 children. It was enlarged in 1950, and is now an internationally famous centre for cardiac surgery. (Bryden, 1988, pp. 158–61; Dormandy, 1999, pp. 321–22.)

56 See also Jelles and Alberts, 1976, p. 3: 'The pavilions and central functions, though fixed on an axis, appear to a visitor to bob up and down like white boats on a dark heath.'

57 See Pearson, 1978, p. 85.

58 Colomina, 1997, p. 60.

59 Heller, 1979, p. 124.

60 Marinetti, 1913; English translation in Apollonio, 1973, p. 97.

61 Letter from Lugano to Sophie Küppers, dated 13 February 1924, translated in Lissitzky-Küppers, 1992, p. 38.

62 See the chapter entitled 'In the Restaurant' in Mann, 1996, pp. 13–18.

63 Mann, 1996, pp. 355–56.

64 Ibid., pp. 10–11.

65 (Kokoschka, 1974, p. 49.) Although Loos and Bruce never married, she took his name. Loos nearly bankrupted himself sending Bruce to a series of expensive sanatoriums before the First World War. Loos took Oskar Kokoschka to Leysin on one of his visits, where he painted portraits of Bruce and a number of other patients. Despite her long spells of expensive – and apparently enjoyable – sanatorium treatment Bruce eventually died from the disease in 1921.

66 The sanatorium in Mann's account is apparently a conflation of the Waldsanatorium, built in 1910, where his wife was treated in 1912, and the International Sanatorium, built in 1899. (Campbell, 1999, p. 341 n. 25.)

67 Mann, 1953, in Mann, 1996, pp. 722–23.

68 'When travel to a better climate was invented as a treatment for tuberculosis in the early 19th century, the most contradictory destinations were proposed. The south, mountains, desert islands – their very diversity suggests what they have in common: the rejection of the city.' (Sontag, 1991, p. 74.)

Chapter 2 The house of health

1 See Heller, 1979, p. 124; Aschenbeck, 1997, passim.

2 Miller, 1992; Campbell, 1999, pp. 327–43.

3 Heller, 1979, p. 124.

4 See Wigley, 1995, p. 346.

5 El Lissitzky – who suffered from (and eventually died from) tuberculosis – wrote of white as 'the colour of hygiene and of space'. (Lissitzky, 1924; English translation, Lissitzky-Küppers, 1992, p. 350.)

6 See Wigley, 1995, passim.

7 Wigglesworth, 1998, p. 282.

8 Giedion, 1929, pl. 76.

9 Colomina, 1997, p. 60.

10 Illustrations in Functional Architecture, 1990, p. 287; Bucharest in the 1920s–1940s, 1994, p. 188. See also the Crucii Rosii Toria Sanatorium at Covasna designed by Grigore Ionescu, 1933–34. (Ibid., p. 187.)

11 See Shorter, 1990, pp. 159–95.

12 For the Purkersdorf Sanatorium, see Sekler, 1985, especially pp. 67–72, 286–89, Topp, 1997, pp. 414–37, Topp, 2004, pp. 63–95.

13 Krafft-Ebing (1840–1902) was the author of *Psychopathia Sexualis* (1886) where he had first introduced the term 'masochism'. In *Über gesunde und kranke Nerven* (On healthy and diseased nerves) published the previous year (1885) he had examined the role of the environment in mental health. (See Topp, 1997, pp. 416–17.)

14 Hoffmann, 1972, p. 116, quoted in translation in Topp, 1997, p. 436.

15 Quoted in translation in Topp, 1997, p. 421.

16 Earlier designs show longer, almost strip windows on the ground floor which would have required a reinforced-concrete frame construction. Illustrated in Sekler, 1985, p. 288 fig. 84/IV.

17 Lux, 1904–5, p. 407, quoted in translation by Topp, 1997, p. 421.

18 Rochowanski, 1959, quoted in translation in Blaschke and Lipschitz, 2003, p. 116. Each room was furnished with a bed with bedside table/chest of drawers, a large washstand fitted with drawers for toiletries and undergarments, a writing desk and chair, and a wardrobe. All except the wardrobe are visible in contemporary photographs. (See Topp, 2004, p. 85 pl. 37.)

19 Illustrated in Sekler, 1985, p. 68 pl. 76.

20 Quoted in translation in Topp, 1997, p. 422.

21 Illustrated in Brandstätter, 2003, pp. 126–27

22 Sekler, 1985, p. 235.

23 Bertha Zuckerkandl, quoted in translation in Topp, 1997, p. 223.

24 After having fallen into decay at the end of the 20th century, in the early years of the 21st century the sanatorium was carefully restored. The extra storey and pitched roof added by Leopold Bauer in 1926 were removed, and a new building constructed beside it. The complex is now run as a private old people's home.

25 Lavin, 2004, p. 26.

26 Entitled *Pròdrŏmŏs* (Altenberg, 1905). *Pròdrŏmŏs* is Greek for forerunner, signpost or antechamber. See Barker, 1996, pp. 107–18.

27 'Werdet einfach!', in Altenberg, 1915.

28 Mann, 1953, reprinted in Mann, 1996, p. 720.

29 For example, the Bella Lui Sanatorium was converted into a hotel by one of its original designers Flora Steiger-Crawford, who had been responsible for the interior where she had employed many standardized furniture designs by Max Ernst Haefeli. In the 1980s, it became a religious institution and many of the furnishings were replaced. (A[rthur] R[üegg], in Janser and Rüegg, 2001, p. 123.)

30 Pommer and Otto, 1991, p. 9.

31 Sanatorium-like features are apparent in old people's homes such as the Budge Home for the Aged in Frankfurt designed by Mart Stam and Werner Moser with Ferdinand Kramer and Erika Habermann (1928–30) as part of Ernst May's neue Frankfurt programme – providing double and single rooms, each with a south-facing balcony overlooking the communal garden – illustrated in Hitchcock and Johnson, 1995, pp. 218–20. See also Otto Haesler and Karl Völker's Old People's Home for the Marie von Boschan Aschrott Stiftung in Kassel (1932), illustrated in Hitchcock and Johnson, 1995, p. 161; Functional Architecture, 1990, pp. 74–75.

32 For Döcker's two houses, see Kirsch, 1989, pp. 147–53. These are little known today as both were destroyed during the Second World War and have not been rebuilt, unlike some of the other houses on the estate.

33 Döcker, in Bau und Wohnung, 1927, translated in Joedicke, 1989, p. 38, translation modified.

34 Döcker, 1929, pp. 68–69. See also the book edited by Hermann Gescheit which grouped together hospitals and hotels. (Gescheit, 1929.)

35 Illustrated in Functional Architecture, 1990, pp. 272–73.

36 Geretsegger and Peintner, 1979, pp. 137–44.

37 Illustrated in Geretsegger and Peintner, 1979, p. 144 ill. 162.

38 Geretsegger and Peintner, 1979, p. 140.

39 Quoted in translation in Geretsegger and Peintner, 1979, p. 140. Drawings for these hotels, including impressions of the austere, hospital-like interiors are illustrated on pp. 142 and 143.

40 See Blau, 1999, pp. 255–56

41 Tim Benton, in Benton and Benton, 1977, p. 65. '*Wohnstadt*' for Taut defined a high-density inner-city estate rather than the more suburban *Siedlung*. For the Wohnstadt Carl Legien, see Deutscher Werkbund Berlin and Brenne, 2005, pp. 140–45.

42 See Buddensieg and Rogge, 1984, p. 80, illustrations p. 80 fig. 69, pp. 320–23 figs A106–A111.

43 More conventional designs by Behrens, Loos, Josef Frank, Oskar Strnad, Margarete Schütte-Lihotzky and other architects were realized as part of the Winarsky Hof/Otto Haas Hof project in Brigittenau, a working-class district in the north of Vienna. (Blau, 1999, pp. 299–31.)

44 Peter Behrens in Bau und Wohnung, 1927, p. 17, quoted in Kirsch, 1989, p. 178.

45 *Blätter des Deutschen Roten Kreuzes*. Behrens wrote to Mies in October 1926 that this was in the 'last issue'. (Behrens to Mies, 6 October 1926, Mies van der Rohe Archives, Museum of Modern Art, New York, cited in Kirsch, 1989, p. 176.)

46 Behrens to Mies, 6 October 1926, Mies van der Rohe Archives, Museum of Modern Art, New York, cited in Kirsch, 1989, p. 176, translation slightly modified.

47 Bau und Wohnung, 1927, p. 17.

48 Kirsch, 1989, p. 18. The 1925 document stated that through the model-housing exhibition and the temporary exhibitions 'it is intended to give as comprehensive a picture as possible of the finest technological, hygienic, and artistic achievements'. (Provisional plan for the execution of the Werkbund exhibition, Stuttgart, 27 June 1925, Mies van der Rohe Archive, Museum of Modern Art, New York, quoted in translation in Kirsch, 1989, p. 17.)

49 One of the principal original aims of the Weissenhofsiedlung was to provide models and types suitable for social housing, although this had to a large extent become lost to sight as the housing exhibition evolved from its inception in 1925 to its realization in 1927. See Kirsch, 1989, passim.

50 Behrens, in Bau und Wohnung, 1927, p. 17, quoted in translation in Benton & Benton, 1977, pp. 17–18.

51 Gravagnuolo, 1995, p. 177. See also Rukschcio and Schachel, 1982, pp. 571–73.

52 Behrens probably knew Loos's design from an illustration in Behne, 1926, in which Garnier's designs for a terraced heliotherapy clinic were also illustrated. (See Behne, 1996, p. 209 and pp. 192–93; also illustrated in Kirsch, 1989, p. 178.)

53 Kirsch, 1989, p. 177.

54 Behrens, in Bau und Wohnung, 1927, pp. 23–24, quoted in translation in Kirsch, 1989, p. 179.

55 Van Doesburg, 1927, pp. 556–59, translated in Van Doesburg, 1990, p. 169.

56 Lüders, 1927, p. 316; English translation, Lüders, 1995, p. 468.

57 Lüders, 1927, p. 316; English translation, Lüders, 1995, p. 468, translation slightly modified.

58 These were similar to the Afrikanische Siedlung in Berlin, the only other social housing Mies designed in Germany, and to apartment blocks by architects who specialized in social housing such as Gropius, Bruno Taut and Otto Haesler.

59 Gans, 1987, p. 128; see also Joedicke and Plath, 1984, p. 71.

60 Behrens, in Bau und Wohnung, 1927, pp. 23–24, quoted in translation in Kirsch, 1989, p. 182.

61 See Schütte-Lihotzky, 2004, pp. 139–41.

62 Ibid., pp. 141–43. In Vienna in the early 1920s Schütte-Lihotzky and other architects working for the settlers' movement had designed allotment huts that could have extra rooms added to provide basic subsistence housing. (Blau, 1999, pp. 118–19.)

63 For the *dom kommuny*, see Buchli, 1999; see also Buchli, 1998.

64 Teige, 1932; English translation *Teige*, 2002, p. 103.

65 Quoted in translation in Svácha, 1995, p. 413.

66 Teige, 1933, p. 76, quoted in translation in Andĕl, 2006, pp. 115, 158, translation modified.

67 Teige, 1933, p. 75, cited and quoted in translation in Andĕl, 2006, p. 152, translation slightly modified.

68 Coates may have known the Narkomfin building through Berthold Lubetkin, who had been working in England since 1931. In an article on a later apartment building he designed in London, Coates referred to the 'three-two' system of planning apartments which Ginzburg had used in the Narkomfin building. (Coates, 1939, quoted in Cohn, 1999, p. 181.) Aalto's sanatorium was reproduced in the *Architectural Review* in November 1932 in an issue devoted to concrete and steel construction.

69 'During the one or two months the official attended the school, the trade union associations would pay a maintenance allowance for himself and his family.' (H[annes] M[eyer], 'Federal School of the General German Trade Unions Federation, Bernau near Berlin, 1928–1930', in Schnaidt, 1965, p. 43.)

70 Meyer, translated in Schnaidt, 1965, p. 43.

71 Illustration in Schnaidt, 1965, p. 49.

72 Quoted in Wingler, 1991, p. 108. Illustrations, Schnaidt, 1965, p. 47, p. 52.

73 Quoted in Wingler, 1991, p. 109.

74 *L'Architecture vivante*, L'Architecture hospitalière: hopitaux, sanatoria, cliniques, maisons de santé, 11 Year, no. 41, Autumn 1933.

75 *Architects' Journal*, 24 June 1925, quoted in 'Introduction', Le Corbusier, 1927, reprint Le Corbusier, 1992, p. xiv, illustration p. xv.

76 In a sonnet that the twenty-year-old Engelmann published in Karl Kraus's magazine *Die Fackel*. (Engelmann, 1911, reprinted in Czech and Mistelbauer, 1984, p. 86.)

77 For the Stonborough-Wittgenstein House, see Leitner, 1976; Wijdeveld, 1994.

78 *Wittgenstein's Neffe* (Frankfurt am Main: Suhrkamp, 1982); English translation *Wittgenstein's Nephew*, London: Quartet, 1986.) Paul Wittgenstein was actually Ludwig Wittgenstein's first cousin once removed. He is not to be confused with his brother Paul, a professional pianist who lost an arm during the First World War and for whom a number of composers (including Maurice Ravel) wrote piano concertos for one hand.

79 For the Tugendhat House, see Hammer-Tugendhat and Tegethoff, 2000.

80 Adolf Loos, 'Heimatkunst', lecture given at the Akademie Architekten Verein, Vienna, 20 November 1912, published in Loos, 1931, reprinted in Loos, 1997b, p. 129; English translation in Loos, 1985, p. 113, translation modified. The sentence quoted is unaccountably omitted from the translation in Loos, 2002, p. 116.

81 Stonborough returned to Vienna in 1947 and lived in the house until her death in 1958.

82 After being occupied at the end of the war by Soviet troops who are said to have stabled horses in the house, it was used as a dance school from 1945 by Karla Hladká, a professor at the Brno Conservatory for her private rhythmics classes. After the Communists came to power in 1950 it was used as part of a children's hospital until the early 1980s. In 1981–85, it was transformed into a conference centre and guesthouse for important visitors to the City of Brno. Since 1994, it has been a museum run by the city. (Ivo Hammer, 'Surface is Interface. History of and Criteria for

the Preservation of the Tugendhat House', in Hammer-Tugendhat and Tegethoff, 2000, p. 119.)

83 Illustrated in Hammer-Tugendhat and Tegethoff, 2000, p. 92 fig. 89. The plate-glass windows had at this time been replaced by windows with smaller panes, which nevertheless let in a great deal of sunlight into the room. The house has now been restored with plate-glass windows similar to the originals. (Hammer, in Hammer-Tugendhat and Tegethoff, 2000, passim.)

84 Edith Farnsworth's unpublished *Memoirs* written in the 1970s, quoted in Friedman, 1996, p. 190. 'Sanatorium' and 'sanitarium' are often used interchangeably, but have different derivations. Sanatorium comes from the Latin *sanare* (to cure) while sanitarium derives from *sanitas* (health). The German founders of the sanatorium movement preferred the former with its implications of medical intervention, whereas in America the latter was employed to express a belief in the benefits of healthy living rather than medical expertise. (Dormandy, 1999, p. 145 n. 1.)

85 With the popularity of sea bathing at the end of the 18th century, a fashionable Quaker physician in London, John Cockley Lettsom, had founded the Royal Sea Bathing Infirmary for Scrofula (an old name for tuberculosis of the lymphatic glands) in Margate on the north-east coast of Kent in 1791, convinced of the medicinal value of the sea air by another physician who had noticed that fishermen did not suffer from the disease. The building was designed so that patients could sleep on open but sheltered balconies and could spend most of the day resting or walking, or bathing on the beach. The infirmary was originally provided with thirty-six beds, enlarged to eight-six in 1800. (Dubos, 1999, p. 173.) The building still exists and has recently been converted into loft-type apartments. For the history of sea bathing as a cure for various illnesses, see Corbin, 1994, pp. 57–96.

86 The north staircase and its steel-and-glass staircase tower were suspended from the roof slab, providing a canopy over the main entrance to the building which shielded those arriving by car or motor coach from the weather.

87 Powers, 2001, p. 79.

88 By this time, however, De La Warr had followed MacDonald into the coalition 'National Government'. He was the first chairman of MacDonald's revisionist National Labour party and later joined the Conservative party, becoming Postmaster General in Winston Churchill's 1951 government.

89 *Bexhill Observer*, 11 May 1935, quoted in De La Warr Pavilion, 1994, p. 23.

Chapter 3 Hygiene & cleanliness

1 Smithson, 1996, in Crimson, Speaks and Hadders, 1999, p. 128. Gropius's *The New Architecture and the Bauhaus* was first published by Faber and Faber (London) in 1935, and reprinted a number of times.

2 See Goubert, 1986, pp. 58ff.

3 International hygiene congresses were held in Brussels (1876), The Hague (1884), Vienna (1887), Berlin (1888) and Budapest (1894). (Goubert, 1986, p. 109.)

4 Olivier, 1908, p.626, quoted in Heller, 1979, p. 128.

5 A Hygiene Act came into force in France in 1902. (Goubert, 1986, p. 109.)

6 Goubert, 1986, p. 256.

7 'Pavillon de l'hygiène', 1937, p. 31. See illustration Mallet-Stevens, 2005, p. 194. Mallet-Stevens also proposed a *maison hygiéniques* (Hygiene House) raised on pilotis with continuous strip windows, a glazed solarium and several terraces and roof terraces, to be built as a show house on a riverside site further along the Seine – although this was never realized. ('Projet de maison hygiéniques pour le Pavillon de l'Hygiène, 1937', Mallet-Stevens, 2005, p. 195.)

8 Compare the diagrams of the human skeleton, nervous system, and circulation of blood and lymph illustrated at the head of the chapter 'Type-Needs Type-Furniture' in Le Corbusier, 1925b; English translation, Le Corbusier, 1987b, p. 69.

9 The description is by an unnamed journalist, quoted in Gebhard, 1945, pp. 44–45. Gebhard was curator of the Dresden Museum until 1937.

10 See Gebhard, 1945, p. 45.

11 A transparent woman, based on the glass man, had been exhibited in the Chicago Museum of Science and Industry. (Gebhard, 1945, p. 45.)

12 See Zukowsky, 1994, pp. 242ff.

13 Zukowsky, 1994, p. 243.

14 Designed by Lubbert and Kammler, this was part of the exhibit of the Reichsforschungsgesellschaft für Wirtschaftlichkeit in Bau- und Wohnungswesen (State Research Insitutute for Economy in Building and Housing).

15 Lüdeke's earlier houses in Dresden such as the Haus eines Geistesarbeiters (House for an Intellectual Worker) and various designs for small houses had been described by Bruno Taut as good examples of functional and economic design. (See Taut, 1927.)

16 For Lissitzky's designs for the 'Internationale Presse-Ausstellung' (generally known as 'Pressa') and the Dresden 'Internationale Hygiene-Ausstellung', see Lissitzky-Küppers, 1992, pp. 203–14.

17 Quoted in translation in Buchli, 1999, pp. 52–53, translation modified.

18 Quoted in translation in Buchli, 1999, translation and punctuation slightly modified.

19 Lux, 1903, p. 64.

20 Kiesler, 1961, p. 106, quoted in Colomina, 1997, p. 69.

21 Our Opinion Concerning the New Architecture, 1924, pp. 157–58, translated in Slapeta, 1987, p.163. *Stavba* was the magazine of the Architectural Club of Prague. Teige was one of the editors from 1923 to 1931 and was probably responsible for this editorial.

22 For a description of the development of such regulating ideas about health and hygiene in the Vaudois canton of Switzerland (Lausanne), see Heller, 1979. See also Forty, 1986, p. 159; Douglas, 1970, passim.

23 Teige, 1932, p. 151, English translation, Teige, 2002, p. 173.

24 Douglas, 1970, p. 12.

25 Wagner, 1896; English translation, Wagner, 1988, pp. 116, 113.

26 Quoted in translation in Ward, 2001, p. 57.
27 Taut, 1929a, p. 136
28 Le Corbusier, 1930; English translation, Le Corbusier, 1991, p. 66, translation modified.
29 Tim Benton, 'The era of great projects', in Le Corbusier, 1987a, p. 170.
30 T[im] B[enton], 'Cité de Refuge, Paris', in Le Corbusier, 1987a, pp. 177–78.
31 Translated in Henkels, 1987, p. 30.
32 Van Doesburg, 1932, pp. 17–19; English translation, Baljeu, 1974, pp. 184–85. Nancy Troy argues that this passage is 'evocative of Bruno Taut's 1919 *Alpine Architecture*'. (Troy, 1983, p. 106.)
33 Van Doesburg, 1932, in Baljeu, 1974, p. 185.
34 Van Doesburg, 1930, pp. 11–12; English translation, Baljeu, 1974, p. 183, translation modified. In the early 1920s, Van Doesburg had edited a Dadaist magazine, *Mécano*, under the Dadaist pseudonym of I. K. Bonset, subtitled 'International Periodical for intellectual hygiene, mechanical aesthetic and Neo-Dadaism'.
35 The three great 'synthesizing' figures of European modernism between the wars – Van Doesburg, Moholy-Nagy and Lissitzky – all died relatively young from major chronic diseases: Van Doesburg of asthma, Moholy-Nagy of leukaemia, and Lissitzky of tuberculosis. For Van Doesburg, Lissitzky and Moholy-Nagy, see Mansbach, 1980; for Lissitzky and Moholy-Nagy, see Margolin, 1997.
36 Writing about Le Corbusier's use of the two-storey height living space, Giedion argued in *Bauen in Frankreich* that: 'The elements of the open, two-storey plan are found in many studios in France.' (Giedion, 1928a; English translation Giedion, 1995, p. 180 n. 91.)
37 Winter, 1922, pp. 1755–58. Dr Winter had worked as a hospital doctor and ear, nose and throat specialist, and played basketball with Le Corbusier every week.
38 The articles written by Winter for *Le Nouveau Siècle* were 'Le Plan Voisin' (1 May 1927), 'La Vie moderne' (8 May 1927), and 'Les quartiers Frugès à Pessac (16 May 1927).
39 See Le Corbusier, 1949; English translation Le Corbusier, 1973, pp. 36ff.
40 Morelli, 1931, quoted in translation in Casciato, 2000, p. 350.
41 *Bulletin du Conseil communal de Lausanne*, 23 December 1924, p. 709, quoted in Heller, 1979, p. 28.
42 Denby, 1944, p. 115, p. 117. The estate, illustrated in pl. 10 (between pp. 112–13), was of brick one-storey houses in a version of the Amsterdam School style. Each had a tiny back yard, indoor toilets, but apparently no bath or shower. Bathing and showering facilities were housed in a central building; a laundry, a children's library, clubrooms, open playing space and sheds for 'hawker's carts' were also provided (p. 116).
43 The estate was designed for the families of 'semi-invalid workers' who were unable to afford more expensive accommodation, rather than 'asocial' families. After building had already started, the municipality allocated 74 dwellings to the Maatschappij voor Volkswoningen, an organization

that sponsored semi-permanent housing in Rotterdam for the poorest members of the population to enable 're-educated' families to move from overcrowded 'transit centres' to affordable housing. (Arnold Reijndorp, 'Het Witte Dorp en de Rotterdamse Volkshuisvesting', in Colenbrander, 1987, p. 62; Taverne, Wagenaar and Vletter, 2001, pp. 249–50.)
44 It has been replaced by a new housing estate.
45 Denby, 1944, pp. 113–14.
46 The phrase 'moral modernism' is employed to characterize the humanist approach of the generation of inter-war modernist architects in The Netherlands such as Oud, Rietveld, Stam and Duiker by Vanstiphout, in Crimson with Speaks and Hadders, 1999, pp. 20–45.
47 Oud, 1924, p. 418, quoted in translation in Taverne, Wagenaar and De Vletter, 2001, p. 195.
48 Pommer and Otto, 1991, p. 122.
49 Between its conception in 1925 and its realization in 1927 the specification for the housing commissioned for the Weissenhofsiedlung moved away from social housing for the working class towards prototypes for middle-class dwellings. (See Kirsch, 1989, pp. 17–18.)
50 Oud in Bau und Wohnung, 1927, p. 87, quoted in Kirsch, 1989, pp. 78–79. This arrangement can be seen in a plan illustrated in Kirsch, 1989, p. 79, at the bottom left-hand corner of the illustration.
51 See illustrations in Grinberg, 1982: cupboard bed, p. 29 fig. 15, and plans of alcove beds in 19th-century tenements in Amsterdam and Rotterdam, p. 32 figs 19 & 20.
52 A number of rooms with alcove beds in modern German interiors are illustrated in Müller-Wulckow, 1932, pp. 14, 19, 50, 5, 57, 59, 123. Some of these would probably have been intended for guest or occasional use.
53 Küper and Van Zijl, 1992, p. 151 (and plan).
54 Grinberg, 1982, p. 30.
55 Baueingabe (Building office submission), 22 March 1927, Bauaktei, Stadtarchiv Stuttgart, quoted in Kirsch, 1989, p. 37.
56 *Bericht über die Siedlung*, Berlin: Reichsforschungsgesellschaft, 1927, p. 88, quoted in Kirsch, 1989, p. 123.
57 The Paris exhibition was officially known as the 'Section allemande' of the 20th annual Salon of the Société des artistes décorateurs. Organized by Gropius with his former Bauhaus colleagues Marcel Breuer, László Moholy-Nagy and Herbert Bayer, it was in effect a Bauhaus exhibition. For further details and discussion of the exhibition, see Overy, 2004, pp. 337–57. The 'Deutscher Bauausstellung' (organized by the Deutscher Werkbund) was originally planned to open in 1930 and to be an international rather than a national exhibition. It was postponed until 1931 because of the worldwide slump, and held on a much smaller site than originally intended. It nevertheless occupied eight exhibition halls on the Berlin Fairgrounds, and included a display of existence-minimum apartments and full-size model houses. (See Schwab, 1931, pp. 206–12; Lotz, 1931, pp. 212–19).
58 See Müller-Lyer, 1912.
59 Lavedan, 1930, p. 234.

60 'Glass and Metal Furniture', 1930, p. 7, reprinted in Ewig, Gaehtgens and Noell, 2002, pp. 345–46.
61 See Pearse and Crocker, 1943, especially Chapter XIV 'Social Poverty', pp. 247–88 and Biologists in Search of Material, 1938, passim. The brief for the centre was drawn up by a young architect, J. M. Richards, who was later to become a distinguished architectural critic and historian, and editor of the *Architectural Review*. (Richards, 1980, pp. 88–89.)
62 See Lewis, 1982, p. 40.
63 Caption to illustration of the cafeteria in Pearse and Crocker, 1943, p. 57 (top).
64 Pearse and Crocker, 1943, p. 241.
65 Ibid., p.68. The well-known biologist, socialist and eugenicist Julian Huxley was scientific adviser to the centre.
66 Biologists in Search of Material, 1938, pp. 43–44.
67 Ibid., p.48.
68 See Lewis, 1982, p.39.
69 Biologists in Search of Material, 1938, pp. 49–50.
70 Ibid., p.43. See also Pearse and Crocker, 1943, p. 82.
71 Pearse and Crocker, 1943, p. 247.
72 The 75- by 35-foot swimming bath occupied the centre of the building rising through all three floors, topped by an angled steel-and-glass roof. As well as the direct lighting and sunlight from the roof, the pool was lit indirectly through the internal windows on the two upper floors, which also provided views over the pool from the adjacent areas.
73 See Pearse and Crocker, 1943, especially Chapter XIV 'Social Poverty', pp. 247–88. For Duiker's Open-Air School, see Chapter 7.
74 Quoted by Kirsty Wark in 'The Peckham Health Centre' in *One Foot in the Past*, TV programme, date unknown.
75 Pearse and Crocker, 1943, p. 49 n. 1.
76 Biologists in Search of Material, 1938, pp. 48–49.
77 Singleton, 1938, quoted in Allan, 1992, pp. 333–34. For a more recent comparison between the two centres, see Darling, 2007. For a detailed reassessment of the Peckham centre, see Lewis and Brookes, 1983.
78 Allan, 1992, p. 334.
79 Lewis, 1982, p. 40.
80 Allan, 1992, p. 334.
81 Ibid., p. 114–18.
82 It was used by Southwark College until the summer of 1996.
83 The development retained the swimming pool but reduced its depth to 1 metre for safety reasons, and divided up the gymnasium and the open spaces that surrounded the pool.
84 A new centre known as the Peckham Pulse Healthy Living Centre, claiming to be inspired by the Pioneer Health Centre, has recently opened in a purpose-built building owned by Southwark Council and run as a partnership between public and private sectors.

Chapter 4 Dirt & decoration
1 Le Corbusier, 1925b; English translation, Le Corbusier, 1987b, p. 188.
2 *Frankurter Zeitung und Handelsblatt*, vol. LXXIV, no. 795, 24 October 1929, evening edition. An

Notes

accompanying footnote read: 'This essay was written in 1908. We dedicate it to the Second Congrès Internationaux d'Architecture Moderne, meeting today in Frankfurt.' (English translation, Loos, 1998, p. 176, translation modified.) Loos's text also appeared in the Czech German language newspaper *Prager Tagblatt* (10 November 1929), and in the Austrian magazine *Neue Zeit* (1930, nos 1–2). Although often dated 1908, the lecture seems not to have been first delivered until 1910.

3 Loos, 1908; English translation, Loos, 1998, pp. 166–71.

4 Loos, 1898; English translation, Loos, 1998, p. 82.

5 Giedion, 1969, p. 701.

6 Loos, 1908; English translation, Loos, 1998, p. 168.

7 See Rukschcio and Schachel, 1982, p. 295.

8 English translation, Loos, 1998, p. 175.

9 'Vorwort zur Erstausgabe', Loos, 1931; reprint Loos, 1997b, p. 19.

10 Loos, 1913, pp. 247–56. A translation of another essay by Loos, 'Architektur', had been published in a previous issue. (See Loos, 1912, pp. 82–92.) *Cahiers d'aujourd'hui* was founded in 1912 by a group that included Octave Mirabeau, Léon Werth and Charles Vildrac. It was edited by Georges Besson and continued to appear until 1926. Besson joined the Parti communiste français after the First World War and remained a member until his death. Before the First World War, the politics of the magazine and its contributors tended to be libertarian and anarchist. (For *Cahiers d'aujourd'hui*, see Troy, 1991, p. 133; see also Suzanne Tise, 'Francis Jourdain', in Barré-Despond, 1988, pp. 241–47.)

11 The reference to Loos was in an advertisement for Jourdain's workshop, Les Ateliers Modernes, the copy for which was probably written by the magazine's editor Georges Besson. (*Cahiers d'aujourd'hui*, no. 5, June 1913, np, reproduced in Troy, 1991, p. 135). This was the issue in which 'Ornement et Crime' appeared. Francis Jordain's father, the architect Frantz Jourdain, was '*correspondent français*' of the Wiener Werkstätte. (Jean-François Pinchon, 'Les débuts de Mallet-Stevens et l'influence de Hoffmann', in Pinchon, 1986, p. 22.)

12 Loos, 1920, pp. 159–68.

13 Augusta Moll-Weiss, *Le Livre du Foyer*, 2nd edition, Paris: A. Colin, 1912, p. 11, quoted in translation in Forty, 1986, p. 169.

14 Oettli, 1892, p. 74, quoted in Heller, 1979, p. 188.

15 Muthesius, 1912, pp. 11–26; translated as 'Where do we Stand', in Benton and Benton, with Sharp, 1975, p. 48.

16 Taut, 1924, pp. 64–70, extract translated in Kaes, Jay and Dimendberg, 1995, pp. 461–62.

17 See Janser and Rüegg, 2001, pp. 45ff.

18 See Kirsch, 1989, p. 20.

19 Robertson and Yerbury, 1927, reprinted in Robertson and Yerbury, 1989, p. 43.

20 Ginzburg, 1928, pp. 1370–72; English translation in Lissitzky, 1970, p. 157.

21 Cited in Kettering, 1997, p. 121, with further references in this vein. See illustrations, p. 122 fig. 1, p. 123 fig. 2, p. 124 fig. 3.

22 See Kettering, 1997, pp. 124–26. The first Five-Year Plan had been completed in four years (1928–32). See also Buchli, 1999, passim.

23 An early example was the Cheap Cottages Exhibition at the new Letchworth Garden City in 1905. Furniture produced by various companies was shown including two cottages furnished by Heal & Son, designed by Ambrose Heal. Heal furnished show houses again at Letchworth in 1907, Hampstead Garden Suburb in 1909, and at Gidea Park and Romford in 1911.

24 Letter from Rietveld to Oud, dated 4 May 1920, quoted in Marijke Küper, 'Gerrit Rietveld', in Blotkamp et al., 1982, p. 267, illustration p. 268 pl. 254.

25 See Petra Timmer, 'Metz and "Nieuwe Bouwen"', in Nieuwe Bouwen: Amsterdam, 1983, p. 130.

26 The settlers' co-operatives were self-help organizations dedicated to providing housing and allotments for growing food for those displaced by the First World War and the subsequent collapse of the Austro-Hungarian empire. The Friedenstadt Siedlung was designed for a cooperative of war veterans and their families.

27 Altman Loos, 1968, p. 105.

28 See Blau, 1999, p. 105.

29 The exhibition 'Ausstellungen Hygiene, 1925: Der neue Haushalt' was on show from 28 April to 30 June 1925 at the Messepalast in Vienna.

30 See Blau, 1999, p. 189, where the model apartment is illustrated.

31 From 1922, the designer Lilly Reich acted as selector for the articles displayed. (Kirsch, 1989, p. 60.)

32 Shütte-Lihotzky, 1924, p. 12, quoted in Blau, 1999, p. 189.

33 The *Register* consisted of numbered sheets grouped by type and listing technical details for use by architects. The artifacts were designed by the Frankfurt city architects for a municipal company Hausrat [Household Equipment] GmbH set up by May, or by approved independent designers. Thirteen of the sheets are illustrated in Hirdina, 1984, p. 191, pp. 193–203. See also Wichert, 1928, reprinted in Hirdina, 1984, pp. 190–92; T[im] B[enton], catalogue entry no. 93, in Wilk, 2006, p. 181.

34 The full name of the organization was the BEratungsSTelle für Inneneinrichtung und Wohnungshygiene (Advice Bureau for Interior Furnishing and Domestic Hygiene). The BEST was the advice centre for interior furnishing of the Österreichischen Verbandes für Wohnungsreform (Austrian Association for Housing Reform). (Podbrecky, 2003, p.101; see also Blau, 1999, pp. 191–92.)

35 For Utility furniture in Britain, see Attfield, 1999, passim. See also Attfield, 2000, pp. 167–68.

36 Le Corbusier, 1923; English translation, Le Corbusier, 1992, p. 122, translation slightly modified.

37 Larbaud, 1913; English translation Larbaud, 1991. pp. 279–80.

38 Ray, who was then living in Vienna and shortly afterwards became the Vienna correspondent of *Le Figaro*, wrote to Larbaud on 30 December 1912 enquiring whether he had read the article on architecture by Loos carefully. (Larbaud and Ray, 1980, p. 208 Letter 211.) In a 'Letter from Paris' written for an English magazine in the summer of 1914, Larbaud referred in detail to what are clearly Loos's writings on ornament and fashion, although misattributing these to Loos's friend and contemporary, the critic and satirist Karl Kraus. ('1er aout 1914', in Larbaud, 2001, pp. 112–13, see also p. 140 n. 4. The original article appeared in English in the *New Weekly* on 1 August 1914.) Larbaud may have written his 'Letter from Paris' in London, where he spent much of his time before the First World War. If so, he probably did not have the issues of *Les Cahiers d'aujourd'hui* with him, which might account for the error. The magazine had also published translations by Ray of aphorisms by Kraus in 1913. (Kraus, 1913, pp. 340–45.)

39 Translated in Larbaud, 1991, p. 280. In 1914, Larbaud wrote a short story about a child who discerns a face in the veined marble of a fireplace which he dedicated to Jourdain. ('L'Heure avec le figure' in Larbaud, 1986, pp. 75–83, translated as 'The Hour with the Face' in Larbaud, 1994, pp. 63–69.)

40 The article was by François Crucy. (Cited by Tise in Barré-Despond, 1988, p. 254.) *L'Humanité* was originally a socialist newspaper and became a communist organ only after the First World War.

41 Although it is not clear exactly what Jourdain's role as a designer for the company was, a photograph and a drawing for a clothes press reproduced by Le Corbusier in *L'Esprit nouveau* are in the Archive Francis Jourdain, which suggests that he might have been the designer. (Tise in Barré-Despond, 1988, p. 342 n. 24.)

42 'The introduction of standard fitments was heralded long ago by office furniture, by "Innovation" style furniture and also by the ingenious, bold and elegant designs of Francis Jourdain.' (Le Corbusier, 1925a, extract translated under the title 'A Single Trade', in Benton and Benton, with Sharp, 1975, p. 137.) Le Corbusier must have been aware that Jourdain had a contract with Innovation as a designer.

43 See [Charlotte Benton], 'Modernist tendencies in French design before 1925: Francis Jourdain (1876–1958)' in Benton and Benton, and Scharf, 1975, p. 53.

44 These consisted of six units in natural wood (pitch-pine, oak, mahogany), which could be used separately, but which had a built-in connecting system that enabled them to form a wall unit or room divider to define different functional areas within a room. The manufacturer was la Société anonyme de pièces détachées pour avions (SAPDA). (Tise in Barré-Despond, 1988, p. 262.)

45 Archives Francis Jourdain, quoted by Tise in Barré-Despond, 1988, p.262.

46 Illustrated by Tise in Barré-Despond, 1988, p. 267, top.

47 There are good illustrations of contemporary hospital furniture in *L'Architecture vivante*, Autumn, 1933, pl. 15.

48 Jacob und Josef Kohn manufactured (and in some cases designed) the furniture for Josef Hoffmann's Westend Sanatorium at Purkersdorf near Vienna in 1904. In 1917, Kohn merged with the Mundus group, which later took over Thonet. The Kohn label disappeared as such in 1930. Hoffmann, their best-known designer, worked

with the firm from 1901 to 1914. For Thonet and other bentwood furniture, see *Bent Wood and Metal Furniture*, 1987.

49 These were model no. 2, made of beech, cane and iron, and model no. 9701, which had an adjustable back and footrest. (Campbell, 1999, p. 330.) Theo van Doesburg was photographed lying on one of these at a Davos sanatorium shortly before his death in 1931. Reproduced in Hoek, 2000, pp. 826–27.

50 Heinrich Graf, Talstrasse 12, Davos-Platz, Switzerland. (Campbell, 1999, p. 340 n. 24, illustration p. 330 fig. 2.)

51 Mann, 1996, p. 67.

52 These included the B15 and B15a Thonet daybeds of chrome steel and ironcloth (a type of canvas), the B25 armchair with upholstered cushions, and the B63 matching footstool with cushion. These were illustrated in the 1930-31 Thonet catalogue (reproduced in Thonet, 1989, np) and originally manufactured by Standard-Möbel from 1927.

53 A version of Breuer's original aluminium recliner is sold as a Garden lounge chair by Isokon Plus today. One of Breuer's Embru designs was the winning entry in a competition in 1933 to find 'the best aluminium chair'.

54 Wilk, 1981, p. 127.

55 Le Corbusier, Jeanneret and Perriand had originally wanted this to be mass produced by the French bicycle manufacturer Peugeot. A later version of the *chaise* was produced in a limited production run by Thonet-France (1929-30). The Mies *chaise longue* was manufactured as the MR100 by Bamberg Metallwerkstatten in Berlin in 1931, and by Thonet as MR535 in 1932.

56 Perriand, 1929, pp. 278–79. Perriand's article was a response to Gloag, 1929, pp. 49–50. The two articles are reprinted in Benton and Benton, with Sharp, 1975, pp. 230–32, pp. 232–33.

57 Quoted in Blaser, 1982, p. 44.

58 'House, 1930', cutting in Archives Charlotte Perriand, exhibited in 'Charlotte Perriand' exhibition, Centre Pompidou, Paris, 2005–6.

59 Musil, 1978; English translation Musil, 1997, quoted in Colomina, 1997, p. 60. Musil's novel first appeared in 1930.

60 Riezler, 1927, p. 262.

61 Düssel, 1927, p. 96, quoted in translation in Kirsch, 1989, p. 123, translation slightly modified.

62 Lavedan, 1930, p. 229.

63 Le Corbusier, 1925b; English translation: Le Corbusier, 1987b, p. 88.

64 Illustrated in Droste, Ludewig and Bauhaus Archiv, 1992, p. 74 fig. 19. The illustration appeared in an article by Hildegard Piscator about the apartment 'Das Heim Piscator' in *Die Dame* (no. 14, 1928, pp. 10–11). See Wilk, 2006, p. 285, cat. no. 190.

65 Quoted in Wilk, 1981, p. 61.

66 Bertolt Brecht and Elizabeth Hauptmann, 'Nordseekrabben oder die moderne Bauhauswohnung', *Münchner Neueste Nachrichten*, January 1927, reprinted in Brecht, 1997. (Brecht's later revised text of the story is reprinted in Brecht, 1983, pp. 50–58.) The other model for the story was the apartment of Friedrich Kroner, editor of the magazine *Uhu*. Brecht and Hauptman's story is

discussed in detail in Schwartz, 1998, pp. 62–63; Schwartz also discusses Joseph Roth's essay 'Architecture' on pp. 58–59 (see next note).

67 Roth, 1929b; English translation: Roth, 2003, pp. 115–18.

68 Ehrenburg, 1927, translated in Bauhaus, 1968, p. 319.

Chapter 5 The domestic clinic

1 Plans illustrated in Functional Architecture, 1990, p. 88.

2 Schlemmer describes the sculpture in a letter of July 1931, where he refers to the work as *Composition in Metal* and describes Zwenkau as being 'rather far from civilization'. He had left the Bauhaus in October 1929, and was then teaching in Breslau – now Wrocław in Poland. (Letter dated 22 July 1931, translated in Schlemmer, 1990, p. 281.) A similar wire sculpture in three parts was on show at the Berlin Building Exhibition of 1931. See Oskar Schlemmer, letter to Otto Meyer, dated 2 July 1931, translated in Schlemmer, 1990, p. 280; see also Von Maur, 1972, pp. 69ff.

3 Schlemmer to Baumeister, translated in Schlemmer, 1990, p. 282.

4 The Maison de Verre (1929–32) is at 31 rue Saint-Guillaume on the Left Bank.

5 Brian Brace Taylor sees Bijvoet's influence in the final organization of the interior space. Like his Dutch architectural partner Jan Duiker, Bijvoet had qualified as an engineer at the Delft Academy (now Delft Technological University) and was considerably more experienced as a practising architect than Chareau, having worked on several major commissions in The Netherlands with Duiker and Wiebenga. Bijvoet had earlier worked with Chareau in 1926 on the clubhouse of the Golf Hotel at Beauvallon in southern France for Annie Dalsace's uncle, Emile Bernheim. (For Chareau and Bijvoet, see Rubino, 1982.)

6 Wiggington, 1996, p. 01.58.

7 This arrangement may have owed something to traditional Dutch bourgeois practice, which would have been familiar to Bijvoet, where professional men and merchants often lived with their families above their practices or businesses. (See Overy et al., 1988, passim.)

8 Wigglesworth, 1998, p. 274.

9 Ibid., p. 275; see also Wilson, 2005, in Heynen and Baydar, 2005, pp. 234–51.

10 Glass lenses (unlike glass blocks or bricks) are a single thickness of glass, and therefore cannot bear a structural load. They can be used only in a non load-bearing wall or curtain wall. The Nevada lenses used in the Maison de Verre (manufactured by the French firm of Saint Gobain) had a blue-green tinge. These were first introduced in 1928, six months before they were adopted in the revised designs by Chareau and Bijvoet for the house. The German firm of Luxfer Prismen had produced similar glass lenses of slightly smaller dimensions since before the First World War. These had been used by Bruno Taut in his Glass Pavilion for the Cologne Werkbund Exhibition in 1914. Glass blocks and bricks had been manufactured since the early

19th century and were frequently used to let light into cellars and basements, where they were often set into pavements. (See Marc Bédarida, 'Liquide surfondu et pierre artificielle', in Chareau, 1994, pp. 57–63.)

11 In the spring of 1934, Walter Benjamin (who had arrived in Paris the previous year as a refugee from Berlin) was due to deliver a series of lectures and seminars on contemporary German literature in the *salle de séjour* of the Maison de Verre. However, the lecture and seminars – which would have been Benjamin's first public performances since leaving Germany – were cancelled because Dr Dalsace had fallen ill with pneumonia. (See Gough, 2002, p. 34.)

12 See Bernard Bauchet, 'Archéologie de la Maison de verre', in Chareau, 1994, p. 107. The external lighting effects at the Maison de Verre were designed by the lighting engineer André Salomon and his architectural lighting company, Perfécla ('Société pour le perfectionnement de l'éclairage'). For Salomon, see Jacob, 2004–5, pp. 93–109.

13 'Chareau's love of theatre is revealed in his architectural masterpiece. The living room seen from this angle and lit by the spotlights outside the glass façade, becomes a space for performers.' (Taylor, 1992, p. 125.)

14 Wigglesworth, 1998, p. 278.

15 Ibid.

16 Ibid., p. 283.

17 See Frampton, 1966; Frampton, 1968.

18 Le Corbusier, 1924; English translation, Le Corbusier, 1971, Chapter XIV, 'Physic or Surgery', pp. 251–71.

19 In *Urbanisme*, Le Corbusier wrote: 'Loos told me one day: "A cultivated man does not look out of the window; his window is a ground glass; it is there only to let the light in, not to let the gaze pass through."' (Le Corbusier, 1924, p. 174, translated in Colomina, 1994, p. 234.) Colomina points out that in Frederick Etchells's English translation Loos's name is omitted and replaced by the phrase 'a friend'. She suggests it may have been at Le Corbusier's instigation that Loos's name was removed from the translated text. (Colomina, 1994, p. 369 n. 2.) For Etchell's translation of this passage, see Le Corbusier, 1971, p. 184, p. 186.

20 According to Taylor, Le Corbusier took a keen interest in the construction of the Maison de Verre. (Taylor, 1992, p. 35.) Marc Bédarida claims that Le Corbusier is reliably reported to have been seen on the construction site of the Maison de Verre, surreptitiously drawing some of the details. (Marc Bédarida, 'Maison de verre: ascendances et filiations', in Chareau, 1994, p. 119 n. 15.) Le Corbusier would have been familiar with the articles published on the house in France – some while it was still in the process of construction. He used Nevada glass lenses in his Armée de Salut building in Paris (completed 1933).

21 According to Brian Housden, who interviewed Mme Dalsace in the late 1950s. The interview remains unpublished. The information given here is based on conversations with Housden on 12 and 14 December 1998.

22 Bauchet, in Chareau, 1994, p. 105.

23 Dr Dalsace was prominent in the anti-fascist movement in France in the early 1930s, and later became a member of the French Communist Party.
24 Duiker, 1933b, pp. 155–64, reprinted in Jelles and Alberts, 1976, pp. 127–28; English translation p. 143. As well as specially designed machine-like 'equipment', the furnishings of the house also included some of the furniture Chareau had designed for an apartment with consulting rooms into which the Dalsaces had moved shortly after their marriage in 1918 – in particular the luxurious furniture in ebony and macassar for Dr Dalsace's consulting rooms, which was installed in the consulting room of the Maison de Verre.
25 *L'Architecture d'aujourd'hui*, May 1933, p. 79, quoted in Clarisse, 2004, p. 71.
26 Schütte-Lihotzky, 2004, p. 225. Schütte-Lihotzky's father died in 1923, her mother in 1924.
27 Schütte-Lihotzky, 2004, p. 225, p. 229.
28 'Ausstellungen Hygiene, 1925: Der neue Haushalt'. See Schütte-Lihotzky, 2004, pp. 107–8.
29 See Schütte-Lihotzky, 2004, pp. 107–8; 'Biographie', in Noever, 1993, p. 54. Lihotzky had married Schütte, who also worked for the neue Frankfurt, in 1927.
30 Schütte-Lihotzky, 1981, p. 22–26, quoted in translation in Kramer, 1989, p. 165.
31 Christine Frederick's book on *Household Engineering: Scientific Management in the Home*, (Frederick, 1919) had been published in a German edition in 1922. Married to an engineer, Frederick based her ideas on the theories of American work-study, time-and-motion techniques, and 'scientific management' developed by Frederick Winslow Taylor and Frank B. Gilbreth. (See Taylor, 1911; Gilbreth, 1911; Gilbreth, 1912.) Frederick's book was advertised as 'the application of the principles of efficiency engineering and scientific management to the every day tasks of housekeeping'. (Quoted in Henderson, 1996, p. 248 n. 9.)
32 Meyer's *Der neue Haushalt. Ein Wegweiser zu wissenschaftliche Hausführung* [The New Household. A Guide to Scientific Housekeeping] first appeared in 1926 and went through innumerable editions. Unlike Frederick's book, Meyer did not take her inspiration from American notions of work management but from consultation with German professional housewives' associations. However, as its title suggests, Meyer wished to give the impression that it was based on 'scientific' ideas.
33 Grete Lihotzky [Margarete Schütte-Lihotzky], 'Rationalisierung im Haushalt', *Das Neue Frankfurt*, no. 5, 1926–27, pp. 120–23, reprinted in Noever, 1993, pp. 16–19, translated as 'Rationalization in the Household', in Kaes, Jay and Dimendberg, 1995, pp. 462–63.
34 See Blau, 1999, p. 118, citing Allmeyer-Beck et al., Vienna, 1993, pp. 52–53, pp. 92–99. See also Blau, 1999, pp. 182ff.
35 Letter of 9 March 1923, Thuringian State Archive, Weimar, quoted in translation in Whitford, 1984, p. 143, translation slightly modified.
36 George Muche (1924) in Wingler, 1993, p. 66.
37 Oud's kitchen for one of his Weissenhofsiedlung houses won approval from Erna Meyer, who

included illustrations in later editions of *Der neue Haushalt*.
38 H[annes] M[eyer], 'Freidorf housing estate, near Basel, 1919–21', in Schnaidt, 1965, p. 7.
39 See for example Taut, 1924, pp.64–70, extract translated in Kaes, Jay and Dimendberg, 1995, pp. 461–62.
40 A short film was also made specifically about the Frankfurt Kitchen, *Die Frankfurter Küche*, directed by Paul Wolf in 1928 and commissioned by the neue Frankfurt. (See frame enlargements in Noever, 1993, pp. 25–27.) Wolf also directed *Die Frankfurter Kleinstwohnung* (The Frankfurt Minimum Dwelling) and *Die Häuserfabrik der stadt Frankfurt-am-Main* for the neue Frankfurt. (See Janser, 1997, p. 38.)
41 The sequences referred to are illustrated as a series of stills with an English commentary in Janser and Rüegg, 2001, pp. 40–53.
42 Janser and Rüegg, 2001, pp. 92–97. The Cona machine was manufactured from 1837 in England.
43 CIAM, 1930, pp. 10–16, translated as 'Flats for subsistence living, 1929' in Benton and Benton, with Sharp, 1975, pp. 203–4, translation slightly modified.
44 The MAK version was reconstructed by the architect Gerhard Lindner in collaboration with Schütte-Lihotzky in 1989–90, based on her 'memory, on her expertise, and on her programmatic convictions'. ('The Frankfurt Kitchen, Margarete Schütte-Lihotzky', in Noever, 1999, p. 151.) The original materials were not adhered to in this reconstruction, which visually corresponds closely to a well-known photograph of a Frankfurt Kitchen from the late 1920s (see p. 91). 'Original' restored examples are in the Stuttgarter Gesellschaft für Kunst und Denkmalpflege, and in the Victoria and Albert Museum, London (from the Am Höhenblick Siedlung, Frankfurt). For the latter, see C[hristopher] W[ilk], 'Frankfurt Kitchen' in Wilk, 2006, p. 180, catalogue entry no. 92.
45 See illustrations in Noever, 1993, p. 28, p. 30. A Cona coffee machine can be seen in both the illustrations on p. 28.
46 Henderson, 1996, p. 232. For Schuster's cupboard kitchen, see Schuster, 1976, p. 43 (illustrations) and Tim Benton 'German design during the Bauhaus period: 3) The "modern kitchen" and convertible space', in Benton, Benton and Scharf, 1975, p. 46 (illustration).
47 Illustrated in Hirdina, 1991, p. 175.
48 The kitchen was not produced directly by the neue Frankfurt itself, but through the manufacturer Georg Grumbach. (Henderson, 1996, p. 237.)
49 The scoop containers for loose food such as flour and sugar would disappear in the post-1945 derivatives of the Frankfurt Kitchen, in the era of packaged products.
50 Catherine Clarisse suggests that this could also be used to boil items of soiled laundry. (Clarisse, 2004, p. 80.)
51 May, 1926, quoted in Kramer, 1989, p. 165.
52 A diagram of the development of the Frankfurt Kitchen from the '*Wohnküche*' (live-in kitchen) through the '*Wohnküche mit Kochnische*' (*Wohnküche* with cooking alcove) was published

in *Das Neue Frankfurt*, vol. 2, no. 7/8, July–August 1928, p. 119. (Cf. Noever, 1993, pp. 8–11.)
53 Henderson, 1996, p. 245. See also Sparke, 1995, p.86. Unlike many of her generation – and despite having twice contracted tuberculosis – Schütte-Lihotzky lived long enough to confront many of her recent critics. (See Schütte-Lihotzky, 1981, pp. 22–26, quoted in translation in Kramer, 1989, p. 167.)
54 Henderson 1996, p. 245.
55 Iain Borden has argued that the Frankfurt Kitchen 'verges on the body-centric'. (Iain Borden, in Borden and Dunster, 1995, p. 219.)
56 See Taut, 1924, pp. 64–70, extract translated in Kaes, Jay and Dimendberg, 1995, p. 461.
57 'Erste die Küche – Dann die Fassade', was the title of a paper by Lüders. (Lüders, 1928).
58 According to Henderson, the BDF had grown 'exponentially on the wave of patriotic sentiment and conservative reaction that followed the First World War'. By the 1920s, it had more than 6,000 adhering groups, representing more than one million women, the largest and most influential women's organization in Weimar Germany. Half the membership was represented by the Reichsverband Deutscher Hausfrauenvereine (the Federal Union of German Housewives Associations) or RDH, initially founded by women coping with 'the servant problem'. (Henderson, 1996, pp. 226–27.)
59 Röttiger, 1925, p. 235, quoted in translation by Henderson, 1996, p. 252 n. 54, translation slightly modified.

Chapter 6 Mountains & the sea

1 See Brunton, 2004a; Brunton, 2004b.
2 Amsterdamsche Woningraad, 1909, pp. 11–12, quoted in translation in Grinberg, 1982, p. 104.
3 For Rikli, see Heller, 1979, pp. 126ff; Giedion, 1969, pp. 671–72.
4 Giedion, 1969, pp. 671ff.
5 Rikli, 1905, p. 35, quoted in Heller, 1979, p. 126.
6 Reproduced from the 5th edition of 1895 in Giedion, 1969, p. 675.
7 Le Corbusier, 1923; English translation, Le Corbusier, 1992, p. 277.
8 See Bourke, 1996, p. 26.
9 See Dormandy, 1999, p. 157. See also Porter, 1997, p. 607.
10 See Rollier, 1936. Rollier first presented his ideas publicly at the Congrès international de tuberculose in Paris in 1905.
11 Heller, 1979, p. 126; Giedion, 1969, p. 674.
12 Dormandy, 1999, p. 158.
13 See Rukschcio and Schachel, 1982, p. 168. For Schwarzwald, see Streibel, 1996.
14 The model was recaptioned 'Le Grand Winter-Sport-Hotel Alpes Maritimes' for the French audience. (Illustration in Lustenberger, 1994, p. 34.)
15 Rukschcio and Schachel, 1982, p. 313.
16 See Taut, 1919. Although dated 1919, this apparently did not appear until early 1920. English translation in Scheerbart, 1972. The illustrations are reproduced with an extensive critical and biographical apparatus in Schirren, 2004.
17 Le Corbusier, 1925b. English translation, Le Corbusier, 1987b, p. 194. For Le Corbusier's father's

passion for mountaineering, see Vogt, 1998, pp. 310ff.

18 See Vogt, 1998, pp. 317–18, illustrations on p. 319 figs 233–35. According to Vogt, Le Corbusier's father was obsessed 'with survival in extreme climatic regions' (p. 318).

19 See Clarisse, 2005, in Perriand, 2005, pp. 141–48; Aujame, 2005, in Perriand, 2005, pp. 123–24.

20 *L'Architecture d'aujourd'hui*, no. 126, June–July, 1966, quoted in Clarisse, 2005, p. 142.

21 Fitzgerald, 2000, p. 11. The novel opens in 1925.

22 Perhaps wisely in hindsight, given the dangers of developing skin cancers.

23 McClintock, 1996, pp. 304–16; 'Commodifying Cleanliness', in Shove, 2003, pp. 89–90. See also Williamson, 2001, pp. 28–29.

24 Fitzgerald, 2000, p. 289.

25 See 'Ten Paintings' in Tomkins, 1972, pp. 129–48.

26 Tomkins, 1972, pp. 37–38; Vaill, 1998, p. 109.

27 Tomkins 1972, p. 38.

28 Vaill, 1998, p. 149, pp. 158–60; illustrations between pp. 214–15, and in Tomkins, 1972, pp. 64–65, p. 75.

29 Tomkins, 1972, pp. 120–21.

30 The designers included Pierre Chareau, Eileen Gray, Theo van Doesburg, Sybold van Ravesteyn, Gabriel Guévrekian, Djo-Bourgeois, Francis Jourdain, Henri Laurens and Louis Barillet. For the Villa Noailles, see Briolle, Fuzibet and Monnier, 1990, passim; Mallet-Stevens, 2005, pp. 102–7.

31 Quoted without reference in Pinchon, 1986, p. 34.

32 This was part of the second phase of the project designed between 1926 and 1927, and completed by the winter of 1927–28. (Briolle, Fuzibet and Monnier, 1990, p. 72.)

33 Illustrated as 'Das amerikanische Freiluftbett des Hausherrn' in Döcker, 1929, p.116 pl. 183. This is shown in a 1928 photograph equipped with a Marcel Breuer tubular steel Club Armchair and bedside table. (Briolle, Fuzibet and Monnier, 1990, p. 48.)

34 The name of the house was a code for Gray and Badovici's intertwined initials: 'following the "E", the numbers 10, 2, and 7 represented the alphabetical order of the letters "J", "B" and "G", respectively.' (Constant, 2000, p. 94.)

35 See Adam, 1987, p. 262, p. 269.

36 Adam, 1987, pp. 311–12. See also Colomina, 1994, pp. 84–89.

37 Schindler was very close to Loos as a young architect, while Neutra attended Loos's architectural school in Vienna for a short period, and worked briefly in Loos's office. (Sack, 1992, p. 21.) Loos encouraged Schindler to go to the United States shortly before the First World War. Neutra later described Loos as 'my master and fountain of ideas in architecture'. (Richard Neutra, unpublished autobiography, quoted in McCoy, 1960, p. 8.) Neutra worked in Berlin with Erich Mendelsohn and moved to the United States in the early 1920s.

38 Lovell's wife Leah ran a kindergarten on progressive principles in an outbuilding of the Lovell Health House in Los Angeles.

39 For details of Schindler's articles, see 'Bibliography' in Gebhard, 1971, p. 205.

40 See for example, Neutra, 1954.

41 Lamprecht, 2004, p. 23.

42 Hines, 1989, in Smith, 1989, p. 88.

43 See Janser and Rüegg, 2001, pp. 75–76.

44 Apparently Van der Leeuw and Neutra had first met at an Efficiency Congress in Basel in 1929. (Wessel de Jonge in Backer, Camp & Dicke, 2005, p. 73.)

45 Van der Leeuw lent Neutra $3,000 of the total cost of $8,000 to build the experimental house. Neutra repaid him with interest nearly twenty years later in the late 1940s. (Lamprecht, 2004, p. 29.) See also and Neutra, 1962, pp. 263–68, Hines, 1982, pp. 94–95, 110–14, and Hines, in Smith, 1989, p. 89, p. 91.

46 See Friedrich Achleitner, 1996, pp. 108–10, illustrations, p. 109 figs 30–31. See also illustrations in Makarova, 2000, p. 46.

47 These have now been restored to their original form in the renovated house. This is a museum and exhibition space, an outstation of the Vienna Museum of Applied Arts (MAK).

48 Letter from Philip Johnson to Robert L. Sweeney, quoted in Robert L. Sweeney, 'His House, Her House, Their House', in Noever, 1995, p. 38. Schindler had written to Johnson inviting him to look at the house with a view to it being included in the exhibition.

49 The house was designed in 1937. Building started in 1938, and it was occupied in early 1939. A few smaller modernist houses were built in or around Dublin in the first part of the 1930s. See Rothery, 1991; Becker, Olley and Wang, 1997.

50 *Ulysses* was serialized in the *Little Review* between 1918 and 1920, and first published in book form by Syliva Beach in Paris in 1922.

51 See John O'Regan, note on 'Geragh' in O'Regan, 1993, p. 10.

52 Joyce, 1937, p. 21.

53 Three survive in Woodlands Avenue, Coombe, Kingston upon Thames. (Collins, 2004, p. 28.) In April 1930, Coates had visited the Weissenhofsiedlung in Stuttgart with Jack Pritchard, who was to commission him to design the Isokon flats in London in 1932. (Grieve, 2004, p. 16.)

54 Advertisement in the Design and Industries Association (DIA) journal *Design for Today*, May 1934, Pritchard Archives, University of East Anglia, Norwich, reproduced in Grieve, 2004, p. 14. The houses came in different sizes: 'a cottage or a mansion at prices ranging from £450 to £4000'.

55 Schmidt, 1927, abridged translation in Charlotte Benton, 1975, p. 20.

56 Riezler, 1927, pp. 258–66, abridged translation in Charlotte Benton, 1975, p. 19.

57 Brick and wood, as processed and employed for building construction, are in practice no more nor less 'natural' materials than steel or concrete.

58 See Lotz, 1932, pp. 179–88.

59 The notion of the *Wachsende Haus* (extendable house) was promoted in Germany during the period of economic instability in the late 1920s and early 1930s – as it had been in immediately post-war Austria. The *Wachsende Haus* was the title of one of the seven Baulehre (Building Construction) courses

taught at the Dessau Bauhaus under Hannes Meyer between 1927 and 1930.

60 Wagner, 1932, p. 23, translated in Tafuri, 1990, p. 228, translation slightly modified.

61 The exhibition was discussed by Adolf Behne in *Das Neue Berlin*, the journal he edited with Martin Wagner to publicize the neue Berlin. (Behne, 1929, p. 20.) See also Giedion, 1954, pp. 48–49; Klonk, 1997, p. 489.

62 Wilhelm Lotz wrote in the Werkbund magazine *Die Form* that it was very curious (*recht merkwürdig*) to find such a didactic display designed by Gropius and Moholy-Nagy in the midst of the Gagfah Siedlung. (Lotz, 1928, p. 297, illustrations pp. 289–90, 292–93. See also Nerdinger, 1997, p. 60.)

63 See Janser, in Janser and Rüegg, 2001, p. 20.

64 The exhibition had been organized by the Allgemeine Häuserbau AG (General House Building Company) or AHAG, which was owned by the Berlin entrepreneur Adolf Sommerfeld. Sommerfeld had sponsored the Sommerfeld House – the experimental wooden house in Berlin designed by Gropius and his partner Adolf Meyer, and constructed and furnished by students at the Weimar Bauhaus in 1922, at a time when the school was still strongly under the influence of expressionist ideas. Sommerfeld continued to be an active financial supporter of the Bauhaus while Gropius remained director, and a patron of Gropius's architectural practice after he moved to Berlin in 1928.

65 See illustrations, Lotz, 1928, p. 289, p. 290.

66 Buchli, 1999, p. 52.

67 Zoshchenko, 2000, p. 61.

68 See Penelope Curtis, 'Modernism & Monumentality', in Curtis, 2003, p. 137, illustration fig. 20.

Chapter 7 Built into the sun

1 Illustrated in Janser and Rüegg, 2001, p. 116. A still of another view of one of the 'outside rooms' of the Rotach houses with cane or rattan furniture is illustrated on p. 118.

2 Other model-housing exhibitions were held at Karlsruhe (1929), Linz (1929), Stockholm (1930) and Milan (1930).

3 Behne, 1926; English translation, Behne, 1996, p. 137, translation slightly modified.

4 Institut national de la propriété industrielle, Paris, brevet no. 439292, quoted in Minnaert, Paris, 2002, p. 161. Although the patent was jointly registered the construction technique is generally recognized to have been the work of Sauvage alone. Sarazin and his brother Paul were property speculators. Sarazin and Sauvage's partnership ended in 1916. (Minnaert, 2002, p. 161.)

5 The Société was founded under the aegis of the HBM (Habitations Bon Marché). This organization regulated the construction and running of accommodation for workers under the Loi Siegfried of 1894, which specified moderate rents and limited annual profits to 4 per cent. (See Dumont, 1991, passim.) Other founders included the publisher Paul Gallimard, two members of the Rothschild family, the chief engineer of the Ponts et Chaussé Horace

Notes

Weill, and the architect Frantz Jourdain. Jourdain's son, the designer Francis Jourdain, was one of the first tenants of the rue Vavin block and designed the interior of his apartment, which still survives. (Minnaert, 2002, p. 91).

6 The rue Admiraux project was directly funded by the HBM. (Minnaert, 2002, pp. 175ff.)

7 The complex consists of 78 two- or three-roomed apartments with kitchen and wc (but no bathrooms) – of which only 38 were provided with a terrace (10 further apartments had a traditional shallow balcony). Another 20 apartments looked onto the light well and 20 received only north light. The cost of building the block was 20 to 25 per cent higher than other similar projects built for the HBM in Paris at this time, and provided less accommodation. (Minnaert, 2002, pp. 174–85.)

8 See Bullock and Read, 1985, pp. 396–410.

9 See Giedion, 1929, p. 14; Giedion, 1954, p. 79.

10 J. J. P. Oud, in Bau und Wohnung, 1927; English translation in Benton, 1976, p. 58.

11 Adam, 1987, pp. 193, 198, 214.

12 Truus Schröder, in Büller and Den Oudsten, 1987, in Overy et al., 1987, p. 42.

13 Wherever possible these were placed so that the ends of the rows faced onto the major roads.

14 Unwin, 1902, p. 3, cited in Grinberg, 1982, p. 104.

15 Amsterdamsche Woningraad, 1909, p. 16, quoted in translation in Grinberg, 1982, p. 104.

16 See Grinberg, 1982, p. 68 figs 53–54. The first estate built on the *strokenbouw* system was the Landlust development in Amsterdam West designed by Ben Merkelbach and C. J. F. Karsten, completed in 1937.

17 This system was championed by Giedion in *Befreites Wohnen*. (Giedion, 1929, p. 14.)

18 The finger plan had first been employed in urban housing by Theodor Fischer in the Siedlung Alte Heide in Munich in 1919, an estate built in traditional style – but 'progressive in all aspects of planning'. (Lane, 1985. p. 245 n. 10.)

19 See Pommer and Otto, 1991, p. 151.

20 Behne, 1930a, pp. 169–70, paraphrased and quoted in translation in Schwartz, 1998, pp. 68–69. See also Colquhoun, 1994, p. 30ff.

21 Behne, 1930a, pp. 169–70, quoted in English translation in Colquhoun, 1994, p. 31, translation slightly modified.

22 See Cockburn, 2005, passim.

23 Adolf Behne, 1930b, p. 494, quoted in translation in Colquhoun, 1994, p. 3. See also Schmidt, 1930, pp. 379–80.

24 De Fries, 1930, p. 189.

25 Quoted in translation in Long, 2002, p. 172.

26 See Lane, 1985, p. 111; Benton and Benton, 1977, p. 68.

27 Illustration in Syring and Kirschenmann, 2004, p. 43. In 1960, Scharoun moved into an apartment in a post-war estate he had designed in Berlin Charlottenburg-Nord (illustration in Syring and Kirschenmann, 2004, p. 65).

28 Rading, 1927, p. 289, quoted in translation in Kirsch, 1989, pp. 159–60. The small bedroom next to the utility room was probably the maid's room. There was no bathroom at this level, although there

was a lavatory with a small washbasin. A maid would have been expected to wash herself more thoroughly in the laundry room, as was common practice at the time. European middle-class families still often employed a live-in maid at this time, or sometimes a woman who came in by the day – for whom a room would be provided to change her clothes and rest during breaks, as in the Rietveld Schröder House in Utrecht. (Paul Overy, 'Introduction', Overy et al., 1988, p. 31, see plan of ground floor of house, p. 60.)

29 Rading, 1927, p. 287, quoted in translation in Kirsch, 1989, p. 160.

30 Wedepohl, 1927, p. 399, quoted in translation in Kirsch, 1989, p. 162.

31 Rading, 1927, p. 289, quoted in translation in Kirsch, 1989, p. 160.

32 Giedion, 1928b, pp. 37–43.

33 Scharoun, 1927, p. 293, quoted in translation in Kirsch, 1989, p. 191.

34 Quoted in translation in Kirsch, 1989, p. 193.

35 The access to the garden in Rading's house was praised in the Swiss magazine *Das Werk* as more successfully designed than in any other Weissenhof house. (*Das Werk*, 1927, no. 9. p. 264, cited in Kirsch, 1989, p. 162.)

36 Worpole, 2000, p. 81.

37 Quoted in Syring and Kirschenmann, 2004, p. 36.

38 Quoted in Pritchard, 1984, p. 97. Agatha Christie lived in the apartment block from 1940 to 1946.

39 Joseph Roth, 1929a, translated as *Right and Left*, in Roth, 1992, pp. 212–13.

40 Bloch, 1995, pp. 733–34, translation slightly modified. *Das Prinzip Hoffnung* was written in the United States between 1938 and 1947 and revised in 1953 and 1959. It was first published in German in 1959.

41 The final paragraph of the quotation is from a translated extract in Kirsch, 1989, p. 133. I have preferred this translation to Bloch, 1995, p. 734.

42 See Lubbock, 1995, pp. 329–33. (Cf. Bloch, 1973, vol. 2, p. 859.)

43 See Bryder, 1992, pp. 72–95; Wyche, 1916.

44 Between 1905 and 1907, W. H. Cowlishaw designed the Cloisters building to house Miss Annie Jane Lawrence's open-air school for theosophical meditation in Letchworth, the first urban development based on Ebenezer Howard's Garden City principles.

45 Duiker, 1932b, pp. 140–43, reprinted in Jelles and Alberts, 1976, pp. 115–16, English translation, p.135. See also details about the school and its heating system in Dutch, p. 64.

46 See Roth, 1950, p. 187.

47 Jelles and Albers, 1976, p. 4; Molema, 1989, pp. 12–17. Duiker and Bijvoet also designed the interior of an apothecary's shop in Zandvoort in 1925. See Jelles and Alberts, 1976, p. 17; Molema, 1989, pp. 58–59.

48 Molema, 1996, p. 20.

49 Duiker, 1932c, p. 166, reprinted in Jelles and Alberts, 1976, pp. 116–17, English translation, p. 136.

50 Duiker, 1932a, pp. 88–92, reprinted in Jelles and Alberts, 1976, pp. 59–60, English translation, pp. 60–61, translation slightly modified.

51 For example, in the information pamphlet on the collection of architectural photographs held by the Architectural Association photographic library in London, a photograph of the Aalsmeer school is captioned as being of Zonnestraal. For Wiebenga, see Molema and Bak, 1987.

52 Ben Rebel, 'The Amsterdam architects association "de 8"', in Nieuwe Bouwen: Amsterdam, 1983, p. 31. As Director of Public Works in Zwolle, Wiebenga also designed a hospital and a swimming pool, although in the design of the school he was compelled to collaborate with an architect, J. van den Linden – which some critics consider to have to some extent compromised the project. (D. van Woerkom, 'J. G. Wiebenga, engineer/architect', in Nieuwe Bouwen: Previous History, 1982, p. 86.)

53 A. P. Smits, *Bouwkundig Weekblad*, no. 29, 1932, p. 261, quoted in translation by Van Woerkom in Nieuwe Bouwen: Previous History, 1982, p. 86.

54 See Jones, 2002, Chapter 4: 'Jan Duiker: Zonnestraal Sanatorium, Hilversum 1926', p. 84.

55 Duiker, 1932b, pp. 140–43, reprinted in Jelles and Alberts, 1976, pp. 115–16, English translation, p.135, slightly modified.

56 'Ingezonder' (Letter to the Editor), *De 8 en Opbouw*, 1933, p. 68, reprinted in Jelles and Alberts, 1976, p. 123, English translation, p. 140, slightly modified. Duiker himself did not live to see it. He died of cancer two years later in 1935.

57 'The isolated class system was developed as the best solution to the rigid requirements of teaching and health.' (Roth, 1946, p. 124, illustration p. 116.)

58 Meyer in Schnaidt, 1965, p. 79, translation modified.

59 Meyer, 1927, reprinted in German and translated into English in Schnaidt, 1965, p. 17.

60 See Schnaidt, 1965, p. 21.

61 Taut seems to have written the English version while on holiday in Lulworth, Dorset. (Taut, 1929a, p. 1.) A German edition was published the same year. (Taut, 1929b.)

62 Caption in Giedion, 1929, fig. 52. Giedion describes the school in Berlin-Neuköln as for 2,000 pupils. Taut gives a figure of 3,000 and describes the school as a 'Municipal (or Karsen) school'. (Taut, 1929a, caption p. 172).

63 Taut, 1929a, p. 173.

64 Giedion, 1929, fig. 52.

65 Ibid., caption to fig. 51. Giedion describes the class as a 'Probeklasse' (experimental class) and the school as a 'Reformschule'.

66 Döcker, 1929, p. 87, illustrations pp. 87–89 pls 138–41.

67 See 'Gemeinschaftsschule am Dammweg, Versuchspavilion, 1928', Deutscher Werkbund Berlin and Brenne, 2005, pp. 136–37.

68 For example, Kingsmead Primary School (2003–4) at Northwich in the north-west of England, designed by the White Design architectural practice (which specializes in eco-friendly buildings) incorporates many of the elements of light, air and openness so highly regarded by inter-war modernists, housing experts and educationists. ('Kingsmead School', *Building*, vol. CCLXIX, No. 31, 6 August 2004, pp. 30–33.)

Chapter 8 The outdoor room

1 Le Corbusier sent the text in June 1927 to his assistant Alfred Roth (who was acting as his site architect in Stuttgart) to be translated into German for publication. It appeared in one of the two official Werkbund publications issued in connection with the exhibition *Bau und Wohnung*, in the Werkbund magazine *Die Form*, in the German construction magazine *Baugilde*, and in Roth's book on Le Corbusier's Weissenhof houses (Roth, 1927, reprint, 1977). For an English translation, see Le Corbusier and Pierre Jeanneret, 'Five Points of a New Architecture', in Benton and Benton, with Sharp, 1975, pp. 153–55.

2 The villa is often described – following Le Corbusier himself – as being in the prosperous Parisian outer suburb of Garches. It is 'actually located in the less prestigious suburb of Vaucresson'. (Tim Benton, 'Six houses', in Le Corbusier, 1987a, p. 60.)

3 Giedion, 1928c, p. 256, quoted in translation by Benton, in Le Corbusier, 1987a, p. 62.

4 See Le Corbusier, 1989.

5 A roof terrace with plants and small trees had been a particular feature of Hennebique's 'demonstration' villa in reinforced concrete at Bourg-le-Reine in the 1890s. (See Giedion, 1941, pp. 246ff.)

6 In 1906, Perret had constructed a terrace on the flat roof of the architect Paul Guadet's Maison Guadet with a roof garden surmounted by a concrete pergola laid out with flower beds filled with soil and concrete containers and pots planted with sage laurel, Spanish broom, irises, roses, grapevines, tomatoes, strawberries and artichokes. (Delorme, 1987, p. 46.)

7 Le Corbusier, 1925a, p. 126.

8 See Colomina, 1997, p. 64.

9 Weissenhof houses which featured terraces of this kind included those by Hans Poelzig, Peter Behrens, Adolf Schneck, Richard Döcker, Bruno Taut, Max Taut and Walter Gropius.

10 For contemporary reactions, see Kirsch, 1989, 'Appendix D', pp. 199–201.

11 Döcker in Bau und Wohnung, 1927, p. 47, quoted in Kirsch, 1989, p. 153.

12 Illustration Kirsch, 1989, p. 151 bottom left.

13 Illustration Giedion, 1929, pl. 83.

14 Mallet-Stevens, 1924, English translation Benton and Benton, with Sharp, 1975, p. 131.

15 Giedion, 1928a, English translation Giedion, 1995, p. 190.

16 See The Müller Villa, 2002, p. 101, illustrations on pp. 99–101 (shower not visible).

17 Hitchcock (1929), 1993, pp. 168–69.

18 See Boudon, 1972, pp. 82–85, illustrations pls 44–47.

19 See Boudon, 1972, pp. 80–82, illustrations pls 15, 24, 25, 36.

20 Le Corbusier and Jeanneret, 1927, pp. 272–74, English translation, Benton and Benton, with Sharp, 1975, pp. 153–55.

21 A radically adapted version, the Maison Guiette, had been erected for a Belgian artist in Antwerp in 1926. (See Gans, 1987, p. 124.) For the links

between the Citrohan type and the Parisian studio house see Banham, 1960, pp. 216–19.

22 Le Corbusier had originally drawn up designs for the Domino system in 1915, although the more sophisticated version on which the Weissenhof house was based dates from 1919.

23 Le Corbusier and Jeanneret, 1927, p. 274, translated in Benton and Benton, with Sharp, 1975, p. 155.

24 The brothers Auguste, Gustave and Claude Perret had established Perret Frères in 1905. Claude was in charge of the business side of the partnership, Gustave was mainly concerned with construction, while Auguste is generally considered to have been responsible for design. (Britton, 2001, p. 20.) Both the Perret firm and Hennébique, the French company that pioneered reinforced-concrete construction, were active in the French North African colonies, presumably because the climate was particularly suitable for this method of building. Perret Frères's projects included dock buildings at Saïda, Tiaret and Sidi-bel-Abbès in Algeria, and Casablanca in Tunisia, erected during the years before the First World War and often illustrated as 'pioneering' examples of reinforced-concrete construction. Between the wars, Auguste Perret designed a house in Cairo and a large villa in Garches near Paris in 1931 (both for the Egyptian politician Nubar Bey) and another villa at Aghun in Alexandria in 1933.

25 Although M. Ballu was the nominal architect of the cathedral, Perret Frères were the contractors and their constructional techniques determined the form of the building

26 Le Corbusier unsuccessfully tried to publish the book in 1912 and 1914. Excerpts from three chapters appeared under the title 'Carnet de Route, 1910' (although the journey had actually taken place in 1911) in *Almanach d'Architecture Moderne* (see Le Corbusier, 1925a, pp. 55–57). An edited version of the text with additions made in 1912 and 1914 prepared by Le Corbusier in 1965 (the year he died) was published in French in 1966 as *Le Voyage d'Orient* (Le Corbusier, 1966). An English translation of the complete text appeared as *Journey to the East* in 1989 (Le Corbusier, 1989).

27 Le Corbusier wrote: 'Arab architecture has a precious lesson for us. You appreciate it on foot, *walking*. Only on foot, in movement, can you see the developing articulation of the architecture. It's the opposite principle to that of Baroque architecture which is conceived on paper, from a theoretical viewpoint. I prefer the lesson of Arab architecture.' (Quoted in English translation in Benton, 1987, pp. 195–96 translation slightly modified.)

28 See Moholy-Nagy, 1965, passim.

29 This experience was graphically represented in a television programme made for the Open University in the 1970s where Tim Benton is seen arriving at the Villa Savoye by car and walking through the interior, following (and commenting) on the 'promenade architectural'. (Le Corbusier, 1975.)

30 For Wiebenga, see Molema and Bak, 1987.

31 Max Risselada, 'Free Plan versus Free Façade:

Villa Savoye and Villa Baizeau revisited', in Risselada, 1988, p. 60.

32 For air-conditioning and its effect on the development of modernist architecture, see Banham, 1970.

33 Benton, 1980, passim; Benton, 1987, p. 193.

34 Risselada, 1988, p. 60. Le Corbusier's comments were: 'Very easy, practicable, allows for combinations'.

35 See T[im] B[enton], 'Cité de Refuge, Paris', in Le Corbusier, 1987a, pp. 177–78.

36 Tim Benton, 'The era of great projects', in Le Corbusier, 1987a, p. 170. See also Benton, 1980, passim.

37 Le Corbusier had elaborated the idea of the *brise-soleil* in 1932 in unrealized designs for a private commission for residential housing, the Domaine Durand in Oued Ouchaia, near Algiers. (R[emy] G[olan], 'Plan Obus, Algiers/Femmes fantasques', in Le Corbusier, 1987a, p. 219.)

38 Costa's assistants included Oscar Niemeyer. Construction began in 1937, but the building was not occupied until 1944. It now houses the Serviço do Patrimônio Histórico e Artístico Nacional.

39 According to Carlos Eduardo Comas, the final design by Costa and his assistants was 'informed by a thorough grasp of Le Corbusier's compositional devices and techniques'. (Comas, 1998, p. 7.)

40 'Le Corbusier, who made two proposals which were not adopted, nevertheless tried on several occasions after the Second World War to take credit for the design.' (Hesel and Kubokawa, 1998, p. 50, see also Comas, 1998, passim.) The misattribution to Le Corbusier can be found as recently as 2001, in the catalogue of the 'Century City' exhibition at Tate Britain. (Paulo Venancio Filho, 'Rio de Janeiro', in Blazwick, 2001, pp. 182–83.)

41 See Rukschcio and Schachel, 1982, p. 154.

42 Adolf Loos, 'Das Grand-Hotel Babylon', *Die Neue Wirtschaft*, 14 February 1924, translated as 'Grand Babylon Hotel', in Loos, 2002, p. 172. A Silesian builder, Samuel Hausler, had devised an insulated flat roof for northern climates in 1851. This type of roof had been further developed in the 'tuberculosis capital' of Davos in the late 19th century to prevent melting snow and icicles falling on passers-by. (See Campbell, 2005, p. 6.)

43 *Wohnungswesen der Stadt Wien*, 1932, p. 8.

44 Apparently, by 1932 there were 33 laundries with 830 wash places serving the municipal blocks throughout the city, and 62 bathhouses providing communal individual baths for tenants. (Ibid., p. 9.)

45 Ibid., p. 9.

46 See Gravagnuolo, 1995, p. 207.

47 Frank, 1932, p. 328.

48 Cited in Friedrich Achleitner, 'Austria', in Lampugnani, 1986, p. 28.

49 Unattributed quotation (probably by Frank himself) in Yorke, 1934, p. 198. Yorke illustrated housing by Frank, Lurçat and Neutra (pp. 198–99).

50 Unlike Le Corbusier's two Weissenhof houses, there was direct connection via the metal staircase between the roof garden and the garden itself.

51 Frank's lecture 'Was ist modern?' was delivered on 25 June 1930. It was reprinted in the August issue of *Die Form* (see Frank, 1930, pp. 399–406).

52 'The puritanism and exclusiveness of the Stuttgart Werkbund Exhibition [Weissenhofsiedlung] prompted him to invite only excluded architects to the Viennese Siedlung of 1932 [...].' Anonymous introductory note to Frank, 1982, p. 5. See also Long, 2002, pp. 178ff.

53 Friedrich Achleitner, quoted in translation in Gravagnuolo, 1995, p. 208.

54 These were destroyed during the Second World War and have not been reconstructed.

55 See Krischanitz and Kapfinger, 1989, p. 94, illustration p. 95.

56 Podbrecky, 2003, p. 111.

57 Benton, in Benton & Benton, 1977, pp. 12–22.

58 Quoted in Barr, 1945, reprinted in Barr, 1986b, p. 172. The article was originally written in May 1933.

59 'Kennst du das Land, wo die Zitronen blühn?' (Goethe, 1999, p. 56.)

60 See Schmidt, 1927, abridged translation in Charlotte Benton, 1975, p. 20; Riezler, 1927, abridged translation in Charlotte Benton, 1975, p. 19; Goldfinger quoted in Elwall, 2006, p. 20.

61 The photomontage was probably first made when the exhibition opened in 1927, and seems to have been available as a postcard until at least the late 1930s. (Willett, 1978, p. 9.) It was illustrated in the yearbook of the Bund für Heimatschutz in Württemberg und Hohenzollern (Association for Heritage Protection in Wurtemberg und Hohenzollern) for 1941 with the caption 'Araberdorf' (Arab Village). (Kirsch, 1989, p. 200 illustration.)

62 Barr, 1945, in Barr, 1986b, p. 173.

63 See Boudon, 1972, pp. 88–90; Curtis, 1975, p. 25.

64 This was to a large extent due to the activities in various fields of art, architecture and design of the 19 former Bauhaus students who worked in British-mandated Palestine. However, there were also architects active in Palestine who had studied or worked with Le Corbusier, Erich Mendelsohn, August Perret, Hans Poelzig and Bruno Taut. (Levin, 1984, p. 9.) 'Bauhaus style' is used in Israel as a generalized descriptive phrase for the white modernist architecture built in the country in the 1930s and 1940s, and particularly in Tel Aviv.

65 Tel Aviv was founded in 1909. There is some dispute as to how it came to be called 'the White City'. According to Michael Levin it was first used by the poet Nathan Alterman. (Levin, 1984, p. 70.) According to Linda Grant, the name was taken from a German utopian novel of the 19th century. (Grant, 2000, p. 70.)

66 May left Africa for Germany in late 1953 and arrived in Hamburg in January 1954. He thus left Kenya at the beginning of the Mau-Mau insurrection and its brutal suppression by the British, although the official reason seems to have been that he was no longer allowed to continue to practice in Kenya as he was not a member of the British professional architectural body, the Royal Institute of British Architects (RIBA).

67 The Aga Khan School is illustrated in Buekschmitt, 1963, pp. 102–4 pls 86–90 and pl. 92. See also illustrations of the Aga Khan Maternity Hospital, p. 104 pl. 91 and p. 105 pl. 93, a model of Aga Khan residence p. 98 pl. 78, and the cultural centre pp. 106–7 pls 94–97.

68 See Buekschmitt, 1963, pp. 99–100 pls 79–83. See also Herrel, 2001, pp. 67–69, p. 129. An article on May's system appeared in the *Architects' Journal* in June 1946. (See May, 1946.)

69 See Herrel, 2001, p. 72 and p. 75, pp. 116–124 (several photographs and plans).

70 These included James Cubitt, the Architects' Co-Partnership, and Godwin + Hopwood. At this time the Architectural Association, the leading avant-garde architectural school in London, set up a School for Tropical Architecture – which was later renamed the Development Planning Unit and incorporated in University College London during the post-colonial 1970s.

71 See Sunand Prasad, 'Le Corbusier in India', in Le Corbusier, 1987a, pp. 278–337.

72 The beginning of Le Corbusier's interest in Algiers coincided and was partly inspired by the centennial of the French conquest of Algeria in 1930, and the Colonial Exhibition held in the Bois de Vincennes in Paris in 1931. (McLeod, 1980, p. 57, p. 59.)

73 In January 1941, Le Corbusier was appointed to the Comité d'Etudes du Batiment (known as the Comité d'Etudes de l'Habitation et de la Construction Immobilière from May 1941) which was charged by the Vichy head of state Marshal Pétain with establishing a national building policy by undertaking studies in metropolitan France, in the French colonies, and abroad. The Algiers plan (Plan Directeur, 1942) was at the head of the committee's list of seven exemplary projects to be undertaken by the Vichy government. (McLeod, 1980, pp. 71–72.) The plan was, however, rejected by the Algiers City Council in June 1942. For an account of Le Corbusier's association with Vichy, see Fishman, 1982, pp. 243ff.

74 R[omy] G[olan], in Le Corbusier, 1987a, p. 217.

75 Le Corbusier began to work on his plans after spending a fortnight in the city in the spring of 1931 where he gave two lectures on modern architecture, urbanism and the future of the Algerian capital at the invitation of the Friends of Algiers.

76 See McLeod, 1980, p. 67, p. 70.

77 Drawing reproduced in ibid., p. 67 fig. 22.

78 Tafuri, 1979, p. 132.

79 Fletcher, 1999, p. 137.

80 Vincendeau, 1998, p. 57.

81 In 1953, Le Corbusier had the idea of interesting the French-Algerian writer Albert Camus in a fictional film set in the building. (Monnier, 2002, p. 74.)

82 Many of these have subsequently closed or been substantially altered due to commercial competition from outside the block. (Monnier, 2002, pp. 66–67.)

83 Quoted in Monnier, 2002, p. 55.

84 Cohen, 2003; see also Cohen and Eleb, 2003, passim.

Chapter 9 Water & bathing

1 Leeuwen, 1998, p. 282 n. 52. One might question the somewhat contradictory and not entirely helpful notion of two 'single great monument[s] of modernism', and take issue with Leeuwen's choices.

2 Lubetkin wrote of presenting animals 'dramatically to the public, in an atmosphere comparable to that of a circus'. (Berthold Lubetkin, 'Dudley Zoo', nd. (c. 1938), unpublished typescript, quoted in Allan, 1992, p. 199.)

3 The undersides of the helical ramps were also painted blue.

4 See Leeuwen, 1998, p. 287 n. 59, citing Kearton, 1930.

5 See Lewis, 2005, p. 91.

6 Allan, 1992, p. 248 n. 31. Allan describes Lane as 'one of the Pool's first admirers'.

7 Poster on the London Underground for the London Zoo, October 2002.

8 Allan notes the 'ironic twist of fate' that: 'While developments in zoological legislation and husbandry have rendered many of the pavilions outmoded, a parallel awareness of their special architectural interest has led to their protection as listed buildings. In an extreme case this could mean that a building could neither be used as it is nor replaced by one more suitable.' (Allan, 1992, p. 245). Many of Lubetkin and Tecton's zoo buildings at London, Whipsnade and Dudley zoos have been converted to uses other than those for which they were originally designed.

9 See Coe and Reading, 1981, p. 127.

10 Writing of the Baroque, Lubetkin argued that 'the architecture is calculated for the onlooker' and that 'all the details, from any viewpoint, blend into the total picture'. (Quoted in Coe and Reading, 1981, p. 42.)

11 Allan, 1992, p. 210.

12 The claim that the penguins suffered aching joints was made by Chris West, a London zoo spokesperson, after they were moved from the pool in 2004. West claimed the pool was 'too shallow for them to dive and swim in', arguing that: 'The black-footed penguins here have been unable to burrow, which is a part of their courting ritual.' (Quoted in Glancey, 2004, p. 10.)

13 Carrier 2005, p. 11. The penguins were at first replaced by alligators, but these were later moved elsewhere.

14 In a section entitled 'Man the Penguin', in Leeuwen, 1998, p. 282.

15 *Mother and Child*, November 1938, quoted in Coe and Reading, 1981, p. 127.

16 Illich, 1986, p. 45. Chadwick, 1887.

17 The American artist Margaret Morgan has satirically superimposed Barr's flow chart over a diagrammatic section through a late-Victorian house with 'modern' plumbing – inverted so that the movements flow into each other from bottom to top – and linking Barr's name with that other great modernist advocate of plumbing, Adolf Loos. See Margaret Morgan, 'Barr/Loos: Portrait of a History of Modern Art as Sanitary System, or: A Place for Everything and Everything In Its Place: (The house that Adolf and Alfred Built)', (1993), illustrated Lahiji and Friedman 1997b, p. 62.

18 See Forty, 1986, pp. 159–61.

19 See Heller, 1979, p. 96.

20 Teige, 1932; English translation, Teige, 2002, p. 245 n. 2.

21 A law of 1846 enabled towns in Britain to tax their populations in order to build public baths. By 1854, London had 13 public baths. (Lupton and Miller, 1992, p. 22.)

22 These first appeared on the Seine in Paris in 1760, on the Main in Frankfurt in 1774, and on the Danube in Vienna in 1781. See Leeuwen, 1998, pp. 20–25.

23 Illustration in Leeuwen, 1998, p. 23 figs 1.4 & 1.5, also pl. 1. It was replaced in 2006 by the *Piscine sur Seine*, a new pool beside the new Bibliothèque de France opposite the Bercy Gardens.

24 Illustrated Leeuwen, 1998, p. 47 fig. 1.29, also pl. 4.

25 A 'floating bath' on the East River is illustrated in Lupton and Miller, 1992, p. 19.

26 'The Story of the Pool' (1977), in Koolhaas, 1994, p. 307.

27 Lissitzky, 1930, English translation, Lissitzky, 1970, pp. 47–49. The bath is illustrated on p. 48 fig. 16.

28 Elizabeth Wright, 'Norwich Lido', information sheet accompanying an exhibition at the Norwich Gallery, Norwich, September 2006.

29 Illustrated in Janser and Rüegg, 2001, pp. 118–19.

30 Hitchcock and Johnson, 1995, pp. 222–23.

31 For British outdoor swimming pools of the inter-war period (generally known as 'lidos') and their destruction in the later decades of the 20th century, see Powers, 1991, and Smith, 2005. For a detailed study of a surviving example, see Smith, 1996.

32 See Nieuwe Bouwen: Rotterdam, 1982, pp. 47ff.

33 For the Freibad Allenmoos, see Roth, 1946, pp. 139–50; for Belle-Rive Plage see Devanthéry and Lamunière, 1998, in Cunningham, 1998, pp. 109–19.

34 Schuster, 1976, p. 59.

35 Described and illustrated in Opel-bad Wiesbaden, 1934, pp. 525–40, Schuster, 1976, pp. 59–62, and in Zukowsky, 1994, p. 97.

36 See Heller, 1979, p. 70. In Lausanne: 'The different types of bathing establishments on the lakes, from the first, constructed in 1861, to Belle-Rive, built in 1937, were undertaken in such a way as to reinforce two fundamental principles: hygiene and morality.' (Heller, 1979, p. 68.)

37 Although as late as 1922 in Lausanne bathing establishments were divided into three separate 'zones' in response to complaints about mixed bathing on the lake: one for women and children, a second for adolescent boys and men, and the third, for mixed bathing by families. (Heller, 1979, p. 74.)

38 'One no longer has to hide in order to swim', commented the Swiss magazine *Habitation* in 1937. (Special issue on the opening of the Belle-Rive Plage baths, quoted in Heller, 1979, p. 77.) Nevertheless, as Heller comments: 'the solicitude of morality, the organization of surveillance, remained present in the sportive and ludic institution of the modern swimming bath.' (Heller, 1979, p. 77.)

39 *ABC*, series 2, no. 2, 1926, p. 1, English translation in 'Commentary' in *ABC*, 1993, p. 13.

40 See Siegfried Kracauer, 'Das Ornament der Masse' (1927) in Kracauer, 1990, pp. 57–67, translated as 'The Mass Ornament', in Kracauer, 1995, pp. 75–86.

41 Diaries of Count Harry Kessler, Deutsches Literatur Archiv, Marbach, entry for 4 June, 1930, translated in Kessler, 1971, p. 36.

42 Kessler's property was sold and his collection dispersed. He died in relative poverty in Paris in 1937.

43 See Toepfer, 1997, passim.

44 Spender, 1977, p. 109.

45 Ibid., p. 107.

46 See 'The Cult of the Body: *Lebensreform*, Sports, and Dance', in Kaes, Jay and Dimendberg, 1995, pp. 673–74.

47 Koch, 1924; translated as 'The Truth about the Berlin Nudist Groups', in Kaes, Jay and Dimendberg, 1995, p. 676, translation slightly modified.

48 Hollaender, 1924, pp. 5–10; translated as 'Ways to Strength and Beauty', in Kaes, Jay and Dimendberg, 1995, p. 677.

49 Kaes, Jay and Dimendberg, 1995, p. 675.

50 Ibid., p. 674.

51 Surén, 1924, preface to the first edition; English translation in Kaes, Jay and Dimendberg, 1995, p. 678.

52 Preface to the 61st edition, translated in Kaes, Jay and Dimendberg, 1995, p. 678.

53 See illustrations in Lavrentiev, 1995, p. 162 fig. 200, p. 163 fig. 201, p. 262 figs 348–49, p. 263 fig. 350.

54 Leeuwen, 1998, pp. 38–39.

55 The main pool is now divided into two 50-metre pools.

56 In 1938, after the Anschluss, 80 per cent of these were deemed to be Jewish-owned according to the Nuremberg laws. (Caption in exhibition 'Riviera an der Donau: Sommerfrische Kritzendorf' [Riviera on the Danube: Kritzendorf Summer Resort], Wien Museum Karlsplatz, Vienna, 22 July to 26 September 2004. See also Fischer, 2004, pp. 101–18.)

57 For the Werkbund Exhibition, see Overy, 2004, pp. 337–57.

58 Giedion, 1930; English translation in Giedion, 1954, p. 50.

59 Giedion, 1969, Part VII 'The Mechanization of the Bath', especially pp. 628–55, pp. 711–12.

60 For open-air swimming baths in Switzerland, see Maurer, 1995, pp. 72–79.

61 Giedion, 1929, fig. 84.

62 Giedion, 1969, pp. 672–75.

63 In most British collieries each man was provided with two towels and a bar of soap.

64 Zola, 1954, pp. 118–20. In the story 'Odour of Chrysanthemums', the mother and wife of a miner killed in a pit accident wash his dead body as they had washed his living body when he was alive. (Lawrence, 1955, pp. 283–302.) See also Lawrence's play on the same subject, *The Widowing of Mrs Holroyd* (1914).

65 The Miners' Welfare Fund had been established in 1920 in response to the Sankey Commission of 1919, set up to investigate the conditions and structure of the mining industry after the threat of strike by the miners' unions. The MWF was created by a levy of one penny on each ton of coal produced. (Allison, 1994, p. 58.)

66 Allison, 1994, p. 59.

67 Quoted in Rich, 2003, p. 6.

Chapter 10 Washing & watching

1 Wagner exhibited the model rooms which included the bathroom with the glass bath at the 1898 Jubilee Exhibition in Vienna that celebrated the fiftieth anniversary of the Emperor Franz Joseph's accession to the Austro-Hungarian throne, and two years later at the Paris 1900 Exposition Universelle. The bathroom fitted with the glass bath in the apartment

at Köstlergasse 3, Vienna (1898–99) was illustrated in *Ver Sacrum* in 1900. (*Ver Sacrum* III, 1900, p. 298, reproduced in Wagner, 2002, p.71.)

2 Paul Asenbaum and Reiner Zettl, 'Wagners "Absteigquartier", VI, Köstlergasse 3', in Asenbaum et al., 1984, p. 181. The 'Absteigquartier' was a series of *pied-à-terre* apartments.

3 The phrase 'indecent nakedness' appeared in an article by A. F. Seligmann in the *Neue Freie Presse* on 16 May 1911, cited in Czech and Mistelbauer, 1984, p. 79. See Haiko, 1994, especially p. 93; Apke, 2005, in Natter and Hollein 2005, pp. 138–46.

4 Schaukal, 1910, quoted in Czech and Mistelbauer, 1984, p. 86.

5 Engelmann, 1911, p. 18; reprinted in Czech and Mistelbauer, 1984, p. 86.

6 The phrase appeared in Auernheimer's article 'Häusertod' (The Death of Buildings) cited in Loos, 1911, English translation, Loos, 2002, p. 99.

7 And often associated with pre-adolescent nakedness, i.e. without body hair. (See Haiko, 1994, p. 93.)

8 *Illustriertes Wiener Extrablatt*, 1 January 1911, illustrated in Haiko, 1994, p. 96.

9 Loos, 1898, English translation, Loos, 1998, pp. 86, translation modified.

10 Loos, 1898, English translation, Loos, 1998, p. 84.

11 Loos went to Chicago to see the World's Columbian Exposition in 1893. He was later in Philadelphia, where he had relatives, and New York, where he worked for a time as a draughtsman.

12 Cited in Glassberg, 1979, p. 7. This began to change however with the provision of public bathhouses, which increased from 6 to 46 in the whole of the United States between 1895 and 1904. (Lupton and Miller, 1992, p. 19.) This was still a relatively small number considering the size of the country and its population. Loos was writing in 1898. In 1895, private baths with hot water were rare. (Goubert, 1986, p. 242.) By 1934, however, 89 per cent of housing units in New York City had a bath or shower. (Glassberg, 1979, p. 5.)

13 Loos, 1898, English translation, Loos, 1998, p. 83.

14 Loos, 1898, English translation, Loos, 1998, p. 85. Loos cites the quotation from Laube's *Die Krieger* (The Warrior), the second volume of a three-volume novel, *Das junge Europa* (Young Europe).

15 Loos, 1898. Here I have preferred to quote the translation in Loos, 1982, p. 49. (Cf. Loos, 1998, pp. 85–86.)

16 Muthesius, 1904–5, extract translated in Benton and Benton, with Sharp, 1975, p. 35, translation modified.

17 'Bathrooms and Civilization', 1917, p. 90, quoted in Lupton and Miller, 1992, p. 17.

18 Quoted in Braham, 1997, in Lahiji and Friedman 1997b, p. 200.

19 Council for Art and Industry, 1937, quoted in Lubbock, 1995, p. 315. The report was produced by the Board of Trade's Council of Art, under chairman Frank Pick, the chief executive of London Transport. Most of the research for this was done by the housing expert Elizabeth Denby.

20 Giedion, 1969, p. 701.

21 Georgiadis, 1993, p. 77. In *Mechanization Takes*

Notes

Command the exhibition is erroneously cited as
'Das Bad im Kulturganzen' (The Bath in its Cultural
Context). (Giedion, 1969, p. 628 n. 1.) This was
probably the title of the section Giedion designed.
The Kunstgewerbemuseum was then housed in the
Landesmuseum (Regional Museum) – opposite which
Max Ernst Haefeli's Rotachhäuser had been built as
model housing for the '*Das neue Heim II*' (The New
Home 2) exhibition at the museum in 1928.

22 Parts of this work in progress were published in
connection with the Zurich exhibition, which ran
from 12 April until 26 May 1935. (Giedion, 1969,
p. 628 n. 1.) Giedion explains that this was
interrupted 'by other work in 1938'. This was
probably the research and writing of the Harvard
lectures that became *Space, Time and Architecture*.

23 See Goubert, 1986, p. 242; Giedion, 1969,
pp. 693–8.

24 See Goubert, 1986, p. 242.

25 By 1940, 77.5 per cent of dwellings in the
urban United States had baths or showers. (Lupton
and Miller, 1992, p. 23.)

26 See Goubert, 1986, p. 242. Only one in ten
Italians had a bathroom in 1931. In France, only
10 per cent of the population had a bath or shower
by 1954. (Goubert, 1986, p. 87.)

27 Lupton and Miller, 1992, p. 25.

28 Enamelled baths were manufactured in a
number of standard sizes in the United States,
commonly 4'6", 5'0", 5'6", 6'0". The 5'0" size was
by far the most popular. (Giedion, 1969, p. 704.)
See also Goubert, 1986, p. 242.

29 The bathroom was illustrated in *Das Frankfurter
Register*, supplement to *Das Neue Frankfurt*, 1929,
no.12, reprinted in Hirdina, 1991, p. 200. The
Sitzbad was 104 cm long, 70 cm wide and 62 cm
deep. The bath (or the bathroom) is credited as
designed by Karl Gutmann in the page from *Das
Frankfurter Register* reproduced in Hirdina (it is not
clear which). Bath and bathroom are sometimes said
to have been designed by Ferdinand Kramer, but
there are no records or patents for these in Kramer's
archives. (Lichtenstein, 1991, p. 182.) According to
the entry in *Das Frankfurter Register*, the bath was
manufactured and distributed by Bamberger, Leroi
& Co. A.-G., Frankfurt am Main. According to
Lichtenstein, it was manufactured by Eisenwerke
Hirzenhain Hugo Buderus GmbH, and distributed
by Bamberger, Leroi & Co. It seems possible that
the bath was designed by Gutmann (who was not
a member of the neue Frankfurt team) while the
bathroom was designed by Kramer. There were also
different configurations, as with the standardized
components of the Frankfurt Kitchen. The bath
was fitted in the bathrooms of the apartment blocks
in the Westhausen Siedlung designed by Kramer
and Blanck, but in a different configuration from
that illustrated in *Das Frankfurter Register*.

30 Schütte-Lihotzky, 1926–27, translated in Kaes,
Jay and Dimendberg, 1995, p. 464.

31 See Adriaansz et al., 2001, p. 123.

32 Oud, 1935, p. 456, reprinted in Taverne, Wagenaar
and De Vletter, 2001, p. 285. Plans of Oud's original
designs and those executed are illustrated in Oud,
1930, p. 362; see also Hans Oud, 1984. p. 91.

33 Hoffmann's was not the only *Gemeindebau* to
have porthole windows to the WCs, but it was one
of the most striking and prominent.

34 See Blau, 1999, pp. 210ff.

35 Blaschke and Lipschitz, 2003, p. 192; Sarnitz,
1998, p. 197.

36 Podbrecky, 2003, p. 63. The baths were named
after Amalie Pölzer, Social Democrat city
councillor and champion of women's rights,
who died in 1924. She and her husband, the
Social Democrat politician Johan Pölzer, were
well-known activists in the working-class district
of Favoriten, where the Amalienbad is located.

37 Blaschke and Lipschitz, 2003, p. 192.

38 The bath complex was carefully restored
between 1979 and 1986 by Erich Schlöss and
Erich Millbacher.

39 Loos was chief architect of the Siedlungsamt
(Settlement Office) – an organization that oversaw
the allocation of land and the construction of
Gartensiedlungen (garden suburbs) by the settlers'
organizations in Vienna – from May 1921 to June
1924. He is often erroneously described as chief
housing architect of the city.

40 'Die Wiener Gemeindebauten vertragen keine
Kritik', a conversation with Adolf Loos in Paris,
translated as 'The Vienna City Council's Tenements
Cannot Tolerate Criticism' in Loos, 2002, p. 195.

41 Giedion, 1969, p. 700.

42 Cited in Weston, 1996, p. 9. For an extended
discussion of the sources of Le Corbusier's use of
the piloti, see Vogt, 1998, passim.

43 In a number of modernist buildings drainage
pipes were designed to run through the structural
columns.

44 Even more extreme was the Italian architect
Luigi Figini's 'Architect's House' (1934–35) in Milan
where the elegant, elongated pilotis become almost
a parody or pastiche of Le Corbusier's practice.
(Illustration in Functional Architecture, 1990, p. 186.)

45 See Lahiji and Friedman, 1997a, pp. 37, 40–41.

46 Rowe, 1994, p. 60.

47 See Van Straaten, 1988, pp. 176–77. The flower-
arranging room was sited in the vestibule of the
villa on the ground floor, next to the lavatory and
separate cloakroom where guests could wash their
hands. It was also directly connected by a short
flight of steps to the garden – presumably so that
Marie-Laure Noailles (or one of the servants) could
bring cut flowers directly from the garden to the
room to be trimmed and arranged.

48 Le Corbusier, 1925b, English translation, Le
Corbusier, 1987b, p. 15 (first published in *L'Esprit
nouveau*).

49 See Rowe, 1994, p. 60.

50 Quoted from Camfield, 1989, p. 39 in Molesworth,
1997, in Lhiji and Friedman, 1997b, p. 80.

51 See Cabanne, 1971, pp. 54–55. But presumably
some members of the society and other privileged
viewers were allowed to inspect the work.

52 The work was apparently lost after being
rejected from the exhibition. A replica, hung by
Duchamp on the wall the 'right' way up – at a level
'where little boys could use it' – was exhibited in an
exhibition entitled 'Challenge and Defy' in New

York in 1950. (Molesworth, 1997, in Lahiji and
Friedman, 1997b, p. 90 n. 9.)

53 'Its total and complete unusability set into play
certain desires about cleanliness (and its potential
impossibility) and certain fantasies about the spaces
where clean and unclean happen: the home, the
institution, the art gallery.' (Molesworth, 1997, p. 83.)

54 Tschumi, 1994, p. 73.

55 Illustrated in Overy, 1996, p. 79 fig. 64.

56 Gerrit Rietveld in an interview recorded in 1963,
quoted in Büller and Den Oudsten, 1988, p. 52.

57 Described in Rietveld, 1971, np., caption to
fig. 99. No date is given for the design, but it is
probably from the late 1930s or early 1940s.

58 See Kirsch, 1989, p. 162.

59 Wedepohl, 1927, p. 399, quoted in translation
in Kirsch, 1989, p. 162.

60 Schwitters, 1927, p. 347, quoted in translation
in Kirsch, 1989, p. 162.

61 Kracauer, 1927, quoted in translation in Kirsch,
p. 62.

62 Kracauer, 1927, quoted in translation in Ward,
2001, p. 62, translation slightly modified.

63 Failures of plumbing or the waterproofing
of flat roofs were notorious among some of the
best-known of modernist architects, including
Le Corbusier, Rietveld and Schindler.

64 Le Corbusier, 1925b, English translation,
Le Corbusier, 1987b, pp. 180ff.

65 Adolf Loos, 1898, English translation, Loos,
1998, p. 87.

66 An exception was the black marble-lined
bathroom Loos designed for the psychiatrist
Theodore Beer's Villa Karma in Switzerland in
1904. The house had both a black and a white
bathroom. (Rukschcio and Schachel, 1982, p. 428)

67 The apartment was at 3 Giselastrasse (now
Bösendorferstrasse), in Vienna's 1st district. Loos
was 12 years older than Lina Obertimpfler, who was
19 when they married in 1902. They were divorced
in 1905.

68 The construction of the bed was described by
Loos in 1918. (Quoted in Rukschcio and Schachel,
1982, p. 81.)

69 Münz and Künstler describe this as a 'rather lush
"sleeping tent".' (Münz and Künstler, 1966, p. 64.)

70 See Dormandy, 1999, p. xiv and passim; Susan
Sontag (1978) in Sontag, 1991, p. 13, pp. 21–22,
pp. 24–26. Patients had a pale complexion because
they suffered from anaemia. For the association
of whiteness with death, see also Dyer, 1997,
Chapter 6, 'White Death', pp. 207–23.

71 Le Corbusier, 1925b, translated in Le Corbusier,
1987b, p. 90.

72 See Haiko, 1994, pp. 89–100; Apke, 2005, in
Natter and Hollein, 2005, pp. 138–46.

73 Illustrated in Teige, 1993, p. 78 figs 1 & 2.

74 Hammann, 1930, p. 121, quoted in Pommer
and Otto, 1991, p. 236.

75 See Ackermann, 2000, in Fiedler and
Feierabend, 2000, p. 133.

76 Theo van Doesburg, *Diary 1928–1930*,
pp. 20–21, 13 June 1928, Van Doesburg Archive,
Netherlands Office for Fine Arts, The Hague, quoted
in translation in Van Straaten, 1994, p. 98. Today,

visitors to the Rietveld Schröder House have to put on felt slippers, to protect the coloured floors.

77 Van Doesburg, 1930, pp. 11–12, English translation, Baljeu, 1974, p. 183, translation modified.

78 See Rothenstein, 1946, p. 159.

79 Ingberman, 1994, p. 91.

80 The colours of the houses in the estate can be seen in a contemporary painting of the Weissenhofsiedlung by Reinhold Nägele, now in the Staatsgalerie, Stuttgart, and a colour postcard from c. 1932. (Reproduced in Pommer and Otto, 1991 pls 1 & 8.)

81 'Since *Weiss* also means white, the name of the Werkbund settlement is peculiarly, if fortuitously, appropriate.' (Searing, 1989, in Smith, 1989, p. 127 n. 50.) However, late 20th-century historians of the Weissenhofsiedlung have been at pains to emphasize that the estate was not painted exclusively in white. (Kirsch, 1989, passim; Pommer and Otto, 1991, passim)

82 At the end of May, Mies wrote to several of the architects (Oud, Rading, Scharoun and Stam) asking them to choose 'the lightest shade of colour possible for the painting of your house, so that through a uniformly light tone the unity of the *Siedlung* can be assured'. (Mies van der Rohe to Oud, 30 May 1927, Mies van der Rohe Archive, MoMA, New York, quoted in translation in Pommer and Otto, 1991, p. 59.) Similar letters were sent to the other architects. Mies made an exception for Bruno Taut and Max Taut who had experimented with colour in earlier architectural designs, although in practice he seems to have allowed some other architects such as Le Corbusier to paint certain parts of their buildings in light tints of colour and off white. (Mies to Stadtschulltheissenamt, 9 June 1927, Stadtarchiv Stuttgart and Mies van der Rohe Archive, New York, quoted in Kirsch, 1989, p. 55.)

83 There has been considerable controversy around exactly what original colours the various buildings were painted. Attempts were made to restore these to what was presumed to be their 1927 colours in the 1980s. However, although these were supposedly based on 'scientific' tests on specimens of old paint, many commentators and contemporary survivors believed that this was not done 'correctly'. (See Kirsch, 1989, p. 56.)

84 *Gehag-Nachrichten*, no. 16 1930, quoted in translation in Pommer and Otto, p. 80.

85 Meyer, 1928, English translation, Schnaidt, 1965, p. 97.

86 For Bauhaus wallpaper, see Bauhaustapete, 1995.

87 Meyer, 1940, English translation in Schnaidt, 1965, p. 111.

88 In his Bundesschule (Trade Union School), designed for the ADGB (Allgemeine Deutsche Gewerkschaftsbund), the General German Trade Union Federation, and built between 1927 and 1930, Meyer insisted that none of the materials were 'camouflaged' by plaster or other surface renderings as they were in Gropius's Dessau Bauhaus building. (For the Bundesschule, see Meyer, 1965, pp. 40–53.)

89 Behne, 1919, quoted in Wigley, 1995, p. 409 n. 57.

90 See Kupinse, 2005, in Cohen and Johnson 2005,

pp. 250–76. See also 'Dirt and Discrimination' in Shove, 2003, pp. 88–89.

91 See Maharaj, 1994, in *Hygiene*, 1994, pp. 14–15.

92 See Le Corbusier, 1925b, English translation 1987b, p. 170; see also Wigley, pp. 294–99.

93 See Dyer, 1997, passim.

94 The plans and elevations for the Baker House are in the Adolf Loos Archive in the Albertina Sammlung, Vienna. See Groenendijk and Vollard, 1985. The project is described in accounts given by Loos's third wife, Claire (Beck) Loos (Claire Loos, 1985, pp. 11–12), and by Loos's students Heinrich Kulka and Kurt Unger. (Kulka, 1931, p. 41; letter from Unger to Ludwig Münz, 23 July 1935, translated in Münz and Kunstler, 1966, p. 178.)

95 For Baker and the *Revue Nègre*, see Gates and Dalton, 1998, in Colin, 1998. For the fascination of modernist artists, writers and composers with black musicians and entertainers in Paris during the 1920s, see Blake, 1999, Archer-Straw, 2000, and Ezra, 2000.

96 Loos was still married to his second wife, the dancer Elsie Altmann, when he moved to Paris in 1924. She did not go with him and they were divorced in March 1926. In 1929, Loos married Claire Beck, the 25-year-old daughter of one of his long-standing clients, Otto Beck of Pilsen.

97 Rukschcio and Schachel, 1982, p. 323.

98 The exhibition toured Germany in 1931. (Rukschcio and Schachel, 1982, p. 323, pp. 365–68.)

99 See Colomina, 1994, p. 260ff, pp. 279ff; Tanzer, 1995, pp. 76–89; Burns, 1997.

100 There are many accounts of Mondrian entertaining visitors with records of jazz and popular music (including some by Baker) in his Montparnasse studio. A group photograph in which Loos and Mondrian can be seen standing next to each other is illustrated in Rukschcio and Schachel, 1982, p. 319. There was some similarity in Loos and Mondrian's thinking. In his early writings Mondrian often describes the vertical as the male and the horizontal as the female principle – from a correct combination of which a harmonious art and design might be constructed. Loos also wrote in this vein, if somewhat more simplistically: 'A horizontal line: a woman. A vertical line: a man penetrating her.' (Loos, 1908, in Loos, 1997b, pp. 78–79, English translation in Loos, 1985, p. 100.) This was a common way of thinking among male artists and writers in the early years of the 20th century. The paragraph that contains these sentences is omitted from the translation in Loos, 1998, p.167. This is based on the text of 'Ornament und Verbrechen' published in the *Frankfurter Zeitung* in 1929, where the paragraph was omitted. It appears, however, in the French translation of 1913 and in the version published in Loos, 1931. (See Stewart, 2000, p. 19.)

101 As recounted by Claire Loos-Beck in 1936. (Claire Loos, 1985, p. 9.)

102 The size of the swimming pool was 4 x 9 x 2 metres and would have contained seven tons of water. It was to be supported by eight large columns. (Münz and Kunstler, 1966, pp. 177–180.)

103 Quoted in translation in Münz and Kunstler, 1966, p. 195.

104 Loos, 1985, p. 11.

105 See Colomina, 1994, pp. 260ff, pp. 279ff; Burns, 1997, passim.

106 Beatriz Colomina has argued that as the swimming pool was lit from a skylight above, from inside the windows 'would appear as reflective surfaces, impeding the swimmer's view of the visitors standing in the passages'. (Colomina, 1994, p. 260.)

107 On her death in 1975 Baker was buried in a black marble tomb in Monte Carlo after a public funeral in the Madeleine in Paris, organized by her patroness, Princess Grace of Monaco – formerly Grace Kelly the film actress. (Tanzer, 1995, p. 88, citing Baker and Chase, 1993, p. 492.)

108 Münz and Künstler, 1966, p. 195; Tournikiotis, 1994, p. 95.

109 See Rukschcio and Schachel, 1982, p. 154

110 See Tanzer, 1995, p. 86.

111 The only house Loos built in Paris (designed for the Dadaist writer Tristan Tzara in Montmartre in 1925) was partly faced with brownish stone, while the white walls of its interior were decorated with 'primitive' artifacts collected by Tzara – many of them from Africa.

112 It has been suggested that Baker may have been the illegitimate daughter of her black mother and a white man. She never used her mother's husband's surname; Baker was the name of the singer's husband. (Baker and Chase, 1993, p. 16, cited in Tanzer, 1995, p. 88, no. 11.) Baker and Chase's speculation is based on hospital records in St Louis, where Baker was born, and on comparison of her skin colour with that of her siblings. Statistically, all African-Americans and Afro-Caribbeans have a relatively high percentage of white blood. 'Mixed' blood is a recurring theme in Baker's work.

113 Quoted in Tanzer 1995, p. 86. Apparently very few copies were printed of the novel, which was badly received by the critics. (Wood, 2000, p. 159.)

Chapter 11 The clean machine

1 Ford, 1924, pp. 113–14.

2 Quoted in Batchelor, 1994, p. 50.

3 In 1932, while staying in Detroit with her husband Diego Riviera (who was working on murals in the Detroit Institute of Arts), Frida Kahlo had a miscarriage in the Henry Ford Hospital. She painted this traumatic event in *Henry Ford Hospital*, 1932 (Museo Dolores Olmedo Patiño, Mexico City), showing herself lying naked after her miscarriage on her hospital bed – depicted out in the open against a background of the Ford River Rouge plant. (See Dexter and Barson, 2005, pp. 98–99 pl. 15.)

4 Ford, 1924, pp. 214–19.

5 In *Der moderne Zweckbau* [The Modern Functional Building] – written in 1923, but not published until 1926 – Adolf Behne makes a connection between Ford's factories and his hospital. (Behne, 1926; English translation, Behne, 1996, p. 104.)

6 See, for example, the photograph by Edmund Lill of 1922 of the power house from Walter Gropius and Adolf Meyer's Fagus factory reproduced in Jaeggi, 2000, p. 70, and the pump room of the boiler house of the Van Nelle factory (1930) illustrated in Backer, Camp & Dicke, 2005, p. 125.

Notes

7 Le Corbusier, 1923; English translation, Le Corbusier, 1992, p. 277.
8 Ibid., p. 279.
9 Steele, 2002, p. 13 n. 4.
10 Mendelsohn went to the United States in 1924. He published a commentary with photographs based on his visit (Mendelsohn, 1926; enlarged edition 1928).
11 See Isaacs, 1983, pp. 412–13. Gropius was to spend the last part of his life living and working in the United States from 1938 to his death in 1969.
12 Le Corbusier, 1923, English translation Le Corbusier, 1992, p. 42.
13 Reyner Banham describes three buildings in Raymond Boulevard along the river in Newark, New Jersey, 'all remarkably similar in build and appearance', two of which are factories – the other 'a well-made tenement for workers'. (Banham, 1986, p. 42.)
14 See Smith, 1993, p. 73.
15 The two Boots factories were designed by Owen Williams, the Austrian State Tobacco factory by Peter Behrens and Alexander Popp, the Wedgwood factory by Keith Murray and C. S. White. For the Boots factory, see Cottam et al., 1988; Yeomans and Cottam, 2001. For the Wedgwood factory, see Taylor, 1994, pp. 53–54. For the Austrian State Tobacco factory at Linz, see Chapter 12.
16 *The American Architect and Building News*, vol. XCIX, no. 1851, 14 June 1911, p. 214, quoted in Banham, 1986, p. 59.
17 Heimstätte deutscher Industrie, 1899, p. 49, quoted in translation in Jaeggi, 2000, p. 12.
18 Robert Mallet-Stevens, 'L'Architecture moderne', *La Gazette des sept arts*, no. 1, 15 December 1922, p. 8.
19 Ginzburg, 1924, English translation, Ginzburg, 1982, p. 108.
20 Ginzburg, 1927, p. 4, quoted in translation in Cohen, 1995, p. 73.
21 Trotsky shared Lenin's view and applied Taylorist principles to railway production. (Cohen, 1995, pp. 70–71.)
22 See Ford, 1923.
23 Ford, 1924, p. 81. Giedion describes the development of the dis-assembly line in *Mechanization Takes Command*. (Giedion, 1969, pp. 214ff.)
24 Duiker, 1933a, pp. 113–18, reprinted in Jelles and Alberts, 1976, pp. 128–29, English translation, p. 142, translation modified.
25 For a wide illustration of examples of early modernist educational buildings, see Taut, 1929a, pp. 172–78.
26 For the Groningen school, see Sam, 2000.
27 Joris Molenaar, in Backer, Camp & Dicke, 2005, p. 88; Wessel de Jonge, in Van der Vlugt, 1993, p. 18. The design of the Groningen schools is now thought to be largely the work of Wiebenga.
28 Usually as a concrete- or steel-framed structure with curtain walls. In fact, the building is a constructed from brick piers from which very large steel-and-glass windows are hung. Le Corbusier misleadingly reproduced the Fagus-Werk among American factories in *Vers une architecture* (Le Corbusier, 1923, Le Corbusier,1992, p. 38.)

29 For a comprehensive recent examination of the Fagus-Werk, incorporating new research, see Jaeggi, 2000. However, much of this has been known since Helmut Weber examined the building history of the factory in some detail in 1961, although his book appeared only in German. (Weber, 1961.) For an excellent account in English, partly based on Weber, see Tim Benton, 'Walter Gropius and Fagus' in Benton, Muthesius and Wilkins, 1975, pp. 53–56.
30 Benton, in Benton, Muthesius and Wilkins, 1975, p. 54.
31 Both father and son gave substantial financial support to orthopaedic research and in the mid-1920s helped found a company that exploited this to manufacture anatomically correct but fashionable shoes. (Jaeggi, 2000, pp. 7–8, p. 67.)
32 Illustrated in Jaeggi, 2000, p. 56.
33 Jaeggi, 2000, p. 56.
34 These were situated in Veldes (Bled, now in Slovenia) and Trieste. Before the First World War, both were part of the Austro-Hungarian empire.
35 The United Shoe Machinery Corporation of Beverley, Massachusetts undertook to contribute 80 per cent of the estimated costs of setting up the Fagus-Werk. Carl Benscheidt was responsible for the remainder and agreed to purchase the machinery for producing shoe lasts from the company, which had recently amalgamated with Goodyear and was looking for a source of lasts for the shoe factories it owned in Germany. (Jaeggi, 2000, p. 15.)
36 Banham, 1986, p. 185.
37 Since the late 1890s Loos had written admiringly of the traditional accoutrements of the English 'gentleman' as exemplifying the high quality achieved by the anonymous designer and craftsman. Le Corbusier's definition of the *objet-type* was similar, and probably derived from Loos: an anonymously designed artefact that had acquired a kind of perfection through gradual modification and improvement over the years. However, the term *objet-type* relates to the German *Typisierung* advocated by Werkbund members like Hermann Muthesius and Bruno Paul. (See James Dunnett, 'Introduction' to Le Corbusier, 1987b, p. ix.) For the *objet-type* see Le Corbusier, 1925b, English translation, 'Type-Needs Type-Furniture', Le Corbusier, 1987b, pp. 69–79. For further illustrations of what Le Corbusier considered to be *objet-types* (including examples of shoes), see Le Corbusier, 1925b, Le Corbusier, 1987b, pp. 84–101.
38 Le Corbusier described these as 'auxiliary limbs' or 'human-limb objects'. (Le Corbusier, 1925b, Le Corbusier 1987b, pp. 72–73, see also pp. 75–79.)
39 See sequence in Jaeggi, 2000, pp. 18–19.
40 These are often believed to date from 1926–27. Jaeggi argues they were taken in April 1928. Renger-Patzsch produced a further series for Karl Benscheidt in 1952. (Jaeggi, 2000, p. 114, p. 149 n. 15.) While it is possible that Renger's original series was intended for use in advertising and publicity, only one image seems to have been employed in this way – in an advertising brochure designed by Herbert Bayer. The depression may have precluded further plans for advertising and publicity campaigns. (Jaeggi, 2000, pp. 115–18)

41 Bat'a had worked in the shoe factories of Lynn, Massachussetts in 1904 as a labourer. He visited America again with his factory executives in 1919–20 before building his 'industrial colony' of factories and workers' housing in Zlín. For Zlín, see Slapeta, 1990, Slapeta, 1992, Pavitt, 1994.
42 Quoted in translation in Pavitt, 1994, p. 36.
43 Ibid.
44 See Pavitt, 1994, pp. 38–39.
45 See Cohen, 1995, pp. 80–81. This idea would have appealed to Le Corbusier, who admired paternalistic and philanthropic industrialists such as Bat'a. Jan Bat'a invited him to submit plans for a new residential complex in Zlín and a new Bat'a factory community at Hellocourt in France, but neither these nor Le Corbusier's design for the Bat'a pavilion for the 1937 Paris International Exhibition were realized. (Pavitt, 1994, p. 40.)
46 Gropius 1911, in Probst and Schädlich, 1988, pp. 28–51; Gropius, 1913, pp. 17–22, English translation, Benton and Benton, with Sharp, 1975, pp. 53–55; Gropius, 1914, pp. 29–32.
47 An early exception was the curtain-walled factory for the Steiff 'Knopf im Ohr' (Button in Ear) teddy-bear manufacturing company in 1903 at Giengen an der Brenz in Württemberg, designed by Richard Steiff – the nephew of the founder of the company, and creator of the original teddy bear.
48 For the Bauhaus building in Dessau, see Sharp, 1993; Bauhaus Dessau Foundation and Kentgens-Craig, 1998.
49 See Gropius, 1926. English translation in Benton and Benton, with Sharp, 1975, pp. 148–49.

Chapter 12 Manufacturing enlightenment

1 See Isaacs, 1983, vol. 1, pp. 412–13. Ise Gropius (Gropius's wife) records in her diary a visit from Van der Leeuw and Van der Vlugt and an engineer (possibly Brinkman or Wiebenga) on 6 May 1926 when the new building was nearing completion, and on 6 April 1927 three months after the official opening of the building. (Typescript, Bauhaus-Archiv, Berlin, quoted in translation by Walter Scheiffele in Bauhaus Dessau Foundation and Kentgens-Craig, 1998, p. 113, p. 115.)
2 Frank Kauffmann, in Backer, Camp & Dicke, 2005, p. 71. Jan Molenaar, however, claims that Van der Leeuw and Wiebenga had no direct contact at this time. (Jan Molenaar, in Backer, Camp & Dicke, 2005, p. 97 n. 4). After the Second World War, Wiebenga joined Kees van der Leeuw on the supervisory board of the Van Nelle company when it became a public company in 1951. (Matthijs Dicke, in Backer, Camp & Dicke, 2005, p. 211.)
3 Van der Leeuw later compared the Van Nelle factory with the Dessau Bauhaus rather than with American factory buildings. (Molenaar, in Backer, Camp & Dicke, 2005, p. 106.)
4 Because of this alternation of steel and glass the façade of the Van Nelle factory was not as 'pure' an example of curtain walling as the all-glass façade of the Bauhaus workshop block.
5 See Wessel de Jonge, in Backer, Camp & Dicke, 2005, p. 284. The steel-and-glass windows were supplied by F. W. Braat of Delft, who were licensed

to manufacture steel window frames designed by the English firm of Crittall. (Molenaar, in Backer, Camp & Dicke, 2005, pp. 111–12.)

6 Wiebenga worked in America for over a year in 1924–25 shortly before collaborating with Van der Vlugt on the Van Nelle factory, but was probably already familiar with American mushroom-column design from photographs and illustrated articles in construction magazines and books.

7 The diameter of the columns is reduced every two floors.

8 Van der Leeuw, 1930, p. 13, quoted in translation by Wessel de Jonge in Van der Vlugt, 1993, p. 21. Brinkman and Van der Vlugt had favoured a more conventional method of concrete-frame construction system, but Van der Leeuw (who had recently returned from his American research trip) opted for the system proposed by Wiebenga.

9 Van der Leeuw shared an interest in theosophy and psychoanalysis with Earl De La Warr, who commissioned the Bexhill Pavilion from Mendelsohn and Chermayeff. De La Warr had known Krishnamurti who, with his brother Nitya, had stayed as a youth for long periods in his mother's house in Ashdown Forest. He later became a devotee of psychoanalysis. Both he and his wife were analysed, and their three children were in Kleinian analysis from a very young age. (Fairley, 2001, pp. 24–25, pp. 53–54.)

10 See Michael Molnar, annotations to Freud's diary entry of Thursday 26 April 1934, 'v.d. Leeuw evening...' in Freud, 1992, p. 170; Kauffmann, in Backer, Camp & Dicke, 2005, p. 72. Further information on this subject, email correspondence with Molnar and Kauffmann, January 2007.

11 For Van der Leeuw and theosophy, see Kauffmann, in Backer, Camp & Dicke, 2005, especially pp. 39–58.

12 Molenaar, in Van der Vlugt, 1993, p. 9.

13 See De Jonge, in Van der Vlugt, 1993, p. 21.

14 Van der Leeuw paid particular attention to the artificial as well as the natural lighting of the factory. He made a special visit to the lighting laboratory of the General Electric Company when he was in the United States, and had numerous brochures sent back to Brinkman and Van der Vlugt. (Molenaar, in Van der Vlugt, 1993, p. 9.)

15 Quoted in translation by Kauffmann in Backer, Camp & Dicke, 2005, p. 47, punctuation altered.

16 Van der Leeuw visited the American Posture League in New York. Among the companies and factories he also visited was the engineering firm of Lockwood Greene & Co., Eastman Kodak, a button factory, a cardboard factory, a coffee factory, General Motors, and various power stations. (Molenaar, in Backer, Camp & Dicke, 2005, p. 104; André Koch, in Backer, Camp & Dicke, 2005, p. 170 n. 7.)

17 See Kauffmann, in Backer, Camp & Dicke, 2005, p. 63. Van der Leeuw also went on study trips to factories in France and Germany.

18 For the Van Nelle garden, see Leo den Dulk, in Backer, Camp & Dicke, 2005, pp. 163–65. The sports fields and tennis courts were turned into a car park and distribution centre in the 1970s.

19 Van der Leeuw, 1930, quoted in translation by Kauffmann in Backer, Camp & Dicke, 2005, p. 72.

20 Michiel Brinkman (the father of Van der Vlugt's partner, J. A. Brinkman) – who had originally been given the commission for the new Van Nelle factory, but had died suddenly in 1925 – wrote on the drawings for his plan of 1923: 'The front of the factory should be favourably positioned with respect to the view from the train, with an eye to illuminated advertising.' (Quoted in translation by Molenaar, in Backer, Camp & Dicke, 2005, p. 85.)

21 Robertson and Yerbury, 1930, reprinted in Robertson and Yerbury, 1989, p. 112.

22 Although the factory as a whole was not completed until 1931, various parts of the plant were in operation from the late 1920s.

23 Report by C. H. [Kees] van der Leeuw, December 1914, Van Nelle Archives, quoted by Frank Kauffmann in Van der Vlugt, 1993, p. 4, translation modified.

24 Quoted in Behne, 1926, English translation, Behne, 1996, p. 105.

25 Initially, the packaging of the company's products encountered resistance from both consumers and retailers, but soon Van Nelle became the market leader in The Netherlands. (Dicke, in Backer, Camp & Dicke, 2005, p. 15, p. 21.)

26 Dingenus van die Vrie, in Backer, Camp & Dicke, 2005, p. 29, and illustration. Over 5,000 copies were printed and another 200 produced in enamelled metal versions. Cassandre worked predominantly for Dutch clients between 1927 and 1931, and had three exhibitions of his work in The Netherlands in 1931.

27 In the early years of the 20th century the Van Nelle company's expenditure on advertising rose exponentially. (Dicke, in Backer, Camp & Dicke, 2005, p. 22.)

28 See for example the advertising campaign for Miss Blanche cigarettes for the Vittoria Egyptian Cigarette Company of Rotterdam, designed by the Hungarian artist and designer Vilmos Huszár who had been closely associated with De Stijl. (White, 2003, pp. 96–100.)

29 Dicke, in Backer, Camp & Dicke, 2005, p. 37. A song from a booklet featuring new words to well-known tunes distributed by Van Nelle sales representatives began:

People, guard against the evils
That come from alcohol;
Become teetotalers forevermore
Men, don't touch that drink.
If you want to succeed in your work,
Drink what you love best,
Always Van Nelle's tea or coffee,
You'll live to be a hundred.

(Quoted in translation by Dicke in Backer, Camp & Dicke, 2005, p. 36.)

30 Behrens returned to Germany in 1936, while Popp joined the Nazi party in 1935 and pursued a successful career as chief architect of the Herman-Goering-Werke steel works in Linz from 1938.

31 This was added at a late stage of construction of the tobacco factory in the autumn of 1927 above the first staircase. (Molenaar, in Backer, Camp & Dicke, 2005, p. 113.)

32 See Kauffmann, in Van der Vlugt, 1993, p. 4;

Kauffmann, in Backer, Camp & Dicke, 2005, p. 45. Van der Leeuw was a freemason as well as a theosophist, a common conjunction at the time. Freemasons also believed in the spiritual qualities of light, and in the symbolic importance of building and construction.

33 See Kuitenbrouwer, 1991, especially pp. 310–26.

34 Kees van der Leeuw's letters written while in Africa and the Dutch East Indies contain remarks that would today be regarded as racist. (See Kauffmann, in Backer, Camp & Dicke, 2005, p. 55; Kauffmann also discusses theosophist racial ideas, p. 53.)

35 Quoted from Posener, 1980, in Burckhardt, 1980, p. 10 (translation slightly modified). Rathenau had become chairman of AEG in 1915 on the death of his father Emil Rathenau, the founder of the company. He was appointed German foreign minister in 1922 and was assassinated by anti-Semitic right-wing militants shortly after signing the German-Soviet treaty in Rapallo that year.

36 Stam worked for Brinkman and Van der Vlugt from the summer of 1926 to April 1928. In a lecture at a meeting of the avant-garde Rotterdam architectural association Opbouw, the speaker apparently referred to the Van Nelle factory 'by Mart Stam'. After the lecture Van der Vlugt asked Stam to correct this statement. Stam refused and Van der Vlugt dismissed him on the spot. The lecture was in connection with an exhibition of International Architecture in Rotterdam, a revised version of the 'Plan- und Modell-Ausstellung neuer Baukunst' exhibition held in Stuttgart in the summer of 1927 to accompany the Weissen-hofsiedlung model-housing exhibition. A drawing of an early version of the Van Nelle factory attributed to Mart Stam was shown in the exhibitions at Stuttgart and Rotterdam. (Molenaar, in Backer, Camp & Dicke, 2005, pp. 121–22, drawing illustrated p. 122.) Van der Leeuw and Stam came into contact again in the 1940s. (Kauffmann, in Backer, Camp & Dicke, 2005, p. 62.) This was after Stam had worked in the Soviet Union in the 1930s and before he went to work in the GDR.

37 Van der Leeuw, 1930, p. 13, quoted in translation in De Jonge, in Van der Vlugt, 1993, p. 21.

38 These were produced by the Crane Company. (Koch in Backer, Camp & Dicke, 2005, p. 174; a photograph of a tobacco-factory washroom is reproduced on p. 126.) See also Molenaar, in Backer, Camp & Dicke, 2005, p. 113.

39 Molenaar, in Backer, Camp & Dicke, 2005, p. 129. Illustration p. 127, p. 262.

40 This was also true of the Steiff Teddy Bear Factory in Giengen an der Brenz (1904–8) which had a largely female workforce.

41 Kees van der Leeuw, quoted in Jeroen Geurst, 'The Van Nelle Factory', in Futagawa, 1994, np. Van der Leeuw was in this instance referring to the office building.

42 Quoted in Koch, in Backer, Camp & Dicke, 2005, p. 175, translation slightly modified.

43 See Housden, 1960, p. 161, p. 167.

44 The open-plan office for the clerical staff in the curving administration building also combined light and airy work conditions with ease of surveillance.

Notes

At one end was a gallery onto which the managers' offices opened, from where they could surveil the clerical staff working on the floor below and 'dominate the whole area of the general office'. (Robertson and Yerbury, 1930, in Robertson and Yerbury, 1989, p. 113, see illustration in Van der Vlugt, 1993, p. 12.)

45 Rob Dettingmeijer, 'The fight for a well built city', in Nieuwe Bouwen: Rotterdam, 1982, p. 44, translation slightly modified.

46 Molenaar, in Backer, Camp & Dicke, 2005, p. 129.

47 Koch, in Backer, Camp & Dicke, 2005, pp. 174–75.

48 Dicke, in Backer, Camp & Dicke, 2005, p. 206.

49 This was contrary to what Ford claimed in his autobiography. (See Chapter 11.)

50 Report now in Van den Broek and Bakema Archives, Rotterdam, quoted in translation by Molenaar, in Van der Vlugt, 1993, p. 9, translation slightly modified.

51 Quoted in translation in Molenaar, in Backer, Camp & Dicke, 2005, p. 124. When Le Corbusier came to Rotterdam to lecture in January 1932 he flew above the port and visited the factory. See also Robertson and Yerbury, 1930, in Robertson and Yerbury, 1989, p. 113.

52 See Wiggington, 1996, p. 01.58. Although Le Corbusier did not visit the factory until the early 1930s, he was probably familiar with photographs of it under construction from as early as 1926 or 1927.

53 Quoted in Curtis, 1986, p. 102. After visiting the factory in 1932 Le Corbusier claimed it had 'removed all the former connotations of despair from that word "proletarian"'. (Le Corbusier, 1933, English translation, Le Corbusier, 1967, p. 177.) Van der Leeuw was the 'ideal' patron Le Corbusier had long sought for his own work, but never found: a man who combined an informed awareness of modern American industrial, commercial and management practices, an 'ethical' approach to manufacture and trade inspired by esoteric beliefs, and an authoritarian paternalism.

54 For Roland Holst's work for the Dutch Diamond Workers' Union, see De Burcht van Berlage, 1991, pp. 24–28, pp. 31–39.

55 Letter from R. N. Roland Holst to M. Elout-Drabbe, 15 January 1933, quoted in translation by Molenaar in Backer, Camp & Dicke, 2005, p. 124, translation slightly modified.

56 For Kees van der Leeuw's house, see Jeroen Geurst in Van der Vlugt, 1993, pp. 28–31; Kauffmann, in Backer, Camp & Dicke, 2005, p. 74.

57 See Molenaar in Backer, Camp & Dicke, 2005, p. 141. The Sonneveld House has recently been restored and can be visited as part of the nearby Nederlands Architectuur Instituut (NAi). See Adriaansz et al., 2001.

58 See Van der Vlugt, 1993, p. 54, illustrated p. 40.

59 Molenaar, in Backer, Camp & Dicke, 2005, p. 141.

60 Molenaar, in Van der Vlugt, 1993, p. 13, translation modified. For the failure of the Van Nelle company as a business enterprise after 1930, see Dicke, in Backer, Camp & Dicke, 2005, pp. 195–212.

61 Molenaar, in Van der Vlugt, 1993, p. 13. Robertson and Yerbury had written in 1930: 'We are told, and we can believe it, that since the plant and offices of Van Nelle have been housed in this new building, output has increased, and the health of the employees maintains an average imcomparably higher than was the case in the former factory.' (Robertson and Yerbury, 1930, in Robertson and Yerbury, 1989, p. 113.) This seems to have been wishful thinking on the part of the Van Nelle management.

62 These were manufactured by the Gispen company, who made the tubular-steel furniture for the factory. Gispen featured the shutters in an advert in a leading Dutch architectural and construction magazine in 1931. (Bouwkundig Weekblad Architectura, vol. LII, no. 25, 1931, cited by Koch in Van der Vlugt, 1993, p. 45.)

63 A series of documentary photographs were commissioned from the photographer E. M. van Ojen recording the construction of the plant and the workings of the completed factory. At about the same time a sequence of 'art' photographs were taken by J. Kammen (Kamann) – a photographer and painter who was a member of the Rotterdam group of avant-garde artists and designers Opbouw – several of which have frequently been reproduced in key modernist texts. The 'factory street' between the factory block and the warehouses and power plant made a dramatic setting for feature and other films, and this was exploited by the Van Nelle company for commercial and promotional ends. The construction of the factory buildings was filmed by Haghe Studios, and in 1930 the Dutch left-wing film-maker Joris Ivens used shots of the factory in operation in one of his documentaries.

64 Van der Leeuw employed the modernist graphic designer Jac (Jacobus) Jongert to design the company's packaging and advertising, and there was a small film department in the basement of the factory. A company film van toured The Netherlands giving promotional shows featuring a film about the building of the factory, Achter glas (Behind Glass).

65 See Dettingmeijer, in Nieuwe Bouwen: Rotterdam, 1982, pp. 43–44.

66 Molenaar, in Van der Vlugt, 1993, p. 10.

Conclusion

1 The factory was decommissioned in 1998 by Sara Lee/Douwe Egberts, who had taken over the Van Nelle company some years previously.

2 Van der Leeuw, 1930, p. 14, quoted by De Jonge in Van der Vlugt, 1993, p. 21.

3 The Van Nelle factory was listed provisionally in 1982, and definitively in 1985. (Marieke Kuipers, in Backer, Camp & Dicke, 2005, pp. 222–23.)

4 This was in response to the attention focused on its plight through DOCOMOMO – the international association devoted to the care and protection of modern-movement buildings. DOCOMOMO is an acronym for the International Working Party for DOcumentation and COnservation of buildings, sites

and neighbourhoods of the MOdern MOvement, and was founded by Hubert-Jan Henket and Wessel de Jonge in 1988 as the direct result of an earlier investigation into the possibility of restoring the Zonnestraal. (Dean, 1992, p. 3.)

5 For the prehistory of attempts to restore Zonnestraal and the notion of 'young monuments' in The Netherlands, see Jelles and Alberts, 1976, p. 2.

6 The surviving original fixtures such as lamps, heating radiators, furniture, washbasins and sinks will be repaired and reinstalled in a few rooms, which will be furnished like the originals. See Wessel de Jonge, 'Zonnestraal Sanatorium, Hilversum (Jan Duiker)', in Cunningham, 1998, p. 156.

7 Wessel de Jonge (who worked on the restoration of both buildings) sees these as representing two different aspects of the modern movement of the early 20th century, rationalism and functionalism – following Adolf Behne's account in Der moderne Zweckbau. See De Jonge, in Backer, Camp & Dicke, 2005, p. 259; Behne, 1926, English translation Behne, 1996, especially Chapter III, pp. 119–46.

8 See Mostafavi and Leatherbarrow, 1993, pp. 82ff.

9 See Jana Horneková, 'A history of the Müller Villa building', in The Müller Villa, 2002, p. 14; illustration of boilers p. 104.

10 Oud's cafe (1924–25) was also intended to have only a ten-year life. It was destroyed in the bombing of Rotterdam in 1940 and reconstructed in 1985–86 on a different site in the city centre, the original site having been built upon during the rebuilding of Rotterdam after the war. For the Barcelona Pavilion and its recreation, see Solà-Morales, Cirici and Ramos, 1998.

11 Wouter Vanstiphout, 'Stories from behind the Scenes of Dutch Moral Modernism', in Crimson, Speaks and Hadders, 1999, p. 39, illustrations p. 177, p. 222.

12 Vanstiphout, in Crimson, Speaks and Hadders, 1999, p. 39, illustration of 1993 reconstruction, pp. 46–47, p. 49.

13 Molema and De Jonge, however, conclude that we should be grateful to Duiker for having the courage continually to apply new techniques and to employ new products and new and often untested materials in his architecture. 'In doing so, and despite the lack of durability of his buildings, Duiker contributed enormously to the development of architecture in the middle of the 20th century.' (Molema and De Jonge, 1985, p. 55.)

14 Mostafavi and Leatherbarrow, 1993, p. 109.

15 See Duiker, 1982, passim. For a counter-argument, see Wim Denslagen 'Over het restaureren en renoveren van jonge mounumenten' (On the restoration and reconstruction of modernism monuments), in Colenbrander, 1987, pp. 83–93.

16 Maristella Casciato and Cristiana Marcosano Dell'Erba, 'Sant'Elia Infant School, Como (Giuseppe Terragni)', in Cunningham, 1998, p. 108.

17 De Jonge, in Cunningham, p. 150.

ABC, 1993. Mart Stam, Hans Schmidt, El Lissitzky and Emil Roth (eds), *ABC: Beiträge zum Bauen 1924-1928*, reprint with commentary, Baden (Switzerland): Lars Müller.

Achleitner, Friedrich, 1996. *Wiener Architektur: Zwischen typologischem Fatalismus und semantischem Schlamassel*, Vienna: Böhlau.

Ackermann, Ute, 2000. 'Bauhaus Parties – Histrionics between Eccentric Dancing and Animal Drama', in Fiedler and Feierabend, 2005, pp. 126-39.

Adam, Peter, 1987. *Eileen Gray: Architect Designer. A Biography*, London: Thames & Hudson.

Adriaansz, Elly et al., 2001. *Brinkman and Van der Vlugt: The Sonneveld House. An Avant-Garde Home from 1933*, Rotterdam: NAi Publishers.

Allan, John, 1992. *Berthold Lubetkin: Architecture and the Tradition of Progress*, London: RIBA Publications, nd.

—— , 2002. *Berthold Lubetkin*, photography by Morley von Sternberg, foreword by Richard Meier, London: Merrell.

Allison, Georgina, 1994. 'The Miners' Welfare Commission and Pithead Baths in Scotland', in Twentieth Century Architecture, 1994, pp. 55-64.

Allmeyer-Beck, Renate et al., 1993. *Margarete Schütte-Lihotzky: Soziale Architektur, Zeitzeugin eines Jahrhunderts*, Vienna: Österreichisches Museum für angewandte Kunst.

Altenberg, Peter, 1905. *Pròdrŏmŏs*, Berlin: Fischer.

—— , 1915. *Fechsung*, Berlin: Fischer.

Altmann Loos, Elsie, 1968. *Adolf Loos: der Mensch*, Vienna and Munich: Herold.

Amsterdamsche Woningraad, 1909. *Rapport over de Volkshuisvesting in de Nieuwe Stad te Amsterdam*, Amsterdam: Amsterdamsche Woningraad.

Anděl, Jaroslav, 2006. *The New Vision for the New Architecture: Czechoslovakia 1918-1938*, Zurich: Scalo.

Apke, Bernd, 2005. 'Adolf Loos and the Naked Architectural Body', in Natter and Hollein, 2005, pp. 38-46.

Apollonio, Umbro (ed.), 1973. *Futurist Manifestos*, London: Thames & Hudson.

Archer-Straw, Petrine, 2000. *Negrophilia: Avant-Garde Paris and Black Culture in the 1920s*, London: Thames & Hudson.

Aschenbeck, Nils, 1997. *Die Moderne, die aus den Sanatorien kam: Reformarchitektur und Reformkultur um 1900*, Delmenhorst: Aschenbeck und Holstein.

Asenbaum, Paul et al., 1984. *Otto Wagner, Möbel und Innenräume*, Salzburg and Vienna: Residenz.

Attfield, Judy (ed.), 1999. *Utility Reassessed: The Role of Ethics in the Practice of Design*, Manchester: Manchester University Press.

—— , 2000. *Wild Things: The Material Culture of Everyday Life*, Oxford and New York: Berg.

Aujame, Roger, 2005. 'Charlotte Perriand et la volumétrie de l'espace', in Perriand, 2005, pp. 123-24.

Backer, Anne Mieke, Camp, D'Laine and Dicke, Matthijs (eds), 2005. *Van Nelle: Monument in Progress*, Rotterdam: De Hef.

Bakema, J. B., 1968. *L. C. Van der Vlugt*, Amsterdam: Meulenhoff.

Baker, Jean-Claude and Chase, Chris, 1993. *Josephine: The Hungry Heart*, New York: Random House.

Baljeu, Joost, 1974. *Theo van Doesburg*, London: Studio Vista.

Banham, Reyner, 1960. *Theory and Design in the First Machine Age*, London: Architectural Press.

—— , 1970. *The Architecture of the Well-tempered Environment*, London: Architectural Press.

—— , 1986. *A Concrete Atlantis: U.S. Industrial Building and European Modern Architecture 1900-1925*, Cambridge, Mass. and London: MIT Press.

Barker, Andrew, 1996. *Telegrams from the Soul: Peter Altenberg and the Culture of Fin-de-Siècle Vienna*, Columbia, South Carolina: Camden House.

Barr, Alfred H., Jr., 1936. *Cubism and Abstract Art*, New York: Museum of Modern Art.

—— , 1945. 'Art in the Third Reich – Preview, 1933', *Magazine of Art*, October 1945, reprinted in Barr, 1986b, pp. 63-175.

—— , 1986a. *Cubism and Abstract Art* (1936), 3rd edition with a foreword by Robert Rosenblum, Cambridge, Mass. and London: MIT Press.

—— , 1986b. *Defining Modern Art: Selected Writings of Alfred H. Barr, Jr.*, edited by Irving Sandler and Amy Newman, New York: Abrams.

Barré-Despond, Arlette, 1988. *Jourdain: Frantz 1847-1935, Francis 1876-1958, Frantz-Philippe 1906*, Paris: Editions du Regard (section on Francis Jourdain by Suzanne Tise).

Batchelor, Ray, 1994. *Henry Ford: Mass Production, Modernism and Design*, Manchester and New York: Manchester University Press.

'Bathrooms and Civilization', 1917. 'Bathrooms and Civilization', *House and Garden*, vol. XXX, no. 2, February.

Bau und Wohnung, 1927. *Bau und Wohnung: Die Bauten der Weissenhofsiedlung in Stuttgart, errichtet 1927 nach Vorschlägen des Deutschen Werkbundes im Auftrag der Stadt Stuttgart und im Rahmen der Werkbundausstellung 'Die Wohnung'*, Stuttgart: Deutscher Werkbund/Wedekind.

Bauhaus, 1968. *50 Years Bauhaus*, exh. cat., London: Royal Academy of Arts.

Bauhaus Dessau Foundation and Kentgens-Craig, Margret (eds), 1998. *The Dessau Bauhaus Building 1926-1999*, Basel and Boston: Birkhäuser.

Bauhaustapete, 1995. *Bauhaustapete: Reklame & Erfolg einer Marke/Advertising and Success of a Name*, Cologne: DuMont.

Becker, Annette, Olley, John and Wang, Wilfred (eds), 1997. *20th Century Architecture, Ireland*, Munich and New York: Prestel.

Behne, Adolf, 1919. *Wiederkehr der Kunst*, Berlin: Wolff.

—— , 1926. *Der moderne Zweckbau*, Munich, Vienna, Berlin: Drei Masken (New Edition, 1964).

—— , 1929. 'Austellung der AHAG am Fischgrund', *Das Neue Berlin*, no. 1, p. 20.

—— , 1930a. 'Dammerstock', *Die Form*, vol. 5, no. 6, 15 March, pp. 169-70.

—— , 1930b. 'Rundschau: Dammerstock-Schlusswort', *Die Form*, vol. 5, no. 18, 15 September, p. 494.

—— , 1996. *The Modern Functional Building*, Santa Monica: The Getty Research Institute for the History of Art and the Humanities (translation of Behne, 1926).

Benton, Charlotte (ed.), 1975. *Documents: A Collection of Source Material on the Modern Movement*, Milton Keynes: Open University.

Benton, Tim, 1976. *History of Architecture and Design 1890-1939: Broadcasting Supplememt Part 1*, Milton Keynes: Open University Press, 2nd edition.

—— , 1980. 'La Matita del Cliente/The Client's Pencil' (on Le Corbusier's Villa Baizeau), *Rassegna*, no. 3, 1980.

—— , 1987. *The Villas of Le Corbusier 1920-1930*, New Haven and London: Yale University Press.

Benton, Tim and Benton, Charlotte, 1977. *The International Style*, Milton Keynes: Open University Press.

—— and Scharf, Aaron, 1975. *Design 1920s: German Design and the Bauhaus 1925-1932; Modernism in the Decorative Arts: Paris 1910-1930*, Milton Keynes: Open University.

—— , with Sharp, Dennis (eds), 1975. *Form and Function: A Source Book for the History of Architecture and Design 1890-1939*, London: Crosby Lockwood Staples/Milton Keynes: Open University Press.

Benton, Tim, Muthesius, Stefan and Wilkins, Bridget, 1975. *Europe 1900-1914: The Reaction to Historicism and Art Nouveau*, Milton Keynes, Open Univeristy Press.

Bent Wood and Metal Furniture, 1987. *Bent Wood and Metal Furniture, 1850-1946*, exh. cat., New York and Washington: American Federation of Arts and University of Washington Press.

Biologists in Search of Material, 1938. *Biologists in Search of Material: An Interim Report on the Work of the Pioneer Health Centre, Peckham*, London: Faber and Faber.

Blake, Jody, 1999. *'Le Tumulte noir': Modernist Art and Popular Entertainment in Jazz-Age Paris, 1900-1930*, University Park, Pennsylvania: Pennsylvania State University Press.

Blaschke, Berthe and Lipschitz, Luise, 2003. *Architecture in Vienna 1850-1930: Historicism-Jugendstil-New Realism*, Vienna and New York: Springer.

Blaser, Werner, 1972. *Mies van der Rohe*, London: Thames & Hudson.

Bibliography

Blau, Eve, 1999. *The Architecture of Red Vienna 1919–1934*, Cambridge, Mass. and London: MIT Press.

Blazwick, Iwona (ed.), 2001. *Century City: Art and Culture in the Modern Metropolis*, exh. cat., London: Tate Publishing.

Bloch, Ernst, 1973. *Das Prinzip Hoffnung*, vol. 2, Frankfurt am Main: Suhrkamp.

——, 1995. *The Principle of Hope*, vol. 2, Cambridge, Mass: MIT Press (translation of Bloch, 1973).

Blotkamp, Carel et al., 1982. *De Stijl 1917–1922: The Formative Years*, Cambridge, Mass. and London: MIT Press.

——, 1994. *Mondrian: The Art of Destruction*, London: Reaktion.

Borden, Iain and Dunster, David (eds), 1995. *Architecture and the Sites of History: Interpretations of Buildings and Cities*, Oxford: Butterworth Architecture.

Boudon, Philippe, 1972. *Lived-in Architecture: Le Corbusier's Pessac Revisited*, London: Lund Humphries.

Bourke, Joanna, 1996. 'The Great Male Renunciation: Men's Dress Reform in Inter-war Britain', *Journal of Design History*, vol. 9, no. 1, pp. 23–33.

Braham, William W., 1997. 'Sigfried Giedion and the Fascination of the Tub', in Lahiji and Friedman 1997b, pp. 200–34.

Brandstätter, Christian, 2003. *Wonderful Wiener Werkstätte: Design in Vienna 1903–1932*, London: Thames & Hudson.

Brecht, Bertolt, 1983. *Über die bildenden Künste*, Frankfurt am Main: Suhrkamp.

——, 1997. *Prosa 4*, Berliner und Frankfurter Ausgabe, vol. 19, Berlin: Aufbau/Frankfurt am Main: Suhrkamp.

Briolle, Cécile, Fuzibet, Agnès, and Monnier, Gérard, 1990. *Rob Mallet-Stevens: La Villa Noailles*, Marseille: Editions Parenthèses.

Britton, Karla, 2001. *Auguste Perret*, London: Phaidon.

Brunton, Deborah, 2004a. *Medicine Transformed: Health, Disease and Society in Europe 1800–1930*, Manchester: Manchester University Press.

——, 2004b. *Health, Disease and Society in Europe 1800–1930: A Source Book*, Manchester: Manchester University Press.

Bryder, Linda, 1988. *Below the Magic Mountain: A Social History of Tuberculosis in Twentieth-Century Britain*, Oxford: Clarendon Press.

——, 1992. 'Wonderlands of buttercup, clover and daisies: Tuberculosis and the Open-Air School Movement in Britain, 1907–1939', in Cooter, 1992, pp. 72–95.

Bucharest in the 1920s–1940s, 1994. *Anii 1920–1940: Între Modernism/Bucharest in the 1920s–1940s: Between Avant-Garde and Modernism*, exh. cat., Bucharest: Simetria/Union of Romanian Architects.

Buchli, Victor, 1998. 'Moisei Ginzburg's Narkomfin Communal House in Moscow', *Journal of the Society of Architectural Historians*, vol. 57, no. 2, June, pp. 160–81.

——, 1999. *An Archaeology of Socialism*, Oxford and New York: Berg.

Buddensieg, Tilmann and Rogge, Henning et al., 1984. *Industriekultur. Peter Behrens and the AEG, 1907–1914*, Cambridge, Mass: MIT Press.

Buekschmitt, Justus, 1963. *Ernst May*, vol. 1 of *Bauten und Planungen*, Stuttgart: Koch.

Büller, Lenneke and den Oudsten, Frank, 1988. 'Interview with Truus Schröder', in Overy et al., 1988, pp. 42–103.

Bullock, Nicholas, 1978. 'Housing in Frankfurt and the new Wohnkultur, 1925 to 1931', *Architectural Review*, vol. 163, no. 976, June.

——, 1984. 'First the Kitchen – Then the Façade', *AA Files*, no. 6, pp. 59–68. Also in *Journal of Design History*, vol. 1, no. 3/4, 1988, pp. 177–92.

—— and Read, James, 1985. *The Movement for Housing Reform in Germany and France 1840–1914*, Cambridge: Cambridge University Press.

Burckhardt, Lucius (ed.), 1980. *The Werkbund: Studies in the History and Ideology of the Deutscher Werkbund 1907–1933*, London: Design Council.

Burns, Karen, 1997. 'A House for Josephine Baker', in Nalbantoglu, Gülsüm Baydar and Wong, Chong Thai (eds), 1997. *Postcolonial Space(s)*, New York: Princeton Architectural Press.

Cabanne, Pierre, 1971. *Dialogues with Marcel Duchamp*, New York: Viking Press.

Campbell, Margaret, 1999. 'From Cure Chair to Chaise Longue: Medical Treatment and the Form of the Modern Recliner', *Journal of Design History*, vol. 12, no. 4, pp. 327–43.

——, 2005, 'What Tuberculosis did for Modernism: The Influence of a Curative Environment on Modernist Design and Architecture', *Medical History*, vol. 49, no. 4, October, pp. 463–88.

Camfield, William, 1989. *Marcel Duchamp: Fountain*, Houston: Houston University Press.

Carrier, Dan, 2005. 'The animal house: builders of London's great ark', *Camden New Journal*, 26 May, p. 11.

Casciato, Maristella, 2000. 'The "Casa all'Italiana" and the Idea of Modern Dwelling in Fascist Italy', *Journal of Architecture*, vol. 5, Winter, pp. 335–53.

Çelik, Zeynep, 1992. 'Le Corbusier, Orientalism, Colonialism', *Assemblage*, no. 17, April, pp. 59–77.

Chadwick, Edwin, 1887. *The Health of Nations*, London: Longman.

Chareau, 1994. *Pierre Chareau: architecte, un art intérieur*, exh. cat., Paris: Centre Pompidou.

CIAM, 1930. *Die Wohnung für Existenzminimum* (Proceedings of the Second CIAM Congress, Frankfurt am Main, 1929), Frankfurt am Main: Englert and Schlosser, 1930.

Clarisse, Catherine, 2004. *Cuisine, recettes d'architecture*, Besançon and Paris: Les Editions de L'Imprimeur.

——, 2005. 'Charlotte Perriand et les Loisirs: L'Aventure des Arcs', in Perriand, 2005, pp. 141–48.

Coates, Wells, 1939. 'Flats in Palace Gate, Kensington', *Architectural Review*, April, p. 173.

Cockburn, Patrick, 2005. *The Broken Boy*, London: Cape.

Coe, Peter and Reading, Malcolm, 1981. *Lubetkin and Tecton: Architecture and Social Commitment, A Critical Study*, London: Arts Council of Great Britain/Bristol: University of Bristol Department of Architecture.

Cohen, Jean-Louis, 1995. *Scenes of the World to Come: European Architecture and the American Challenge 1893–1960*, Paris: Flammarion/Montreal: Canadian Centre for Architecture.

——, 2003. 'Colonial Architecture in Algiers and Casablanca', Annual Lecture of the Society of Architectural Historians, Courtauld Institute, 17 November.

—— and Eleb, Monique, 2003. *Casablanca. Colonial Myths & Architectural Venues*, New York: Monacelli Press.

Cohen, William A. and Johnson, Ryan (eds), 2005. *Filth: Dirt, Disgust, and Modern Life*, Minneapolis and London: University of Minnesota Press.

Cohn, Laura, 1999. *The Door to a Secret Room: A Portrait of Wells Coates*, London: Scolar Press.

Coleman, Debra, Danze, Elizabeth and Henderson, Carol, 1996. *Architecture and Feminism*, New York: Princeton Architectural Press (Yale Publications on Architecture).

Colenbrander, 1987. Bernard Colenbrander (ed.), *Oud Mathenesse: Het Witte Dorp, 1923–1987*, Rotterdam: De Hef, 1987.

Colin, Paul, c. 1998. *Josephine Baker and La Revue nègre: Paul Colin's Lithographs of Le tumulte noir in Paris, 1927*, introduction by Henry Louis Gates, Jr. and Karen C. C. Dalton, New York: Abrams.

Collins, Nick, 2004. 'Combing through the Houses of Coombe, 21 February 2004', *Twentieth Century Society Newsletter*, Spring, pp. 28–29.

Colomina, Beatriz, 1994. *Privacy and Publicity: Modern Architecture as Mass Media*, Cambridge, Mass. and London: MIT Press.

——, 1997. 'The Medical Body in Modern Architecture', *Daidalos*, June, no. 64, pp. 60–71.

Constant, Caroline, 2000. *Eileen Gray*, London: Phaidon.

Colquhoun, Alan, 1994. 'Criticism and Self-Criticism in German Modernism', *AA Files*, no. 28, Autumn, pp. 26–33.

——, 2002. *Modern Architecture*, Oxford: Oxford University Press.

Comas, Carlos Eduardo, 1998. 'Modern Architecture, Brazilian Corollary', *AA Files*, no. 36, Summer, pp. 3–13.

Conrads, Ulrich (ed.), 1970. *Programmes and Manifestoes on 20th-Century Architecture*, London: Lund Humphries.

Cooter, Roger (ed.), 1992. *In the Name of the Child: Health and Welfare, 1880–1940*, London and New York: Routledge.

Corbin, Alain, 1994. *The Lure of the Sea*, London: Penguin. (First published as Alain Corbin, *Le Territoire du vide*, Paris: Aubier, 1988.)

Cottam, David et al., 1988. *Sir Owen Williams 1890–1969*, exh. cat., London: Architectural Association.

Council for Art and Industry, 1937. *The Working Class Home: Its Furnishing and Equipment*, London: HMSO.

Crimson, with Speaks, Michael and Hadders, Gerard, 1999. *Mart Stam's Trousers*, Rotterdam: 010 Publishers.

Cunningham, Allen (ed.), 1998. *Modern Movement Heritage*, London and New York: Spon.

Curtis, William, 1975. *Le Corbusier/English Architecture 1930s*, Milton Keynes: Open University Press.

——, 1986. *Le Corbusier: Ideas and Forms*, Oxford: Phaidon.

Curtis, Penelope (ed.), 2003. 'Modernism & Monumentality', in *Sculpture from Fascist Italy*, Leeds: Henry Moore Institute.

Czech, Hermann and Mistelbauer, Wolfgang, 1984. *Das Looshaus*, 3rd rev. edition, Vienna: Löcker.

Darley, Gillian, 2003. *Factory*, London: Reaktion.

Darling, Elizabeth, 2007. *Re-forming Britain: Narratives of Modernity before Reconstruction*, London and New York: Routledge.

Dean, Christopher, 1992. 'Docomomo-UK: The First 2 Years', in *Docomomo UK Newsletter*, no.1, Summer, p. 3.

De Back, Aimée, Berndsen, Sabine and Berns, Camiel, 1996. *Een zeer aangenaam verblijf: Het dienstbodenhuis van J. Duiker op het sanatorium Zonnestraal/A space of their own: The servants' house by J. Duiker at Zonnestraal sanatorium*, Rotterdam: 010 Publishers.

De Burcht van Berlage, 1991. *De Burcht van Berlage: van bondsgebouw tot vakbondsmuseum*, Amsterdam: Nationaal Vakbondsmuseum.

De Fries, H., 1930. 'Problematik des Städtebaues', *Die Form*, vol. 5, no. 7, 1 April, pp. 189–93.

De Jonge, 1998. Wessel de Jonge, 'Zonnestraal Sanatorium, Hilversum (Jan Duiker)', in Cunningham, 1998, pp. 149–58.

De La Warr Pavilion, 1994. *The De La Warr Pavilion*, Bexhill-on-Sea: Pavilion Trust.

Delorme, Jean-Claude, 1987. *Les Villas d'Artistes à Paris*, Paris: Les Editions de Paris.

Denby, Elizabeth, 1944. *Europe Re-housed* (1938), London: Allen and Unwin.

Derwig, Jan and Mattie, Erik, 1995. *Functionalism in the Netherlands/Functionalisme in Nederland*, Amsterdam: Architectura & Natura.

Deutscher Werkbund Berlin and Winifried Brenne (eds), 2005. *Bruno Taut: Meister des farbigen Bauens in Berlin*, Berlin: Verlagshaus Braun.

Devanthéry, Patrick and Lamunière, Inès, 1998. 'Belle-Rive Plage (Marc Picard)', in Cunningham, 1998, pp. 109–19.

Dexter, Emma and Barson, Tanya (eds), 2005. *Frida Kahlo*, exh. cat., London: Tate Publishing.

Döcker, Richard, 1929. *Terrassentyp*, Stuttgart: Wedekind.

Dormandy, Thomas, 1999. *The White Death: A History of Tuberculosis*, London and Rio Grande, Ohio: Hambledon Press.

Douglas, Mary, 1970. *Purity and Danger*, Harmondsworth: Penguin.

Dreysse, D. W., 1994. *May-Siedlungen: Architekturführer durch Acht Siedlungen des neuen Frankfurt 1926–1930*, Frankfurt am Main: König.

Droste, Magdalena, Ludewig, Manfred and the Bauhaus Archiv (Berlin), 1992. *Marcel Breuer: Design*, Cologne: Taschen.

Dubos, René and Dubos, Jean, 1953. *The White Plague: Tuberculosis, Man and Society*, London: Gollancz.

Duiker, Jan, 1932a. 'Een gezonde school voor het gezonde kind', *8 en Opbouw*, pp. 88–92, reprinted in Jelles and Alberts, 1976, pp. 59–60, English translation on pp. 60–61.

——, 1932b. 'De Nieuwe Zakelijheid in zomer en winter', *8 en Opbouw*, pp. 140–43, reprinted in Jelles and Alberts, 1976, pp. 115–16; English translation on p. 135.

——, 1932c. 'Hoe is het met onze kleeding?', *8 en Opbouw*, p. 166, reprinted in Jelles and Alberts, 1976, pp. 116–17; English translation on p. 136.

——, 1933a. 'De nieuwe Fordfabriek te Amsterdam: Een oriënteering', *8 en Opbouw*, pp. 113–18; reprinted in Jelles and Alberts, 1976, pp. 126–27; English translation on p. 142.

——, 1933b. 'Het huis van Dr Dalsace in de Rue St Guillaume te Parijs: Architecten P. Chareau en ir. B. Bijvoet', in *8 en Opbouw*, pp. 155–64, reprinted in Jelles and Alberts, 1976, pp. 127–28; English translation on pp. 142–43.

——, 1982. *J. Duiker bouwkundig ingenieur. Constructeur in stuc en staal*, Rotterdam: Stichting Bouw.

Dumont, Marie-Jeanne, 1991. *Le Logement social à Paris 1850–1930, les habitations à bon marché*, Liège, Mardaga.

Düssel, Karl Konrad, 1927. 'Die Stuttgarter Weissenhofsiedlung', *Deutsche Kunst und Dekoration*, vol. 21, no. 1, October, p. 96.

Dyer, Richard, 1997. *White*, London and New York: Routledge.

Ehrenburg, Ilya, 1927. 'About the Bauhaus', *Frankfurter Zeitung*, 28 May, translated in Bauhaus, 1968, pp. 318–20.

Elwall, Robert, 2006. 'The Outsiders', *RIBA Journal*, vol. 113, no. 4, April, p. 20.

Engelmann, Paul, 1911. 'Das Haus auf dem Michaelerplatz', *Die Fackel*, nos 317/318, 3 March, p. 18, reprinted in Czech and Mistelbauer, 1984, p. 86.

Ewig, Isabelle, Gaehtgens, Thomas W. and Noell, Matthias (eds), 2002. *Das Bauhaus und Frankreich. Le Bauhaus et la France. 1919–1940*, Berlin: Akademie.

Ezra, Elizabeth, 2000. *The Colonial Unconscious: Race and Culture in Interwar France*, Ithaca and London: Cornell University Press.

Fairley, Alastair, 2001. *Bucking the Trend: The Life and Times of the Ninth Earl De La Warr*, Bexhill-on-Sea: Pavilion Trust.

Fiedler, Jeannine (ed.), 1990. *Photography at the Bauhaus*, London: Nishen.

—— and Feierabend, Peter (eds), 2000. *Bauhaus*, Cologne: Könemann.

Fischer, Lisa, 2004. *Die Riviera an der Donau: 100 Jahre Strombad Kritzendorf*, Vienna: Böhlau.

Fishman, Robert, 1982. *Urban Utopias in the Twentieth Century: Ebenezer Howard, Frank Lloyd Wright, and Le Corbusier* (1977), Cambridge, Mass. and London: MIT Press.

Fitzgerald, F. Scott, 2000. *Tender is the Night* (1934), London: Penguin.

Fletcher, Yaël Simpson, 1999. '"Capital of the Colonies": Real and Imagined Boundaries between Metropole and Empire in 1920s Marseilles', in Felix Driver and David Gilbert, *Imperial Cities: Landscape, Display and Identity*, Manchester and New York: Manchester University Press.

Ford, Henry, 1923. *Mein Leben und Werk*, Leipzig.

——, 1924. *My Life and Work* (1922), in collaboration with Samuel Crowther, London: Heinemann.

Forty, Adrian, 1986. *Objects of Desire: Design and Society, 1750–1980*, London: Thames & Hudson.

Frampton, Kenneth, 1966. 'Maison de Verre', *Arena*, The Architectural Association Journal, vol. 81, no. 901, April.

——, 1968. 'Maison de Verre', *Perspecta*, no. 12.

——, 1985. *Modern Architecture: A Critical History*, rev. edition, London: Thames & Hudson.

Frank, Josef, 1930. 'Was ist modern?', *Die Form*, vol. 5, no. 15, 1 August, pp. 399–406.

——, 1932. 'International Housing Exposition, Vienna, Austria', *Architectural Forum*, vol. 57, no. 4, October, pp. 325–28.

——, 1982. 'Flippancy for the Comfort of the Soul and Flippancy as a Problem', *9H*, no. 3, pp. 5–6. (English translation of 'Der Gschnas fürs G'müt und der Gschnas als Problem', in Bau und Wohnung, 1927, pp. 48–57.)

Frauen im Design, 1989. *Frauen im Design: Berufsbilder und Lebenswege seit 1900/Women in Design: Careers and Life Histories since 1900*, exh. cat., vol. 1., Stuttgart: Haus der Wirtschaft/ Design Center.

Frederick, Christine, 1919. *Household Engineering: Scientific Management in the Home*, Chicago: American School of Home Economics.

Freud, Sigmund, 1992. *The Diary of Sigmund Freud 1929–1939: A Record of the Final Decade*, translated, annotated, with an introduction by Michael Molnar, London: The Freud Museum/ New York: Scribner.

Friedmann, Alice T., 1996. 'Domestic Differences: Edith Farnsworth, Mies van der Rohe, and the Gendered Body', in Reed, 1996.

Functional Architecture, 1990. *Functional Architecture: The International Style, Funktionale Architektur, Le Style Internationale*, Cologne: Taschen.

Futagawa, Yukio (ed.), 1994. *J. A. Brinkman and L. C. van der Vlugt: The Van Nelle Factory, Rotterdam, The Netherlands*, GA (Global Architecture), Tokyo: A. D. A. Edita.

Gans, Deborah, 1987. *The Le Corbusier Guide*, New York: Princeton Architectural Press.

Gates, Henry Louis, Jr., and Dalton, Karen C. C., 1998. 'Josephine Baker and *La Revue nègre*', in Colin, 1998.

Gebhard, Bruno, 1945. 'Art and Science in a Health Museum', *Bulletin of the Medical Library Association*, vol. 33, no. 1, January, pp. 39–45.

Bibliography

Gebhard, David, 1971. *Schindler*, London: Thames & Hudson/New York: Viking.

Georgiadis, Sokratis, 1993. *Sigfried Giedion: An Intellectual Biography*, translated by Colin Hall, Edinburgh: Edinburgh University Press.

Geretsegger, Heinz and Peintner, Max, 1979. *Otto Wagner 1841–1918: The Expanding City, The Beginning of Modern Architecture*, associate author Walter Pichler, introduction by Richard Neutra, translated by Gerald Onn, London: Academy Editions.

Gescheit, Hermann, 1929. *Neuzeitliche Hotels und Krankenhäuser*, Berlin: Pollak.

Geurst, Jeroen and Molenaar, Joris, 1983. *Van der Vlugt Architect, 1894–1936*, Delft: Delft University Press (2nd edition, 1984).

Giedion, Sigfried, 1928a. *Bauen in FRANKREICH – Bauen in EISEN – Bauen in EISENBETON*, Leipzig and Berlin: Klinkhardt and Biermann.

——, 1928b. 'La Leçon de L'Exposition du "Werkbund" à Stuttgart 1927', *L'Architecture vivante*, Spring & Summer 1928, pp. 37–43.

——, 1928c. 'Le Problème du luxe dans l'architecture', *Cahiers d'Art*, vol. 3, nos 5–6, pp. 254–56.

——, 1929. *Befreites Wohnen*, Zürich and Leipzig: Orell Füssli.

——, 1930. 'Der Deutsche Werkbund in Paris', *Neue Zürcher Zeitung*, 17 June, 8–18.

——, 1941. *Space, Time and Architecture: The Growth of a New Tradition*, Cambridge, Mass: Harvard University Press.

——, 1954. *Walter Gropius, Work and Teamwork*, London: The Architectural Press/New York: Reinhold.

——, 1969. *Mechanization Takes Command: A Contribution to Anonymous History* (1948), New York: W. W. Norton.

——, 1995. *Building in France – Building in Iron – Building in Ferro-Concrete* (translated by J. Duncan Berry, introduction by Sokratis Georgiadis), Santa Monica: The Getty Center for the History of Art and the Humanities.

Gilbreth, Frank B., 1911. *Motion Studies: A Method for Increasing the Efficiency of the Workman*, New York: Van Nostrand.

——, 1912. *Primer of Scientific Management*, New York: Van Nostrand.

Ginzburg, Moisei, 1924. *Stil' i Epokha: problemy sovremennoi Arkhitektury*, Moscow: Gosudarstvennoe Izdatelstvo (English translation, Ginzburg, 1982).

——, 1927. 'Tselevaya ustanovka v sovremennoi arkhitekture', *Sovremennaia Arkhitektura*, vol. 2, no. 1, pp. 4–10.

——, 1928. 'Contemporary Architecture in Russia', *Die Baugilde*, October 1928, pp. 1370–72 (English translation in Lissitzky, 1970, pp. 157–59).

——, 1982. *Style and Epoch*, foreword by Kenneth Frampton, introduction and translation by Anatole Senkevitch, Jr., Cambridge, Mass. and London: MIT Press (translation of Ginzburg, 1924).

Glancey, Jonathan, 2004. 'Waddling off: Penguins Moved from Listed Pool', *Guardian*, Saturday 3 July, p. 10.

Glass and Metal Furniture, 1930. H. F. E., 'Glass and Metal Furniture. Hygienic but not Beautiful', *Daily Mail*, Continental Edition, Saturday, 24 May, p. 7, reprinted in Ewig, Gaehtgens and Noell, 2002, pp. 345–46.

Glassberg, David, 1979. 'The Public Bath Movement in America', *American Studies*, vol. XX, no. 2, pp. 5–21.

Gloag, John, 1929. 'Wood or Metal?' *Studio*, vol. 97, pp. 49–50, reprinted in Benton and Benton, with Sharp, 1975, pp. 230–32.

Goethe, Johann Wolfgang von, 1999. *Selected Poetry*, London: Libris.

Goubert, Jean-Pierre, 1986. *The Conquest of Water*, Princeton: Princeton University Press.

Gough, Maria, 2002. 'Paris, Capital of the Soviet Avant-Garde', *October*, no. 101, Summer.

Grant, Linda, 2000. *When I Lived in Modern Times*, London: Granta.

Gravagnuolo, Benedetto, 1995. *Adolf Loos*, preface by Aldo Rossi, photography by Roberto Schezen, London: Art Data.

Grieve, Alastair, 2004. *Isokon*, London: Isokon Plus.

Grinberg, Donald I., 1982. *Housing in the Netherlands 1900–1940*, Delft: Delft University Press.

Groendijk, Paul and Vollard, Piet, 1985. *Adolf Loos: House for Josephine Baker*, Rotterdam: 010 Publishers.

Gropius, Walter, 1911. 'Monumentale-Kunst und Industriebau', lecture given at the Folkwang Museum in Hagen, published in Probst and Schädlich, vol. 3, 1988, pp. 28–51.

——, 1913. 'Die Entwicklung moderner Industrie-baukunst', in Jahrbuch des Deutschen Werkbundes, 1913, pp. 17–22; translated as 'The Development of Modern Industrial Architecture', in Benton and Benton, with Sharp, 1975, pp. 53–55.

——, 1914. 'Der stilbildende Wert industrieller Bauformen', in Jahrbuch des Deutschen Werkbundes, 1914, pp. 29–32.

——, 1926. *Bauhaus Dessau. Grundsätze der Bauhausproduktion*, printed sheet published by the Bauhaus, Dessau, March, translated as 'Bauhaus Dessau – Principles of Bauhaus Production', in Benton and Benton, with Sharp, 1975, pp. 148–49.

——, 1935. *The New Architecture and the Bauhaus*, translated by P. Morton Shand with an introduction by Frank Pick, Faber and Faber (new edition, 1965).

Haiko, Peter, 1994. The "Obscene" in Viennese Architecture', in Patrick Werkner (ed.), *Egon Schiele: Art, Sexuality, and Viennese Modernism*, Palo Alto, California: The Society for the Promotion of Science and Scholarship, pp. 89–100.

Hammann, J. E., 1930. 'Weiss, alles weiss: Von der Wertstellung der Farbe "Weiss" in unserer Zeit', *Die Form*, vol. 5, no. 5, 1 March, pp. 121–23.

Hammer-Tugendhat, Daniela and Tegethoff, Wolf (eds), 2000. *Ludwig Mies van der Rohe: The Tugendhat House*, Vienna and New York: Springer.

Heimstätte deutscher Industrie, 1899. 'Ein Heimstätte deutscher Industrie', in *Der Schuhmarkt*, no. 13, 31 March, pp. 45–54.

Heller, Geneviève, 1979. *Propre en ordre. Habitation et vie domestique 1850–1930: l'exemple vaudois*, Lausanne: Editions d'en Bas.

Henderson, Susan H., 1996. 'A Revolution in the Woman's Sphere: Grete Schütte-Lihotzky and the Frankfurt Kitchen', in Debra Coleman, Elizabeth Danze and Carol Henderson, *Architecture and Feminism*, New York: Princeton Architectural Press (Yale Publications on Architecture), pp. 221–53.

Henkels, Herbert, 1987. *From Figuration to Abstraction*, London: Thames & Hudson.

Henket, Hubert-Jan, 1998. 'The icon and the ordinary', in Cunningham, 1998, pp. 13–17.

Herrel, Eckard, 2001. *Ernst May: Architekt und Stadtplaner in Afrika 1934–1953*, Frankfurt am Main: Deutsches Architektur-Museum.

Hesel, Michael, and Kubokawa, Rumi, 1998. 'Building Brazil, Part 1: 1900–1964', *AA Files*, no. 37, Autumn, pp. 48–54.

Heynen, Hilde, 1999. *Architecture and Modernity: A Critique*, Cambridge, Mass. and London: MIT Press.

—— and Baydar, Gülsüm, 2005. *Negotiating Domesticity: Spatial Productions of Gender in Modern Architecture*, London and New York: Routledge.

Hines, Thomas, 1982. *Richard Neutra and the Search for Modern Architecture: A Biography and History*, New York: Oxford University Press.

——, 1989. 'Case Study Trouvé: Sources and Precedents Southern California, 1920–1942', in Smith, 1989, pp. 83–104.

Hirdina, Heinz, 1991. *Neues Bauen, Neues Gestalten: Das neue Frankurt/Die neue Stadt. Eine Zeitschrift Zwischen 1926 und 1933* (1984), 2nd edition, Dresden: Verlag der Kunst.

Hitchcock, Henry-Russell, 1929. *Modern Architecture, Romanticism and Reintegration*, New York: Payson and Clarke, reprint New York: Da Capo: 1993.

—— and Johnson, Philip, 1932. *The International Style: Architecture since 1922*, New York: W. W. Norton.

—— and Johnson, Philip, 1995. *The International Style*, with a new foreword by Philip Johnson, New York and London: W W Norton.

Hoek, Els (ed.), 2000. *Theo van Doesburg: Oeuvre catalogue*, Utrecht: Centraal Museum Otterlo: Kröller-Müller Museum.

Hoffmann, Josef, 1972. 'Selbstbiographie', in *Ver Sacrum*, Neues Heft für Kunst und Literatur.

Hollaender, Felix, 1924. *Wege zur Kraft und Schönheit*, Film Programme, Berlin, pp. 5–10, translated as 'Ways to Strength and Beauty', in Kaes, Jay and Dimendberg, 1995, p. 677.

Housden, Brian, 1960. 'M. Brinkman, J. A. Brinkman, L. C. van der Vlugt, J. H. van den Broek, J. B. Bakema', *Architectural Association Journal*, LXXVI, no. 847, December.

House, Martha, 1930. 'Sheen of glass and metal in hyper modern sitting rooms', *Daily Telegraph*, 12 March.

Hygiene, 1994. *Hygiene: Writers and Artists Come Clean and Talk Dirty*, exh. cat., Birmingham: Ikon Gallery.

Illich, Ivan, 1986. *H2O and the Waters of Forgetfulness*, London: Marion Boyars.

Ingberman, Sima, 1994. *ABC: International Constructivist Architecture, 1922–1939*, Cambridge, Mass. and London: MIT Press.

Isaacs, Reginald, 1983. *Walter Gropius: der Mensch und sein Werk*, vol. 1, Berlin: Mann.

—, 1984. *Walter Gropius: der Mensch und sein Werk*, vol. 2, Berlin: Mann.

—, 1991. *Gropius: An Illustrated Biography of the Creator of the Bauhaus*, Boston and London: Little, Brown.

Jacob, Delphine, 2004–2005. 'André Salomon, éclairagiste de l'architecture moderne', *Les Cahiers du Musée national d'art moderne*, no. 90, Winter, pp. 93–109.

Jaeggi, Annemarie, 2000. *Fagus: Industrial Culture from Werkbund to Bauhaus*, translated from the German by Elizabeth M. Schwaiger, New York: Princeton Architectural Press.

Jahrbuch des Deutschen Werkbundes, 1912. *Jahrbuch des Deutschen Werkbundes*, no. 1, 'Die Durchgeistigung der deutschen Arbeit: Wege und Ziele im Zusammenhang von Industrie/Handwerk', Jena: Diederichs.

Jahrbuch des Deutschen Werkbundes, 1913. *Jahrbuch des Deutschen Werkbundes*, no. 2, 'Die Kunst in Industrie und Handel', Jena: Diederichs.

Jahrbuch des Deutschen Werkbundes, 1914. *Jahrbuch des Deutschen Werkbundes*, no. 3, 'Der Verkehr', Jena: Diederichs.

Janser, Andres, 1997. 'Only Film Can Make the New Architecture Intelligible: Hans Richter's *Die neue Wohnung* and the Early Documentary Film on Modern Architecture', in François Penz and Maureen Thomas, *Cinema & Architecture: Méliès, Mallet-Stevens, Multimedia*, London: British Film Institute, 1997, pp. 34–46.

—, and Rüegg, Arthur, 2001. *Hans Richter, New Living, Architecture, Film, Space*, Baden (Switzerland): Lars Müller Publishing.

Jelles, E. J. and Alberts, C. A., 1976. 'Duiker 1890–1935', Special double issue of *Forum*, (Amsterdam), Year 22, January 1972, reprinted 1976 (includes writings by Duiker with English translations).

Joedicke, Jürgen, 1989. *Weissenhofsiedlung*, Stuttgart: Krämer.

—, and Plath, Christian, 1984. *Die Weissenhofsiedlung/The Weissenhof Colony/La Cité de Weissenhof*, Stuttgart: Krämer.

Jones, Peter Blundell, 2002. *Modern Architecture through Case Studies*, London: Architectural Press.

Joyce, James, 1937. *Ulysses*, London: The Bodley Head.

Kaes, Anton, Jay, Martin and Dimendberg, Edward (eds), 1995. *The Weimar Republic Sourcebook* (1994), Berkeley, Los Angeles, London: University of California Press.

Kearton, Cherry, 1930. *The Island of Penguins*, London: Longman.

Kessler, Count Harry, 1971. *In the Twenties: The Diaries of Harry Kessler*, New York: Holt, Rinehart and Winston.

Kettering, Karen, 1997. '"Ever More Cosy and Comfortable": Stalinism and the Soviet Domestic Interior, 1928–1938', *Journal of Design History*, vol. 10, no. 2, pp. 119–35.

Kiesler, Friedrich, 1961. 'Kiesler: Pursuit of an Idea', interview with Thomas H. Creighton, *Progressive Architecture*, July.

King, Anthony D., 1984. *The Bungalow: The Production of a Global Culture*, Oxford: Oxford University Press.

Kirsch, Karin, 1989. *The Weissenhofsiedlung: Experimental Housing for the Deutscher Werkbund, 1927*, New York: Rizzoli.

Klonk, Charlotte, 2005. 'Patterns of Attention: From Shop Windows to Gallery Rooms in Early 20th-Century Berlin', *Art History*, vol. 28, no. 4, September.

Koch, Adolf, 1924. 'Die Wahrheit über die Berliner Gruppen für Freie Körperkultur', *Junge Menschen*, no. 5, August, translated as 'The Truth about the Berlin Nudist Groups', in Kaes, Jay and Dimendberg, 1995, p. 676.

Kokoschka, Oskar, 1974. *My Life*, London: Thames & Hudson.

Koolhaas, Rem, 1994. *Delirious New York: A Retroactive Manifesto for Manhattan*, new edition, Rotterdam: 010 Publishers.

Kracauer, Siegfried, 1927. 'Das neue Bauen. Zur Stuttgarter Werkbund-Ausstellung: "Die Wohnung"', *Frankfurter Zeitung*, 31 July.

—, 1990. 'Das Ornament der Masse', *Frankfurter Zeitung*, vol. 71, no. 420, 9 June and no. 423, 10 June 1927, reprinted in Siegfried Kracauer, *Schriften*, vol. 5, edited by Inka Mülder-Bach, Frankfurt am Main: Suhrkamp, pt. 2, pp. 57–67.

—, 1995. *The Mass Ornament: Weimar Essays*, translated, edited and with an introduction by Thomas Y. Levin, Cambridge, Mass. and London: Harvard University Press, pp. 75–86.

Kramer, Lore, 1989. 'Die Frankfurter Küche: Zeitgenössische Kritik und Perspektiven/The Frankfurt Kitchen: Contemporary Criticism and Perspectives', in Frauen im Design, 1989, vol. 1.

Kraus, Karl, 1913. 'Aphorismes', *Les Cahiers d'aujourd'hui*, no. 7, October, pp. 340–45.

Krischanitz, Adolf and Kapfinger, Otto, 1989. *Die Wiener Werkbundsiedlung: Dokumentation einer Erneuerung*, Vienna: Beton.

Kuitenbrouwer, Maarten, 1991. *The Netherlands and the Rise of Modern Imperialism: Colonies and Foreign Policy, 1870–1902*, New York and Oxford: Berg.

Kulka, Heinrich (ed.), 1931. *Adolf Loos: Das Werk des Architekten* (vol. IV of the series 'Neues Bauen in Der Welt', edited by Joseph Gantner), Vienna: Schroll. (Reprinted, Vienna: Löcker, 1985.)

Küper, Marijke and Van Zijl, Ida, 1992. *Gerrit Th. Rietveld, 1888–1964: The Complete Works*, exh. cat., Utrecht: Centraal Museum.

Kupinse, William, 2005, 'The Indian Subject of Colonial Hygiene', in Cohen and Johnson, 2005, pp. 250–76.

Kurzke, Hermann, 2002. *Thomas Mann: Life as a Work of Art*, London: Allen Lane.

Lahiji, Nadir and Friedman, D. S., 1997a. 'At the Sink: Architecture in Abjection', in Lahiji and Friedman, 1997, p. 36.

— (eds), 1997b. *Plumbing: Sounding Modern Architecture*, New York: Princeton Architectural Press.

Lamprecht, Barbara, 2004. *Richard Neutra, 1892–1970*, Cologne, London: Taschen.

Lampugnani, Vittorio Magnago (ed.), 1986. *Encyclopaedia of 20th-Century Architecture*, London: Thames & Hudson.

Lane, Barbara Miller, 1985. *Architecture and Politics in Germany 1918–1945* (1968), Cambridge, Mass. and London: Harvard University Press.

Larbaud, Valery, 1913. *A.O. Barnabooth: Oeuvre complète*, Paris: Gallimard/NRF.

—, 1986. *Enfantines* (1918), Paris: Gallimard.

—, 1991. *A. O. Barnabooth: His Diary*, translated by Gilbert Cannan, London: Dent, 1924, republished London: Quartet.

—, 1994. *Childish Things*, translated by Catherine Wald, Los Angeles: Sun & Moon Press.

—, 2001. *Lettres de Paris pour le* New Weekly *(mars-aout 1914)*, translated by Jean-Louis Chevalier, introduction and notes by Anne Chevalier, Paris: Gallimard/NRF.

— and Ray, Marcel, 1980. *Correspondance 1899–1937*, vol. II, 1910–1920, Paris: Gallimard.

Lavedan, Pierre, 1930. 'Le Salon des décorateurs', *L'Architecture*, vol. XLIII, no. 7, pp. 229–36.

Lavin, Sylvia, 2004. *Form Follows Libido: Architecture and Richard Neutra in a Psychoanalytic Culture*, Cambridge, Mass. and London: MIT Press.

Lavrentiev, Alexander, 1995. *Alexander Rodchenko: Photography 1924–1954*, Cologne: Könemann.

Lawrence, D. H., 1955. *The Complete Short Stories*, vol. II, London: Heinemann.

Le Corbusier, 1923. *Vers une architecture*, Paris, Crés (2nd enlarged edition, 1925).

—, 1924. *Urbanisme*, Paris: Crès.

—, 1925a. *Almanach d'architecture moderne*, Paris: Crès.

—, 1925b. *L'Art décoratif d'aujourd'hui*, Paris: Crès.

—, 1930. *Précisions sur un état présent de l'Architecture et de l'urbanisme*, Paris: Crès.

—, 1933. *Le Corbusier, La ville radieuse*, Paris: Fréal.

—, 1949. *Le Modulor*, Boulogne-sur-Seine: Editions de l'Architecture d'Aujourd'hui.

—, 1966. *Le Voyage d'Orient*, Paris: Forces Vives.

—, 1967. *The Radiant City*, translated by P. Knight, E. Levieux and D. Coltman, New York: Orion Press/London: Faber and Faber (translation of Le Corbusier, 1933).

—, 1971. *The City of Tomorrow and its Planning*, translated from the 8th French edition of *Urbanisme* (1929) by Frederick Etchells, London: Architectural Press. *See* Le Corbusier, 1924.

—, 1973. *The Modulor: A Harmonious Measure to the Human Scale Universally Applicable to Architecture and Mechanics* (1961), London: Faber and Faber.

—, 1975. 'Le Corbusier, Villa Savoye', presented by Tim Benton, Videorecording, Programme 13, Open University Course A305, *History of Architecture and Design, 1890–1939*, Milton Keynes: Open University/BBC.

245

Bibliography

——, 1987a. *Le Corbusier: Architect of the Century*, exh. cat., London: Hayward Gallery/Arts Council of Great Britain.

——, 1987b. *The Decorative Art of Today*, Cambridge, Mass: MIT Press (translation of Le Corbusier, 1925b).

——, 1989. (Charles-Edouard Jeanneret), *Journey to the East*, edited by Ivan   , translated by Ivan   in collaboration with Nicole Pertuiset, Cambridge, Mass. and London: MIT Press.

——, 1991. *Precisions on the Present State of Architecture*, translated by Edith Schreiber Aujame, Cambridge, Mass. and London: MIT Press (translation of Le Corbusier, 1930).

——, 1992. *Towards a New Architecture*, English translation by Frederick Etchells of the 13th edition of *Vers une architecture* (1927), London: Butterworth Architecture.

—— and Jeanneret, Pierre, 1927. 'Fünf Punkte zu einer neuen Architektur', *Die Form*, vol. 2, no. 9, pp. 272–74, translated as 'Five Points of a New Architecture', in Benton and Benton, with Sharp, 1975, pp. 153–55.

Leeuwen, Thomas A. P. van, 1998. *The Springboard in the Pond: An Intimate History of the Swimming Pool*, Chicago: Graham Foundation for Advanced Studies in the Fine Arts/Cambridge, Mass. and London: MIT Press.

Leitner, Bernhard, 1976. *The Architecture of Ludwig Wittgenstein: A Documentation*. With excerpts from the family recollections by Hermine Wittgenstein, New York: New York University Press.

Lenin, V. I., 1970. *Imperialism, the Highest Stage of Capitalism: A Popular Outline* (1916), Peking: Foreign Languages Press.

Levin, Michael, 1984. *White City: International Style Architecture in Israel. A Portrait of an Era*, Tel Aviv: Tel Aviv Museum.

Lewis, Jane, 1982. 'The Peckham Health Centre: "An Inquiry into the Nature of Living"', (Paper presented at the Annual General Meeting, Wellcome Institute, London, 4 December 1981), *The Society for the Social History of Medicine Bulletin*, no. 30–31, June & December, pp. 39–43.

——, and Brookes, Barbara, 1983. 'A Reassessment of the work of the Peckham Health Centre, 1926–1951', *The Millbank Memorial Fund Quarterly, Health and Society*, vol. 61, no. 2, Spring, pp. 307–50.

Lewis, Jeremy, 2005. *Penguin Special: The Life and Times of Allen Lane*, London: Viking.

Lichtenstein, Claude (ed.), 1991. *Ferdinand Kramer: Der Charme des Systematischen: Architektur, Einrichtung, Design*, exh. cat., Giessen: Anabas.

Lissitzky, El, 1924. 'Element und Erfindung', *ABC*, no. 1, np [pp. 3–4], translated as 'Element and Invention' in Lissitzky-Küppers, 1992, pp. 349–51.

——, 1930. *Russland: Die Rekonstruktion der Architektur in der Sowjetunion* (vol. I in the series 'Neues Bauen in der Welt', edited by Joesph Gantner), Vienna: Schroll.

——, 1970. *Russia: An Architecture for World Revolution*, translated by Eric Dluhosch, Cambridge, Mass: MIT Press/London: Lund Humphries. (Translation of Lissitzky, 1930.)

Lissitzky-Küppers, Sophie (ed.), 1992. *El Lissitzky: Life, Letters, Texts*, translated by Helene Aldwinckle and Mary Whittall, introduction by Herbert Read, London: Thames & Hudson (1968).

Long, Christopher, 2002. *Josef Frank: Life and Work*, Chicago: University of Chicago Press.

Loos, Adolf, 1898. 'Die Plumber', *Die Neue Freie Presse*, 17 July 1898, reprinted in Loos, 1997a, pp. 101–7; translated as 'Plumbers' in Loos, 1998, pp. 82–88.

——, 1902. 'Damenmode', *Dokumente der Frau* 1 March 1902; reprinted in Loos, 1997, pp. 126–32' translated as 'Ladies Fashion', in Loos, 1998, pp. 106–11.

——, 1908. 'Ornament und Verbrechen', first published in German in *Frankfurter Zeitung* in 1929, reprinted in Loos, 1997b, pp. 78–79, translated as 'Ornament and Crime' in Loos, 1985, pp. 100–3, and in Loos, 1998, pp. 167–76.

——, 1911. 'Mein Haus am Michaelerplatz 12', lecture, Vienna, 11 December 1911, reprinted in Loos, 1988, pp. 55–71; English translation 'My Building on Michaelerplatz', in Loos, 2002, pp. 92–107.

——, 1912. 'Architecture et le style moderne', *Cahiers d'aujourd'hui*, no. 2, December, pp. 82–92.

——, 1913. 'Ornement et Crime', translated by Marcel Ray, *Cahiers d'aujourd'hui*, no. 5, June, pp. 247–56.

——, 1920. 'Ornement et Crime', *L'Esprit nouveau*, no. 2, 15 November, pp. 159–68.

——, 1931. *Trotzdem 1990–1930*, Innsbruck: Brenner.

——, 1982. *Spoken into the Void: Collected Essays 1897–1900*, Cambridge, Mass. and London: MIT Press.

——, 1985. *The Architecture of Adolf Loos*, edited by Yehuda Safran and Wilfried Wang, exh. cat., London: Arts Council of Great Britain.

——, 1988. *Konfrontationen: Schriften von und über Adolf Loos*, edited by Adolf Opel, Vienna: Prachner.

——, 1997a. *Ins Leere Gesprochen: Gesammelte Schriften, 1897–1900*, Vienna: Prachner.

——, 1997b. *Trotzdem: Gesammelte Schriften 1900–1930*, edited by A. Opel, Vienna: Prachner.

——, 1998. *Ornament and Crime: Selected Essays*, selected and with an introduction by Adolf Opel, translated by Michael Mitchell, Riverside, California: Ariadne Press.

——, 2002. *On Architecture*, selected and introduced by Adolf and Daniel Opel, translated by Michael Mitchell, Riverside, California: Ariadne Press.

Loos, Claire, 1985. *Adolf Loos Privat*, edited by Adolf Opel, Vienna: Böhlaus. (First edition: Claire Loos, *Adolf Loos Privat*, Vienna: Johannes-Presse, 1936.)

Lotz, Wilhelm, 1928. 'Die Gagfah-Siedlung' in *Die Form*, 1928, vol. 3, no. 10, October, pp. 289–98.

——, 1931. 'Kritik der Bauausstellung', *Die Form*, vol. 6, no. 6, 15 June, pp. 212–19.

——, 1932. 'Sonne, Luft und Haus für Alle!', *Die Form*, Year 7, no. 6, 15 June, pp. 179–88.

Lubbock, Jules, 1995. *The Tyranny of Taste: The Politics of Architecture and Design in Britain 1550–1960*, New Haven and London: Yale University Press, for the Paul Mellon Centre for British Art.

Lüders, Marie-Elizabeth, 1927. 'Baukörper ohne Wohnung', *Die Form*, vol. 2, no. 10, October, pp. 316–19, translated as 'A Construction, Not a Dwelling', in Kaes, Jay and Dimendberg, 1995, pp. 468–69.

——, 1928. 'Erst die Küche – Dann die Fassade', in *Die Küche der Klein- und Mittel-wohnung*, Berlin: Reichsforschungsgesellschaft für Wirtschaftlichkeit im Bau- und Wohnungswesen E. V., Sonderheft 2, Group II 6, Year 1, no. 2, June.

Lupton, Ellen and Miller, J. Abbott, 1992. *The Bathroom, The Kitchen and the Aesthetic of Waste: A Process of Elimination*, exh. cat., Cambridge, Mass: MIT/List Visual Arts Center.

Lustenberger, Kurt, 1994. *Adolf Loos*, Zurich and London: Artemis.

Lux, Joseph August, 1904–1905. 'Sanatorium', *Hohe Warte*, no.1, pp. 406–7.

——, 1903. *Das Moderne Landhaus: Ein Beitrag zur neuen Baukunst*, Vienna: Scholl.

McClintock, Anne, 1996. 'Soft-Soaping Empire: Commodity Racism and Imperial Advertising', in Nicholas Mirzoeff (ed.), *The Visual Culture Reader*, London: Routledge, pp. 304–16.

McCoy, Esther, 1960. *Richard Neutra*, New York: George Braziller/London: Mayflower.

——, 1962. *Modern California Houses: Case Study Houses 1945–1952*, New York: Reinhold Publishing; republished as *Case Study Houses 1945–1962*, Los Angeles: Hennessey & Ingalls, 1977.

McLeod, Mary, 1980. 'Le Corbusier and Algiers', *Oppositions*, nos 19–20, Winter-Spring.

Maharaj, Sarat, 1994. 'Up Hearthead for Apartheid: The Peace Committee commends both Award Winners', in Hygiene, 1994, pp. 14–15.

Makarova, Elena, 2000. *Friedl Dicker-Brandeis*, Paris: Somogy.

Mallet-Stevens, Robert, 1924. 'Architecture est un art essentiellement géometrique', *Bulletin de la vie artistique*, no. 23, 1 December, pp. 532–34, translated as 'Architecture and Geometry' in Benton and Benton, with Sharp, 1975, p. 131.

——, 1926. 'Une rue nouvelle à Paris', à l'invitation de J.-E. Blanche, *Art et industrie*, Urbanisme, May, no. 3, pp. 11–12.

——, 2005. *Robert Mallet-Stevens: L'oeuvre complète*, Paris: Centre Pompidou.

Mann, Thomas, 1924. *Der Zauberberg*, Berlin: Fischer.

——, 1953. 'The Making of *The Magic Mountain*', *Atlantic*, January (reprinted in Mann, 1996).

——, 1996. *The Magic Mountain*, London: Minerva.

Mansbach, Steven A., 1980. *Visions of Totality: László Moholy-Nagy, Theo van Doesburg, and El Lissitzky*, Ann Arbor: Research Press.

Margolin, Victor, 1997. *The Struggle for Utopia*,

Rodchenko, Lissitzky, Moholy-Nagy, 1917–1946, Chicago: Chicago University Press.

Marinetti, F. T., 1913. 'Distruzione della sintassi – Immaginazione senza fili – Parole in liberta', dated 11 May and first published in *Lacerba*, 15 June; translated as 'Destruction of Syntax – Imagination without Strings – Words-in-Freedom 1913' in Apollonio, 1973, pp. 95–105.

Maurer, Bruno, 1995. 'From "Public Baths" to "Park Pools": Neues Bauen Open-air Swimming Facilities in Switzerland', *Daidalos*, no. 55, March, pp. 72–79.

May, Ernst, 1926. 'Wohnpolitik in Wien und Frankfurt', *Frankfurter Volksstimme*, 22 September.

—— , 1946. 'Hook-On Slab Reinforced Concrete System Designed by E. May', *Architects' Journal*, 13 June, vol. 103, no. 2681, pp. 453–55.

Mendelsohn, Erich, 1926. *Amerika, Bilderbuch eines Architekten*, Berlin: Mosse, 6th enlarged edition, 1928. (For abridged English version, see Benton and Benton, 1975.)

—— , 1987. *Erich Mendelsohn 1887–1953*, exh. cat., Bexhill-on-Sea: De La Warr Pavilion/London: Bartlett School of Architecture and Planning, University College London.

Mendelsohn and Chermayeff, c. 1990s. *Mendelsohn and Chermayeff: De La Warr Pavilion 1933–35 Bexhill-on-Sea*, fold-out exhibition card, Bexhill-on-Sea: De La Warr Pavilion, nd.

Mercer, Kobena, 2005. *Cosmopolitan Modernisms*, London: Institute of International Visual Arts (inIVA)/Cambridge, Mass. and London: MIT Press.

Meyer, Erna, 1926. *Der neue Haushalt. Ein Wegweiser zu wissenschaftliche Hausführung*, Stuttgart: Franck'sche Verlagshandlung.

Meyer, H[annes] M[eyer], 1927. 'Projekt für die Petersschule, Basel, 1926', in *bauhaus*, vol. 1, no. 2, p. 5, reprinted in German and translated into English in Schnaidt, 1965, p. 17.

—— , 1928. 'Bauen', *bauhaus*, vol. 2, no. 4, p. 12, reprinted in Schnaidt, 1965, pp. 94 and 96; translated as 'Building' in Schnaidt, 1965, pp. 95 and 97.

—— , 1940. 'Bauhaus Dessau 1927–30: Erfahrungen einer polytechnischen Erziehung', in Schnaidt, 1965, pp. 106, 108, 110, 112; translated as 'Bauhaus Dessau 1927–1930: My Experience of a Polytechnical Education', in Schnaidt, 1965, pp. 107, 109, 111, 113.

—— , 1965. 'Bundesschule des Allgemeinen Deutschen Gewerkshaftsbundes, Bernau bei Berlin, 1928–1930', nd., in Schnaidt, 1965, pp. 40, 48, translated as 'Federal School of the General German Trade Unions Federation, Bernau near Berlin, 1928–1930', pp. 43, 49.

Meyer, Esther da Costa, 1995. *The Work of Antonio Sant'Elia. Retreat into the Future*, New Haven and London: Yale University Press.

Miller, Quintus, 1992. *Le sanatorium: architecture d'un isolement sublime*, Lausanne: Ecole polytechnique fédérale de Lausanne, Département d'architecture.

Minnaert, Jean-Baptiste, 2002. *Henry Sauvage ou l'exercice du renouvellement*, Paris: Editions Norma.

Moholy-Nagy, László, 1925. *Malerei, Fotografie, Film*, Munich: Albert Langen

—— , 1965. *Vision in Motion*, Chicago: Paul Theobald (1947).

—— , 1967. *Painting, Photography, Film*, London: Lund Humphries. (English translation of Moholy-Nagy, 1925.)

Molema, Jan, 1989. *Ir. J. Duiker*, Rotterdam: 010 Publishers.

—— , 1996. *The New Movement in the Netherlands 1924–1936*, with contributions by Maristella Casciato, Leonard K. Eaton and Chistopher Vernon, Rotterdam: 010 Publishers.

—— and Bak, Pieter (eds), 1987. *Jan Gerko Wiebenga. Apostel van het Nieuwe Bouwen*, Rotterdam: 010 Publishers.

—— and de Jonge, Wessel, 1985. 'Johannes Duiker', *Architectural Review*, vol. CLXXVII, no. 1055, January, pp. 48–55.

Molesworth, Helen, 1997. 'Bathrooms and Kitchens: Cleaning House with Duchamp', in Lahiji and Friedman, 1997b, pp. 74–92.

Monnier, Gérard, 2002. *Le Corbusier: Les unités d'habitation en France*, Paris: Belin-Herscher.

Morelli, Lidia, 1931. *La casa che vorrei avere: come ideare, disporre, arredare, abbellire, rimodernare la mia casa*, Milan: Hoepli.

Mostafavi, Mohsen and Leatherbarrow, David, 1993. *On Weathering: The Life of Buildings in Time*, Cambridge, Mass. and London: MIT Press.

The Müller Villa, 2002. *The Müller Villa in Prague*, Prague: City of Prague Museum.

Müller-Lyer, Franz, 1912. *Die Entwicklungstufen der Menschheit*, Munich: Lehmanns.

Müller-Wulckow, Walter, 1932. *Die deutsche Wohnung der Gegenwart*, Königstein im Taunus and Leipzig: Langewiesche.

Mumford, Eric, 2000. *The CIAM Discourse on Urbanism, 1928–1940*, Cambridge, Mass. and London: MIT Press.

Münz, Ludwig and Künstler, Gustav, 1966. *Adolf Loos, Pioneer of Modern Architecture*, London: Thames & Hudson.

Musil, Robert, 1978. *Der Mann ohne Eigenschaften*, Neu-Edition, Reinbeck bei Hamburg: Rowohlt.

—— , 1997. *Robert Musil, The Man Without Qualities*, translated by Sophie Wilkins and Burton Pike, London: Picador.

Muthesius, Hermann, 1904–5. Das Englische Haus, Berlin: Wasmuth, 2 vols.

—— , 1912. 'Wo Stehen Wir', 1911, in Jahrbuch des Deutschen Werkbundes, pp. 11–26.

Natter, Tobias G. and Hollein, Max (eds), 2005. *The Naked Truth: Klimt, Schiele, Kokoschka and Other Scandals*, exh. cat., Munich and London: Prestel.

Nerdinger, Winfried, 1997. 'Walter Gropius: permanenze dell' effimero' (with English translation), *Casabella*, vol. 61, no. 643, pp. 56–67.

Neutra, Richard, 1954. *Survival Through Design*, New York: Oxford University Press.

—— , 1962. *Life and Shape*, New York: Appleton-Century Crafts.

Nieuwe Bouwen: Amsterdam, 1983. *Het Nieuwe Bouwen: Amsterdam 1920–1960*, text in Dutch and English, exh. cat., Amsterdam: Stedelijk Museum/Delft: Delft University Press.

Nieuwe Bouwen: Rotterdam, 1982. *Het Nieuwe Bouwen in Rotterdam, 1920–1960*, text in Dutch and English, exh. cat., Museum Boymans-van Beuningen, Rotterdam/Delft: Delft University Press.

Nieuwe Bouwen: Previous History, 1982. *Het Nieuwe Bouwen (Previous History)*, exh. cat., text in Dutch and English, Museum Boymans-van Beuningen, Rotterdam/Delft: Delft University Press.

Noever, Peter (ed.), 1993. *Die Frankfurter Küche von Margarete Schütte-Lihotzky*, Berlin: Ernst.

—— , 1995. *MAK Center for Art and Architecture R. M. Schindler*, Munich and New York: Prestel.

—— , 1999. *MAK: Austrian Museum of Applied Arts*, Vienna, 3rd rev. edition, Munich, London, New York: Prestel.

Oettli, Jacques, 1892. *Cours d'économie domestique: Manuel et livre de lecture à l'usage des écoles et des familles*, Lausanne.

Olivier, Dr Charlotte, 1908. 'L'enseignement ménager et la lutte contre la tuberculose', in *Congrès international d'Enseignement ménager et la lutte contre la tuberculose*, vol. I, Fribourg.

Opel-bad Wiesbaden, 1934. 'Opel-bad Wiesbaden', *Moderne Bauformen*, vol. XXXIII, pp. 525–40.

O'Regan, John (ed.), 1993. *Michael Scott 1905–1989*, Dublin: Gandon Editions.

Oud, Hans, 1984. *J. J. P. Oud: Architekt 1890–1963. Feiten en herinneringen gerangschikt*, The Hague: Nijgh & Van Ditmar.

Oud, J. J. P., 1924. 'Semi-permanente woningbouw "Oud-Mathenesse" te Rotterdam', in *Bouwkundig Weekblad*, vol. 45, no. 43, pp. 418–21.

—— , 1930. 'Die Städtische Siedlung "Kiefhoek" in Rotterdam: Bericht des Architekten J. J. P. Oud', *Die Form*, vol. 5, no. 14, 15 July, pp. 357–69.

—— , 1935. 'The £213 House. A Solution to the Re-housing Problem for Rock-bottom Incomes in Rotterdam'. *Studio*, no. 101, p. 456, reprinted in Taverne, Wagenaar and De Vletter, 2001, p. 285.

Our Opinion Concerning the New Architecture, 1924. 'Our Opinion Concerning the New Architecture', *Stavba*, vol. 3, no. 4, pp. 157–58, translated in Slapeta, 1987, p. 163.

Overy, Paul, 1991. *De Stijl: Art, Architecture, Design*, London: Thames & Hudson.

—— , 1996. 'Designing for the Modern World – De Stijl: The Red Blue Chair and the Schröder House', in Liz Dawtrey et al., *Investigating Modern Art*, New Haven and London: Yale University Press in association with the Open University, the Arts Council of England and the Tate Gallery.

—— , 2004. 'Visions of the Future and the Immediate Past: The Werkbund Exhibition, Paris 1930', *Journal of Design History*, vol. 17, no. 4, pp. 337–57.

—— , 2005. 'White Walls, White Skins: Cosmopolitanism and Colonialism in Inter-war Modernist Architecture', in Mercer, 2005, pp. 50–67.

Bibliography

Overy, Paul et al., 1988. *The Rietveld Schröder House*, Guildford, Surrey: Butterworth Architecture/Cambridge, Mass: MIT Press.

Pavillon de l'hygiène, 1937. 'Pavillon de l'hygiène', *L'Architecture d'aujourd'hui*, no. 8, August, p. 31.

Pavitt, Jane, 1994. 'The Bata Project: A Social and Industrial Experiment', in Twentieth Century Architecture, 1994, pp. 31–44.

Pearse, Innes H. and Crocker, Lucy H., 1943. *The Peckham Experiment: A Study in the Living Structure of Society*, London: George Allen and Unwin, for the Sir Halley Stewart Trust.

Pearson, Paul David, 1978. *Alvar Aalto and the International Style*, New York: Whitney Library of Design/Watson-Guptill Publications.

Perriand, Charlotte, 1929. 'Wood or Metal? A Reply', *Studio*, vol. 97, pp. 278–79, reprinted in Benton and Benton, with Sharp, 1975, pp. 232–33.

Perriand, 2005. *Charlotte Perriand*, exh. cat., Paris: Centre Pompidou.

Pevsner, Nikolaus, 1936. *Pioneers of the Modern Movement*, London: Faber and Faber.

——, 1960. *Pioneers of Modern Design: from William Morris to Walter Gropius*, Harmondsworth: Penguin. (Revised and partly rewritten edition of Pevsner, 1936.)

Pinchon, Jean-François (ed.), 1986. *Robert Mallet-Stevens*, Paris: Action Artistique de Paris/Sers.

Podbrecky, Inge, 2003. *Rotes Wien: Gehen & Sehen: 5 Routen zu gebauten Experimenten von Karl-Marx-Hof bis Werkbundsiedlung*, Vienna: Falter.

Polano, Sergio, 1988. *Hendrik Petrus Berlage, Complete Works*, Guildford: Butterworth.

Pommer, Richard and Otto, Christian F., 1991. *Weissenhof 1927 and the Modern Movement in Architecture*, Chicago and London: Chicago University Press.

Porter, Roy, 1997. *The Greatest Benefit to Mankind*, London: Harper Collins.

Posener, Julius, 1980. 'Between Art and Industry: The Deutscher Werkbund', in Burckhardt, 1980.

——, 1992. *Hans Poelzig: Reflections on his Life and Work*, edited by Kristin Feireiss, New York: The Architectural History Foundation, Inc./Cambridge, Mass. and London: MIT Press.

Powers, Alan (ed.), 1991. *Farewell My Lido*, London: Thirties Society.

——, 2001. *Serge Chermayeff: Designer, Architect, Teacher*, London: RIBA Publications.

Pritchard, Jack, 1984. *View from a Long Chair: The Memoirs of Jack Pritchard*, London: Routledge & Kegan Paul.

Probst, Hartmut and Schädlich, Christian (eds), 1988. *Walter Gropius. Der Mensch und sein Werk*, vol. 3, Berlin: Ernst.

Rading, Adolf, 1927. 'Das Haus von Adolf Rading', *Die Form*, vol. 2, no. 9, 1927, pp. 287–89.

Reed, Christopher (ed.), 1996. *Not at Home: The Suppression of Domesticity in Modern Art and Architecture*, London: Thames & Hudson.

Renger-Patzsch, 1997. *Albert Renger-Patzsch: Photographer of Objectivity*, edited by Ann and Jürgen Wilde and Thomas Weski, introductory text by Thomas Janzen, London: Thames & Hudson.

Rich, Laurence, 2003. 'Casework. Forest Fruit: The Pithead Baths of the former Princess Royal Colliery, Gloucestershire', *Twentieth Century Society Newsletter*, Spring, pp. 6–7.

Richards, J. M., 1980. *Memoirs of an Unjust Fella*, London: Wiedenfeld & Nicolson.

Richter, Hans (director), 1930. *Die neue Wohnung*, Zurich: Praesens Films.

Rietveld, Gerrit, 1932. 'Nieuwe zakelijkheid in de Nederlandsche architectuur', *De Vrije Bladen*, vol. 9, no. 7, pp. 1–27; translated as 'New Functionalism in Dutch Furniture', in Küper and Van Zijl, 1992, pp. 33–39.

——, 1948. Typescript dated 1947 of a lecture given in March 1948 at the Academy of Visual Arts, Rotterdam, published as 'Het interieur' in *Bouwkundig Weekblad*, vol. 66, no. 25, pp. 188–201, and no. 26, pp. 206–9; translated as 'Interiors' in Küper and Van Zijl, 1992, pp. 40–47.

Rietveld, 1971. *G. Rietveld, Architect*, exh. cat., Amsterdam: Stedlijk Museum/London: Hayward Gallery, 1971–72.

Riezler, Walter, 1927. 'Die Wohnung', *Die Form*, vol. 2, no. 9, September, pp. 258–66.

Rikli, Arnold, 1905. *Médécine naturelle et bains de soleil*, Lausanne: Bridel.

Risselada, Max (ed.), 1988. *Raumplan versus Plan Libre: Adolf Loos and Le Corbusier, 1919–1930*, Delft: Delft University Press.

Robertson, Howard and Yerbury, F. R., 1927. 'The Housing Exhibition at Stuttgart', first published in three parts in *The Architect & Building News*, 11, 18, and 25 November, reprinted in Robertson and Yerbury, 1989, pp. 40–49.

——, 1930. 'A Poem in Glass and Steel: The Van Nelle Factory in Rotterdam', in *The Architect and Building News*, 30 May, reprinted in Robertson and Yerbury, 1989, pp. 110–13.

——, 1989. *Travels in Modern Architecture*, London: Architectural Association Publications.

Rochowanski, L. W., 1959. *Josef Hoffmann. Eine Studie geschrieben zu seinem 80. Geburtstag*, Vienna: Österreichische Staatsdruckerei.

Rollier, Auguste Rollier, 1936. *La cure de soleil* (1915), 2nd edition, Paris: Baillière et fils.

Roth, Alfred, 1927. *Zwei Wohnhäuser von Le Corbusier und Pierre Jeanneret*, Stuttgart: Wedekind, reprint Stuttgart: Krämer, 1977.

——, (ed.), 1946. *La nouvelle architecture/ Die neue Architektur/The New Architecture*, 2nd edition, Erlenbach-Zurich: Les Editions d'Architecture.

——, 1950. *The New School/Das neue Schulhaus/ La nouvelle école*, Zurich: Girsberger.

Roth, Joseph, 1929a. *Rechts und Links*, Berlin: Kiepenheuer.

——, 1929b. 'Architektur', *Münchner Illustrierte Presse*, 27 October, translated as 'Architecture' in Roth, 2003, pp. 115–18.

——, 1992. *Right and Left. The Legend of the Holy Drinker*, translated by Michael Hofmann, Woodstock, New York: Overlook Press.

——, 2003. *What I Saw: Reports from Berlin 1920–33*, translated with an introduction by Michael Hofmann, London: Granta Books.

Rothenstein, Michael, 1946. 'Colour and Modern Architecture, or the Photographic Eye', *Architectural Review*, June, vol. XCIX, no. 594, p. 159.

Rothery, Seàn, 1991. *Ireland and the New Architecture, 1900–1940*, Dublin: Lilliput Press.

Röttiger, Helene, 1925. 'Erfahrungen nach dem hauswirtschaftlichen Volljahr', *Die Frau*, no. 32, p. 235.

Rowe, Colin, 1994. *The Architecture of Good Intentions: Towards a Possible Retrospect*, London: Academy.

Rubino, Luciano, 1982. *Pierre Chareau and Bernard Bijvoet*, Rome: Kappa.

Rüegg, Arthur, 2005. 'Les "Cellules Vitales": Cuisson et Sanitaire', in Perriand, 2005, pp. 136–37.

Rukschcio, Burkhardt and Schachel, Roland, 1982. *Adolf Loos: Leben und Werk*, Salzburg and Vienna: Residenz.

Sack, Manfred, 1992. *Richard Neutra*, Zurich and London: Verlag für Architektur.

Sam, Eleonoor Jap (ed.), 2000. *Het Wiebengacomplex: hergebruik en restauratie van de Nijverheidsscholen in Groningen (1922–1923)/ The Wiebenga Complex: Conversion and Restoration of the Technical Schools in Groningen (1922–1923)*, Rotterdam: 010 Publishers.

Sant'Elia, Antonio and Marinetti, Filippo Tommaso, 1914. *L'Architettura futurista. Manifesto*, Milan: Tipografia Taveggia, 11 July 1914, translated as 'Futurist Architecture' in Conrads, 1970, p. 38.

Sarnitz, August (ed.), 1998. *Architecture in Vienna*, Vienna and New York: Springer.

Scharoun, Hans, 1927. 'Haus Scharoun', *Die Form*, vol. 2, no. 9, September, pp. 293–94.

Schaukal, Richard, 1910. 'Ein Haus und seine Zeit', *Der Merker: Österreichische Zeitschrift für Musik und Theater*, 10 December.

Scheerbart, Paul, 1914. *Glasarchitektur*, Berlin: Der Sturm.

——, 1972. *Glass Architecture*, and Bruno Taut, *Alpine Architecture*, with an introduction by Dennis Sharp, New York and Washington: Praeger (translation of Scheerbart, 1914 and Taut, 1919).

Schirren, Matthias, 2004. *Bruno Taut, Alpine Architektur: A Utopia·Eine Utopie*, Munich, London, New York: Prestel.

Schlemmer, Oskar, 1990. *The Letters and Diaries of Oskar Schlemmer*, Selected and edited by Tut Schlemmer (1970), Evanston, Illinois: Northwestern University Press.

Schmidt, Hans, 1927. 'Die Wohnung', *Das Werk*, Basel, vol. XIV, abridged translation in Charlotte Benton, 1975, p. 20.

——, 1930. 'Rundschau: Zum Zeilenbau der Dammerstock Siedlung', *Die Form*, vol. 5, no. 14, 15 July, pp. 379–80.

Schnaidt, Claude, 1965. *Hannes Meyer: Bauten, Projekte und Schriften/Buildings, Projects and Writings*, London: Tiranti.

Schütte-Lihotzky, Margarete, 1924. 'Beratungsstelle für Wohnungseinrichtung', in *Die Neue Wirtschaft*, 31 January, p. 12.

—— (Grete Lihotzky), 1926–27. 'Rationalisierung im Haushalt', *Das Neue Frankfurt*, no. 5, pp. 120–23.

——, 1981. 'Arbeitsküche', in *form + zweck*, vol. 4, no. 13, pp. 22–26.

——, 2004. *Warum ich Architektin wurde*, Vienna: Residenz.

Schuster, 1976. *Franz Schuster, 1892–1972*, exh. cat., Hochschule für angewandte Kunst, Vienna: Löcker.

Schwab, Alexander, 1931. 'Anmerkungen zur Bauausstellung', *Die Form*, vol. 6, no. 6, 15 June, pp. 206–12.

Schwartz, Frederic J., 1996a. *The Werkbund: Design Theory & Mass Culture before the First World War*, New Haven and London: Yale University Press.

——, 1996b. 'Commodity Signs, Peter Behrens, the AEG and the Trademark', *Journal of Design History*, vol. 9, no. 3, pp. 153–84.

——, 1998. 'Form Follows Fetish: Adolf Behne and the Problem of Sachlichkeit', *Oxford Art Journal*, vol. 21, no. 2, pp. 45–77.

——, 2001. 'The Eye of the Expert: Walter Benjamin and the Avant-Garde', *Art History*, vol. 4, no. 3, June, pp. 401–44.

Schwitters, Kurt, 1927. 'Stuttgart, "Die Wohnung"; Werkbundausstellung', *i10*, no. 10, 1927, pp. 345–48.

Searing, Helen, 1989. 'Case Study Houses: In the Grand Modern Tradition', in Smith, 1989, pp. 107–29.

Sekler, Eduard, 1985. *Josef Hoffmann: The Architectural Work*, Princeton: Princeton University Press.

Sharp, Dennis, 1993. *Bauhaus, Dessau: Walter Gropius*, London: Phaidon.

Shorter, Edward, 1990. 'Private Clinics in Central Europe, 1850–1933', *Social History of Medicine*, vol. 3, no. 3, pp. 159–95.

Shove, Elizabeth, 2003. *Comfort, Cleanliness and Convenience: The Social Organizaion of Normality*, Oxford and New York: Berg.

Singleton, Frank, 1938. 'Health Centres – Two Styles', *Spectator*, 28 October.

Slapeta, Vladimir, 1987. *Czech Functionalism*, London: Architectural Association.

——, 1990. 'Bat'a Architecture', *Rassegna*, no. XII, September.

——(ed.), 1992. *Bat'a: Architecture and Urbanism, 1910–1950*, exh. cat., Zlin: State Gallery.

Smith, Elizabeth A. T. (ed.), 1989. *Blueprints for Modern Living: History and Legacy of the Case Study Houses*, Cambridge, Mass. and London: MIT Press.

Smith, Janet, 1996. *Tooting Bec Lido*, London: South London Swimming Club.

——, 2005. *Liquid Assets: The Lidos and Open-air Swimming Pools of Britain*, London: English Heritage.

Smith, Terry, 1993. *Making the Modern: Industry, Art and Design in America*, Chicago: University of Chicago Press.

Smithson, Peter, 1996. '"Mart Stam's Trousers": A Conversation between Peter Smithson & Wouter Vanstiphout', London, 29 November 1996, in Crimson, with Speaks and Hadders, 1999, pp. 128–38.

Smithson, Alison and Smithson, Peter, 1981. *The Heroic Period of Modern Architecture*, London: Thames & Hudson. (Originally published as a section of *Architectural Design* in December 1965.)

Solà-Morales, Ignasi, Cirici, Cristian and Ramos, Fernando, 1998. *Mies van der Rohe: Barcelona Pavilion*, Barcelona: Gili.

Sontag, Susan, 1991. *Illness as Metaphor* (1978) in Susan Sontag, *Illness as Metaphor and Aids and Its Metaphors*, London: Penguin.

Sparke, Penny, 1995. *As Long as it's Pink: The Sexual Politics of Taste*, London and San Francisco: Pandora.

Spender, Stephen, 1977. *World Within World: The Autobiography of Stephen Spender* (1951), London: Hamish Hamilton.

Stam, Mart, 1930. 'Das Projekt Habermann-Kramer-Moser-Stam für das neue Altersheim in Frankfurt am Main', in *Das Neue Frankfurt*, vol. V, no. 7 July.

Steele, Brett, 2002. 'Absolut Mies, Absolute Modern: Building Good Copy', *AA Files*, no. 48, Winter, pp. 2–14.

Stewart, Janet, 2000. *Fashioning Vienna: Adolf Loos's Cultural Criticism*, London and New York: Routledge.

Streibel, Robert (ed.), 1996. *Eugenie Schwarzwald und ihr Kreis*, Vienna: Picus.

Surén, Hans, 1924. *Der Mensch und die Sonne*, Stuttgart: Dieck.

Svácha, Rotislav, 1995. *The Architecture of New Prague, 1895–1945*, Cambridge, Mass. and London: MIT Press.

Syring, Eberhard and Kirschenmann, Jörg C., 2004. *Scharoun 1893–1972*, Cologne: Taschen.

Tafuri, Manfredo, 1979. *Architecture and Utopia: Design and Capitalist Development* (1976), Cambridge, Mass. and London: MIT Press.

——, 1990. *The Sphere and the Labyrinth: Avant-Gardes and Architecture from Piranesi to the 1970s*, Cambridge, Mass. and London: MIT Press.

Tanzer, Kim, 1995. 'Baker's Loos and Loos's Loss: Architecting the Body', *Center*, vol. 9, pp. 76–89.

Taut, Bruno, 1919. *Alpine Architektur*, Hagen: Folkwang Verlag. English translation in Scheerbart, 1972. See also Schirren, 2004.

——, 1924. *Die neue Wohnung: Die Frau als Schöpferin*, Leipzig: Klinkhardt & Biermann.

——, 1927. *Ein Wohnhaus*, Stuttgart: Keller.

——, 1929a. *Modern Architecture*, London: The Studio Limited/New York: Boni.

——, 1929b. *Die neue Baukunst in Europa und Amerika*, Stuttgart: Hoffmann.

Taverne, Ed, Wagenaar, Cor and de Vletter, Martien (eds), 2001. *J. J. P. Oud: Poetic Functionalist, 1890–1963, The Complete Works*, Rotterdam: Netherlands Architecture Institute.

Taylor, Frederick Winslow, 1911. *The Principles of Scientific Management*, New York and London: Harper & Brothers.

Taylor, Brian Brace, 1992. *Pierre Chareau: Designer and Architect*, Cologne: Taschen.

Taylor, Diane, 1994. 'Keith Murray, Architect and Designer for Industry', in Twentieth Century Achitecture, 1994, pp. 53–54.

Teige, Karel, 1932. *Nejmenší byt*, Prague: Petr.

——, 1933. *Práce Jaromíra Krejcara*, Prague: Petr.

——, 1993. *Rassegna*, vol. 15, no. 53/1, March Special Issue: Karel Teige: Architecture and Poetry.

——, 2002. *The Minimum Dwelling*, translated by Eric Dluhosch, Cambridge, Mass. and London: MIT Press (translation of Teige, 1932.)

Thonet, 1989. *Thonet Tubular Steel Furniture: Card Catalogue, First Complete Collection of German and French Models, 1930–31*, with an introduction by Sonja Günther, Vitra Design Museum, Weil am Rhein: Vitra Design Publications.

Toepfer, Karl, 1997. *Empire of Ecstasy: Nudity and Movement in German Body Culture, 1910–1935*, Berkeley, Los Angeles, London: University of California Press.

Tomkins, Calvin, 1972. *Living Well is the Best Revenge: Two Americans in Paris 1921–1933*, London: André Deutsch.

Topp, Leslie, 1997. 'An Architecture for Modern Nerves: Josef Hoffmann's Purkersdorf Sanatorium', *Journal of the Society of Architectural Historians*, vol. 56, no. 4, December, pp. 415–37.

——, 2004. *Architecture and Truth in Fin-de-Siècle Vienna*, Cambridge: Cambridge University Press.

Tournikiotis, Panayotis, 1994. *Adolf Loos*, New York: Princeton Architectural Press.

Troy, Nancy J., 1983. *The De Stijl Environment*, Cambridge, Mass. and London: MIT Press.

——, 1991. *Modernism and the Decorative Arts in France: Art Nouveau to Le Corbusier*, New Haven and London: Yale University Press.

Tschumi, Bernard, 1994. 'Architecture and Transgression', in Bernard Tschumi, *Architecture and Disjunction*, Cambridge, Mass. and London: MIT Press, 1994.

Twentieth Century Architecture, 1994. *Twentieth Century Architecture*, Journal of the Twentieth Century Society, no. 1, Industrial Architecture.

Unwin, Raymond, 1902. *Cottage Plans and Common Sense* (Fabian Tract no. 109), London: Fabian Society.

Vaill, Amanda, 1998. *Everybody Was So Young: Gerald and Sara Murphy. A Lost Generation Love Story*, New York: Houghton Mifflin/London: Little, Brown.

Van der Leeuw, C. H., 1930. *Bouw eener nieuwe fabriek: Factoren bij de keuse van terreinen en fabriekstype*, Purmerend: Nederlands Instituut voor Efficiency, Publication no. 48, November.

Van der Vlugt, 1993. *Leen van der Vlugt*, issue edited by Elly Adriaansz, Joris Molenaar and Joost Meuwissen, *Wiederhall*, no. 14.

Van Doesburg, Theo, 1924. 'Tot een Beeldende Architectuur', *De Stijl*, vol. 6, no. 6–7, pp. 78–83, translated as 'Towards plastic architecture', in Baljeu, 1974, pp. 142–47.

——, 1925. 'Vernieuwingspogingen der Oostenrijksche en Duitsche architectuur', *Het Bouwbedrijf*, vol. 2, no. 6, June, pp. 225–27, reprinted in Van Doesburg, 1986, pp. 57–62; translated as 'The Significance of Glass: Toward transparent structures', in Van Doesburg, 1990, pp. 63–69.

——, 1927. 'Stuttgart-Weissenhof 1927: "Die Wohnung"', *Het Bouwbedrijf*, vol. 4, no. 24, November, pp. 556–59, reprinted in Van Doesburg, 1986, pp. 144–51; translated as 'Stuttgart-Weissenhof 1927: Die Wohnung', in Van Doesburg, 1990, pp. 164–72.

——, 1930. 'Vers la peinture blanche', *Art Concret*, April, pp. 11–12; translated as 'Towards White Painting' in Baljeu, 1974, p. 183.

——, 1932. 'Elementarisme (les éléments de la nouvelle peinture)', *De Stijl*, Van Doesburg Memorial Issue, pp. 17–19, translated as 'Elementarism (the Elements of the New Painting)', in Baljeu, 1974, pp. 184–85.

——, 1986. *De Stijl en de Europese architectuur. De architectuuropstellen in Het Bouwbedrijf 1924–1931*, Nijmegen: SUN.

——, 1990. *On European Architecture: Complete Essays from Het Bouwbedrijf 1924–1931*, Basel, Berlin and Boston: Birkhäuser.

Van Straaten, Evert, 1988. *Theo van Doesburg: Painter and Architect*, The Hague: SDU Publishers.

——, 1994. *Theo van Doesburg: Constructor of the New Life*, Otterlo: Kröller-Müller Museum.

Vanstiphout, Wouter, 1999. 'Stories from behind the Scenes of Dutch Moral Modernism', in Crimson, with Speaks and Hadders, 1999, pp. 20–45.

Vickery, Robert, 1971. 'Bijvoet and Duiker', *Perspecta*, no. 13, pp. 130–61.

Vincendeau, Ginette, 1998. *Pépé Le Moko*, London: British Film Institute.

Vogt, Adolf Max, 1998. *Le Corbusier, the Noble Savage: Toward an Archaeology of Modernism*, Cambridge, Mass. and London: MIT Press.

Von Maur, Karin, 1972. *Oskar Schlemmer*, Thames & Hudson, London.

Wagner, Martin, 1932. *Das wachsende Haus. Ein Beitrag zur Lösung der städtischen Wohnungsfrage*, Berlin and Leipzig: Bong.

Wagner, Otto, 1896. *Modern Architektur*, Vienna: Schroll.

——, 1988. *Modern Architecture. A Guidebook for his Students to this Field of Art* (1896), Santa Monica: The Getty Foundation (translation of Wagner, 1896).

——, 2002. *Villen, Wohn- und Geschäftshäuser Interieurs, Ausgeführte Bauten*, Vienna: Album.

Wainwright, Milton, 1990. *Miracle Cure: The Story of Penicillin and the Golden Age of Antibiotics*, Oxford: Blackwell.

Ward, Janet, 2001. *Weimar Surfaces: Urban Visual Culture in 1920s Germany*, Berkeley, Los Angeles, London: University of California Press.

Weber, Helmut, 1961. *Walter Gropius und das Faguswerk*, Munich: Callwey.

Wedepohl, Edgar, 1927. 'Die Weissenhofsiedlung der Werkbundausstellung,' *Wasmuths Monatshefte für Baukunst und Städtebau*, vol. 11, no. 8, August, pp. 391–402.

Werkbundsiedlung Breslau 1929, 1996. *Auf dem Weg zum neuen Wohnen: die Werkbundsiedlung Breslau 1929/Towards a New Kind of Living: the Werkbund Housing Estate Breslau 1929*, edited by the Institut für Auslandsbeziehungen (ifa), Basel and Boston: Birkhäuser.

Weston, Richard, 1996. *Modernism*, London: Phaidon.

White, Michael, 2003. *De Stijl and Dutch Modernism*, Manchester: Manchester University Press.

Whitford, Frank, 1984. *The Bauhaus*, London: Thames & Hudson.

Wichert, Fritz, 1928. 'Der Neue Hausrat', *Das Neue Frankfurt*, no. 1, reprinted in Hirdina, 1984, pp. 190–92.

Wiggington, Michael, 1996. *Glass in Architecture*, London: Phaidon.

Wigglesworth, Sarah, 1998. 'Maison de Verre: Sections through an In-Vitro Conception', *Journal of Architecture*, vol. 3, Autumn, pp. 263–86.

Wigley, Mark, 1995. *White Walls, Designer Dresses: The Fashioning of Modern Architecture*, Cambridge, Mass. and London: MIT Press.

Wijdeveld, Paul, 1994. *Ludwig Wittgenstein, Architect*, London: Thames & Hudson.

Wilk, Christopher, 1981. *Marcel Breuer: Furniture and Interiors*, New York: Museum of Modern Art.

—— (ed.), 2006. *Modernism: Designing a New World*, exh. cat., London: Victoria & Albert Museum.

Williamson, Judith, 2001. 'The Rise of the White King', *New Statesman*, 13 August 2001, pp. 28–29 (review of 'Dirty Washing: The Hidden Language of Soap Powder Packaging' exhibition, Design Museum, London).

Willett, John, 1978. *The New Sobriety 1917–1933: Art and Politics in the Weimar Period*, London: Thames & Hudson.

Wilson, Alan, 1981. *Peter Behrens: Architect and Designer, 1868–1940*, London: Architectural Press.

Wilson, Christopher, 2005. 'Looking at/in/from the Maison de Verre', in Heynen and Baydar, 2005, pp. 234–51.

Wingler, Hans M., 1991. *The Bauhaus-Archives Berlin: Museum of Design*, Braunschweig: Westermann.

——, 1993. *The Bauhaus* (first published 1969, revised edition 1976), Cambridge, Mass. and London: MIT Press.

Winter, Dr [Pierre], 1922. 'Le Corps nouveau', *L'Esprit nouveau*, no. 15, February, pp. 1755–58.

Wohnungswesen der Stadt Wien, c. 1932. Das Wohnungswesen der Stadt Wien/Housing in Vienna/L'Habitation à Vienne, Frankfurt am Main: Veröffentlichung des Int. Verbandes für Wohnungswesen/Stuttgart: Hoffmann, nd.

Wood, Ean, 2000. *The Josephine Baker Story*, London: Sanctuary.

Worpole, Ken, 2000. *Here Comes the Sun: Architecture and Public Space in Twentieth-Century European Culture*, London: Reaktion.

Wyche, E. M., 1916. 'Open-Air Education for Ailing Children', *Child*, vol. 7.

Yeomans, David and Cottam, David, 2001. *Owen Williams*, London: Telford.

Yorke, F. R. S., 1934. *The Modern House*, London: Architectural Press.

Zola, Emile, 1954. *Germinal* (1885), Harmondsworth: Penguin.

Zoshchenko, Mikhail, 2000. *The Galosh: And Other Stories*, translated by Jeremy Hicks, London: Angel.

Zukowsky, John (ed.), 1994. *The Many Faces of Modern Architecture: Building in Germany between the World Wars*, Munich and New York: Prestel.

Acknowledgments

I would like to acknowledge the help of Jeremy Aynsley, Lutz Becker, László Beke, Charlotte Benton, Tim Benton, Lenneke Büller, Guy Brett, Monika Buch, Simon Caulkin, David Cottington, David Craven, Barry Curtis, Peter Graham, Theresa Zugmann Gronberg, Leslie Gronberg, Brian Housden, Margaret Housden, Adrian Forty, John Furse, Frank Kauffmann, Wessel de Jonge, Julie Lawson, Jana Lloyd, Sarat Maharaj, Mary Macleod, Roger Malbert, Kobena Mercer, Michael Molnar, Bertus Mulder, Simon Ofield, Jaap Oosterhoff, Frank den Oudsten, Claire Pajaczkowska, Alan Powers, Adrian Rifkin, Jan Schriefer, Dennis Sharp, Jenny Stein, Aldina Terzi, Lisa Tickner, Nancy Troy, Renzo Vecchiato, Ginette Vincendeau, Dennis Walder, John Walker, Michael White, Sarah Wigglesworth, Christopher Wilk, Wim de Wit and Ida van Zijl.

I also thank the staff of the following institutions and libraries for individual help and access to their resources: the Institut für Geschichte und Theorie der Architektur of the Eidgenössische Technische Hochschule (ETH) Zürich; the Bibliothèque nationale and the library of the Musée des arts décoratifs in Paris; in Vienna, the Wienbibliothek im Rathaus (formerly Wiener Stadt- und Landesbibliothek) and the library of the Freud Museum; the Nederlands Architectuur Instituut, Rotterdam, and the Centraal Museum, Utrecht. In London, I have benefited from the resources of the British Library, the London Library, the Library and Photographic Collection of the Architectural Association, the National Architecture Library and Photographic Collection at the Royal Institute of British Architects, the National Art Library at the Victoria & Albert Museum, the Freud Museum, and the Wellcome Library.

Initial research for the project was undertaken with the assistance of a Leverhulme Fellowship and a grant from the Elephant Trust; study leave from Middlesex University enabled me to complete the text. I also wish to acknowledge the help and support at Thames & Hudson of Thomas Neurath, Jamie Camplin, Sam Ruston and Naomi Pritchard, with special thanks to my editor Julia MacKenzie, the picture researcher Pauline Hubner and designer Rowena Alsey. The book was commissioned by the late Nikos Stangos, without whose patient encouragement and enthusiasm it would not have been finished. My biggest debt is to my wife Tag Gronberg for her unsparing help, criticism and support.

Sources of illustrations

Index

Index